Career Counseling

CAREER COUNSELING

A Holistic View of Lifespan and Special Populations

Rebecca R. Sametz and Mary-Anne M. Joseph, Editors

Texas Tech University Health Sciences Center | Alabama State University

cognella®

SAN DIEGO

Bassim Hamadeh, CEO and Publisher
Amy Smith, Senior Project Editor
Abbey Hastings, Associate Production Editor
Emely Villavicencio, Senior Graphic Designer
Stephanie Kohl, Licensing Coordinator
Natalie Piccotti, Director of Marketing
Kassie Graves, Vice President of Editorial
Jamie Giganti, Director of Academic Publishing

www.cognella.com   800-200-3908

Brief Contents

Contents

6   **Career Counseling for Adult Clients**   **63**

Jina Chun, Gloria K. Lee, and Hung Jen Kuo

7   **Career Counseling for Older Adults: Retirement and Preretirement**   **79**

Mary-Anne Joseph and Bernadette Williams York

PART III   Career Counseling forSpecial Populations   95

8   Career Counseling for Multicultural Groups   96

Myshalae Euring

9   Career Counseling for Gender Differences and Dual Careers   114

Roxanna Pebdani, Serene Lin-Stephens, and Erin Fearn-Smith

10   Career Counseling for LGBT+ Clients   132

Erica L. Wondolowski, Michelle McKnight-Lizotte, and Emily Lund

11   Career Counseling for Individuals With Disabilities   152

Michelle McKnight-Lizotte, Trenton Landon, and Emily Lund

12   Career Counselingfor Veterans   170

Rebecca R. Sametz and Tyler A. Riddle

13   Career Counseling for Individuals Recovering From Substance Abuse   179

Sara P. Johnston and Susan Lingle

14   Career Counseling for Individuals With Mental Health Disorders   194

Allison Levine and Catherine Troop

15   Career Counselingfor Ex-Offenders   205

Brenna Breshears

18 Advocating and Marketing to Employers and Human Resources   262

Rebecca R. Sametz and Danielle Ami Narh

Preface

Career counseling and development can assist individuals with understanding themselves in the world of work to make the best career, life, and education decisions (Palladino Schultheiss, 2003). Career development goes beyond what major an individual should pursue; our careers and life decisions are what shape us as individuals and how we understand ourselves in the world. This textbook will provide an overview of the historical context of career counseling, assessments, models, and theories, as well as ethical and legal issues related to career development and employment. Further, the book provides insight, guidance, and resources for the implementation of career counseling with a wide range of special populations.

The organization of this textbook is purposeful in that it attempts to walk the career counselor through the foundations behind all career counselors and then move them into specific topics that can become resources for them when practicing! By starting out with a historical reference, career counseling theories, and ethical and legal considerations, the book allows career counselors to feel that they have a foundation before moving too quickly into the life span section. That section of the book helps to prepare career counselors for the diverse ages they may be working with and techniques that can be helpful for each of these groups. The bulk of the textbook is spent discussing career counseling for special populations. These specific populations are ones career counselors may encounter in their work. The information contained in the associated chapters can be used as a resource guide to increase their understanding of and techniques in assisting these different populations. The last part of the textbook is focused on how to do group career counseling and a variety of assessments and intakes, as well as advocating and marketing to employers—all of which are important for career counselors to understand!

This book attempts to capture events that affect the workplace and workforce within the current climate. Keeping up-to-date has been an inclusive process involving a close look at a broad range of historical events and research results from many different academic disciplines. This process also includes taking into account social-economic trends and other factors that have affected the workforce and workplace (i.e., legislative changes, labor market). When structuring this textbook, I attempted to ensure that populations that have been missing from other textbooks concerning career counseling were included. Many of the populations that counselors are seeing are no longer traditional but tend to have diverse barriers—ones that textbooks need to pay more attention to in order to prepare counselors for the workforce.

In addition, this book provides information and resources that promote the advocacy and marketing of clients in the workforce. The purpose of this is to assist the counselor in potentially understanding the needs of employers, as well as what human resource employees and managers are going to be looking for when reviewing applicants.

This textbook is well suited to serve as a core textbook for career, clinical rehabilitation, and general counseling, as well as human resources, students at the graduate and undergraduate levels. This textbook can be used for the instruction of courses such as career counseling, vocational development and placement, and other career, employment, or vocation courses.

References

Palladino Schultheiss, D. E. (2003). A relational approach to career counseling: Theoretical integration and practical application. *Journal of Counseling and Development*, 301–310.

PART I

Foundations of Career Counseling

CHAPTER 1

Introduction to Career Counseling and Development

Danielle Ami Narh

CHAPTER OVERVIEW

Career counseling and development can assist individuals with understanding themselves in the world of work to make the best career, life, and education decisions (Niles & Harris-Bowlsbey, 2002). Career development goes beyond what major an individual should pursue; our careers and life decisions are what shape us as individuals and how we understand ourselves in the world. This chapter will provide a brief historical development of career counseling, discuss the skills that a counselor must have to provide career counseling, outline the goals of career counseling, and share the necessary ethical considerations when providing career counseling.

CHAPTER OBJECTIVES

After reading this chapter, the student will be able to complete the following:

1. Discuss the historical development of career counseling and landmarks of the career counseling specialty area.

2. Identify the goals of career counseling.

3. Identify the skills needed to provide career counseling successfully to diverse populations.

4. Explain and discuss ethical and legal considerations when providing career counseling.

In modern-day America *work* has become a major part of an individual's identity. Super (1957) reported, "If the average adult's twenty-four-hour day is examined to ascertain how he spends his time, we note that his occupation absorbs more of his time than does any other type of activity" (p. 17). In most western cultures, work and productivity of the population have contributed to the success of producing wealth and economic rewards for citizens. Havighurst (1982), commenting on the meaning and importance of work, put it this way:

> The job orients and controls the behavior of those persons who participate in it. It sets a goal for the worker, determines the manner in which the goal may be attained, and the reward offered for

its achievement, and affects the whole range of his or her participation in the society of which s/he is a member. Its influences extend even beyond the actual work life of the individual. We also find that the part of his/her adult life not spent in work is, nonetheless, affected. In short, the job in our society exerts an influence which pervades the whole of the adult life span. (p. 780)

Parsons (1909) stated that the choice of an occupation is one of the most important steps in a person's life. Today, work is viewed as an imperative not only for socioeconomic well-being but also for physical and psychological well-being, where work affords many with purpose and identity. Questions regarding the fundamental concept of a career, specifically on how individuals can negotiate different job changes successfully without necessarily losing their identities or who they are have become prominent in the 21st century because of the changes to the world economy (Savickas, 2005). In the United States, one of the first questions anyone will ask you is, "What do you do?" This social identity related to occupation has certainly become a defining characteristic in the American class structure (Lind, 1995).

Career development and career choice are very important for all individuals, as well as career counselors. Career development can be seen as a life span process that begins in childhood. This includes the formal and informal experiences that give rise to talents, interests, values, and knowledge of the world of work, which continue into adulthood through the progression of one's career behavior and culminates the transition into and adjustment to retirement. Career development is a concept designed to capture the dynamic change in nature of career or work behavior and is sometimes used as a method for incorporating career choice. At other times, it refers to one's experience before, during, and after one's career choice, which may overlap with one's educational life.

With the many standpoints on describing, viewing, explaining, approaching, and facilitating career choice and career development (Engels et al., 1995), there are also a variety of definitions, theories, approaches, and strategies of career counseling (Brown et al., 1990; Gysbers & Moore, 1987; Herr & Cramer, 1992; Peterson et al., 1991; Spokane, 1991).

Defining Career Counseling

Career counseling is the pursuit of any therapeutic intervention whose scope is to affect the career decision-making process based on elements/theories of traditional counseling. These types of interactions between a counselor and an identified client have been noted in the exigent literature to have positive outcomes (Oliver & Spokane, 1988). Career counseling typically takes place between an individual client and counselor; however, some career counseling involves playgroups or workshops, particularly in educational settings in which clients are dealing with common developmental challenges (Brown & Lent, 2013). These challenges may largely be captured within three categories: making and implementing career-related decisions, adjusting to work, and negotiating career transitions and work-life balance (Brown & Lent, 2013).

Goals of Career Counseling

The goal of career counseling is to help individuals better understand their personalities, interests, values, and skills. This self-understanding will allow for individuals to make knowledgeable decisions throughout their lives regarding the world of work, such as requirements, opportunities, and limitations. Career counseling will equip individuals with the capabilities to make confident choices about their goals to be more successful going forward into the world.

Another goal of career counseling is to help individuals with career planning, decision making, implementation of career choice, career adjustment, and interplay between career and personal issues. The career planning process focuses on self-understanding and awareness and may use professional instruments, exploratory questionnaires, and inventories, as well as a variety of other information-gathering tools to assess personality traits, interests, and values. Assessment instruments aid in the awareness process and are often a necessary component of career planning. The individual seeking career counseling becomes empowered to continually reassess and reevaluate career goals in relation to changing circumstances. The second goal is to assist the client in clarifying a direction in life, where more specific decisions and exploratory activities become more meaningful.

Historical Development of Career Counseling

The call for one-stop career centers to address the nation's career needs by President Bill Clinton reiterated the importance of career development and the need for career counseling in a rapidly changing society and world (Engels et al., 1995). The field of career development and the practice of career counseling have since evolved rapidly. Results from polls sponsored by the National Career Development Association (NCDA) and the National Occupational Information Coordinating Committee (Brown & Minor, 1992) found that 7% of adults surveyed needed job-seeking assistance in 1991, two thirds would seek more occupational information if they could plan their work lives again, 29% expected job changes within 3 years, and 22% of those who sought assistance got it from professional counselors.

The first scientific approach to career counseling is credited to Frank Parson, who in 1908 founded the first documented career counseling program, the Vocation Bureau, in Boston, Massachusetts. The purpose of the bureau was to help any young and old who seek council to opportunities and resources for the betterment of their condition and the means of increasing their economic efficiency (Parsons Statement). In Parsons's (1909) book titled *Choosing a Vocation*, he outlined the factors involved in the choice of a vocation as "a clear understanding of yourself your aptitude abilities intersects emissions resources limitations in their causes; Knowledge of the requirements and conditions success advantages in disadvantages compensation opportunities and prospects in different lines of work; True reasoning on the relations of these two groups of facts" (p. 5).

In a historical analysis of vocational guidance, Brewer (1942) concluded that Parsons

1. Furnished the idea for the Vocation Bureau and began its execution;
2. Paved the way for vocational guidance in schools and colleges by advocating their role in it and offering methods they could use;
3. Began the training of counselors;
4. Used all the scientific tools available to him at the time;
5. Developed "steps" to be followed in the vocational progress of the individual;
6. Organized the work of the Vocation Bureau in a way that laid the groundwork for groups to model in schools, colleges, and other agencies;
7. Recognized the importance of his work and secured for it the appropriate publicity, financial support, and endorsements from influential educators, employers, and other public figures; and
8. Laid the groundwork leading to the continuance and expansion of the vocational guidance movement by involving friends and associates in the work and preparing the manuscript for *Choosing a Vocation*.

Among the numerous significant accomplishments that have defined career counseling as a specialty area, the following developments seem especially pertinent. First, Parsons's (1909) landmark approach to career counseling has helped clients develop an understanding of self and of the world of work, followed by true reasoning about self and work. Second, there is a growing body of heuristically based theories of career development, career choice, and career counseling. Third, the establishment and subsequent revision of career counseling competencies by the National Vocational Guidance Association (NVGA), now the NCDA Professional Standards Committee, helped define career counseling as a specialty. Fourth, the establishment and subsequent revision of career counselor credentialing by the National Council for Credentialing Career Counselors (Smith & Karpati, 1985), which evolved into the National Certified Career Counselor specialty certification sanctioned by NBCC (Sampson & Loesch, 1991), further defined career counseling as a specialty. Fifth, the establishment and subsequent revision of preparation standards by the Association for Counselor Education and Supervision (ACES) and the Council for Accreditation of Counseling and Related Educational Programs (CACREP) include life span and career development as a core counseling element, as well as the establishment of specialty preparation standards for career counseling. And sixth, the establishment of ethical standards by NCDA and selected state and federal laws aimed at promoting career development and regulating career counseling practice also expanded the career specialty definition. The consensus expressed in these landmark developments, standards, competencies, and credentials provides yet another context for operationally defining the specialty of career counseling.

Herr (1997) explained that for much of its history, career counseling was rarely differentiated from vocational or career guidance and that it was not until the 1960s and 1970s that the term "career guidance and counseling" sufficiently differentiated the two elements. It is only in the last 20 years that calls have been made for expanded views of career counseling in response to changes in society, and increasing attention is being paid to changing definitions of career counseling. Herr (1997) distinguished five observations about the changes in career counseling.

1. Career counseling's principal content is the perceptions, anxieties, information deficits, work personalities, competencies, and motives that people experience in their interactions with their external environment.
2. Career counseling is not a singular process but a term used to summarize a range of interventions.
3. Career counseling is no longer conceived as a process principally focused on ensuring that adolescents make a wise choice of an initial job.
4. Career counseling may be considered the preferred intervention of choice but may also be one of a program of interventions to deal with emotional or behavioral disorders that accompany or confound the career problem.
5. Career counseling may best be thought of as a continuum of intervention processes (pp. 85–86).

Career Counseling Competencies

Career counseling can be seen as an evolving profession. In the past years, it has emerged as a profession of its own. The active role of the individual in the career counseling process is emphasized as career counselors aim to work collaboratively with individuals, focusing on well-rounded and all-inclusive approaches to life and career and encouraging individuals to reflect actively on, revise, and reorient their life-career relationship (McMahon & Patton, 2002).

Professional competency statements provide guidance for the minimum competencies necessary to perform effectively in an occupation or job within a particular field. Professional career counselors or persons in career development positions must have or be able to demonstrate the knowledge and skills for a specialty in career counseling that the generalist counselor may not necessarily have. Skills and knowledge are represented by designated competency areas, which have been developed by professional career counselors and counselor educators. Career counseling competency statements can serve as a guide for career counseling training programs or as a checklist for persons wanting to acquire or to enhance their skills in career counseling.

Minimum Competencies

According to the 1997 career counseling competencies presented by the NCDA, to work as a professional engaged in career counseling, an individual must demonstrate minimum competencies in 11 designated areas. These 11 areas are as follows: (1) career development theory, (2) individual and group counseling skills, (3) individual/group assessment, (4) information/resources, (5) program management and implementation, (6) consultation, (7) diverse populations, (8) supervision, (9) ethical/legal issues, (10) research/evaluation, and (11) technology. In 2009, these career counseling competencies were updated as the multicultural career counseling and development competencies. The update was done to ensure that individuals in training or practicing career counseling and development are aware of the expectation that they have to practice in ways that promote the career development and functioning of individuals of all backgrounds in accordance with the American Counseling Association (ACA) and NCDA policy. The introductory statement of this new document reads

> The purpose of the multicultural career counseling and development competencies is to ensure that all individuals practicing in, or training for practice in the career counseling and development field are aware of the expectation that we, as professionals, will practice in ways that promote the career development and functioning of individuals of all backgrounds. Promotion and advocacy of career development for individuals is ensured regardless of age, culture, mental/physical ability, ethnicity, race, nationality, religion/spirituality, gender, gender identity, sexual orientation, marital/partnership status, military or civilian status, language preference, socioeconomic status, any other characteristics not specifically relevant to job performance, in accordance with NCDA and ACA policy. Further, they will provide guidance to those in the career counseling and development field regarding appropriate practice with regard to clients of a different background than their own. Finally, implementation of these competencies for the field should provide the public with the assurance that they can expect career counseling and development professionals to function in a manner that facilitates their career development, regardless of the client's/student's background. (NCDA, 2009, p. 1)

In the following sections, we will briefly discuss the 11 areas in which career counseling professionals should demonstrate a minimum level of competency according to the NCDA.

Career Development Theory

This competency requires a theory base and knowledge considered essential for professionals engaging in career counseling and development. To provide career counseling to individuals, the multicultural career professional should understand the strengths and limitations of career theory and use the theory for the appropriate population. An individual must demonstrate knowledge of counseling theories and associated techniques, theories, and models of career development; individual differences related to gender, sexual, orientation, racial ethnicity, and physical and mental capacities; development of relationships throughout the life span; and facilitation of working plans, information techniques, and models related to career planning and placement.

Individual and Group Counseling Skills

This competency requires individual and group counseling skills that are considered essential for effective career counseling. To provide career counseling to individuals, the multicultural career professional should be (a) aware of his/her own cultural beliefs and assumptions and incorporate that awareness into his/her decision making about interactions with clients/students and other career professionals, (b) continually develop his/her individual and group counseling skills to enhance his/her ability to respond appropriately to individuals from diverse populations, and (c) be cognizant when working with people with different group demographics and monitor those differences to ensure that appropriate respect and confidentiality are maintained.

Individual/Group Assessment

This competency requires individual/group assessment skills that are considered essential for professionals engaging in career counseling. To provide career counseling to individuals, the multicultural career professional should understand the psychometric properties of the assessments he/she is using to select and administer assessments effectively and interpret and use results with the appropriate limitations and cautions.

Information/Resources and Technology

This competency requires an information/resource base and knowledge that are essential for professionals engaging in career counseling. To provide career counseling to individuals, the multicultural career professional should (a) evaluate the information, resources, and use of technology to determine that these tools are sensitive to the needs of diverse populations, amending and/or individualizing for each client as required; (b) provide resources in multiple formats to ensure that clients/students are able to benefit from needed information; and (c) provide targeted and sensitive support for clients/students in using the information, resources, and technology.

Program Promotion, Management, and Implementation

This competency requires the skills necessary to develop, plan, implement, and manage comprehensive career development programs in a variety of settings. To provide career counseling to individuals, the multicultural career professional should be able to (a) incorporate appropriate guidelines, research, and experience in developing, implementing, and managing programs and services for diverse populations; (b) use the principles of program evaluation to design and obtain feedback from relevant stakeholders in the continuous improvement of programs and services, paying special attention to feedback regarding the specific needs of the population being served; and (c) apply his/her knowledge of multicultural issues in dealing with other professionals and trainees to ensure the creation of a culturally sensitive environment for all clients.

Coaching, Consultation, and Performance Improvement

This competency requires knowledge and skills that are considered essential in enabling individuals and organizations to impact effectively upon the career counseling and development process. To provide career counseling to individuals, the multicultural career professional should be able to engage in coaching, consultation, and performance improvement activities with appropriate training and incorporate knowledge of multicultural attitudes, beliefs, skills, and values. Such a professional should also seek awareness and understanding about how to best match diverse clients/students with suitable, culturally sensitive employers.

Supervision

This competency requires knowledge and skills that are considered essential in critically evaluating counselor performance, maintaining and improving professional skills, and seeking assistance for others when needed in career counseling. To provide career counseling to individuals, the multicultural career professional should be able to accomplish the following: (a) Gain knowledge of and engage in evidence-based supervision and pursue educational and training activities on a regular basis inclusive of both counseling and supervision topics. Further, the multicultural career professional should be aware of his/her limitations, cultural biases, and personal values, as well as seek professional consultative assistance as necessary; (b) infuse multicultural/diversity contexts into his/her training and supervision practices, make supervisees aware of the ethical standards and responsibilities of the profession, and train supervisees to develop relevant multicultural knowledge and skills.

Research/Evaluation

This competency requires knowledge and skills that are considered essential in understanding and conducting research and evaluations in career counseling and development. To conduct research, the multicultural career professional should be able to design and implement culturally appropriate research studies with regard to design, instrument selection, and other pertinent population-specific issues.

Ethical/Legal Issues

This competency requires an information base and knowledge essential for the ethical and legal practice of career counseling. In accordance with the NCDA and the ACA codes of professional ethics, career development professionals must perform only activities for which they "possess or have access to the necessary skills and resources for giving the kind of help that is needed." If a professional does not have the appropriate training or resources for the type of career concern presented, an appropriate referral must be made. Career counselors or practitioners should never attempt to use skills for which he/she has not been trained. For additional ethical guidelines, refer to the NCDA Ethical Standards for Career Counselors. To provide career counseling to individuals, the multicultural career professional should follow three basic steps. (1) Continuously update his/her knowledge of multicultural and diversity issues and research and apply new knowledge as required. (2) Employ his/her knowledge and experience of multicultural ethical and legal issues within a professional framework to enhance the functioning of his/her organization and the image of the profession. (3) Use supervision and professional consultations effectively when faced with an ethical or legal issue related to diversity to ensure that he/she provides high-quality services for every client/student.

Multicultural Career Counseling Skills

In the book *Gaining Cultural Competence in Career Counseling*, Evans (2008) discussed the awareness, techniques, attitudes, knowledge, and multicultural skills that make up the framework for developing multicultural career counseling competencies. In this discussion, Evans (2008) proposed certain skills and characteristics that a multiculturally competent career counselor should have, including

1. The ability to establish trusting relationships to help clients feel at ease during the counseling process;
2. The ability to maintain a culturally sensitive group by taking care to choose members of the group to maximize the benefits of group counseling and minimize conflicts. This is accomplished by facilitating cultural understanding among group members;
3. An awareness that in some collectivist cultures, client goals may be communal rather than personal;
4. The ability to choose techniques that best fit their clients' problems and cultural backgrounds;
5. The understanding that personality and personal characteristics are influenced by race, ethnicity, gender, sexual orientation, and ability status and that these characteristics must be assessed accurately;
6. A political awareness and understanding that clients are affected by societal and institutional policies;
7. An understanding of the expectations that families and cultural structures place on clients in their work environments;
8. An awareness that each client is different and that acculturation will dictate the need for family members and/or other important members of the community to become involved in the process;
9. The ability to identify and understand clients' attitudes toward work and workers;
10. The ability to identify and understand clients' biases toward work and workers based on gender, race, and cultural stereotypes;
11. An understanding of how poverty, discrimination, racism, and so forth limit client access to information, inhibit client ability to take action, and limit the scope of possibilities clients may see for themselves;
12. An awareness of discriminatory practices at social and community agencies that may affect the psychological welfare of the client; and
13. Support and challenge clients to examine life-work roles, including the balance of work, leisure, family, and community in their careers. Multiculturally competent career counselors must realize that clients may need to be assisted in finding time for leisure and community to balance their busy lives (pp. 145–146).

As a multicultural career counselor/professional, it is important to enhance your culturally appropriate initiatives and services. Ward and Bingham (1993) proposed (a) counselor preparation, (b) exploration and assessment, and (c) negotiation and working consensus as three main areas to assess your multicultural career counseling competency.

Summary

Career counselors dedicate their time to helping individuals to get a better understanding of themselves and the world of work to make important occupational, education, and life decisions. During this process, career counselors provide clients with skills and tools that help them make future career and life decisions independently.

Without a doubt, career counseling has evolved over the years since Frank Parsons founded the first documented program. The establishment and subsequent revision of career counseling competencies, the establishment and subsequent revision of career counselor credentialing, and the establishment of ethical standards by NCDA to regulate career counseling practice further defined career counseling as a specialty.

It is therefore important for professional career counselors or persons in career development positions to have or be able to demonstrate the knowledge and skills for a specialty in career counseling that the generalist counselor may not necessarily have. All career counselors must be multiculturally competent and should demonstrate a minimum level of competency according to the 11 areas in which career counseling professionals should practice as outlined by the NCDA.

Discussion Questions

1. What is your professional identity as a career counselor?
2. As a career counselor/practitioner in training, what skills have you acquired so far in your program, and what skills have you yet to acquire?
3. Looking at the population you intend to work with, which of the competency areas will you use the most?

References

Brewer, J. M. (1942). *History of vocational guidance.* Harper.

Brown, D., Brooks, L., & Associates. (1990). *Career choice and development.* Jossey-Bass.

Brown, D., & Minor, C. W. (Eds.) (1992). *Career needs in a diverse workforce: Implications of the NCDA Gallup survey.* National Career Development Association.

Brown, S. D., & Lent, R. W. (Eds.). (2013). *Career development and counseling: Putting theory and research to work.* John Wiley & Sons.

Engels, D. W., Minor, C. W., Sampson, Jr., J. P., & Splete, H. H. (1995). Career counseling specialty: History, development, and prospect. *Journal of Counseling & Development, 74*(2), 134–138.

Evans, K. (2008). *Gaining cultural competence in career counseling.* Lahask Press.

Gysbers, N. C., & Moore, E. J. (1987). *Career counseling: Skills and techniques for practitioners.* Prentice-Hall

Havighurst, R. J. (1982). The world of work. In B. B. Wolman (Ed.), *Handbook of developmental psychology* (pp. 771–787). Prentice Hall.

Herr, E. L., & Cramer, S. H. (1992). *Career guidance & counseling through the lifespan* (4th ed.). Harper Collins.

Herr, E. L. (1997). Career counselling: A process in process. *British Journal of Guidance and Counselling, 25*(1), 81–93.

Lind, M. (1995). *The next American nation: The new nationalism and the fourth American revolution.* Simon & Schuster Inc.

McMahon, M., & Patton, W. (2002). *Supervision in the helping professions: A practical approach.* Pearson Education.

National Career Development Association. (NCDA). (2009). *Minimum competencies for multicultural career counseling and development.*

Niles, S. G., & Harris-Bowlsbey, J. A. (2002). *Career development interventions in the 21st century.* Merrill Prentice Hall.

Niles, S. G., & Harris-Bowlsbey, J. (2005). *Career development interventions in the 21st century* (2nd ed.). Pearson.

Oliver, L. W., & Spokane, A. R. (1988). Career-intervention outcome: What contributes to client gain? *Journal of Counseling Psychology, 35*(4), 447.

Parsons, F. (1909). *Choosing a vocation.* HardPress Publishing.

Peterson, G. W., Sampson, J. P., & Reardon, R. C. (1991). *Career development and services: A cognitive approach*. Brooks/Cole.

Sampson, J. P., Jr., & Loesch, L. C. (1991). *National career counselor certification examination technical manual*. National Board for Certified Counselors.

Savickas, M. L. (2005). Life design: A paradigm for career interventions in the 21st century. *Journal of Counseling and Development*, *90*, 13–19.

Smith, R. L., & Karpati, F. S. (1985). Credentialing career counselors. *Journal of Counseling & Development*, *63*(10), 611.

Spokane, A. (1991). *Career interventions*. Prentice Hall.

Super, D. E. (1957). The psychology of careers. Harper & Row

Ward, C., & Bingham, R. (1993). Career assessment of ethnic minority women. *Journal of Career Assessment*, *3*, 246–257.

CHAPTER 2

Career Counseling Theories and Models

Quiteya Walker and Nykeisha Grant

CHAPTER OVERVIEW

The purpose of this chapter is to introduce the basic elements of career development theories. This chapter describes the specific traditional and contemporary theories of career counseling from which counseling students may select to inform their career counseling approaches. Counselors can use career theories to guide their career interventions.

The theories of career counseling covered in this chapter are trait and factor theory, person-environment-correspondence, Holland's theory of types, Myers-Briggs type theory, Krumboltz's social learning theory, Super's model of career development, Super's life-span, life-space approach, Roe's personality development theory, and family systems theory in career counseling. The theories will be divided into subclasses: trait-oriented theories, social learning and cognitive theories, developmental theories, and relational theories. For each of the theories, the chapter outlines the key theorists, essential principles and concepts, key terms, the primary goal of the career counseling approach, and the outcomes. The chapter concludes with a discussion of how counselors can integrate their personal counseling styles into career counseling theories and approaches.

CHAPTER OBJECTIVES

After reading this chapter, the student will be able to complete the following:

1. Discuss the various types of career counseling models and theories.

2. Discuss the key concepts of each career counseling model and theory.

3. Identify limitations and strengths for each career counseling model and theory.

4. Integrate personal counseling styles into career counseling theories and approaches.

Trait and Factor Theory

The trait-and-factor approach is one of the oldest and most widely used career development theories. Trait and factor theory principles were first proposed in Frank Parsons's book, *Choosing a Vocation*. Parsons (1909) identified three domains that contribute to choosing an occupation: (1) understanding one's personhood, (2) analysis of occupations, and (3) development of a match between the person and the occupation. A later proponent of Parsons's trait and factor theory was Edmund G. Williamson (1965), who designed a six-step counseling approach to help clients make better career choices.

The term *trait* describes a distinguishing quality or characteristic that is unique to each individual. The term *factor* describes a characteristic that is required for successful job performance. Herr et al. (2004) identified the assumptions of trait and factor theory as follows: (a) there is a single career goal for everyone, and (b) career decisions are based primarily on measured abilities. As Flanigan (2011) noted, individuals have certain unique traits that can be matched to the requirements of different types of occupations. The likely satisfaction of the person with his/her vocational goal depends on the relationship between the occupation and the individual's traits. An individual's traits must be adequately assessed for an occupational match to occur.

Parsons's (1909) three-step approach included developing an understanding of one's personhood, conducting an analysis of occupations, and developing a match between the person and the occupation. To assist with gaining an understanding of one's personhood, step one involves the assessment of aptitude, achievement, interests, values, and personality. There are various assessments a counselor can use to assist a person with self-understanding. The trait and factor theory has been instrumental in the development of these assessments and is often scrutinized because of an overreliance on test results. Chapter 17 goes into more detail about career counseling intakes, assessments, and measurements.

Williamson's (1939) six-step counseling approach includes analysis, synthesis, diagnosis, prognosis, counseling, and follow-up. *Analysis* involves collecting data from many sources through structured and unstructured interviews about the person's attitude, aptitude, interests, family background, knowledge, and so on. An example of analysis would be asking the client background questions or administering a career assessment. Once all the information is collected about the individual, *synthesis* of the data takes place. An example of synthesis is compiling all the information you have collected into one document. *Diagnosis* involves the interpretation of the data to identify the nature and causes of a problem. The information the counselor has gathered will tell a story about the client, which will be used to make a diagnosis or understand the career development issues. *Prognosis* is the process of making a judgment about the future development of the problem in an effort to identify alternative actions and adjustments for the client. An example of prognosis is the counselor and client working together to identify different ways in which the client can rectify the career issues. *Counseling* involves working with the client to make adjustments and readjustments in relation to the problem in an effort to reach the desired outcome. The counselor and client will work to determine ways to reach the identified goal, which is also known as career counseling. Finally, *follow-up* involves repeating the previous steps as new problems arise or further assisting the client with reaching the identified goal. Follow-up can be seen when the counselor contacts the client 3 months following the final appointment to check in on progress. Through careful assessment of a person's unique traits and exploration of various occupations that match the person's traits, an individual can be successfully matched to a meaningful occupation.

The trait-and-factor approach has had a significant influence on career development. While it has been several decades since the creation of the theory, it is still useful today and has influenced many other career theories, such as person-environment-correspondence (PEC). Another major criticism of the theory is the directive and authoritarian nature of the counselor during the process.

PEC

PEC has also been referred to as the theory of work adjustment (TWA). Its theoretical roots branched from vocational rehabilitation research, which focused on securing the most suitable employment for individuals with disabilities. This influential theory laid the foundation to evaluate the congruence between a person and his/her work environment. Research has confirmed that the match between the two constructs predicts job satisfaction and tenure (Leonard & Schimmel, 2016).

Rene Dawis and Lloyd Lofquist (1984), as theorists of this model, defined the following terms to provide insight into the theory. *Work adjustment*, a significant component of TWA, is defined as a fluid process in which an individual achieves harmony within the workplace (Renfro-Michel et al., 2009). *Satisfaction* is the validity of a person's needs being met, and *satisfactoriness* occurs when the person has the skill set to meet the demands of the job. With the successful combination of satisfaction and satisfactoriness, *tenure* is developed and defined as the length of time these components coexist in the workplace (Hansen, 2013).

The underlying assumption of PEC theory is that every individual must secure and maintain a positive relationship with his/her work environment. Essential tenets of the theory are summarized as follows: (a) The workplace has a need, and the individual delivers a specific skill set to respond to the need; (b) the individual is required to be compensated for his/her experience, which may or may not be tangible; (c) the environment and individual must harmonize to guarantee satisfaction and longevity; (d) the individual's needs and expectations are the primary influences on the fit; (e) both the individual and the environment should expect change over time; and (f) flexibility of the person and/or the environment is necessary to determine to what extent he/she may adjust and/or tolerate change.

The implications of PEC theory begin after the vocational goal is selected. If a person becomes overwhelmed by his/her current job, he/she may reach out to a counselor for assistance. The counselor will complete the following three steps: (1) assess the individual's abilities, values, personality, and interests; (2) measure the conditions of the occupation; and (3) match abilities, values, and reinforcers. Assessments provide rich data for counseling sessions and are often incorporated for a more in-depth insight into the presented concern.

The General Aptitude Test Battery (U.S. Department of Labor, 1982) was a historical assessment used to measure work-related cognitive abilities; however, it was revised and is now known as the Ability Profiler. The new version yields 11 timed tests that measure nine work-related abilities. CareerScope is an interest and aptitude assessment that has been used extensively by the Department of Veterans Affairs with veterans who are transitioning from military to civilian life (Hart, 1999), but it can also be used with the general population. The Minnesota Importance Questionnaire (MIQ) (Rounds et al., 1981) is known as the assessment that measures the individual's needs, thus providing insight into an individual's satisfaction with his/her job. MIQ evaluates the individual's happiness explicitly with current working conditions, leadership, responsibility, and extrinsic rewards. Although it is essential to assess the individual, the work environment must also be evaluated.

The Minnesota Job Description Questionnaire (MJDQ) is a widely used assessment that asks individuals to indicate the relative importance of 21 vocationally relevant reinforcers (Borgen et al., 1968). The 21 needs may be grouped into six value dimensions. The MJDQ measures the occupational side, whereas the MIQ examines the personal side of values (McCloy et al., 1999). MJDQ and MIQ assessments match personal values with occupational values.

The outcome of PEC theory is to find the perfect blend between the individual and his/her work environment. The more closely the individual's abilities correspond with his/her place of employment, the more likely he/she will perform well at the job, which will generate favorable feedback from supervisors. There are many assessments to help a counselor guide an individual through career development to tenure. The bottom line is that both individuals and work environments experience ongoing changes; therefore, both must be able to adjust.

Holland's Career Typology Theory of Vocational Behavior

John Holland (1992) proposed the career typology theory of vocational behavior. The premise of the theory is that a successful employment outcome depends on a match between personality, background variables, and a specific career. He posited that career choice and career adjustment are an extension of one's personality. Holland's view on career development differed from other theorists, such as Super, because he believed personality factors lead to a career choice as opposed to a developmental process. The assumption of the theory is that career choice is determined by an individual's personality and several variables. According to Holland, individuals choose a career to satisfy their *modal personal style*, which is defined as congruence between the view of self and occupational preference. Holland defined *stereotypes* as a person's impressions and generalizations about work. He assigned people and work to different categories based on stereotypes.

Holland's theory of career development is supported by the Vocational Preference Inventory (VPI; Holland, 1985) and the Self-Directed Search (SDS; Holland et al., 1994). Both instruments can be used to measure an individual's personality. Another instrument specific to Holland's typology is called My Vocational Situation (Holland et al., 1980), which measures the concept of identity.

Holland's theory described how the individual and the environment interact through the development of six vocational personality and work environment types: (1) realistic, (2) investigative, (3) artistic, (4) social, (5) enterprising, and (6) conventional (R-I-A-S-E-C). The realistic environment requires more physical work. Realistic individuals are more likely to enjoy using tools and machines and are typically more practical and mechanical. The investigative environment requires more analytical work. Investigative environments require the ability to solve math and science problems, which investigative individuals are good at understanding. Artistic environments require creative and expressive thinking. The artistic individual has good artistic abilities in areas such as writing, drama, craft, music, or arts. The social environment requires the ability to engage with people. Social individuals enjoy helping people, solving social problems, and imparting information. The enterprising environment requires the ability to lead and persuade people. The enterprising individual is a good leader and excels at selling ideas and items. The conventional environment involves working with numbers, records, and machines. The conventional individual is orderly and excels at following a set plan. The six types are arranged in a hexagonal structure in the order of R-I-A-S-E-C (see Figure 2.1). Types that are more proximal to one another on the hexagon are more similar than those that are farther apart on the hexagon. The theory also accounts for a combination of types because the belief is that many individuals do not fit into a single Holland psychological type.

Holland's theory includes four important constructs that are helpful in counseling individuals: (1) congruence, (2) differentiation, (3) consistency, and (4) identity. *Congruence* refers to the relationship between personality and the environment. The more similar a person's personality is to the environment, the

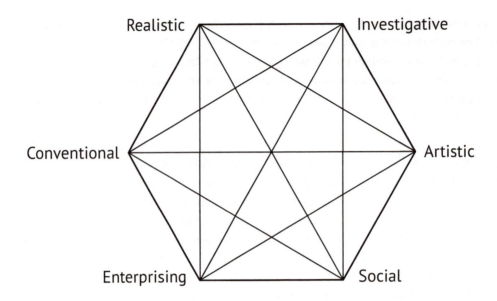

Figure 2.1 *Holland's Hexagonal Structure of the Six Types (Holland, 1997)*

more congruent the relationship. *Differentiation* refers to the difference between the personality and the environment. There are instances in which an individual may closely relate to one personality type or be undifferentiated and relate to several different types. The formula for establishing differentiation involves subtracting the lowest score of any type from the highest score of any type on the SDS or VPI. *Consistency* refers to the differences and similarities of the types in regard to an individual's personality and environments. As shown in Figure 2.1, enterprising and conventional environments are more consistent with one another, and they are closer together on the hexagonal shape, whereas social and realistic are farther apart, and the personality types are more inconsistent. *Identity* is the clarity and stability of an individual's goals and the working environment. Identity is formed when a person is clear about what he/she wants to do and has garnered the necessary information to be successful in that occupation. An environment has achieved identity when the intended outcome of the employee does not vary widely; the tasks are specific.

Holland's theory has been widely researched and proven to be effective. The theory provides a useful framework for understanding career satisfaction. This theory can be used as a vocational guide for those who wish to study different careers and offer information about why individuals are not satisfied with certain careers. Strengths of the theory include the ease of understanding the different concepts, clear definitions, and consistency of the structure (Holland & Gottfredson, 1976). Holland and Gottfredson noted a weakness of the theory to be inaccurate information provided in some publications of the theory. As such, it is important to be careful about the various interpretations of the theory.

Myers-Briggs Type Theory

Myers-Briggs Type Theory originated from the work of Jung (1971) and was later adapted by Briggs and Myers in their development of the Myers-Briggs Type Indicator (MBTI) assessment, a well-known and widely used tool (Myers, 1962). The basic premise of the theory is that individuals observe their worlds and make decisions based on their perceptions. Myers-Briggs type theory was not originally created to be a theory of counseling but is used as such by counselors.

The Myers-Briggs theory includes the four bipolar dimensions: (1) extraversion-introversion, (2) sensing-intuition, (3) thinking-feeling, and (4) judgment-perception. Briggs and Myers were responsible for adding the fourth dimension of judgment and perception to Jung's previous concepts. *Perception* occurs when an individual takes in information. Perceptive individuals are spontaneous, curious, and open to change (Blodgett, 2017). The perceiving dimension has two modes: *sensing* and *intuition. Sensing* involves taking in information using the five senses to perceive the physical world. Individuals who have a sensing attitude prefer to observe using their senses. These individuals focus on current events and are observant and detail-oriented. *Intuition* is the process of an individual using the unconscious to evaluate the natural world. Intuitive individuals are more judgmental, imaginative, and future-oriented. These individuals focus on future events and ways to connect one event to another. Intuitive individuals have a tendency to be creative, imaginative, and abstract. *Judgment* is the process of decision making. Individuals who have a judging attitude are organized and decisive (Blodgett, 2017). The judging dimension has two different modes: *thinking* and *feeling. Thinking* involves using a rational and logical process to evaluate information, resulting in the process of analysis and objectivity. *Feeling* is more value-oriented and factors in others' points of view. Feeling involves the evaluation of information based on emotional response.

The concept of perceiving and judging can be combined to understand individual behavior. *Sensing-* and *thinking*-oriented individuals are more practical and pragmatic. *Sensing-* and *feeling*-oriented individuals make decisions based on their feelings. *Intuition-* and *feeling*-oriented individuals are more likely to be future-oriented. *Intuition-* and *thinking*-oriented individuals make rational decisions after careful thought.

Extraversion and introversion are additional factors that add to the understanding of perception and judgment. While both extroverts and introverts deal with the inner world and outer world in their own ways (Boeree, 2006), extroverts are motivated by outwardly focused behaviors, whereas introverts are motivated by inwardly focused behaviors. Extroverts prefer people and activities. Introverts prefer their own thoughts and feelings.

Myers-Briggs typology is often used with trait and factor theory and an assessment of aptitude, achievement, or interest. When conducting career counseling, the counselor would consider the listing of environments from the MBTI manual and the client's personality type to assist with integrating information about the person and the world of work. Each of the concepts can interact with each other to yield different types, known as the 16 personality types. In an effort to categorize the individual personality type codes, Myers and Briggs created the Systematic Type Table (see Figure 2.2).

The 16 personality types include the four bipolar dimensions divided into 16 combinations. Introverts (I) appear at the top half of the table and extroverts (E) at the bottom half. The sensing (S) dimension appears at the left side of the table and intuition (N) on the right side of the table. The thinking (T), feeling (F), judgment (J), and perception (P) dimensions are disbursed systematically throughout the table. The information in Figure 2.2 provides a system for understanding different personality types and occupations when conducting career counseling.

			Sensing Types		Intuitive Types	
			Thinking	Feeling	Feeling	Thinking
			-ST-	-SF-	-NF-	-NT-
Introvert	Judging	I – J	ISTJ	ISFJ	INFJ	INTJ
Introvert	Perceiving	I – P	ISTP	ISFP	INFP	INTP
Extravert	Perceiving	E – P	ESTP	ESFP	ENFP	ENTP
Extravert	Judging	E – J	ESTJ	ESFJ	ENFJ	ENTJ

Figure 2.2 *MBTI Systematic Type Table (Myers & Briggs, 1995)*

Krumboltz's Social Learning Theory

John Krumboltz, along with his colleagues (Krumboltz et al., 1975; Mitchell & Krumboltz, 1996), developed a social learning theory approach that emphasized behavior and cognition in career decision making. The theory assumes that life events are influential in determining career decision making. Specifically, learning experiences affect occupational selection, and this learning takes place through both observation and direct experiences. It is believed that each individual's unique learning experiences over the course of life lead to career decision making.

Krumboltz's social learning theory (KSLT) assumed that four factors play a central role in career decision making: (1) genetics and special qualities, (2) environmental conditions and events, (3) learning experiences, and (4) task-approach skills. Task-approach skills and learning experiences are unique qualities of KSLT that make it different from other career development theories. Genetics and special qualities are those inherited and innate traits that allow them to grasp concepts in certain areas more quickly. For example, some individuals are born with strengths in math and science that they may have inherited from a parent; these individuals may be more likely to go into those professions or have more knowledge about particular occupations in science, technology, engineering, and math.

Environmental experiences and events are social, cultural, political, and economic conditions that are outside the control of individuals. Environmental conditions include social conditions, parents and caretakers, peer groups, structured learning settings, and occupational conditions. An example of an environmental condition would be an individual who lives in a rural area and has limited job opportunities, which may create limited access to specific job skills and result in limited career choices.

Learning experiences are how individuals' previous learning affects their career decision making. There are two types of learning experiences: instrumental learning and associative learning. Instrumental learning experiences include the antecedents, behaviors, and consequences of an event. Associative learning experiences include observation and classical conditioning. Classical conditioning is the generalization of an event, whereas observation is the actual observation of the event.

Task-approach skills describe the process of completing a task. Examples of task-approach skills are researching jobs, setting goals to acquire employment, problem-solving strategies to overcome unemployment, and identifying current work skills. Task-approach skills are essential for understanding an individual's ability to make career decisions.

Super's Model of Career Development

Developmental theories of careers assume that "career development is a process that takes place over the life span" (Super et al., 1996, p. 128). Arthur et al. (1989) noted that individuals progress through distinct career stages, each characterized by unique concerns, psychological needs, and developmental tasks. Super (1957) defined a career as a sequence of positions occupied by a person during the course of a lifetime. Super's career development theory also includes the notions of self-concept (Betz, 1994) and career maturity. Self-concept is how individuals view themselves (Super, 1957). It has been defined as "the constellation of self attributes considered by the individual to be vocationally relevant" (Super, 1963, p. 20). Super (1963) suggested that individuals attempt to implement their self-concept through occupational choice. Vocational self-concept develops through observations of work, identification with working adults, general environment and experience, and physical and mental growth. Career maturity is the successful accomplishing of developmental tasks within a continuous series of life stages.

Super (1990) described five stages individuals go through in their careers. The five stages are (1) growth, (2) exploration, (3) establishment, (4) maintenance, and (5) disengagement.

Stage 1: Growth. The growth stage spans from birth to age 14 or 15. In the growth stage, an individual begins to develop his/her self-concept (Super, 1957). The growth stage involves an individual's first introduction to the world of occupations (Super, 1990).

Stage 2: Exploration. The exploration stage spans from ages 15 to 24. Individuals in the exploration stage gather more specific information about themselves and the world of work. The stereotypes learned in the growth stage are refined as adolescents and young adults learn more about the world of work and more accurate information is obtained about specific occupations. Individuals then act on this information by matching their interests and capabilities to occupations in an attempt to implement their self-concept at work and in other life roles (Super, 1957). The substages of exploration are crystallizing, specifying, and implementing. Crystallizing is the process of making and implementing a decision about employment. Specifying is the process of identifying one's preference to aid in selecting a specific job or occupation. The last part of the exploration process before working is implementing. This involves making specific plans to meet one's career goals.

Stage 3: Establishment. The establishment stage spans from ages 25 to 44. During the establishment stage, individuals are concerned with career advancement in their chosen occupation. They are trying to establish a stable work environment with the potential for growth and the opportunity for promotions. The substages of the establishment phase are stabilizing, consolidating, and advancing. Stabilizing is the process of becoming permanent on a job; it involves settling down in a job and meeting the minimum requirements. During the consolidation stage, an individual is comfortable with employment, and the goal is to prove dependability and competence. Advancement involves moving ahead in one's current employment.

Stage 4: Maintenance. The maintenance stage spans from ages 45 to 64. During the maintenance stage, individuals are concerned with maintaining their self-concept and their present job status. In the maintenance stage, individuals are faced with career choices, such as whether to remain in their chosen occupation and whether to continue working for their present company. The substages of maintenance are holding, updating, and innovating. Holding involves staying in one's current position. Updating involves enhancing content knowledge in one's specific occupational area. This can involve attending conferences, workshops, and professional meetings, whereby individuals can gain knowledge in their specific content areas. Innovating involves making contributions to the field in which one works.

Stage 5: Disengagement. The disengagement stage spans from age 65+. During the disengagement stage, individuals are focused on developing a self-image and a self-concept that are independent of and separate from work. Advances in health care, the aging of the workforce, and the desire to remain active in the workplace throughout one's 60s and 70s suggest that people today may spend a long time in the maintenance stage and delay disengaging from work more than was true of their parents and grandparents (Brewington & Nassar-McMillan, 2000). The substages of the disengagement stage are decelerating retirement planning and retirement living. Decelerating is minimizing work roles and responsibilities. This could involve training others to do the required task in one's specific area. Retirement planning is the process of making financial, familial, and social decisions about plans postemployment. Retirement living is the change one experiences postemployment.

Recycling. The process of transitioning through the various stages does not always occur in an ordered pattern; sometimes, a person can recycle through one or more stages. For example, individuals may be downsized from their current employment and thus need to recycle back to the exploratory stage.

Super's career development theory is the most widely known view of career development. The theory allows for an individual to change over time depending on his/her stage of development. Super views the entire process as unfolding throughout a person's life (Šverko, 2006).

Super's Life-Space, Life-Span Approach

Super's life-space, life-span approach (1980) refined the concepts of life span and life space to incorporate the various personal and social determinants of the use of life space in occupying career positions and fulfilling roles during the course of a career. This approach is based on the premise that career development is a process that unfolds gradually over the life span and is a continuous process that involves multiple life space roles. Herr (1997) noted that people live in multiple-role environments where roles (work, family, education, and community) vary in demand during different periods of development.

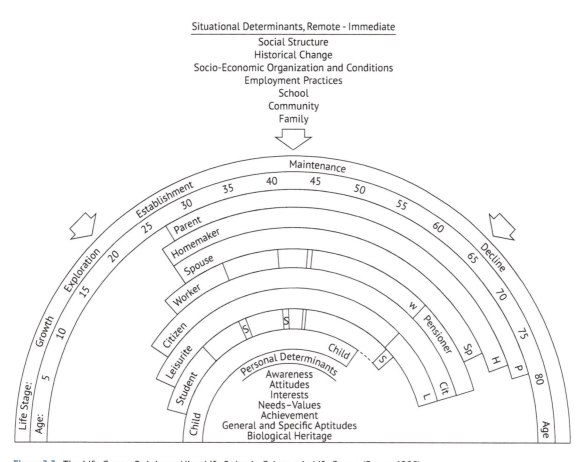

Figure 2.3 *The Life Career Rainbow: Nine Life Roles in Schematic Life Space (Super, 1980)*

Super (1980) developed the life career rainbow, as shown in Figure 2.3, also known as the life-stage model. In the model, the maxicycle is a description of the five major life stages and thus is a representation of a longitudinal dimension of the life span. Minicycles represent major life stages that can occur within any of the stages in the maxicycle. A second component of the approach is life space, which is defined as the variety of roles individuals play throughout their lifetimes. According to Super, life space includes nine roles: (1) child, (2) student, (3) leisurite, (4) citizen, (5) worker, (6) spouse, (7) homemaker, (8) parent, and (9) pensioner. The bands of the rainbow identify the current or past life career roles. Super (1980) used the life career rainbow device to provide information on the longitudinal nature of roles that most people play across their lives; how these roles emerge, interact, and possibly conflict; and how these roles shape decision points that occur before and at the time of taking on a new role, giving up an old role, and making significant changes in the nature of an existing role.

Super identifies the four principal theaters where the nine life space roles are played as (1) the home, (2) the community, (3) the school, and (4) the workplace. There are other theaters that are not considered the principal theaters; they include the church, the retirement community, and so on. It is essential to note that not everyone enters all theaters. For example, some people never attend a traditional school but are homeschooled, and some individuals may never work because of a disability or some other factor that limits their ability to work. All roles affect each other in the various theaters; for example, individuals can be involved in several roles within several theaters simultaneously, and success in one role can facilitate success in other roles. Super (1990) also developed the archway model to differentiate between the various life roles an individual encounters over the life span (see Figure 2.4).

The archway model includes material from the life career rainbow but reaffirms the interaction of the individual and society in the base and two vertical columns of the archway. The archway model was designed to be more descriptive than the life career rainbow. The models provide a depiction of how biographical,

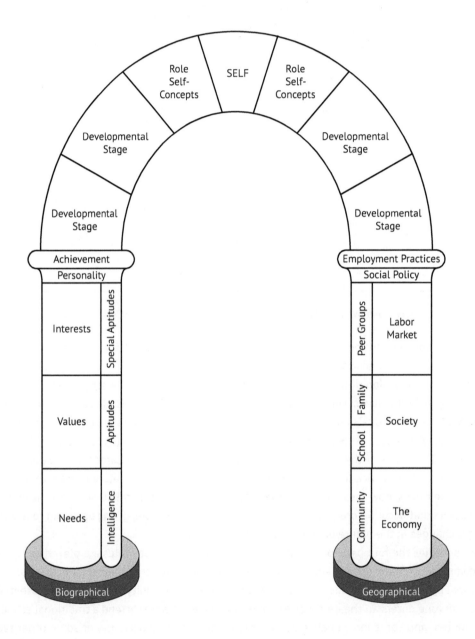

Figure 2.4 *Archway of Career Determinants (Super, 1990)*

psychological, socioeconomic, and other environmental determinants influence the development of apti-tudes, interests, values, and careers.

A strength of Super's life-space, life-span approach is the ability of individuals to make changes as they evolve. A limitation of this approach is the lack of focus on ethnic and gender differences. The theory originated during a time when women worked as homemakers or were in sexually segregated occupations; as such, the theory is predominantly based on white male subjects who hold a social value of independence.

Roe's Personality Development Theory

Roe's personality development theory, proposed by Anne Roe (1956), is very individualistic; however, Roe believed childhood experiences influence an individual's career choice (Brown, Lum, & Voyle, 1997). She demonstrated that people's choices of careers are based on a common background of how they were raised and may be based on an individual's unmet needs during childhood. The tenets of this theory are that (a) children's experiences are defined by their environment; (b) the environment has the following modes: emotional concentration, avoidance, and acceptance; and (c) each of the aforementioned modes generates different parenting styles.

Emotional concentration is a parenting style in which the child's physical needs are met; however, responses to psychological needs are concerning. Emotional concentration can produce either an overly protective parent or a demanding parent. Although in both cases, the parents want the best for their chil-dren, the environment encourages dependence or demands perfectionism, respectively. Avoidance and acceptance parenting styles are opposites. Avoidance is when parents may neglect or reject their children's physical and psychological needs. In this parenting style, the parents are overly critical of their children and may ignore their children's needs because of their life stressors. On the opposite side of the spectrum is acceptance. According to Roe, this type of parenting style produces independent children because their parents are supportive.

Roe's personality development theory proposed that parental style was correlated with occupational selection. Individuals' career choices may be fostered by how they develop attitudes toward or away from people. They may choose a career that requires either a lower or a higher level of interactions with others. For example, a child raised by supportive parents may select a career in the helping professions. On the other hand, if a child is raised in an environment that was nonsupportive, he/she may want to work independently.

Roe was unhappy with the classification of occupational careers; therefore, she developed a list of eight occupational groups divided into six levels of responsibility, capability, and skills needed to perform on each level. Table 2.1 highlights the occupational groups with examples.

After Roe identified the occupational categories, she subdivided them into the following six classification levels: (1) independent responsibility, (2) less independence and responsibility, (3) semiprofessional, (4) skilled, (5) semiskilled, and (6) unskilled. An individual was classified into eight categories and six levels based on how much skill was required for the job.

The outcome of this theory is to help clients understand how their childhood environment shapes them to align with a specific career path. The tenets of the theory can help an individual who may be struggling with a career choice; however, the theory does not discuss vocational development after the career choice. The theory is underused in the counseling profession because of questions of validity. However, studies

Table 2.1. ROE'S EIGHT OCCUPATIONAL CATEGORIES

Occupation	Examples
Service	Maids, teachers, nurses
Business	Salesmen, buyers, brokers
Organizations	Accountants, bankers, analysts
Technology	Engineers, mechanics, web developers
Outdoor	Farmers, miners, landscapers
Science	Technicians, pharmacists, chemists
Culture	Curators, historians, anthropologists
Arts and entertainment	Singers, actors, comedians

continue to use this framework and support Roe's key proposals (Brown et al., 1997). Therefore, the author of this chapter suggests that this theory will move to the forefront in the counseling profession. It is essential that members of this helping profession understand the importance of clients' career choices, as the selection will impact clients and their families. The clients will be in a better position to understand their choices and positively influence generational career choices.

Family Systems Theory

Family systems theory was one of the first comprehensive theories of family systems functioning. Murray Bowen, the founder of family systems theory (Bowen, 1966), proposed that a family is an emotional unit that is interconnected and interdependent. To truly understand a family dynamic, the family must be analyzed instead of the individuals within the unit. Although career counseling is not the focal point of family counseling, research has confirmed that family dynamics influence career choices.

In Bowen's theory, there are two types of families. The enmeshed family is a dysfunctional family dynamic in which the family responsibilities are unclear. This dynamic tends to work against the family system as a unit and focuses on one individual. Enmeshed families tend to prevent children from developing their unique identities, and boundaries are continuously overlooked, which becomes problematic in career selection. Enmeshment may be developed and passed down through generations. On the opposite spectrum, there is the disengaged family. These families are detached and share little to nothing within the family unit. The family members are typically living independently under one roof. Also, they see their solutions as keeping their concerns from their family members. The ideal is a balanced family. In this type of family, each family member recognizes that each person has emotions and may make independent decisions. They respect each other's differences, emphasize nurturing, and support growth. Regardless of the type of family dynamics, career selection is being affected.

Within this paragraph, the author of this chapter provides a scenario of how career selection looks from each dynamic. For example, Noah Jones decides he would like to become an engineer. His mother supports his choice; however, his father advises him that he must become a doctor. His mother helps Noah identify top engineering programs, while his father will not entertain any conversations about his choice to pursue engineering. In the disengaged dynamic, the father uses his authoritative role and tells Noah that he must study to become a doctor because all the Jones men are doctors. The father may even refuse to provide any financial support to Noah if he chooses to become an engineer. His mother has no opinion. During a family conversation, Noah's younger brother, Brandon, teases him for being a nerd and states that nerds should become doctors. The parents do nothing to correct Brandon's statements. Within the same scenario, a balanced family will listen to Noah's choice and gain more insight into his selection. As a family, they will determine if engineering is the best choice for Noah as they look at the job market, local schools, and his current academic strengths. If the parents are unsure how to help Noah, they may reach out to a family therapist. He/she will use theoretical techniques to support the family.

Genograms are three-generational graphic representations of family relationships. However, a career genogram takes this idea one step further. A career genogram looks at established career patterns, or a lack thereof, in a family unit (Paquette, 2019). A counselor or a family member may use a genogram to help the individual determine family patterns, solidify their inner meaning of work, and determine viable career choices.

Career choices are decisions that individuals must make as they enter adulthood. It is recommended that families create a safe atmosphere for their children to feel safe to explore. When in doubt about where to begin, the family may start this conversation by developing a genogram. This technique has proven to be a resource that may add unique value to every family. The expected outcome is a family unit that is balanced and will allow the fostering of career exploration and selection in a supportive environment.

Integrating Personal Counseling Style Into Career Counseling

Each of the career counseling theories described earlier has roots in personality theory. For example, Krumboltz's social learning theory is rooted in behavioral principles. Furthermore, theories such as those of Roe and Holland can be considered mini-personality theories. Super's and Roe's theories propose developmental concepts related to child development and the role of early experiences. Given the different career counseling theories that are rooted in personality theories, the incorporation of personal counseling style into career counseling can be seen as a seamless process.

Career development theories can help individuals understand themselves and either their chosen careers or other career options. Integrating career theories with personality theories can be beneficial for clients. For example, career theories can be integrated with cognitive theory. Holland's career typology theory of vocational behavior and cognitive theory can be used together to understand how people with heightened work experience develop different views of themselves that lead to job changes (Holland & Gottfredson, 1976). The use of story in career and personal counseling is another beneficial integration. The narrative approach involves dialogue between the client and counselor. The client is allowed to tell his/her story and reauthor their stories. Gysbers et al. (1998) noted that the use of story in career counseling is a way to identify and analyze life career themes. The integration of career and personal counseling can be a useful tool in career counseling and beneficial for client success.

Summary

Career counseling theories is a useful roadmap counselors can use when assisting individuals with career counseling. Counselors possess the skills to help clients prepare for career decision making and utilizing career counseling theories will serve as a guide throughout the process. In this chapter we have identified traditional and contemporary theories of career counseling and how counselors can integrate their personal counseling styles into career counseling theories and approaches. We have outlined the key theorists, essential principles and concepts, key terms, the primary goal of the career counseling approach, and the outcomes for each theory discussed. We have identified limitations and strengths for each career counseling model and theory.

Discussion Questions

1. Discuss your opinion on the importance of utilizing career counseling theories as a factor related to successful employment outcomes.
2. Compare and contrast two career counseling theories or models. In your response, describe the benefits and drawbacks in applying each perspective.
3. Discuss the five stages in Super's career development theory.
4. Discuss how you would integrate your personal counseling styles into career counseling.

Table 2.2. OVERVIEW OF CAREER COUNSELING THEORIES

Theories	Key Theorist	View of Human Occupational Behavior	Goal/Outcome
Trait-Oriented Theories			
Trait and Factor Theory	Frank Parsons	Trait and factor theory asserts that there is a single career goal for everyone and career decisions are based primarily on measured abilities. The three domains that contribute to choosing an occupation are (1) understanding one's personhood, (2) analysis of occupations, and (3) development of a match between the person and the occupation.	Through careful assessment of a person's unique traits and exploration of various occupations that match the person's traits, an individual can be successfully matched to a meaningful occupation. Counseling involves working with the client to make adjustments and readjustments in relation to the problem in an effort to reach the desired outcome.
PEC Theory	Rene Dawis and Lloyd Lofquist	Career choice and development is an ongoing process. This includes individuals seeking to achieve and maintain a positive relationship with their work environment. The perfect match equates to tenure.	The goal is to find the positive correlation between the individual and his/her work environment. Thus it will increase the individual's satisfaction and the company's satisfactoriness.

Theories	Key Theorist	View of Human Occupational Behavior	Goal/Outcome
Trait-Oriented Theories			
John Holland's Typology	John Holland	Holland believed that career choice and career adjustment are an extension of one's personality. Career choice is determined by a fit between the individual's personality type and work type. Individuals choose a career to satisfy their modal personal style and occupational preference. Holland defined *stereotypes* as a person's impressions and generalizations about work. Most people can be categorized as one of the six stereotypes: realistic, investigative, artistic, social, enterprising, and conventional.	The goal of Holland's theory is to match occupations and work environments with individuals' personality types. Thus individuals will be more satisfied with their jobs and experience other positive work outcomes.
Myers-Briggs Type Theory	Carl Gustav Jung Isabel Briggs Myers Katharine Briggs	Individuals observe their worlds and make decisions based on their perceptions. Myers and Briggs outlined 16 personality types based on the four personality preferences from which individuals perceive their world. The four bipolar dimensions are (1) extraversion-introversion, (2) sensing-intuition, (3) thinking-feeling, and (4) judgment-perception.	The goal of Myers-Briggs type theory is to help individuals understand how they perceive and judge the world and how they perceive their inner world and the outer world as they relate to career decision making. The counselor should help the client examine how the Myers-Briggs types interact to assist with career decision making.
Social Learning and Cognitive Theories			
Krumboltz's Social Learning Theory	John D. Krumboltz	This theory emphasizes behavior and cognition in career decision making. The theory assumes that life events are influential in determining career decision making and that social learning takes place through observation and direct learning experiences. Learning experiences affect occupational selection, and this learning takes place through both observation and direct experiences. Four factors play a central role in career decision making: (1) genetics and unique qualities, (2) environmental conditions and events, (3) learning experiences, and (4) task-approach skills.	The goal of Krumboltz social learning theory is to explore the individual learning experience and task-approach skills over the life span to assist in making a career choice. Counselors use cognitive and behavioral counseling strategies to assist the client in career counseling.

continues on next page

Theories	Key Theorist	View of Human Occupational Behavior	Goal/Outcome
Developmental Theories			
Super's Model of Career Development	Donald Super	Career development takes place over the life span. Individuals progress through distinct career stages in which each stage is characterized by unique career concerns, psychological needs, and developmental tasks. Super's theory outlines the five stages individuals go through in their careers: (1) growth, (2) exploration, (3) establishment, (4) maintenance, and (5) disengagement.	The goal of the theory is to provide an overall mastery of tasks unique to each stage of development. Individuals who gain strong foundational experience at each stage will be more successful as they transition through the stages, thus reaching career maturity.
Life-Span, Life-Space Approach	Donald Super	Super's life-space, life-span approach refined the concepts of life span and life space to incorporate the various personal and social determinants of the use of life space in occupying career positions and fulfilling roles during the course of a career. This approach is based on the premise that career development is a process that unfolds gradually over the life span, and it is a continuous process that involves multiple life-space roles. In this concept, Super identifies nine life roles and four life spaces.	The goal of the theory is to help individuals capture their vocational identities and self-concepts. It is important to clarify an individual's self-concept because this will increase a person's successful occupational choice.
Relational Approaches			
Roe's Personality Development Theory	Ann Roe	Focuses on psychological needs that develop between the interaction of parent and child. Career choice is developed from child and parent interactions.	The goal of Roe's personality development theory is to provide insight into how parental influence affects the career choices of children. Counselors analyze past relationships to help a client effectively deal with career exploration and choice in a supportive environment.
Family Systems Theory	Murray Bowen	Family is a unit and may not be viewed as individual parts. The family should work together to relieve family strain and promote growth.	The goal of family systems theory is to gain individuality while maintaining togetherness. A family unit that is balanced will foster career exploration and selection in a supportive environment.

References

Arthur, M. B., Hall, D. T., & Lawrence, B. S. (1989). Generating new directions in career theory: The case for a transdisciplinary approach. In M. B. Arthur, D. T. Hall, & B. S. Lawrence (Eds.), *Handbook of career theory* (pp. 7–25). Cambridge University Press.

Betz, N. E. (1994). Basic issues and concepts in career counseling for women. In W. B. Walsh & S. H. Osipow (Eds.), *Contemporary topics in vocational psychology. Career counseling for women* (pp. 1–41). Lawrence Erlbaum Associates, Inc.

Blodgett, J. (2017). *Exploring the Myers-Briggs Type Indicator.* https://shareok.org/bitstream/handle/11244/317246/oksd_blodgett_HT_2017.pdf

Boeree, C. G. (2006). *Personality theories: Carl Jung.* http://webspace.ship.edu/cgboer/jung.html

Borgen, F. H., Weiss, D. J., Tinsley, H. E. A., Dawis, R. V., & Lofquist, L. H. (1968). *Minnesota Job Description Questionnaire.* University of Minnesota, Psychology Department, Vocational Psychology Research.

Bowen, M. (1966). The use of family theory in clinical practice. *Comprehensive Psychiatry, 7*(5), 345–374.

Brewington, J. O., & Nassar-McMillan, S. (2000). Older adults: Work-related issues and implications for counseling. *The Career Development Quarterly, 49,* 2–15.

Brown, M., Lum, J., & Voyle, K. (1997). Roe revised: A call for the reappraisal of theory of personality development and career choice. *Journal of Vocational Behavior, 51,* 283–294.

Dawis, R. V., & Lofquist, L. H. (1984). *A psychological theory of work adjustment.* University of Minnesota Press.

Flanigan, D. (2011). *The influence of cultural context on vocational assessment with bicultural Latina/o college students* [Doctoral dissertation]. University of Florida.

Gysbers, N. C., Heppner, M. J., & Johnston, J. A. (1998). *Career counseling: Process, issues and techniques.* Allyn & Bacon.

Hansen, J.-I. C. (2013). A person-environment fit approach to cultivating meaning. In B. J. Dik, Z. S. Byrne, & M. F. Steger (Eds.), *Purpose and meaning in the workplace* (pp. 37–55). American Psychological Association.

Hart, J. (1999). Interest vs. aptitude in career assessments. *Tech Directions, 58*(9), 26.

Herr, E. L. (1997). Super's life-span, life-space approach and its outlook for refinement. *The Career Development Quarterly, 45*(3), 238–246.

Herr, E. L., Cramer, S. H., & Niles, S. G. (2004). *Career guidance and counseling through the life span: Systemic approaches* (6th ed.). Pearson Education, Inc.

Holland, J. L. (1985). *Manual for the Vocational Preference Inventory.* Psychological Assessment Resources.

Holland, J. L. (1992). *Making vocational choices* (2nd ed.). Psychological Assessment Resources.

Holland, J. L. (1997). *Making vocational choices* (3rd ed.). Psychological Assessment Resources, Inc.

Holland, J. L., Daiger, D., & Power, P. G. (1980). *My vocational situation.* Psychological Assessment Resources.

Holland, J. L., & Gottfredson, G. D. (1976). Using a typology of persons and environments to explain careers: Some extensions and clarifications. *The Counseling Psychologist, 6*(3), 20–29.

Holland, J. L., Powell, A. B., & Fritzsche, B. A. (1994). *The SDS: Professional users guide.* Psychological Assessment Resources.

Jung, C. G. (1971), *Psychological types: The collected work of C. G. Jung* (Vol. 6, H. B. Baynes, Trans., R. F. Hull, rev.). Princeton University Press. (Original work published 1921)

Krumboltz, J. D., Mitchell, A., & Gelatt, H. G. (1975). Applications of social learning theory of career selection. *Focus on Guidance, 8*(3), 1–16.

Leonard, J., & Schimmel, C. (2016). Theory of work adjustment and student-athletes' transition out of sports. *Journal of Issues in Intercollegiate Athletics, 9,* 62–85.

McCloy, R., Waugh, G., Medsker, G., Wall, J., Rivkin, D., & Lewis, P. (1999). *Determining the occupational reinforcer patterns for O* NET occupational units.* https://www.onetcenter.org/dl_files/ORP.pdf

Mitchell, K. E., & Krumboltz, J. D. (1996). Krumboltz's learning theory of career choice and counseling. In D. Brown, L. Brooks, & Associates (Eds.), *Career choice and development* (3rd ed., pp. 233–280). Jossey-Bass.

Myers, I. B. (1962). *Manual: The Myers-Briggs Type Indicator.* Educational Testing Service.

Paquette, E. W. (2019, August 28). *Career genogram. Career Consulting Concepts.* http://www.careerconsultingconcepts.com/blog/career-genogram

Parsons, F. (1909). *Choosing a vocation.* Houghton Mifflin.

Renfro-Michel, E. L., Burlew, L. D., & Robert, T. (2009). The interaction of work adjustment and attachment theory: Employment counseling implications. *Journal of Employment Counseling, 46,* 18–26.

Roe, A. (1956). *The psychology of occupations.* John Wiley & Sons.

Rounds, J. B., Henley, G. A., Dawis, R. V., Lofquist, L. H., & Weiss, D. J. (1981). *Manual for the Minnesota Importance Questionnaire.* University of Minnesota, Psychology Department, Work Adjustment Project.

Super, D. E. (1957). *The psychology of careers.* Harper & Row.

Super, D. E. (1963). Self-concepts in vocational development. In D. E. Super, R. Starishevski, N. Matkin, & J. P. Jordaan (Eds.), *Career development: Self-concept theory* (pp. 1–16). College Entrance Examination Board.

Super, D. E. (1980). A life-span, life-space approach to career development. *Journal of Vocational Behavior, 13,* 282–298.

Super, D. E. (1990). A life-span, life-space approach to career development. In D. Brown, L. Brooks, & Associates (Eds.), *Career choice and development: Applying contemporary theories to practice* (2nd ed., pp. 197–261). Jossey-Bass.

Super, D. E., Savickas, M. L., & Super, C. M. (1996). The life-span, life-space approach to careers. In D. Brown, L. Brooks, & Associates (Eds.). *Career choice and development* (3rd ed., pp. 121–170). Jossey-Bass.

Šverko, B. (2006). Super's career development theory. In J. H. Greenhaus & G. A. Callanan (Eds.), *Encyclopedia of career development* (pp. 790–792). Sage Publications.

U.S. Department of Labor. (1982). *Manual for the USES General Aptitude Test Battery: Section II. Occupational aptitude pattern structure.* U.S. Government Printing Office.

Williamson, E. G. (1939). *How to counsel students: A manual of techniques for clinical counselors.* McGraw-Hill.

Williamson, E. G. (1965). *Vocational counseling: Some historical, philosophical, and theoretical perspectives.* McGraw-Hill.

Figure Credits

CHAPTER 3

Ethical and Legal Considerations for Career Counselors

Mary-Anne Joseph

CHAPTER OVERVIEW

Ethical and legal issues in the workplace are of significant importance when working with minority groups and special populations (Corey et al., 2011). Those working with varied populations in the areas of career counseling and vocational development are responsible for ensuring that they understand the ethical and legal issues associated with employment and career development. This chapter will discuss the legal and ethical considerations of providing career counseling to a diverse group of clients. The American Counseling Association (ACA) and Certified Rehabilitation Counselors Code of Ethics will be discussed as the two main ethical standards that a career counselor may encounter in their career. Further, a case study will be provided as an example of a situation that a career counselor may encounter.

CHAPTER OBJECTIVES

After reading this chapter, the student will be able to complete the following:

1. Define ethics.

2. Identify ethical considerations a career counselor may encounter.

3. Understand how to resolve ethical and legal considerations in career counseling.

4. Identify the code of ethics that a career counselor may encounter.

In recent decades, career counseling has grown substantially because of the increased levels of vocational competition on a global scale (Habbal & Habbal, 2016). Career counseling has gained notoriety in schools, businesses, and communities, resulting in the development of a range of theoretical approaches aimed at directing career counseling. As this profession expands and gains notoriety, so too does the ethical obligations of the counselors charged with serving clients in this specialty area. As inferred earlier, vocational choices and career development have a global impact that reaches far beyond the individual.

The vocational choices and career development of a single person affect his/her family, community, and society, as well as the economy and the environment (International Association for Education and Vocational Guidance (IAEVG), 2017a).

Therefore, career counselors and those serving in the field of career counseling should recognize that they have the potential to improve the societal injustices, stereotypes, and misnomers that shape the nature of public policy. In addition, career counselors and related professionals can also have a positive effect on the molding of societal norms by minimizing and potentially eliminating inequitable service provision and enhancing theoretical frameworks, techniques, and resources to ensure that they are applicable for diverse populations (IAEVG, 2017a). By attending to the practical ethical issues that arise during the service delivery process, career counselors will ultimately reach a higher level of service provision and skill proficiency.

Defining Ethics

Ethics is a code of moral values that guides a person's behavior. More specifically, Neulicht et al. (2010) define ethics as "referring to characteristics or customs, generally described how to evaluate life through a set of standards and how to regulate behavior." In addition, Weston (2008) indicates that ethics are solely focused on a person's actions and values as they relate to the things that we believe in that results in our behavior. As we venture into this discussion about ethics, it is essential to clarify the difference between our ethical obligations and our legal obligations.

As previously discussed, ethics are codes of moral values (Neulicht et al., 2010; Weston, 2008). However, the law overtakes ethical guidelines and codes. Ethics and ethical responsibilities do vary from the law and legal requirements. Unlike ethics, the law is "the system of rules that a particular country or community recognizes as regulating the actions of its members and may enforce by the imposition of penalties" (Wheeler & Bertram, 2015). There are two sources of laws that govern our society: (1) laws that are passed by governmental bodies and (2) laws that are made by courts.

Types of Ethics

There are three primary types of ethics: (1) mandatory ethics, (2) aspirational ethics, and (3) positive ethics. Mandatory ethics deals with the minimum level of professional practice (Corey, 2016). While this may be seen as a novel concept, one might consider that when people work in fear, meaning they are always focused on avoiding punishment, they often use a significant amount of energy that yields minimal returns if any. "Additionally, practicing in fear potentially interferes with clinician's self-care and can prevent competent practice. Practicing in fear can also sap the energy, motivation, and fulfillment related to practice, leading to impairment or burnout" (Vandevender, 2015).

Aspirational ethics is a higher level of ethical practice. Aspirational ethics "entails an understanding of the spirit behind the code and the principles on which the code rest" (Corey, 2016, p. 38). Aspirational ethics is intended to incorporate prevention, holistic case conceptualization, and social justice (Gelso et al., 2014). Positive ethics is described as "an approach taken by practitioners who want to do all they can to assist their clients as opposed to simply doing the minimum requirements of their job that will keep them out of trouble" (Corey, 2016; Knapp & VandeCreek, 2005).

Ethical Principles

Each profession follows a group of laws, ethical codes and principles, and policies that guide their ethical behavior. Likewise, career counselors are governed by the National Career Development Association's (NCDA) Code of Ethics. In addition, depending on their academic training and professional licensure and certification acquisition, some career counselors may also be held to the ACA's Code of Ethics and/or the Commission on Rehabilitation Counseling's (CRCC) Code of Professional Ethics. As such, it is essential for career counselors to ensure that they are familiar with the ethical principles and codes that guide their profession.

The three aforementioned governing bodies have presented a total of eight ethical principles, which include (1) autonomy, (2) beneficence, (3) nonmaleficence, (4) veracity (American Counseling Association (ACA), 2014; Beauchamp & Childress, 2012; Coughlin, 2008; CRCC, 2017; Kitchener, 1984;), (5) justice, (6) fidelity, (7) objectivity, and (8) accountability (National Career Development Association (NCDA), 2015). These ethical principles are viewed as central to the process of ethical decision making within career counseling. In the following section, we will describe each of these principles.

The first four principles of autonomy, beneficence, nonmaleficence, and veracity are ethical principles that are recognized by all three of the previously mentioned governing bodies (ACA, 2014; CRCC, 2017; NCDA, 2015). The first principle is *autonomy*, and it requires professionals to respect the rights of clients to be independent and have self-determination. This principle highlights the significance of allowing clients to make their own decisions. A vital component of the job search process is client involvement, which requires career counselors to educate, empower, and encourage clients to act independently.

The second principle is beneficence. The principle of *beneficence* states that professionals have an obligation to do good when working with clients (ACA, 2014; CRCC, 2017; NCDA, 2015). Doing good is synonymous with contributing to the welfare of the client. This principle is a guideline that emphasizes the need for professionals to act in the best interest of the client. In the spirit of beneficence, career counselors also have an ethical obligation to do no harm to clients; this is in line with the third ethical principle of *nonmaleficence*. The application of this principle is to be holistic in nature and requires career counselors to avoid physical, psychological, or societal harm to their clients. The fourth ethical principle is *veracity*. This principle requires professionals to be honest when working with their clients. As is the societal norm, deception and deceitfulness are bound to disrupt the equilibrium of any relationship; thus it is essential that career counselors embrace the importance of this ethical principle.

The fifth and sixth ethical principles, justice and fidelity, are presented by the CRCC and ACA. The ethical principle of *justice* calls for professionals, such as career counselors, to operate fairly when serving all clients. This speaks to the spirit of the provision of equitable service in a continuous manner that is accessible to all in need. The ethical principle of *fidelity* indicates that professionals are to be faithful to their clients by keeping their promises and honoring the trust placed in them by their clients.

This brings us to the final two ethical principles, objectivity and accountability. These two ethical principles are specifically addressed by the NCDA and are not directly identified as "ethical principles" in the ethical codes set forth by the ACA and the CRCC. The seventh ethical principle of *objectivity* calls for career counselors to treat individuals equitably, which can be considered in alignment with the ethical principle of justice. Last is the eighth ethical principle of *accountability*: "*accountability*, or honoring commitments and keeping promises, including fulfilling one's responsibilities of trust in professional relationships" (NCDA, 2015, p. 1).

Two additional principles that are often included in the discussion of ethics is privacy and confidentiality (Beauchamp & Childress, 2001). ***Privacy*** allows individuals to limit access to information about themselves. ***Confidentiality*** is a guarantee to the client by the service provider that information disclosed during the helping process will be kept between the service provider and the client. There are two essential times when confidentiality can be broken. First, when clients pose a threat to themselves or someone else, human services and rehabilitation professionals have a "duty to warn" (p. 125). More specifically, this is a "situation in which a helping professional must violate the confidentiality promised to a client to warn others that the client is a threat to self or others." The second instance in which confidentiality can be broken is when it is necessary to report child abuse and elder abuse.

Codes of Ethics

A code of ethics guides the professional behavior of those serving in a particular field or profession (ACA, 2014; Corey et al., 2007; Tarvydas & Cottone, 2000). Referred to as ethical codes, guidelines, or standards, these professional documents are often established by an appropriate field-related governing body. The aim of ethical codes is to minimize harm to clients and the general public through the establishment of professional norms and expectations. Career counselors and aspiring career counselors would do well to gain a working knowledge of the codes of ethics that govern their professional behavior. In this section, we will review brief descriptions of five codes of ethics that are applicable to career counselors. Before engaging in this discussion, it is noteworthy to indicate that while ethical codes are intended to serve as guides and effective standards that professionals can use to govern their professional behaviors, ethical codes are not comprehensive in nature, and they are always superseded by the law.

The NCDA Code of Ethics

The NCDA provides professional development, publications, standards, and advocacy to practitioners and educators who inspire and empower individuals to achieve their career and life goals. "The *NCDA Code of Ethics* (Code) has been designed as a guide and resource for career practitioners" (NCDA, 2015, p. 1). The sections in this code include (Section A) *The Professional Relationship*; (Section B) *Confidentiality, Privileged Communication, and Privacy*; (Section C) *Professional Responsibility;* (Section D) *Relationships With Other Professionals*; (Section E) *Evaluation, Assessment, and Interpretation*; (Section F) *Providing Career Services Online, Technology, and Social Media*; (Section G) *Supervision, Training, and Teaching*; (Section H) *Research and Publication;* and (Section I) *Resolving Ethical Issues*.

The ASCA Ethical Standards for School Counselors

The American School Counselor Association (ASCA) is a professional organization supporting school counselors, school counseling students/interns, school counseling program directors/supervisors, and school counselor educators. The purpose of the ASCA ethical standards is to serve as a guide to practitioners and to provide support, direction, and information to practitioners and stakeholders. The ASCA provides ethical standards for school counselors that include (Section A) *Responsibility to Students*; (Section B) *Responsibilities to Parents/Guardians, School, and Self*; (Section C) *School Counselor Administrators/ Supervisor*; (Section D) *School Counselor Intern Site Supervisor*; (Section E) *Maintenance of Standards;* and (Section F) *Ethical Decision Making*.

The CRCC Code of Professional Ethics

Rehabilitation counselors are guided by the CRCC Code of Professional Ethics, which is intended to guide their professional behavior (CRCC, 2017). The CRCC is the world's largest rehabilitation counseling organization dedicated to improving the lives of individuals with disabilities. The CRCC Code of Professional Ethics consists of 12 sections (A–L), which addresses a variety of areas, including *the counseling relationship* (Section A); *confidentiality and privileged communication* (Section B); *privacy, advocacy, and accessibility* (Section C); *professional responsibility* (Section D); *relationships with other professionals and employers* (Section E); *forensic services* (Section F); *assessment and evaluation* (Section G); *supervision, training, and teaching* (Section H); *research and publication* (Section I); *technology, social media, and distance counseling* (Section J); *business practices* (Section K); and *resolving ethical issues* (Section L).

The ACA Code of Ethics

The ACA Code of Ethics was established by the ACA professional and educational organization, which is dedicated to the growth and enhancement of the counseling profession. Founded in 1952, ACA is the world's largest association exclusively representing professional counselors in various practice settings. The ACA Code of Ethics consists of nine sections that are intended to guide the professional behavior of counselors. These sections address the following areas: *the counseling relationship* (Section A); *confidentiality and privacy* (Section B); *professional responsibility* (Section C); *relationships with other professionals* (Section D); *evaluation, assessment, and interpretation* (Section E); *supervision, training, and teaching* (Section F); *research and publication* (Section G); *distance counseling, technology, and social media* (Section H); and *resolving ethical issues* (Section I). The ACA and CRCC codes of ethics have a multitude of similarities and often mirror one another in the spirit and presentation of many of their respective ethical codes.

The IAEVG Ethical Guidelines

An additional set of ethical guidelines that warrant inclusion in this discussion was developed by the IAEVG. The IAEVG engages in leadership and advocacy for guidance on a global stage through the promotion of ethically and socially just best practices to ensure the competent provision of educational and vocational guidance and counseling by qualified practitioners (International Association for Education and Vocational Guidance (IAEVG), 2019). The IAEVG presents ethical guidelines that are intended to stimulate the professional development of their members' ethical behaviors. These ethical guidelines identify the minimum aspirational goals for the practice of ethical behavior. More specifically

> the Guidelines provide a reference for (a) making decisions and actions as individual practitioners, (b) planning agency policies and services, (c) informing the public of expected standards of professional practices and behaviour, (d) providing evaluative criteria for self-assessments, peer evaluation, and supervision to ensure quality standards in service provision, and (e) seeking organizational support for professional development. (IAEVG, 2017a, p. 1)

The IAEVG ethical guidelines are separated into five distinct sections: (1) *ethical responsibility to clients*; (2) *attitude toward colleagues and professional associates*; (3) *behaviors toward government, employers, community agencies, and community members*; (4) *responsibility to theory and research*; and (5) *responsibility for professional learning and development*.

As previously stated, it is noteworthy to indicate that while ethical codes are intended to serve as guides and effective standards that professionals can use to govern their professional behaviors, ethical codes are not comprehensive in nature, and they are always superseded by the law.

The Law and Career

The 20th century brought the inception of a variety of legislative actions focused on employee rights, which have expanded exponentially over the past decades and have evolved into approximately 180 worker-protection laws. Such legislation addresses issues from pay requirements to parental leave benefits that are overseen by the Department of Labor. The Department of Labor is a cabinet-level U.S. agency responsible for enforcing federal labor standards. The following is a list of some common legislation with which career counselors should become familiar.

Table 3.1

Legislation/Program	Description
The Fair Labor Standards Act	Ensures that American workers receive a minimum wage for their work. Since 2009, most private and public employers have had to pay staff members at least $7.25 per hour, although some legislators have tried to increase that amount. In addition, the Fair Labor Standards Act (FLSA) ensures that nonexempt workers receive time and a half for any overtime they perform. The law offers special protections for minors as well. For nonagricultural positions, it limits the number of hours that children under the age of 16 can work. In addition, the FLSA prohibits businesses from hiring those under 18 for certain high-risk jobs. The FLSA prescribes standards for wages and overtime pay, which affect most private and public employment. The act is administered by the Wage and Hour Division. It requires employers to pay covered employees who are not otherwise exempt at least the federal minimum wage and overtime pay of one-and-one-half times the regular rate of pay. For nonagricultural operations, it restricts the hours that children under age 16 can work and forbids the employment of children under age 18 in certain jobs deemed too dangerous. For agricultural operations, it prohibits the employment of children under age 16 during school hours and in certain jobs deemed too dangerous (Department of Labor (DOL), 2018).
The Occupational Safety and Health (OSH) Act of 1970	The OSH legislation created a number of specific safety provisions, including industry-specific guidelines for construction, maritime, and agricultural jobs. It also includes a "general duty clause" that prohibits any workplace practice that represents a clear risk to workers. The OSH Act is administered by the Occupational Safety and Health Administration (OSHA). Safety and health conditions in most private industries are regulated by OSHA or OSHA-approved state programs, which also cover public-sector employers. Employers covered by the OSH Act must comply with the regulations and the safety and health standards promulgated by OSHA. Employers also have a general duty under the OSH Act to provide their employees with work and a workplace free from recognized serious hazards. OSHA enforces the act through workplace inspections and investigations. Compliance assistance and other cooperative programs are also available (DOL, 2019).

Legislation/Program	Description
The Longshore and Harbor Workers' Compensation Act (LHWCA)	Administered by the Office of Workers' Compensation Programs, the LHWCA provides for compensation and medical care to certain maritime employees (including longshore workers or other people in longshore operations and any harbor workers, including ship repairers, shipbuilders, and ship breakers) and to qualified dependent survivors of such employees who are disabled or die because of injuries that occur on the navigable waters of the United States or in adjoining areas customarily used in loading, unloading, repairing, or building a vessel.
The Energy Employees Occupational Illness Compensation Program Act (EEOICPA)	EEOICPA provides a compensation program that offers a lump-sum payment of $150,000 and prospective medical benefits to employees (or certain of their survivors) of the Department of Energy and its contractors and subcontractors diagnosed with cancer caused by exposure to radiation or certain illnesses caused by exposure to beryllium or silica incurred in the performance of duty, as well as a payment of $50,000 and prospective medical benefits to individuals (or certain of their survivors) determined by the Department of Justice to be eligible for compensation as uranium workers under Section 5 of the Radiation Exposure Compensation Act.
The Federal Employees' Compensation Act (FECA)	FECA established a comprehensive and exclusive workers' compensation program that pays for the disability or death of a federal employee resulting from personal injury sustained while in the performance of duty. The FECA, administered by the Office of Workers' Compensation Programs, provides benefits for wage loss compensation for total or partial disability, scheduled awards for permanent loss or loss of use of specified members of the body, related medical costs, and vocational rehabilitation.
The Black Lung Benefits Act (BLBA)	BLBA provides monthly cash payments and medical benefits to coal miners who are totally disabled by pneumoconiosis ("black lung disease") arising from their employment in the nation's coal mines. The statute also provides monthly benefits to a deceased miner's survivors if the miner's death was because of black lung disease.
The Employee Retirement Income Security Act (ERISA)	ERISA regulates employers who offer pension or welfare benefit plans for their employees. Title I of ERISA is administered by the Employee Benefits Security Administration (EBSA) (formerly the Pension and Welfare Benefits Administration) and imposes a wide range of fiduciary, disclosure, and reporting requirements on fiduciaries of pension and welfare benefit plans and on others having dealings with these plans. These provisions preempt many similar state laws. Under Title IV, certain employers and plan administrators must fund an insurance system to protect certain kinds of retirement benefits, with premiums paid to the federal government's Pension Benefit Guaranty Corporation. EBSA also administers reporting requirements for continuation of health care provisions, required under the Comprehensive Omnibus Budget Reconciliation Act of 1985 and the health care portability requirements on group plans under the Health Insurance Portability and Accountability Act.
The Labor-Management Reporting and Disclosure Act (LMRDA) of 1959 (also known as the Landrum-Griffin Act)	The LMRDA deals with the relationship between a union and its members. It protects union funds and promotes union democracy by requiring labor organizations to file annual financial reports; by requiring union officials, employers, and labor consultants to file reports regarding certain labor relations practices; and by establishing standards for the election of union officers. The act is administered by the Office of Labor-Management Standards.

continues on next page

Legislation/Program	Description
Social Security Act (SSA) of 1935	The SSA established a system of old-age benefits for workers, benefits for victims of industrial accidents, unemployment insurance, and aid for dependent mothers and children, the blind, and the physically handicapped. The SSA provides retired and disabled Americans with a financial safety net. In 2019, about 64 million people received Social Security checks each month, with an average amount of $1,461 for retirees and $1,234 for citizens with disabilities.
Family and Medical Leave Act (FMLA) of 1993	Administered by the Wage and Hour Division, the FMLA requires employers of 50 or more employees to give up to 12 weeks of unpaid job-protected leave to eligible employees for the birth or adoption of a child or for the serious illness of the employee or a spouse, child, or parent. Eligible employees are afforded up to 12 weeks of unpaid leave per year if they decide to stay home in the wake of their child's birth, an adoption, or a family member's serious illness. To receive FMLA benefits, one must have been with a company for at least 12 months and worked at least 1,250 hours during the past year. The law applies only to businesses that employ at least 50 employees within a 75-mile radius.
The Civil Rights Act of 1964	The Civil Rights Act made it illegal for businesses to discriminate based on "race, color, religion, sex or national origin."
Lilly Ledbetter Fair Pay Act of 2009	The Lilly Ledbetter Fair Pay Act prohibits wage discrimination based on age, religion, national origin, race, sex, and disability.
Age Discrimination in Employment Act of 1967	The Age Discrimination in Employment Act prohibits discrimination of workers 40 years of age and older on the basis of age in hiring, promotion, discharge, compensation, terms, conditions, or privileges of employment.
Americans With Disabilities Act (ADA) of 1990	The ADA prohibits discrimination against people with disabilities in several areas, including employment, transportation, public accommodations, communications, and access to state and local governments' programs and services.
Uniformed Services Employment and Reemployment Rights Act	Certain persons who serve in the armed forces have a right to reemployment with the employer they were with when they entered service. This includes those called up from the reserves or National Guard. These rights are administered by the Veterans' Employment and Training Service.
Employee Polygraph Protection Act	This law bars most employers from using lie detectors on employees but permits polygraph tests only in limited circumstances. It is administered by the Wage and Hour Division.
Migrant and Seasonal Agricultural Workers Protection (MSAWP) Act	The MSAWP regulates the hiring and employment activities of agricultural employers, farm labor contractors, and associations using migrant and seasonal agricultural workers. The act prescribes wage protections, housing and transportation safety standards, farm labor contractor registration requirements, and disclosure requirements. The Wage and Hour Division administers this law.
FLSA	FLSA is the federal law that establishes minimum wage, overtime pay eligibility, record keeping, and child labor standards affecting full-time and part-time workers in the private sector and in federal, state, and local governments.

Legislation/Program	Description
The Immigration and Nationality Act (INA)	The INA requires employers who want to use foreign temporary workers on H-2A visas to get a labor certificate from the Employment and Training Administration certifying that there are not sufficient, able, willing, and qualified U.S. workers available to do the work. The labor standards protections of the H-2A program are enforced by the Wage and Hour Division.
Unemployment Benefits	Even though each state has its own unemployment insurance agency, jobless benefits are actually offered through a joint federal-state program. States manage payments to the unemployed but have to meet certain federal guidelines in terms of how they do so. To qualify for payments, individuals must have been unemployed for reasons outside their control—for example, a layoff or firing—and meet state-specific requirements. In most cases, workers are eligible to receive benefits for up to 26 weeks, although payments are sometimes extended during periods of economic turmoil. While not as generous as unemployment payments in some European countries, the U.S. unemployment system ensures that Americans have at least a few months of security when they temporarily leave the workforce.
Whistleblower Protection	A patchwork of federal statutes helps protect whistleblowers who report their employers for violations of the law. Often, whistleblower protections are built into other pieces of legislation that govern an industry. For example, the Clean Air Act safeguards those who highlight violations of environmental law and the Consumer Product Safety Improvement Act offers protection to those who uncover unlawful manufacturing policies. OSHA's Whistleblower Protection Program is the main body responsible for protecting the rights of employees who may fear losing their jobs or other reprisals if they speak up. Workers who feel they have suffered retribution for reporting company violations should file a complaint with their local OSHA office within 30 days of the incident.
Equal Employment Opportunity Commission (EEOC)	The EEOC investigates charges of discrimination brought against employers.

Ethical Decision Making

The discussion of ethical and legal issues related to career counseling would be incomplete without the inclusion of the exploration of ethical decision-making models. The culmination of knowledge about ethics, the law, ethical principles, and various codes of ethical standards and guidelines are a direct avenue to the exploration of ethical decision-making models. An ethical decision-making model is a framework or guide that aids professionals in resolving ethical dilemmas through the application of a step-by-step process.

Over recent decades, a variety of ethical decision-making models have been presented for use by practitioners (Corey et al., 2015; Forester-Miller & Davis, 1996; Frame & Williams, 2005; Hill & Mamalakis, 2001; Sileo & Kopala, 1993; Wheeler & Bertram, 2015). Hauck & Ling (2016) posited that professionals should use an ethical decision-making model that is "theoretically grounded and accessible, considers relevant literature, is widely applicable, and addresses the complexity of decision making in practice" (p. 2). Such a decision model should also encompass a multitude of perspectives. Three such perspectives are (1) utilitarianism, (2) moral relativism, and (3) moral absolutism (Hauck & Ling, 2016). The steps of the ETHICS model presented by Hauck & Ling (2016) include evaluate the dilemma, think ahead, help, information, calculate risk, and select an action. While this ethical decision-making model was developed for use by licensed professional counselors, it is certainly applicable to the work of career counselors and career counseling professionals.

Identifying and evaluating an ethical dilemma is an essential component of the ETHICS model (Hauck & Ling, 2016). This step requires career counseling professionals to evaluate the problem and survey their professional code of ethics to assess the validity of their ethical concerns. It is, however, essential to note that all ethical codes are not clear-cut. While some codes provide specific guidelines for professional behavior, other codes present broad and unspecified guidelines.

Once career counseling professionals have been able to identify and evaluate an ethical dilemma success-fully, it is then time for them to think ahead and consider the potential outcomes of the possible course of action they may take regarding the ethical dilemma (Hauck & Ling, 2016). This assessment should include consideration of both positive and negative repercussions of their actions. These professionals should also consider the effect their decisions will have on direct and indirect parties/stakeholders. In essence, professionals are weighing the pros and cons of their possible actions before they act.

During the third step of the ETHICS model, help, career counselors are to engage in consultation (Hauck & Ling, 2016). This involves career counseling professionals seeking input and feedback from other professionals regarding the ethical dilemma and the actions they are considering. The developers of the model warned against professionals depending on or allow others to make the ethical decisions for them. Consultation is to be treated as another form of assessment and information gathering. All in all, the responsibility for the ethical decisions lie with the career counseling professionals, not those they consult.

The fourth step of the ETHICS model is information. "The information step involves considering litera-ture, regulations, and law that pertain to the dilemma and combining it with analysis from the other steps of the model. The counselor should think of this as seeking information from available written sources" (Hauck & Ling, 2016, p. 4). This information is to be used by career counseling professionals to support or negate the course of action they are considering.

The last two steps of the ETHICS model require career counseling professionals to calculate the risk and select an action (Hauck & Ling, 2016). When calculating the risk, career counseling professionals are essentially revisiting "the various stakeholders identified in the think ahead step" (Hauck & Ling, 2016, p. 4). It is very likely that each of these stakeholders may be exposed to a certain level of risk pending the actions the professionals take to address the ethical dilemma. To select an action, career counseling professionals must determine the most ethical and unethical courses of action (Hauck & Ling, 2016). The developers of this ethical decision-making model urged professionals to progress through all the steps of the model to ensure that an ethical decision is made. The authors posit that premature decision making can lead to bias in the ethical decision-making process.

Summary

As a final overview and point of interest, career counselors would do well to consider the six strategies for best practice presented by Oramas as they apply the information presented in the body of this chapter. Oramas (2017) recommended that while going through the ethical decision-making process, professionals should ensure that they (1) engage in supervision and consultation; (2) exercise ethical reflection; (3) be self-aware to ensure that bias is not involved in their decisions; (4) practice assessment and maintenance of their core principles, values, and qualities; (5) expand their level of cultural competence; and (6) ensure that they are adequately equipped to work with the lesbian, gay, bisexual, transgender, queer or questioning (LGBTQ), and other vulnerable populations.

Ethical issues arise on a routine basis; thus, it is vital that career counselors and related professionals are equipped to handle such issues effectively. As stipulated in the NCDA, ASCA, CRCC, ACA, and IAEVG, these professionals have an ethical obligation to ensure that they are well versed in their respective ethical principles and codes of conduct. Likewise, career counselors should continually work to remain abreast of national and local legislation that affects their clientele. In addition, career counselors should seek out continuing education opportunities that allow them to expand their ethical decision-making skills.

Discussion Questions

1. Compare and contrast the different types of ethics.
2. List and describe the ethical principles presented in this chapter.
3. Identify the code of ethics for which you are responsible, and list and describe the difference sections of the code.
4. List and describe the benefits of the Energy Employees Occupational Illness Compensation Program Act (EEOICPA).
5. List and describe the benefits of the Federal Employees' Compensation Act (FECA).
6. List and describe the benefits of the Migrant and Seasonal Agricultural Workers Protection (MSAWP) Act.
7. List and describe the benefits of the Age Discrimination in Employment Act of 1967.
8. List and describe the benefits of the Americans With Disabilities Act (ADA) of 1990.
9. List and describe the benefits of Lilly Ledbetter Fair Pay Act of 2009.
10. List and describe the steps of the ethical decision-making model.

References

Beauchamp, T. L., & Childress, J. F. (2001). *Principles of biomedical ethics* (5th ed.). Oxford University Press.

Beauchamp, T. L., & Childress, J. F. (2012). *Principles of biomedical ethics* (7th ed.). Oxford University Press.

Commission on Rehabilitation Counselor Certification (CRCC). (2017). *Code of professional ethics for rehabilitation counselors.* https://www.crccertification.com/code-of-ethics-3

Corey, G. (2016). *Theory and practice of group counseling* (10th ed.). Cengage Learning.

Corey, G., Corey, M. S., & Callanan, P. (2003). *Issues and ethics in the helping professions* (6th ed.). Thomson, Brooks/Cole.

Corey, G., Corey, M., & Callahan, P. (2011). *Issues and ethics in the helping profession* (8th ed.). Cengage Learning, Brooks/Cole.

Corey, G., Corey, M. S., Corey, C., & Callanan, P. (2015). *Issues and ethics in the helping professions* (9th ed.). Brooks/Cole.

Corey, G., Corey, M. S., & Callanan, P. (2007). *Issues and ethics in the helping professions.* (7th ed.). Thomson Higher Education.

Coughlin, S. (2008). How many principles for public health ethics? *Open Public Health Journal, 1,* 8–16.

Department of Labor. (DOL). (2019). Summary of the major laws of the department of labor. https://www.dol.gov/general/aboutdol/majorlaws

Forester-Miller, H., & Davis, T. (1996). *A practitioner's guide to ethical decision making.* American Counseling Association. http://www.counseling.org/docs/ethics/practitioners_guide.pdf?sfvrsn=2

Frame, M. W., & Williams, C. B. (2005). A model of ethical decision making from a multicultural perspective. *Counseling and Values, 49*, 165–179. doi:10.1002/j.2161-007X.2005.tb01020.x

Gelso, C. J., Williams, E. N., & Fretz, B. R. (2014). *Counseling psychology* (3rd ed.). American Psychological Association.

Habbal, Y., & Habbal, H. B. (2016). Identifying aspects concerning ethics in career counseling: Review on the ACA code of ethics. *International Journal of Business and Public Administration, 13*(2), 115.

Hauck, J., & Ling, T. (2016). The DO ART model: An ethical decision-making model applicable to art therapy. *Art Therapy: Journal of the American Art Therapy Association, 33*(4), 1–6.

Hill, M. R., & Mamalakis, P. M. (2001). Family therapists and religious communities: Negotiating dual relationships. *Family Relations, 50*, 199–208. doi:10.1111/j.1741-3729.2001.00199.x

International Association for Education and Vocational Guidance. (IAEVG). (2017a). IAEVG ethical guidelines. https://www.vkotocka.si/wp-content/uploads/2018/09/IAEVG-EthicsNAFeb2018Final.pdf

International Association for Education and Vocational Guidance. (IAEVG). (2017b). Mission and vision. https://iaevg.com/About

Kitchener, K. S. (1984). Intuition, critical evaluation and ethical principles: The foundation for ethical decisions in counseling psychology. *Counseling Psychologist, 12*, 43–55.

Knapp, S., & VandeCreek, L. (2005). *Practical ethics for psychologists: A positive approach.* American Psychological Association.

Neulicht, A. T., McQuade, L. J., & Chapman, C. A. (2010). *The CRCC desk reference on professional ethics: A guide for rehabilitation counselors.* Elliot & Fitzpatrick.

Oramas, J. E. (2017). Counseling ethics: overview of challenges, responsibilities and recommended practices. *Journal of Multidisciplinary Research (1947-2900), 9*(3), 47–58.

Sileo, F. J., & Kopala, M. (1993). An A-B-C-D-E worksheet for promoting beneficence when considering ethical issues. Counseling *and Values, 37*, 89–95. doi:10.1002/j.2161-007X.1993.tb00800.x

Society of Counseling Psychology. (2015). Positive ethics and counseling psychology. https://www.div17.org/scp-connect/op-eds/positive-ethics-and-counseling-psychology/

Tarvydas, V. & Cottone, R. R. (2000). The code of ethics for professional rehabilitation counselors: What we have and what we need. *Rehabilitation Counseling Bulletin, 43*(4), 188–196.

Vandevender, A. (2015). Positive ethics and counseling psychology. *Society of Counseling Psychology.* https://www.div17.org/scp-connect/op-eds/positive-ethics-and-counseling-psychology/

Weston, A. (2008). *A 21st century ethical toolbox* (2nd ed.). Oxford University Press.

Wheeler, A. M., & Bertram, B. (2015). *The counselor and the law: A guide to legal and ethical practice.* American Counseling Association.

PART II

Career Counseling Across the Life Span

CHAPTER 4

Career Counseling in Childhood

Rebecca R. Sametz and Logan Winkelman

CHAPTER OVERVIEW

The early experiences in childhood have been shown to have a significant impact on career development over the life span (Prime, et al., 2010). Factors such as positive experiences and relationships to early career exposure helps to shape one's career path from an early age. This chapter will provide an overview of career counseling strategies in childhood, taking into account cultural differences when providing career counseling in childhood and adolescence, and the role of assessment instruments.

CHAPTER OBJECTIVES

After reading this chapter, the student will be able to complete the following:

1. Discuss the factors that influence career development in childhood.

2. Identify and discuss diversity and contextual differences in childhood.

3. Discuss the role of career-related programming and activities when providing career counseling in childhood.

Introduction to Career Counseling in Childhood

From a developmental perspective on careers, vocational development constitutes a lifelong process from infancy through childhood, adolescence, adulthood, and old age affected by both personal and contextual factors (Gottfredson, 1981; Super, 1957; Vondracek et al., 1986). Contrary to the focus of most career counseling research, the early experiences in childhood have been shown to have a significant effect on career development over the life span (Prime et al., 2010). Factors such as positive experiences and relationships to early career exposure help to shape one's career path from an early age. This chapter will provide an overview of career counseling strategies in childhood, taking into account cultural differences when providing career counseling to children and the role of career-related programming and activities.

Early childhood has been recognized as a time where career development is pivotal (Kyle & Hennis, 2000). In childhood, we are encouraged to begin thinking about work, engage in processes of learning about the world of work, project ourselves into the future, and develop career awareness, exploration, aspirations, and interests (Prime et al., 2010). When a child reaches high school, they have likely already solidified their career choices (Knight et al., 2011). Yet when reviewing the literature on career development and counseling, there is little research in the area of childhood since the majority of the literature focuses on late adolescence, young adulthood, and adulthood. In this chapter, childhood is considered to be those ages 14 and younger. Therefore, the target population when speaking of childhood is elementary to middle school age.

When reviewing the vocational literature, the common theme that continuously surfaces when discussing vocational guidance and development in childhood is that "children should focus on being children" (Zinnecker, 1995). In other words, some literature implies that child development and career development should be mutually exclusive. Children learn about vocations mainly through exposure from school, family, and interactions with friends (Kyle & Hennis, 2000). Further, children will often use their personal interests, beliefs, and values to explore the world of work and to develop their initial tentative occupational goals (Erikson, 1963). In the following case example, let's explore ways we might integrate personal interests, beliefs, and values with career-related activities when providing career counseling in childhood.

Case Example

Daniel is a 13-year-old middle school student from a Latino family with a middle to upper socioeconomic status who is about to enter high school. In this school, students are encouraged to identify a career track to follow to prepare them for postsecondary education or the workforce after graduation. This student is coming to you, a career counselor, with his mother to seek guidance on how he can narrow down his decision and select a track where he will "thrive." During your initial session, Daniel expresses that he does not like math but feels pressure from his family to pursue an engineering track similar to his father, who works as a construction engineer. He describes his interests in art and music but says his parents are discouraging him from pursuing this as a career because "It is just a hobby, and he will not be able to make a living." Daniel's mom describes how he has always been creative and enjoys autonomy. As you brainstorm your approach to this case, consider the following:

1. What factors stood out to you in this case study?

2. What techniques would you employ to entice Daniel to explore his childhood interests further?

3. What activities could you integrate that could help Daniel identify possible career tracks that might be satisfying?

4. What age-appropriate career resources might you use to foster career development with Daniel?

5. What cultural or other contextual factors might you consider in your approach with Daniel?

Now that you have examined a case example, let's take a deeper look into the diversity and contextual differences in childhood that may influence career development.

Diversity and Contextual Differences in Childhood

Research indicates the family as the primary context of vocational development (Hartung et al., 2005). Reflecting on your own childhood, what occupations and vocational areas were you familiar with? These were usually ones that parental figures in your life held. In particular, parental figures appear to be a much stronger influence on a child's vocational development than their peer network or the school

(Davos-Klosters, 2014). However, while parents play an important role in career choices for their children, their lack of knowledge of the workforce can hinder recruitment into and interest in other vocations (Knight et al., 2011).

Counselors need to be sensitive to the values and traditions of culturally diverse families (Byars-Winston & Fouad, 2006). The values and traditions of the family system can shed light on the child's unique thinking and development. For example, Africans, Asians, and Hispanics expect and accept that all members of the family contribute to its welfare and survival (Zunker, 2016). This can leave an individual's goals and aspirations behind as the focus is on the contribution to the family and its survival.

In Asian and Hispanic families, the husbands are typically seen as the head of the family (Zunker, 2016). The family dynamics of these two populations lend themselves to typical male-female stereotypical gender roles, as well as male-female relationships. Another factor that can influence career choices and goals is religion. All of these factors can affect an individual family member's approach to work, the way that they think about work, the way that they view work, and the meaning of work (Liu et al., 2014).

Gender and Sex-Role Influences

Preadolescent girls, in comparison to boys of the same age, appear to aspire to a more restricted range of occupations and engage in less career exploration during the primary school years (Zinnecker, 1995). While there is no clear reason for this, what is clear is that more preadolescent girls lag in career exploration and development at this age than boys of the same age. In contrast, preadolescent girls do tend to have greater career decidedness at an earlier age (Dorr & Lesser, 1980). Some research indicates that society influences a child's career aspirations (Zinnecker, 1995). The research on the effect of society on the career development of children found that boys seek out and aspire toward male-dominant occupations and girls aspire and pursue female-dominated occupations (Zinnecker, 1995).

Media Influences

While a parent's influence is among the strongest influences on a child's career development, another major influence to be considered is the media (Kyle & Hennis, 2000). For example, the occupations of children's favorite characters in movies and television shows may influence or spark interest in those specific professions. Cartoon watching has been found to relate inversely to 6- to 10-year-old children's positive perceptions of scientific professions (Potts & Martinez, 1994). Developmentally, second- and fifth-grade children can distinguish between documentary and fictional televised material, which selectively shape their beliefs about real-world occupations (Kyle & Hennis, 2000).

Emotional Maturity and Self-Identity

As children engage in career-related activities and programs, they experience emotional reactions that are combined with cognition (Oliveira et al., 2015). Emotions triggered by career exploration are also tied to individuals' positive or negative performance feedback and could potentially spark motivation for or avoidant attitudes toward the process (Flum & Blustein, 2000). This is implying that a child needs to develop strong decision-making abilities and emotional maturity to navigate the career development process successfully. Emotional maturity is the ability to handle situations without unnecessarily escalating them. Instead of seeking to blame someone else for their problems or behaviors, emotionally mature people seek to fix the problems or behaviors; they accept accountability for their actions.

Further, the period of transition where children of early adolescence are attempting to search for their identities is often one where they are at risk of role confusion, and it is a critical period of development (Erikson, 1963). Super (1957) suggested that strong relationships between identity and career commitment are variables of career maturity. Career maturity refers to "a measure of readiness to make career decisions on the bases of attitudes toward and knowledge of career decision making" (Powell & Luzzo, 1998, as cited by Patton et al., 2001, p. 338). When one thinks of career maturity, independence and the ability to make decisions come to mind, as well as knowledge of occupational information and acquiring planning and decision-making skills.

Having an increased self-awareness allows the child to focus on personal attributes and how he/she could fit in an occupational environment. The key point is that when the child takes time to invest in the skills needed for various occupations, the child becomes more aware of the skills that are necessary to obtain a job.

Career Development and the School Curriculum

In addition to learning about career opportunities from their parents, children also learn a great deal about occupational choices while at school. For career counselors or school personnel, the focus may be to organize an occupational information program for young children (Hartung et al., 2008)—for example, career days where parents come in to speak about their occupations and the children ask questions. This is a common method seen in elementary schools to incorporate opportunities for children at this age to learn about various occupations outside of the family system.

A technique used by Knight et al. (2011) was to promote health through awareness of a career in nursing for middle-school-age children. The content of the program focused on individual health and the role nurses play in health promotion. At the end of the program, the students had an increased interest in the nursing profession, and most students identified that they learned new information (Knight et al., 2011). Thus such educational programs have been found to be most beneficial when working with children.

In addition, a study conducted by Palladino Schultheiss (2005) examined children's experiences and descriptions of gaining information through occupational exploration, connecting school learning to work, and exploring through play. Children reported how teachers exposed them to experiences and information—for example, visiting museums on field trips or observing others in their working environments to see what they do as part of their jobs. By exposing children at young ages to various types of occupations that are not performed by their parents, a family member, or a friend's family member, children are allowed to become curious as to what other types of occupations exist.

The idea of integrating career development concepts into the existing curricula is referred to as infusion (Hiebert, 1993). This calls for teachers to expand the existing curriculum and incorporate vocational concepts, activities, and subjects to stimulate career development. This would require school counselors and teachers to be active in engaging and keeping up with changes in the workforce and labor market (Zunker, 2016).

Counseling programs at all school levels typically require counselors to justify program content and materials (Zunker, 2016). For elementary schools, it is crucial to have the investment of teachers, administrators, and parents in career-related activities and programs (Knight, 2014). Further, having community investment in the career-related activities and programs can assist in the development of and the quality of such career-related programming for elementary and middle school age children.

Knight (2014) provided additional suggestions that allow school and career counselors to create and modify career programs and activities to address career development at the elementary level, which can easily be applied at the middle school level. The first recommendation is university-elementary partnerships, particularly with school counselor educators. With limits on school and career counselors' time, resources, and funding, Knight (2014) recommended, when possible, fostering community partnerships for counseling students to mitigate these concerns and promote hands-on learning where school counselors in training deliver "classroom guidance lessons on career development topics, host parent workshops, meet one-on-one with students to discuss career plans, or full implementation of a career development program" (p. 80).

An additional recommendation provided by Knight (2014) is incorporating age-appropriate resources, materials, experiences, and information, emphasizing the need for counselors to become familiar with tools that aid their work. Knight (2014) discussed a free website resource maintained by the Virginia Employment Commission that provides a wealth of career development information for students, parents, and counselors called the Virginia Career View. This resource offers career-related assessments, games, and activities specific to school-age children.

Knight (2014) went on to offer a list of three questions school counselors can consider asking when developing and evaluating data-driven, developmental, and comprehensive career interventions. These three questions are as follows: "(1) What are the career development needs of students at each grade? (2) How can the skills taught in my career guidance program build on one another? (3) Based on the data for my individual schools, what are some particular career competencies that I need to address?" (p. 81). Now that we have reviewed this chapter's contents, let's explore career counseling strategies with another case example while taking into account cultural differences and the role of career-related programming and activities with children.

Case Example

A Montessori middle school recently hired a new principal who is very interested in exposing students to various types of occupations through field trips. However, the budget for the school is tight, and they are unable to spend money on field trips. The principal approaches the school counselor and asks her to form a committee that can brainstorm methods for infusing career-related materials and trips into the already existing curriculum. The school counselor must report to the principal in the next 2 weeks what the committee has come up with and how they are planning to infuse this into the current curriculum with no allocated budget. The principal asked the school counselor to handpick her committee. The only requirement is that one of the committee members must be a parent of one of the children from the school.

1. If you were the school counselor, what would be your approach to incorporating career development opportunities into the already existing curriculum?

2. How would you, as the school counselor, get the other teachers to invest in joining your committee?

3. What types of activities would be beneficial that would cost little to no money to implement? Why did you choose these activities?

4. How would you engage the students in the activities and field trips that the committee decided to incorporate into the curriculum?

Summary

It is clear that vocational development begins during childhood (Dorr & Lesser, 1980). Curiosity, fantasy, interests, and capacities are stimulated and take form as children playfully construct possible future selves projected in work and other social roles (Super, 1957). While parents and family are considered to have a high impact on a child's overall career development, other factors need to be taken into account. However, more and more individuals are delaying a career commitment until they better understand their interests, skills, and values (Zunker, 2016). Career development and activities should be highly interactive to promote engagement (Knight et al., 2011).

Discussion Questions

1. As a career counselor, how you would take into account the child's age, and what strategies and/or techniques you would use?
2. How can school programs compliment or meet the career needs of children?
3. What other contextual influences might a child experience that could affect their career development?

References

Byars-Winston, A. M., & Fouad, N. A. (2006). Metacognition and multicultural competence: Expanding the culturally appropriate career counseling model. *Career Development Quarterly, 54*(3), 187–201.

Davos-Klosters. (2014). Matching skills and labour market needs: Building social partnerships for better skills and better jobs. *World Economic Forum*, 1–28. https://www3.weforum.org/docs/GAC/2014/WEF_GAC_Employment_Matching-SkillsLabourMarket_Report_2014.pdf

Dorr, A., & Lesser, G. S. (1980). Career awareness in young children. Communication Research & Broadcasting, *3*, 36–75.

Erikson, E. H. (1963). *Childhood and society* (2nd ed.). W. W. Norton.

Flum, H., & Blustein, D. L. (2000). Reinvigorating the study of vocational exploration: A framework for research. *Journal of Vocational Behavior, 56*, 380–404.

Gottfredson, L. S. (1981). Circumscription and compromise: A developmental theory of occupational aspirations. *Journal of Counseling Psychology, 28*, 545–579.

Hartung, P. J., Porfeli, E. J., & Vondracek, F. W. (2005). Child vocational development: A review and reconsideration. *Journal of Vocational Behavior, 66*, 385–429.

Hartung, P., Porfeli, E., & Vondracek, F. (2008). Career adaptability in childhood. *Career Development Quarterly, 57*(1), 63–74.

Hiebert, B. (1993). Career education: A time for infusion. *Guidance & Counselling, 8*(3), 5–10.

Knight, J. L. (2014). Preparing elementary school counselors to promote career development: Recommendations for school counselor education programs. *Journal of Career Development, 42*(2), 75–85.

Knight, M., Abdallah, L., Findeisen, M., Devereaux, K., & Dowling, J. (2011). Making healthy connections: Introducing nursing as a career choice to middle school students. *Nursing Forum, 46*(3), 146–151.

Kyle, M. T., & Hennis, M. (2000). Experiential model for career guidance in early childhood education. In N. Peterson, & R. C. Gonzalez (Eds.), *Career counseling models for diverse populations* (pp. 1–7). Brooks/Cole.

Liu, J., McMahon, M., & Watson, M. (2014). Childhood career development in mainland China: A research and practice agenda. *Career Development Quarterly, 62*, 268–279.

Oliveira, I. M., Taveira, M., & Porfeli, E. J. (2015). Emotional aspects of childhood career development: Importance and future agenda. *International Journal of Education and Vocational Guidance, 15*, 163–174.

Palladino Schultheiss, D. E. (2003). A relational approach to career counseling: Theoretical integration and practical application. *Journal of Counseling and Development*, 301–310.

Patton, W., & Creed, P. A. (2001). Developmental issues in career maturity and career decision status. *Career Development Quarterly, 49*(4), 336–351.

Potts, R., & Martinez, I. (1994). Television viewing and children's beliefs about scientists. *Journal of Applied Developmental Psychology, 15*, 287–300.

Powell, D. F., & Luzzo, D. A. (1998). Evaluating factors associated with the career maturity of high school students. *Career Development Quarterly, 47*, 145–158.

Prime, D. R., Nota, L., Ferrari, L., Schultheiss, D. E. P., Soresi, S., & Tracey, T. J. G (2010). Correspondence of children's anticipated vocational, perceived competencies, and interests: Results from an Italian sample. *Journal of Vocational Behavior, 77*(1), 58–62.

Super, D. E. (1957). *The psychology of careers*. Harper and Row.

Vondracek, F. W., Lerner, R. M., & Schulenberg, J. E. (1986). *Career development: A life-span developmental approach*. Erlbaum.

Zinnecker, J. (1995). The cultural modernisation of childhood. In L. Chisholm, P. Buchner, H. H. Kruger, & M. du Bois-Reymond (Eds.), *Growing up in Europe: Contemporary horizons in childhood and youth studies* (pp. 85–94). Walter de Gruyter.

Zunker, V. G. (2016). *Career counseling: A holistic approach*. Cengage Learning.

Career Counseling for Adolescence and Transition-Age Clients

Rene Gonzalez, Brandi N. Cruz, and Klarissa Trevino

CHAPTER OVERVIEW

As young adults move into their primitive years of identity development and self-exploration, they engage in key activities that often relate to career development (Arbona & Novy, 1991). During this stage of life, young adults can conceptualize realistic career paths and begin to develop a plan for carrying out their career goals. This chapter will provide an overview of strategies for career counseling for transition-age youth (TAY), as well as discuss the available career-related programs. Further, placement services and work- and experience-based programs for youth will be discussed.

CHAPTER OBJECTIVES

After reading this chapter, the student will be able to complete the following:

1. Discuss factors that affect the career development of TAY.

2. Discuss strategies for career counseling for TAY.

3. Outline career-related programs.

4. Identify placement services and work- and experience-based programs for TAY.

Introduction

Career development is a lifelong process, as adolescents' interests, likes, and dislikes will expand and change as they read about occupations, take new classes in school, and gain real-life experience through volunteer work, part-time jobs, and extracurricular activities (Super, 1990). As such, if an adolescent did not have the benefit of early career orientation while in elementary school, it is critical for the career counselor to cultivate awareness of the world of work, careers, and occupations while the adolescent is in middle school and high school.

Career counseling can help answer the age-old question, "What will I be when I grow up?" Career counselors have an upper hand in helping adolescents answer this question as they transition from school to work and/or postsecondary training by facilitating self-awareness and occupational knowledge for decision making concerning critical life choices. Self-awareness and occupational knowledge may entail a variety of formal career assessments and inventories to examine the adolescent's interests, personality, and work values (Brooks, 1990). Career counselors also inform and discuss important decision-making factors. Further, the adolescent may acquire occupational information through exploration endeavors, such as volunteer work or interviewing workers from various industries.

Who Is Considered a TAY?

The transition from youth to adulthood is a critical stepping-stone among all young people. According to the Federal Partners in Transition (FPT) Workgroup (FPT Workgroup, 2016), a transition age is a time when adolescents are moving into adulthood and are typically concerned with planning for postsecondary education, careers, health care, financial benefits, housing, and more.

TAY is defined differently among agencies, organizations, and researchers. For instance, the Workforce Innovation and Opportunity Act (WIOA) Youth Program serves two distinct target populations. The *in-school youth* population must not be younger than 14 years of age or older than age 21. The *out-of-school youth* population must not be younger than 16 years of age or older than age 24 (U.S. Department of Labor, n.d.). The World Health Organization (n.d.) described "adolescents" as "individuals in the 10- to 19-year age group" and "youth" as the "15- to 24-year age group" (p. B-5). Whereas, researchers described TAY as 14- and/or 16-year-olds to 25- and/or 30-year-olds across multiple child service agencies (e.g., foster care and juvenile detention facilities) and adult service agencies (e.g., mental health agencies and career centers) (Davis & Sondheimer, 2005; FTP Workgroup, 2016; Manteuffel et al., 2008). Conversely, other researchers described TAY as older adolescent (15- to 16-year-olds) to young adult (24- to 26-year-olds) because of the transition of the developmental stages from childhood into adulthood (Martel & Fuchs, 2017; Wilens & Rosenbaum, 2013). Because TAY acquire knowledge, learn important skills, and develop an understanding of the need to maximize their independence to be self-sufficient in their communities (FPT Workgroup, 2015), this chapter will focus on TAY who are in middle to late adolescence (14-year-olds to 18-year-olds).

Strategies for Career Counseling TAY

Employment is a valued adult role in that it serves as a primary indicator of adult success in the United States (Eisenman, 2003). As such, career counselors should begin their initial meetings with TAY by assessing barriers and providing appropriate guidance and support to adolescents as they take their next steps toward their career or educational goals. It is important for a career counselor to work closely with TAY to ensure that a plan addresses preferences, strengths, and needs before an adolescent exits school. For instance, career counselors may emphasize how high school course selection plays a major role in postsecondary options. Therefore, it is important for career counselors to help the adolescent choose courses that allow for a range of postsecondary options and provide more exposure to career plans of interest.

Adult outcomes for youth are undoubtedly influenced by transition planning and services. The school-to-work transition for youth is a complex process and a collaborative working alliance between the career counselor and the adolescent to bridge the gap from school to adult life. Transition planning must encompass all of the major areas of adult functioning, such as employment, postsecondary education, daily living, health, leisure, communication, interpersonal skills, self-determination, and community participation. Hence, the ultimate goal of school-to-work transition is community adjustment through careful planning of

CHAPTER 5 CAREER COUNSELING FOR ADOLESCENCE AND TRANSITION-AGE CLIENTS   53

transitional services. Career counselors may approach transitional services as outcome-oriented processes that encompass postsecondary education, college and vocational training, community living, living arrangements and community participation, and competitive employment. The transition process is treated in a holistic manner, as all these factors can affect a youth's career outcome. To this end, the career counselor may apply different strategies in the career exploration process to assist TAY in affectively transitioning into adulthood (Lechner et al., 2016; Lindsay et al., 2015; Setlhare-Meltor & Wood, 2016; Wehmeyer et al., 2019). Accordingly, career counselors may use the following strategies when providing career guidance to TAY: (a) the ecological approach, (b) the life-design counseling approach, or (c) the postmodern era approach.

Ecological Approach

Career counselors may use the ecological approach to understand the barriers to employment (e.g., age discrimination, family, and work) among adolescents (Lindsay et al., 2015). In understanding an adolescent's ecological barriers to employment, career counselors can help the adolescent bridge the gap (Lindsay et al., 2015) to enhance a successful employment outcome. Moreover, identifying the adolescent's specific barriers (e.g., lack of work experience, transportation, and qualifications) can further assist in the development of the adolescent's career and education goals by gaining information relative to the barriers that need to be addressed. For instance, relative to "age" and "limited work" barriers, employers may have a preference for hiring someone of perceived greater maturity (i.e., an older applicant) and with more work experience. In this case, the career counselor may need to assess the adolescent's volunteer experience alongside any work experience to highlight the transferability of skills and desired characteristics, such as work ethic, integrity, and ambition, which may benefit the youth's employability despite limited work experience.

Life-Design Counseling

As youth may be uncertain about which career path to follow, using tools such as the life-design process, career mapping, and development of goals has been demonstrated as useful for their preparation for transition into adulthood (Lechner et al., 2016; Setlhare-Meltor & Wood, 2016). For instance, using a life-design process (Savickas et al., 2009) allows for youth to use past experiences to understand the present and enables them to construct a future career identity (Setlhare-Meltor & Wood, 2016). The past experiences may include part-time employment (e.g., fast-food industry, customer service, or clothing departments), volunteer experiences (e.g., nursing homes, homeless shelters, or pet shelters), and skills learned through school clubs joined during the middle and high school years.

Life-design counseling is a narrative approach to career counseling and affords the career counselor an opportunity to make the working alliance with youth more personal. Undoubtedly, a working alliance is essential to the partnership that the career counselor and adolescent establish, as it facilitates "dialogues to reconstruct vocational identity and 're-story' decision making" (Savickas, 2019a, p. 38). As such, the career counselor initiates a working alliance with the question, "How can I be useful to you as you construct your career?" (Savickas, 2016). If the adolescent expresses interest in academic advice, vocational direction, or career counseling, then the career counselor can proceed with the interview. Thereafter, the career counselor maintains a working alliance through attending to behaviors through storytelling and by being authentic, genuine, empathetic, and encouraging.

Life-design counseling is a continuous process whereby a youth's professional identity is shaped by self-organization over time, which allows for the ordering of multiple experiences of daily life (Savickas et al., 2009) with narratives that emphasize the future (Savickas, 2013). Life-design counseling evolves throughout three counseling sessions (Cardoso et al., 2016; Savickas, 2019b). In the first session, the career counselor uses the Career Construction Interview to facilitate narratives of the youth's life story. The Career Construction Interview is a good baseline for adolescents to discuss past experiences that will transition into future goals. The Career Construction Interview consists of five questions that ask about (1) role models that individuals admired when they were young for self-construction, (2) magazines or television shows they watch regularly or websites for manifest interest, (3) a current favorite story from a book or movie, (4) the saying or motto they like most for self-advice, and (5) early recollections from around the age of 6 (Cardoso et al., 2016). As adolescents answer the interview questions and engage in self-reflection, the career counselor prompts them to elaborate on their feelings, beliefs, and goals. This, in turn, affords youth an opening to ask questions of their lives. Consequently, the questions direct youth to consider what their experiences mean for the self and identity.

After completing the interview and prior to meeting with the youth for the second counseling session, the career counselor studies the youth's constructs in the small stories, or micro-narratives, told during the Career Construction Interview to reconstruct a provisional larger story by combining the micro-narratives into a meaningful pattern. It is essential that the career counselor conceptualize the macro-narratives, as they are fundamental to the construction of a narrative in which past, present, and future are continuously and coherently connected and integrated (Savickas, 2011). To enhance the development of narrative competence, the career counselor must be empathetic to the youth's micro-narratives, demonstrate a genuine understanding of these small stories, and elaborate on their underlying meanings, which leads to interpretation and narrative reframing.

In the second session, the career counselor's objective is to help the youth in the construction of a narrative that provides coherence to micro-narratives referred to in the previous session. Hence, the second session entails narrating to the client a reconstructed story and serves as the beginning of the co-construction of a reconceptualized identity narrative. The macro-narratives serve as a point of dialogue with the youth to invoke meaning by assimilating experiences and reframing causality to accommodate new understandings. To illustrate, youth may not realize the importance of previous experiences, as they may not seem relevant, but in reality, those experiences may be of value when introduced from a macro-narrative perspective. Accordingly, the macro-narrative should invigorate the youth to engage in activities that realize their intentions. The career counselor may assist the youth in exploring their choices and their positive or negative consequences through planned activities. Ultimately, the youth will crystallize their preferences for a group of occupations that are within their ability and interest. Career counselors may then generate a list of occupations or academic majors and identify local resources (e.g., certification training, community colleges, placement centers, and nonprofit organizations) to assist the youth's plan and actualize their goals.

Finally, in the third and final session, the focus is on completing counseling and the termination of services. The career counselor ascertains if the youth has indeed taken action to actualize the plan "through weekly activities, intermediate projects, and long-term goals" (Savickas, 2019c, p. 149). In addition, the career counselor may need to address attitudes toward the choice or barriers (e.g., feelings, circumstances, and relationships) that may impede the youth from taking action. As the counseling concludes, the career counselor summarizes what has been accomplished by reinforcing the reconceptualized story and reiterating how it relates to the initial reason for seeking career counseling (e.g., academic advice, vocational direction, and/or career counseling). Conversely, the career counselor may ask the youth to explain how they achieved their goal. The youth may compare and contrast the micro-narratives to the reconceptualized story.

Postmodern Era

In a new era of a postmodern world understanding, the trends in secondary education, self-determined learning, and transition planning allow for career counselors to offer a more suitable approach to the current era of the 21st-century world of work (Wehmeyer et al., 2019). Implementing a transition plan may include early planning, career culture, college culture, and adult roles/responsibilities (Morningstar et al., 2017). Similar to the life-design process, postmodern techniques used by career counselors should discuss career plans early on with their TAY. Transition plans should be individualized to their needs (e.g., accommodations for disability, housing, funding to pay for postsecondary education, or part-time employment) to develop an effective plan prior to their transition into young adulthood. Career counselors can begin early planning as soon as eighth grade to encourage youth to begin formulating ideas about their future career goals. During this planning stage, transition youth should begin with trying new career-related experiences to develop career goals based on service learning or volunteering outside of school (Morningstar et al., 2017). For example, when a youth informs a career counselor that they would like to be a nurse, the counselor should encourage and recommend that youth to volunteer/shadow at a clinic, hospital, or nursing home. This will give the youth a better understanding of the different settings nurses work in and allow the youth to gather a nurse's perceptive on the daily job tasks they may encounter on a day-to-day basis. Allowing transition youth to take an active role in their career goals and life planning, as well as identify educational services, encourages greater autonomy and self-determination (Wehmeyer et al., 2019). Furthermore, allowing transition youth control of their career goals can be beneficial during the career development process (Hamm et al., 2013).

Career-Related Programs

Tech-Prep Programs

According to U.S. Department of Education, tech-prep programs are nationwide and federally supported through the Carl D. Perkins Career and Technical Education Act of 2006 (Perkins Act): Title II 20.*U.S.C.*2371, as amended by P.L. 109-270, which empathizes career and technical education for the transition between high school and community college (U.S. Department of Education, n.d.). The purpose of tech-prep programs is to apply a sequenced program of study that combines at least 2 years of high school and 2 years of postsecondary education, specifically for 11th and 12th graders. Students gain academic knowledge and technical skills earned through college credit for their secondary coursework; essentially, students earn college credit (U.S. Department of Education, n.d.).

Tech-prep programs were first used for career guidance and counseling. For example, high school counselors taught transition youth about the changes in the labor market in their local areas, broadened youth knowledge and skills in their areas of interest, and maximized youth career opportunities by encouraging them to take dual enrollment classes relating to career and technical education (U.S. Department of Education, 2014). Now, career and technology programs have replaced tech-prep programs by expanding on career pathways that relate to the current labor market.

Career and Technology Programs

The purpose of career and technology programs, also known as career and technology education (CTE), is to align the challenges of academic standards and relevant technical knowledge and skills needed to prepare for further education and a career in current or emerging professions (e.g., finance, hospitality, information technology, manufacturing, health science, and human services) (Texas Education Agency, n.d.a). Ideally, students in middle school participate in CTE courses to learn more about options for school, complete a career assessment, and work closely with the middle school transition counselor to review/finalize their 4-year plans based on their career goals. High school students take their first introductory course and discuss their interests with their high school counselors or campus career advisors to continue on their chosen pathways and to ensure that they pass all their classes and stay on target for their career goals.

The Strengthening Career and Technical Education for the 21st Century Act (Perkins V) H.R.2353, as amended by P.L. 115-224, is the largest source of federal funding for CTE (Higher Learning Advocates, 2019). Funding to states and local communities support the following activities: developing new and innovative programs of study, professional development and technical assistance, career exploration, guidance and advisement, data collection and analysis, and implementation and continuous improvement of existing programs of study (Higher Learning Advocates, 2019).

According to Higher Learning Advocates (2019), 60% of companies reported having difficulty filling job openings because of the lack of qualified applicants. Specifically, the state of Texas implements the Pathways in Technology Early College High School (P-TECH) program. Currently, Texas has 34 designated P-TECH/Industry Cluster Innovative Academies (ICIA) high schools and 28 planning P-TECH/ICIA high schools. To illustrate, one of the 28 designated P-TECH/ICIA high schools offers 10 career pathways for students to choose from based on their career interests: (1) advanced architectural design, (2) automotive technology, (3) construction technology, (4) culinary arts, (5) digital design, (6) health science, (7) industrial robotics, (8) information technology, (9) veterinary science, and (10) welding, thus allowing ninth through 12th graders the opportunity to complete a course of study that combines high school and postsecondary credits (Texas Education Agency, n.d.b). During secondary education, TAY earn their high school diplomas, an associate's degree, or a 2-year postsecondary certificate/industry certification and complete work-based training. This allows students to gain work experience through apprenticeships, internships, or other job training programs.

Partnerships and Programs Between High Schools and Colleges

During President Barack Obama's administration, the first White House Summit on Community Colleges was held on October 5, 2010, to discuss the best practices for improving the outcome of student enrollment and graduation rates at community colleges across the country, which was one of the president's priorities (The White House, 2011).

The three important milestones that align with the White House Summit on Community Colleges are (1) enrollment in college, (2) college readiness at enrollment, and (3) persistence in college (Barnett & Hughes, 2010). For example, for students to attend college, they must first enroll; this can be done with the partnerships between local community colleges and high schools to increase enrollment. Hence outreach/recruitment, dual enrollment, early assessment, CTE pathways, summer bridge programs, and early and middle college high schools are vital in developing partnerships between colleges and high schools (Barnett & Hughes, 2010). For instance, in a South Texas community, the purpose of the CTE program is to increase students' options for professional licenses and certifications, meet the needs of current the labor market, and enhance college and career readiness skills. In doing so, the CTE program provides dual enrollment opportunities with postsecondary institutions (e.g., South Texas College and University of Texas–Rio Grande Valley) and offers 32 professional licenses and certifications, job shadowing, and wage-earning internship opportunities; students are also afforded an opportunity to participate in national student organizations (e.g., FIRST Robotics, Business Professionals of America, Distributive Education Clubs of America, Health Occupations Students of America, and Future Farmers of America).

In the state of California, California State University (CSU) offers outreach and student academic preparation programs that provide information and academic support to California's elementary, middle, secondary, and postsecondary students (CSU, 2017). For instance, the California Academic Partnership Program endeavors to improve the academic quality of public secondary schools and improve access and preparation of all students for college, while the College-Going Culture Extension Grant's main focus is to build strong academic partnerships with middle schools as they enhance the academic rigor at high schools.

Placement Services

The National Fund for Workforce Solutions (2017) discussed the importance and strategies of promoting youth skills and job training. The National Fund developed the Young Adult Initiative, which allows the use of sectoral strategies to provide employment opportunities to 18- to 25-year-olds who are not employed or enrolled in school (National Fund for Workforce Solutions, 2017). In 2013, New York City established the Young Adult Sectoral Employment Project (YASEP), which was the nation's first sectoral strategy focused on youth and young adults. YASEP's intermediary focus is to allow partnerships within the community in an effort to have local organizations provide support services to at least one training institution with connections to the employer. When assisting youth in sectoral employment programs, one needs to understand that strong community partnerships are essential during the preparation process (National Fund for Workforce Solutions, 2017). Doing so creates a connection between employer(s) and career counselor(s) that will better serve the youth during the process. For example, once a career counselor understands the job tasks and needs of a specific employer, the career counselor can provide a more efficient service to their clients.

The U.S. Department of Labor's Employment and Training Administration (ETA) offers a wide variety of programs to assist youth in developing skills and provides the training they need to transition into adulthood and their careers successfully. For instance, the WIOA Youth Program is a comprehensive youth employment program. This program is specifically designed to address barriers youth may encounter in the area of education, training, and employment. The WIOA Youth Program provides an array of services, such as paid and unpaid work experiences, pre-apprenticeship programs, on-the-job training, and occupational skill training. Further, Job Corps is the largest and most comprehensive residential education and job training program for at-risk youth. Job Corps works closely with private companies, state and federal agencies, and unions in which youth can be trained and assisted in securing employment. Similarly, the YouthBuild program helps at-risk youth who have previously dropped out of high school to acquire the knowledge and skills they need to obtain and maintain employment.

Noteworthy, of the aforementioned youth programs, the YouthBuild program serves 6,000 youth in 40 states every year. The entities eligible for YouthBuild grant funding include workforce development boards, school districts, community colleges, nonprofit and community-based organizations, housing development agencies, Indian tribes, and youth service or conservation corps (U.S. Department of

Labor, 2018). As the YouthBuild program is a community-based, pre-apprenticeship program, it offers an array of services to afford youth an opportunity to acquire vocational skills in construction, health care, information technology, and hospitality. Furthermore, the YouthBuild program affords youth an opportunity to earn a high school diploma or general educational development (GED) certificate. Of the youth completing the YouthBuild program, 70% earned a degree or certificate, 62% increased their literacy or numeracy skills, and 54% entered higher education or employment. While YouthBuild is offered at certain locations, such as American YouthWorks (Austin, Texas), AMIkids Baton Rouge (Baton Rouge, Louisiana), and Asian Media Access (Minneapolis, Minneapolis), career counselors in rural areas may not have access to these types of programs because of a lack of grant funding. Nonetheless, it is important for career counselors to explore such programs, as the youth may not need to live in the immediate area of the YouthBuild program to be eligible for services. For example, American YouthWorks in Austin, Texas, offers counseling, assistance in employment readiness, college readiness, and a reentry track for young people exiting the criminal justice system, regardless of whether the youth and/or career counselor live in the immediate area of Austin.

Career counselors may be challenged in finding appropriate state or local placement resources. The U.S. Department of Labor's ETA has a web page specifically for youth under the Division of Youth Services that includes resources, policies, programs, and links for career counselors to access. Six ETA regional offices monitor programs, services, and benefits provided under the WIOA, including the unemployment insurance program, trade adjustment assistance program, and other targeted grant investment. For instance, a new career counselor in New York can contact their acting regional administrator by locating the region they are in (U.S. Department of Labor, 2018) and gain information on current youth placement and/or employment services in their state.

Online Resources

When it comes to providing services to youth, there are web-based applications that career counselors can use to assist youth with career development. For example, Workforce is a national organization that has state/local agencies throughout the United States. Through the U.S. Department of Labor's ETA, CareerOneStop provides career exploration, job search and training, tool kits, resources, and local assistance. In the young adult section, GetMyFuture offers a range of tools and resources that are available for career counselors to use with their transition youth. Not only does CareerOneStop provide a variety of tools and resources for career counselors, but there is also a specific section on young adults. GetMyFuture has sections on career exploration, education, employment, support, and tool kits.

The "find support" section in GetMyFuture is unique, as it has tools for job search help, banking/credit, transportation, parenting, foster system, criminal record, addiction recovery, food/money, and other supports to assist youth in their transition from high school to adulthood. However, a great starting point for career counselors when using this website is the "explore careers" section. This section has multiple tools to assist youth in guiding them in the decision-making process. Specifically, the "choose your career" section provides a chart with links for an interest assessment, skills checklist, and occupational profile. Once an interest assessment and skills checklist are completed, the career counselor and youth can check on the occupation profile skills section to determine if the outcome of their interest assessment and skills checklist align with each other. From there, the youth can review the education that is required, average wages/

salary, and employment outlook. Each of these sections can be reviewed in the youth's local community or elsewhere, depending on the youth's employment and personal goals.

Other resources on GetMyFuture is the "tool kit" section, which offers easy access for more experienced career counselors. This section has quick links to the interest assessment, occupation profile, salary finder, job finder, and much more. Experienced career counselors can use the tool kit for finding local training (e.g., vocational careers), scholarships for those transitioning into college, and apprenticeships for gaining work experience, as well as access to the American Job Center Finder. Other great tools in the tool kit include the State Resource Finder and Youth Program Finder. This makes it easier for career counselors to direct youth to other resources in their communities.

Another online resource sponsored by the U.S. Department of Labor's ETA is the WorkforceGPS. This website benefits career counselors, as it allows one to browse resources in education and training, employment retention and advancement, and management and operations. Career counselors can use geographic locations to search their local areas for updated information on the labor market. Changing the search criteria to better fit each client is recommended, as the available information is broad.

Placement Centers

As a career counselor, being aware of placement centers in one's local area is vital for providing efficient services to clients. One way to find services is to locate the Youth Program Finder on CareerOneStop and search by state. A list of locations for specific states is available for career counselors to find additional resources at placement centers. Lastly, career counselors may want to use their local workforce agencies, along with nonprofit organizations (specific to employment services).

Summary

In efforts to assist young adults with determining their career of choice, it is important for career counselors to consider key factors of this developmental stage. Adolescence is often characterized by feelings of uncertainty, as youth discover who they are and who they'd like to become. As adolescents contemplate their future, an array of emotions may be experienced by the youth. The idea of a new chapter in their lives may bring out feelings of excitement and anticipation, yet youth may simultaneously feel overwhelmed by fear of the unknown. Thus the career development process can be intimidating as they transition from youth to adulthood. A career counselor must be well grounded in his/her theoretical approach yet flexible to address the unique characteristics of youth.

The application of counseling techniques must be practiced in a manner that promotes an effective working alliance and allows youth to gain self-awareness and knowledge about the world of work. Career counselors have such an important role in this decision-making process that they can influence the direction in which youth decide to go. The counselor must appropriately draw out youth strengths and abilities while considering their preferences and needs. Barriers (e.g., readiness, first-generation graduates, and family support) must be validated and approached with empathy, warmth, and unconditional positive regard. Counselors must also be comfortable moving through this journey with youth, as adolescents may experience periods of indecisiveness. Ultimately, a collaborative working alliance will empower youth as they answer the infamous question, "What will I be when I grow up?"

Case Study

A case study serves to illustrate real-life situations and allows students to analyze them critically.

Robert is a 16-year-old high school junior who has a 4.0 grade point average. He plays the saxophone in the marching and jazz bands. Robert feels that music is a very important aspect of his life, but he also enjoys the science and automotive clubs. Most recently, he started to volunteer at the local food bank. He reports that his parents are pressuring him to join the Junior Reserve Officer's Training Corps and, upon graduation from high school, enroll in the local university and major in military science to keep with the family tradition of serving in the armed forces. Lately, Robert has been thinking about his future goals and feels very anxious, as he does not know what he wants to do after high school and fears he will have no choice but to major in military science. In response to the question of how counseling might be useful to him, he replied, "I want to figure out what I am supposed to do with my life after I graduate from high school."

Questions

1. Describe how you, as the career counselor, will proceed with this case.
2. What are the issues the youth is facing?
3. What kinds of activities would you suggest, and why?
4. What are some short-term goals you would use to assist this youth?
5. What are some long-term goals you would use to assist this youth?
6. What additional information would you like to have regarding this case?

Discussion Questions

1. How can career and technology programs be beneficial to this population in terms of their career development?
2. What issues are youth facing that career counselors need to take into consideration?
3. How can career counselors capitalize on partnerships between high schools and colleges?

References

Arbona, C., & Novy, D. M. (1991). Career aspirations and expectations among Black, Mexican American, and white college students. *Career Development Quarterly, 39*, 231–239.

Barnett, E., & Hughes, K. (2010.). *Community college and high school partnerships*. https://www2.ed.gov/PDFDocs/college-completion/09-community-college-and-high-school-partnerships.pdf

Brooks, L. (1990). Career counseling methods and practice. In D. Brown & L. Brooks (Eds.), *Career choice and development* (2nd ed., pp. 455–472). Jossey-Bass.

California State University, Office of the Chancellor. (CSU). (2017). *Student academic outreach programs: 2016–2017 annual report*. https://www2.calstate.edu/attend/student-services/student-outreach-admissions-and-financial-aid-resources/Documents/2016-2017_OutreachReport.pdf

Cardoso, P., Duarte, M. E., Gaspar, R., Bernardo, F., Janeiro, I. N., & Santos, G. (2016). Life design counseling: A study on client's operations for meaning construction. *Journal of Vocational Behavior, 97*, 13–21. https://doi-org.ezhost.utrgv.edu/10.1016/j.jvb.2016.07.007

Davis, M., & Sondheimer, D. L. (2005). State child mental health efforts to support youth in transition to adulthood. *Journal of Behavioral Health Services & Research, 32*(1), 27–42.

Eisenman, L. T. (2003). Theories in practice: School-to-work transitions-for-youth with mild disabilities. *Exceptionality, 11*, 89–102.

Federal Partners in Transition Workgroup (FPT Workgroup). (2015). *The 2020 federal youth transition plan: A federal interagency strategy.* https://www.dol.gov/odep/pdf/20150302-FPT.pdf

Federal Partners in Transition Workgroup (FPT Workgroup). (2016). *What to know about youth transition services for students and youth with disabilities.* https://www2.ed.gov/about/offices/list/osers/transition/products/fpt-factsheet-transitionservices-swd-ywd-3-9-2016.pdf

Hamm, J. M., Stewart, T. L., Perry, R. P., Clifton, R. A., Chipperfield, J. G., & Heckhausen, J. (2013). Sustaining primary control striving for achievement goals during challenging developmental transitions: The role of secondary control strategies. *Basic and Applied Social Psychology, 35*(3), 286–297. https://doi.org/10.1080/01973533.2013.785404

Higher Learning Advocates. (2019). *101: Career technical education.* https://ejm0i2fmf973k8c9d2n34685-wpengine.netdna-ssl.com/wp-content/uploads/2019/06/CTE-101-Career-Technical-Education-FINAL2.pdf

Lechner, C. M., Tomasik, M. J., & Silbereisen, R. K. (2016). Preparing for uncertain careers: How youth deal with growing occupational uncertainties before the education-to-work transition. *Journal of Vocational Behavior, 95–96,* 90–101. https://doi.org/10.1016/j.jvb.2016.08.002

Lindsay, S., McDougall, C., Menna-Dack, D., Sanford, R., & Adams, T. (2015). An ecological approach to understanding barriers to employment for youth with disabilities compared to their typically developing peers: Views of youth, employers, and job counselors. *Disability and Rehabilitation, 37*(8), 701–711. https://doi.org/10.3109/09638288.2014.939775

Manteuffel, B., Stephens, R. L., Sondheimer, D. L., & Fisher, S. K. (2008). Characteristics, service experiences and outcomes of transition-aged youth in systems of care: Programmatic and policy implications. *Journal of Behavioral Health Services & Research, 35*(4), 469–487.

Martel, A., & Fuchs, D. C. (2017). *Transitional age youth and mental illness: Influences on young adult outcomes.* https://doi.org/10.1016/j.chc.2017.01.001

Morningstar, M. E., Lombardi, A., Fowler, C. H., & Test, D. W. (2017). A college and career readiness framework for secondary students with disabilities. *Career Development and Transition for Exceptional Individuals, 40*(2), 79–91. https://doi.org/10.1177/2165143415589926

National Fund for Workforce Solutions, Resource, Young Adults. (2017). *Connecting young adults to skills and jobs: Lessons from the National Fund's sectoral strategies.* https://nationalfund.org/wp-content/uploads/2017/04/ConnectingYouth-Report-Final-4-11-1.pdf

Savickas, M. L. (2011). *Career counseling.* American Psychological Association.

Savickas, M. L. (2013). Career construction theory and practice. In S. D. Brown & R. W. Lent (Eds.), *Career development and counseling: Putting theory and research to work* (2nd ed., pp. 147–183). Wiley.

Savickas, M. L. (2016). Reflection and reflexivity during life-design interventions: Comments on career construction counseling. *Journal of Vocational Behavior, 97,* 84–89. https://doi-org.ezhost.utrgv.edu/10.1016/j.jvb.2016.09.001

Savickas, M. L. (2019a). *Career counseling* (2nd ed., pp. 37–55). American Psychological Association.

Savickas, M. L. (2019b). *Career counseling* (2nd ed., pp. 71–88). American Psychological Association. https://doi.org/ezhost.utrgv.edu/10.1037/0000105-005

Savickas, M. L. (2019c). Career counseling (2nd ed., pp. 145–157). American Psychological Association. https://doi-org.ezhost.utrgv.edu/10.1037/0000105-009

Savickas, M. L., Nota, L., Rossier, J., Dauwalder, J.-P., Duarte, M. E., Guichard, J., Soresi, S., Van Esbroeck, R., & van Vianen, A. E. M. (2009). Life designing: A paradigm for career construction in the 21st century. *Journal of Vocational Behavior, 75*(3), 239–250. https://doi-org.ezhost.utrgv.edu/10.1016/j.jvb.2009.04.004

Setlhare-Meltor, R. & Wood, L. (2016). Using life design with vulnerable youth. *Career Development Quarterly, 64,* 64–74. https://doi.org/10.1002/cdq.12041

Super D. (1990). A life-span approach to career development. In D. Brown & L. Brooks (Eds.), *Career choice and development* (2nd ed., pp. 197–261). Jossey-Bass.

Texas Education Agency, College, Career, and Military Prep. (n.d.a). *CTE Texas essential knowledge and skills from 2017–2018*. https://tea.texas.gov/Academics/College,_Career,_and_Military_Prep/Career_and_Technical_Education/CTE_Texas_Essential_Knowledge_and_Skills_for_2017–2018/

Texas Education Agency, College, Career, and Military Prep. (n.d.b). *Pathways in technology early college high school (P-TECH)*. https://tea.texas.gov/PTECH/

The White House. (2011). *The White House summit on community colleges*. https://obamawhitehouse.archives.gov/sites/default/files/uploads/community_college_summit_report.pdf

Wehmeyer, M. L., Nota, L., Soresi, S., Shogren, K. A., Morningstar, M. E., Ferrari, L., Sgaramella, T. M., & DiMaggio, I. (2019). A crisis in career development: Life designing and implications for transition. *Career Development and Transition for Exceptional Individuals, 42*(3), 179–187. https://doi.org/10.1177/2165143417750092

Wilens, T. E., & Rosenbaum, J. F. (2013). Transitional age youth: A new frontier in child and adolescent psychiatry. *Journal of the American Academy of Child & Adolescent Psychiatry, 52*(9), 887–890. https://doi.org/10.1016/j.jaac.2013.04.020

World Health Organization, Department of Child and Adolescent Health and Development. (n.d.). *Orientation programme on adolescent health for health-care providers*. https://www.who.int/maternal_child_adolescent/documents/pdfs/9241591269_op_handout.pdf

U.S. Department of Education, DTI Associates Inc. (DTI), and the Community College Research Center, Teachers College, Columbia University (CCRC). (n.d.). *Fact sheet: Tech-prep program*. https://www2.ed.gov/about/offices/list/ovae/pi/cclo/cbtrans/techprep.pdf

U.S. Department of Education, Office of Career, Technical, and Adult Education. (2014). *Career guidance and counseling program*. https://www2.ed.gov/about/offices/list/ovae/pi/cte/cgcp.html

U.S. Department of Education, Office of Career, Technical, and Adult Education. (2017). *Postsecondary career and technical education: Demographic differences in enrollment, departure, and completion*. https://files.eric.ed.gov/fulltext/ED583036.pdf

U.S. Department of Labor. (n.d.b). *Resources*. WorkforceGPS. https://www.workforcegps.org/resources.

CHAPTER 6

Career Counseling for Adult Clients

Jina Chun, Gloria K. Lee, and Hung Jen Kuo

CHAPTER OVERVIEW

In an ever-changing workforce, adults must continually ensure that they are marketable and tech-savvy in today's workforce (Kroger, 2007) by having relevant skill sets and effective work-related skills for a successful career. Just keeping up with societal demands and technological changes alone makes keeping a job and staying relevant in one's field a full-time job. This chapter will discuss the changes in life roles for adult clients, as well as considerations in terms of barriers to employment as related to career counseling process and development. Specifically, what it means to go through the interview and application process and how to survive and thrive in a competitive job market will be discussed. Lastly, career counseling approaches will be examined with special attention and application to career decision making and motivational interviewing (MI).

CHAPTER OBJECTIVES

After reading this chapter, the student will be able to complete the following:

1. Discuss life roles and stages for adult clients.

2. Discuss factors that affect career development and growth in adults.

3. Identify barriers to employment for adults.

4. Develop strategies for addressing a competitive job market.

5. Discuss counseling approaches for helping adult clients with career development, pursuit, and maintenance.

Super's Life Roles and Stages for Adults

Super's (1980, 1990) life-span, life-space theory to career development has been widely used as a comprehensive developmental framework for career counseling. The concepts of life roles and life stages represent an interactive system called the "life career rainbow model" (Super, 1980). In Super's theory, career development can be viewed in the context of all life roles enacted by an individual.

Life Roles

Super indicated six primary roles people play at specific points throughout their lifetime: (1) child, (2) student, (3) leisurite, (4) citizen, (5) worker, and (6) homemaker. These roles are played in four theaters: (1) home, (2) school, (3) workplace, and (4) community. While the roles of child, student, and leisurite are important in childhood, the roles of citizen, worker, and homemaker are particularly important for adults. Super's life career rainbow model shows how a person's roles vary within their lifetime (Sharf, 2014). For example, particularly focusing on working-age adult groups, some individuals may participate in their education or training at some point in their lives for job advancement. They may have found an appropriate field and thus put effort into making a permanent place in it. Some individuals may also participate in community service activities, such as religious, social, and political groups. Depending on the age of the person, the role of home and family can vary. Taking the lead role as caregiver for children and/or aging adults may become more important later in life than it is in earlier years. Lastly, the role of leisure is an important activity for many individuals across the life span. During early childhood or adolescence, activities such as sports and clubs can help individuals explore curiosity and refine their interests, whereas for adults, leisure activities can be work or family related.

In some stages of an individual's life, they may play multiple roles at the same time, such as studying, working, and participating in community services and leisure activities. Individuals' participation in these life roles can fluctuate depending on age and other circumstances across the life span. Some roles are more important than others during certain ages. Super further indicated that as a person moves through life stages and juggles various life roles, the individual's self-concept is initiated and developed (Okocha, 2001). Self-concept is the belief a person has about themselves that is developed early in life, but it goes through constant evaluation and adjustment throughout the life span (Super, 1980). For most people, engaging employment opportunities can affect self-concept, personal development, and satisfaction with life.

Life Stages

Another major concept of Super's theory of career development is life stages. The concepts of life stages and substages are both age specific and non-age specific (Sharf, 2014). In other words, those stages are age specific in the sense that there are typical times when people go through stages of growth, exploration, establishment, maintenance, and decline or disengagement. It is also possible, however, for an individual to experience one or more particular stages at any moment in their lifetime. For example, a client who is already in the establishment stage of a career may look for ways to maintain themselves in their current work. On the other hand, the person may want to explore other career options or opportunities for growth at the same time. This is described as "recycling" in Super's theory, which reflects a new, growing segment of the workforce.

Super (1990) proposed the following five major life stages: (1) growth, (2) exploration, (3) establishment, (4) maintenance, and (5) disengagement. Since the focus of the current chapter is on adults, only three of the life stages will be discussed, and they are (1) exploring oneself in identifying job interests and capabilities, (2) establishing oneself in one's career, and lastly, (3) maintaining one's position or transitioning into a different/new career. The last stage, disengagement, will be discussed in the next chapter.

Exploration

Exploration is the period when individuals attempt to understand themselves and find their place in the world of work. Typically, the exploration stage ranges from 15 to 24 years of age. Through school, work experiences, and hobbies, individuals may try to identify their interests and capabilities and learn how they fit with various occupations. The exploration stage includes three substages: (1) crystallizing and making an occupational choice, (2) becoming more specific in the choice, and (3) implementing it by finding and choosing a job. During the *crystallizing* substage, people clarify what they want to do. They learn about entry-level jobs that may be appropriate for them and acquire skills that are needed for the jobs. They also explore to identify their abilities, interests, and values through work experience during this stage. In the second substage, *specifying*, people tend to determine their preferences, so they may find an employer or an appropriate graduate training program. Some must specify an occupation while others must specify a job within an occupation. Lastly, during the *implementing* substage, people make plans to develop their career objectives. They may expand their network by meeting people in their desired fields, write resumes and job applications, arrange job interviews, and decide between potential employers.

Establishment

The establishment stage, which ranges from the age of 25 to 45 years, pertains to the time when an individual starts a job. During this time, individuals learn the basic elements of the job and where they fit in a field. Those who change their careers later in life also go through this stage at a more advanced age. Substages within the establishment period are (a) stabilizing, (b) consolidating, and (c) advancing. In the *stabilizing* substage, people begin to settle into a job and are able to meet the job requirements to stay in the field. They may be apprehensive about whether they have certain required or desired knowledge, skills, and abilities that are essential for becoming successful on the job. During the *consolidating* substage, people strive to be more productive and feel more comfortable with their jobs. As the employment status becomes more stabilized, an individual may seek a promotion or advancement within his/her organization. The final substage, *advancing*, occurs as the individual moves ahead into a position with more responsibility and higher pay based on his/her success on the job.

Maintenance

Super (1990) proposed that individuals age 45 to 65 years maintain what they have achieved. During this stage, workers may have become comfortable with their job duties and found a balance between work and other aspects of life. Substages within maintenance include (a) holding, (b) updating, and (c) innovating. The individuals may maintain their status in their chosen fields, update their competencies, and/or find innovative ways of performing their job routines. Having obtained a secure and recognized position, the first substage, *holding*, occurs as people seek to maintain their place and status in light of competition from others, family concerns, and other demands. On the other hand, in some fields of work and for some individuals, holding their own is not enough. During the *updating* substage, workers may seek professional development opportunities. In other cases, some fields may require employees to keep themselves current in the field, such as a counselor and a teacher. The last substage, *innovating*, presents when a person desires to have a new spark in their career. Some individuals may feel the need to learn new things and explore so as to make new contributions to the field, whereas they may already be well established.

While Super's theory is informative for individuals at any given age or stage, it is particularly applicable to career counseling for working-age adult groups. The concept of career maturity can be helpful in considering the job-readiness of individuals with stage disruption, and areas of experiential deficiency can be identified. The life-space segment of Super's life career rainbow model is also useful in identifying and normalizing an imbalance of life roles and creating a projected balance of life roles (Okocha, 2001). By comparing the time spent in current life roles with the ideal work-life balance and the projected balance, the client can be motivated toward changes, and goals can be developed accordingly. Exploring some possible changes and developing goals can help the client make a smooth transition into a new role.

Factors Affecting Career Development and Growth in Adults

In this part of the chapter, we will consider people between the age of 25 and 54 as working-age adults because they are mostly finished with schooling but not near retirement age, and they have the highest participation rate in the labor force as reported by the Congressional Budget Office (CBO, 2017). This working-age group consists of approximately two thirds of the labor force participation (CBO, 2017). According to the Bureau of Labor Statistics (2018), 6.6 million people were counted as "unemployed," with an additional 5.1 million indicating that they wanted a job but were not counted as part of the labor force. However, six million jobs remained unfilled, with 13,000 openings during the month of January in 2018 (Express, 2018). There are many factors that contribute to this trend, including economic and political factors that interact with personal and demographic factors. Furthermore, it is worth noting that even for workers who are actively participating in the workforce, the environment can affect low labor force participation, thus underscoring the importance of a healthy work environment and the psychosocial aspects of work. Given the complexity of how these personal, psychosocial, and environmental factors may affect working-age adults' career development, growth, and participation, career counselors must be mindful of such challenges and help clients understand these challenges. More importantly, counselors must be equipped to help addressing challenges not only at the personal but also at societal and systemic levels.

Economic and Political Factors

Economic conditions, such as recessions and outsourcing, as well as fiscal policies, such as earned income tax credits, raise in the minimum wage, and Social Security Disability Insurance programs, can have an effect on one's ability and decision to work. During economic weakness, the reduced availability of jobs may discourage labor force participation and make finding work more competitive, thus distorting the significance of the unemployment rate. Between the end of the 2007–2009 recession and 2017, the unemployment rate for ages between 25 and 54 fell by 4.5%. The slow recovery of the labor market reflects the reduction in the demand for goods and services, thus slowing the growth in gross domestic product. This causes sharp increases in unemployment. This recession continued to have a lingering effect on the economy and contributed to a slow recovery, particularly for people aged 25 to 54 (CBO, 2017).

The economic crisis period affected the labor market where employers reduced the number of workers to compensate for their expenditure, thus reorganizing the internal structure to maintain the same level of efficiency and competitiveness and to employ workers based on outsourcing (Pew Research Center, 2016). Furthermore, employers increasingly offer contracts, freelancing, and hourly work (e.g., Karamessini, Symeonaki, & Stamatopoulou, 2016; Mucci et al., 2016), resulting in job insecurity (e.g., Felstead & Gallie, 2004; Mauno et al., 2005). The federal earned income tax credit substantially pushes up the labor force participation of single mothers without a college degree. The Affordable Care Act raises effective tax rates, thus reducing workers' take-home pay and potentially discouraging labor force participation (CBO, 2017).

Also, education policy can affect the education of the population, and immigration policies have affected the racial and ethnic composition of the workforce.

Another policy that directly affects the economy and the workforce is raising the minimum wage, and the debate has continued since 2016 (Maverick, 2016). Raising the minimum wage comes with both positive and negative effects on the economic system. As we will discuss next, for the working-age populations that come with additional expenses and considerations for childcare, elderly care, and inflation of living, minimum wage increases would improve the overall standard of living. Maverick's article cited a 2013 CBO report that stated an estimated 900,000 people would live above the poverty line with an increase in the minimum wage. This trend will also increase employee morale and retention, as well as encourage employees to put maximum effort into their jobs. However, an increase in the minimum wage could pose challenges for the economy, employers, and employees. Raising the minimum wage means increasing wages and salaries. This is especially true for workers whose job duties may not require high skill sets, thus, making them less competitive for those who have the skill sets. The situation, in turn, increases operating costs and thereby the price of services and products, as well as then the cost of living. Although we discussed earlier that an increase in the minimum wage could help to attract workers who are qualified, it could also cause job losses, especially if employers turn to outsourcing to reduce labor expenses and maintain profits. Furthermore, this could also increase the competition for minimum wage jobs in the labor market, with a larger number of overqualified workers taking jobs that would have gone to those with less experience.

Demographic and Psychosocial Factors

Because of the economic factors affecting the labor market, a discussion about the perception of work is important to better support workers to enter and maintain the workforce. The Pew Research Center (2016) indicated that American workers perceive a job as an activity to earn a living, particularly workers who have lower-than-average income and those with less education. Similarly, individuals with a higher education who work full-time and earn a higher income tend to report more satisfaction with their financial situation, family life, and general happiness. Younger workers see jobs as stepping-stones, and workers in certain occupations see jobs as a career (health care, education, science, technology, engineering, and mathematics (STEM)/teaching). Workers with higher education attainment also reported a better sense of work identity. In 2017, the labor force participation rate for men aged 25–54 with at least a college degree was 9% higher compared to those without a degree, while the difference was 13% for women (CBO, 2017). Individuals who are more educated (63% with a bachelor's degree or higher) recognize the importance of further education (Pew Research Center, 2016).

Meaningful work motivates people to go above and beyond the requirements of their work. Nonetheless, there are some demographic characteristics that affect labor force participation more negatively with this working-age group, and these are often intertwined with other psychosocial factors. In regard to race and ethnicity, African American men of working age were more likely to work than other racial and ethnic groups, but Hispanic women were the least likely to be in the labor force (CBO, 2017). Men have lower levels of work participation because of illness or disability as compared to women in general. Mothers with children under the age of 5 have lower labor force participation compared to men, but this trend varies based on marital status. Married women with young children are less likely to work than those without young children, while unmarried women with young children are more likely to work. The issues on gender and marital and parental status are tied to childcare expenses, as 71% of parents reported finances as a serious problem (Express, 2018).

Caring for a family member or having an illness or a disability may prohibit an individual from finding or keeping a job. Illness or disability has been the primary reason that men have been out of the workforce, while a key reason for women is caring for family members. The CBO (2017) reported that people with disabilities participate less in the labor force because of a combination of having a limited amount of work and the need to receive Social Security disability benefits or other health care benefits (Pew Research Center, 2016). An increase in incarceration, especially among men, has contributed to a decline in work participation, primarily because of the tenuous connection to employment and the existence of a criminal record. A staggering 65% of applicants fail drug tests, and more than 70 million individuals (one in three adults) have criminal records that pose employment-related stigma (Express, 2018). Reductions in health care insurance and retirement funds have also contributed to aging Americans staying in the workforce longer or needing to find other means to cover their health care needs. People work on average 5 years longer before retirement and have to work longer hours and find alternative employment, such as independent contracting and freelancing (Pew Research Center, 2016).

Employment and Work Environmental Factors

Factors directly related to employment and the work climate also affect one's desire and motivation to work. Specifically, the Pew Research Center (2016) reported that the U.S. economy continues to emphasize the knowledge-focused age, thus rewarding jobs that require social, communication, and analytical skills. Thus adults are under constant pressure to make a lifetime commitment to retraining and upgrading their skills. The report also indicated that young adults and those in the service sectors are more likely than their older counterparts to seek new skills and training as they pursue their careers. Sixty percent of those between 18 and 29 and 56% of those between 30 and 49 indicated the need for ongoing training. Sixty percent of workers in the STEM-related industries and 62% of workers in the health care industry see the importance of ongoing training and skills development, compared to other fields, such as hospitality, manufacturing, farming, and retail. Furthermore, employment has been rising faster in jobs that require higher levels of education, training, and experience. The number of workers in occupations that require average to above-average education has increased by 65% since 1980. Employment increased by 77% for jobs that require higher levels of analytic skills, including critical thinking and computer usage. Thus workers also see the combination of soft skills and technical skills as crucial to success in today's economy. Express (2018) noted that 37% of businesses reported a lack of applicants with experience as the most common reason for having difficulty filling jobs with 34% stating that there is a lack of available applicants. About 22% reported applicants lacking hard skills with 13% stating applicants lack soft skills. Given the diversity of immigrants coming to the United States, the workforce also consists of workers from countries where English is not their first language. The report indicated that some workers in certain industries may have communication and language skills that limit core job functions.

As discussed earlier, job insecurity often makes workforce participation less appealing. Job insecurity not only depends on objective conditions but also on workers' perceptions of their situations. From a healthy work perspective, work-related stress can have a significant psychological effect on a worker, thus leading to poor job performance and possibly leaving the workforce (De Sio et al., 2018). The World Health Organization defines work-related stress as a condition that is characterized by physical, psychological, or social dysfunction that results from the feeling of not being able to respond to expectations (EU-OSHA-European Agency for Safety and Health at Work, 2001). Work-related stress and a multitude of psychosocial risk factors interact with each other. These risk factors stem from a combination of personal issues, such as the workers' resources, needs, skills, work organizations/environmental conditions, and technological factors (Leka & Jain, 2010). The psychosocial risks that influence the perception of stress are excessive workloads, a lack of decisional autonomy in the management of one's work, a lack of support by colleagues or superiors, the presence of relational conflicts in the workplace, the under evaluation of one's role within the company, and the lack of involvement in the company's organizational changes (Leka et al., 2008). Chronic exposure to psychosocial risks has been associated with a wide range of mental and physical conditions, such as anxiety, depression, back pain, chronic fatigue, impaired immune function, and cardiovascular diseases (e.g., Cohen et al., 2012; Mucci et al., 2016). Finn et al.'s (2016) study further confirmed the importance of organizational factors that affect workers, suggesting that decision control, role conflict, positive challenge, support from immediate superiors, fair leadership, predictability, commitment to the organization, rumors of change, human resource primacy, and social climate all contribute to mental distress, thus highlighting the importance of a positive and supportive work environment in the contributing to health and well-being of people at work.

Technology

As mentioned earlier, in this digital age, technology has become a part of our daily lives. According to a study conducted by the Pew Research Center (2019), approximately 81% of Americans own at least a smartphone or something alike compared to 35% just a few years ago in 2011. In addition, nearly three quarters of American adults own at least a desktop or a laptop computer. Although the possession rate of a personal computer fluctuated in recent years because the line between a smart device (e.g., Android tablet or iPad) and a computer has become blurry, it is clear that information technology has become mainstream and that almost everyone can enjoy the convenience that technology can bring. The mainstreaming of modern technology has several benefits; for example, the U.S. Census Bureau (2014) reported a positive relationship between the ownership of a computer and higher education attainment. A similar positive association was also found in computer possession, employment status, and household income. However, while technology can be beneficial and promising, it also has its downsides. Imagine a situation in which a person is seeking employment opportunities. This person might have included computer skills, such as operating a Word processor or email software, on their resume as a "selling point" a few years ago. These once "icing on the cake" skills seem to have become basic in today's labor market. As Hamer (2016) claimed, Microsoft Word is a "super basic" skill and should not be included on a resume anymore.

While the full analysis of the benefit and risk of technology advancement is much needed, it is beyond the scope of the current chapter. However, it is important for practitioners to be aware of some of the consequences associated with the advancement of technology and provide training and counseling accordingly. The following paragraphs will discuss two key impacts resulting from technology evolving: they are (1) job destruction or technological unemployment and (2) demand for more skilled employees.

Job destruction or technological unemployment pertains to business owners choosing to replace their low-skilled employees with automated machinery, and as a result, workers are forced to move to other positions or retire earlier than expected. As Silva and Lima (2017) described, the change in technology has raised some concerns about the decline in low-skilled jobs. This is somewhat consistent with the prediction by Frey and Osborne (2017) in which they pointed out that 47% of occupations in the United States will face a high risk of decreased employment rates within the next 10–25 years as a result of computerization. From a business owner's perspective, there are many reasons to rely heavily on automatic machinery instead of human workers. For example, the technological devices are consistent and flexible, have less turnover rate, and require little to no on-the-job training. These effects are even more robust for production businesses. Lachenmaier and Rottmann (2011) reported that the adoption of these innovative devices has helped manufacturing businesses by producing more products with fewer workers. As a result, the traditional blue-collar workers are forced to choose between transforming into more skilled white-collar positions or leaving the labor force. It is, however, worth noting that the relationship between technological advancement and employment is still considered paradoxical (Bogliacino & Pianta, 2010). In fact, many believe that process innovation can lower the cost of production and increase profit. In turn, employers may be able to generate more jobs and thus more opportunities for labor force participation. This "compensation theory" has attracted lots of attention among economic professionals and can be traced back as far as the '60s and '70s (Say & Prinsep, 2000). Although the overall effect of technological change is still inconclusive, career counselors should keep these possibilities in mind.

Another consequence of technology advancement is the demand for highly skilled employees—a direct result of the reliance on the technology discussed earlier. Since the 1990s, a new phenomenon has emerged: With the technological changes, the labor market began to favor high-skilled over middle-skilled workers (Silva & Lima, 2017)—as discussed in the section on demographic trends. This is largely because of the so-called technology-skill complementarity in which technology enhances productivity and changes the dynamics of the workforce. In turn, these changes create more job opportunities and higher wages for more skilled workers. This situation was first observed in the 1940s (Goldin & Katz, 1998) and continues to be true today (Vivarelli, 2014). While the increase in opportunities for workers with higher skills is encouraging, a decrease in the demand for low- to mid-skilled workers may pose a serious issue to those seeking entry-level jobs. The situation is particularly important for career counselors to be aware of, as the counseling process will no longer be a passive or simple process of matching clients' skills and abilities to the right jobs. In fact, enhancing clients' skills via formal education or training will be pivotal (Kim et al., 2017).

Interview and Job Application Process

Given the unique political, demographic, work/environmental, and technological landscapes that have become workforce participation barriers, workers may find themselves having to prepare to shift and change jobs. This poses a challenge for all working ages, but there are some unique challenges for those workers who have been in the workforce—that is, at the establishment and maintenance stages of their career development. Because the application and interviewing processes have changed since these workers first began their careers, there are strategies that can better prepare them for current job preparation.

Experienced workers, although not always, often span the age range of 25–45 (establishment) or even 45–65 (maintenance) and can be subject to age discrimination. Doyle (2019) discussed important tips to help more experienced workers reduce barriers during the job search process. (1) Emphasize your experience. Experienced workers have a previous work history that younger workers simply do not have; thus, it is imperative to highlight the years of experience in job materials and interviews. (2) Highlight your skills. In addition to specific skills that are important for the job functions, experienced workers often have transferable skills that are required and useful in almost any job. Reade (2015) indicated that experienced workers were rated as being more patient, reliable, detail oriented, and possessing leadership skills. (3) Be open to learning new skills. Workers at the establishment or maintenance stages may or may not have the most current skills. Therefore, being open to identifying relevant skills they potentially lack or may not have used for a while will enhance their marketability and value. Consistent with the technology section discussed earlier, Doyle (2019) suggested that a common skill that may be lacking for experienced workers is technology, thus learning and knowing the right technology skills has become imperative in the digital age. (4) Network. Although seasoned workers may have existing contacts in their industries or fields, it is suggested that joining or rejoining professional associations and updating or learning the use of newer networking tools, such as LinkedIn, will allow workers to stay connected with others.

Doyle (2019) further discussed tips related to the job search process. (1) Age-proof/update your resume and cover letter. While it is important to highlight enriched work experience, having a resume that lists all work experience or uses outdated terms should be avoided. (2) Update your professional image. There are many practical tips that make a worker presentable by noting the appropriate dress code, including types of clothes, shoes, makeup, hairstyles, and accessories for an interview, as a presentable image makes a positive first impression. (3) Prepare for your job interview. Working-age adults should be prepared to provide reasons for job changes. The barriers section presented earlier in the chapter highlighted many reasons for a working-age adult to change jobs (e.g., not ready to retire, focus on the future, unemployed, career change). Being able to discuss unique issues, such as being overqualified and the willingness to work for a younger manager, will allow potential employers to consider the job seeker as a valued member of the workplace. (4) Get job search help. Seasoned workers must be cognizant of the many resources and outlets available for conducting a job search, including libraries, job search workshops, job clubs, and job transition tools (online job search and career exploration tools; https://library.nashville.org/content/career-transitions), as well as other online revenues such as LinkedIn, Indeed (see the following), and personal networks.

Workers in the establishment and maintenance stages often have many strengths, including their work and life experiences. However, they can also face some unique challenges, such as age, reasons for job shifts, and outdated etiquette in their job search process and interviewing skills. Being open to learning the nuances of the current world of work, as well as being able to highlight one's strengths and explain potential challenges, can make the job seeker appealing to employers.

Strategies for Addressing a Competitive Job Market

Frank Parsons, many call him the father of guidance, has been one of the most impactful pioneers leading the field of career guidance. His famous creation, the trait and factor theory, has provided a systematic way for career counselors to match a person's abilities to the occupations that share the same requirements. Numerous job seekers have benefited from the implementation of the approach. One of the biggest criticisms against Parsons's theory is that it conceptualizes a person's traits as stable and lacking plasticity. As such, the education and training that a person receives may not be in the matching equation. Instead, the matching process is passive and static. Despite its weaknesses, the trait and factor theory has led to the development of numerous assessments that are used to identify people's traits, and it provided a solid ground for later constructions, such as person-environment fit and Occupational Information Network (O*Net). As the science of career guidance evolved, occupational training and vocational rehabilitation were emphasized and promoted to address the weaknesses of the traditional trait and factor theory.

Table 6.1

Resource	Brief Description	Link
O*Net	O*Net was developed as a replacement for the *DOT*. The system details specific jobs with tasks, work behaviors, abilities, skills, knowledge areas, and work context.	https://www.onetonline.org/
Occupational Outlook Handbook (OOH)	The OOH is a government-owned website that provides thousands of occupations with information such as average salary, educational level, and projected growth rate.	https://www.bls.gov/ooh/
USA Jobs	USA Jobs not only provides job opening information but also offers a platform for job seekers to upload their resumes and profiles for applying for federal jobs. The hiring paths help job seekers with diverse backgrounds.	https://www.usajobs.gov/
CareerOneStop	The website is sponsored by the U.S. Department of Labor. CareerOneStop provides job seekers with a variety of free online tools, information, and resources.	https://www.careeronestop.org/
Monster	Monster is a job search engine that job seekers can use to identify employment opportunities based on key words and location. The career advice option is available for users with resume and interview questions.	https://www.monster.com/
Indeed	Indeed is a job search engine with millions of job listings. Users can also upload their resumes and create a link to share with potential employers.	https://www.indeed.com/

However, the challenges of Parsons's technique do not stop there. In fact, the assumption that occupation requirements are stable and can be documented in an encyclopedia-like book, such as the *Dictionary of Occupational Titles* (*DOT*), may not be practical nowadays. An attempt to fully understand the labor market is similar to aiming at a moving target. With all the economic changes, such as automatic machinery evolution and the outsourcing trend, if career counselors are not equipped with occupational information and guidance, then attempts to match job seekers may not be as successful as it once was. Apparently, it may not be practical to expect every career counseling practitioner to study global economic factors and be ready to deal with an economic crisis; however, knowing where to find occupational information is critical serving and preparing their clients to face these challenges.

Gore et al. (2013), in their book chapter, Structure, Sources and Uses of Occupational Information, presented a plethora of resources and classification systems for career counselors to better understand occupational information. For example, they introduced the use of Holland's hexagon and the *Dictionary of Holland Occupational Codes* for better use of occupational information with job seekers. While similar information can be easily accessed on the internet, the intention of this chapter is to highlight a few resources so that readers can quickly reference them when needed. These resources will be discussed in more detail in Chapter 17. Table 6.1 includes the resources for occupational information and brief descriptions of each.

Career Counseling and Approaches

Practitioners need appropriate counseling and related strategies for facilitating clients' career transitions across all stages of career development and achieving their goals. This facilitation requires counselors to be equipped with methods for promoting clients' autonomy and career decision-making abilities, responding to client resistance, and addressing clients' self-efficacy, as well as the ability to identify and assist in the reduction or alleviation of any personal and/or environmental barriers to promote career decision making and successful job or career pursuits. Career decision making and MI provide practical methods to accomplish a client-centered approach in the context of career counseling where the evidence supports specific vocational behavior changes and the most appropriate action is dependent on the client's preferences.

Career Decision Making

Making an effective career decision can often be stressful because each prospective career decision can have a variety of effects on an individual's life (Lustig et al., 2012; Reardon et al., 2000). Research on career development has shown that an individual's vocational behavior is cognitively mediated by the interaction between their vocational cognitions, behaviors, and environment (Lustig et al., 2012). As mentioned earlier in this chapter, a number of individual factors, such as cognitions regarding careers, self-esteem, self-efficacy and family involvement, as well as environmental factors, such as decision-making opportunities, work experience, and economic conditions, affect career decision-making abilities in the process of career development (Yanchak et al., 2005).

Career decision making was originally characterized by Parsons in 1909. The three components of career decision making are (1) clear self-understanding, (2) knowledge of occupations, and (3) an ability to draw a relationship between self and occupational knowledge. If the client demonstrates faulty self-efficacy beliefs and/or self-defeating assumptions, these negative career thoughts may lead to distorted and misinformed career beliefs. Such negative career beliefs can result in self-defeating behaviors, which may, in turn, cost the person relationships, jobs, and other opportunities that require him/her to take some risks. Therefore, practitioners should help clients not only learn about their job interests, values, abilities, and employment preferences but also understand the way they think and how that influences their career decision-making abilities (Sharf, 2014).

The Career Thought Inventory (CTI; Sampson et al., 1996) measures negative career thinking. Research has found that the CTI is useful in identifying problem areas in thinking, determining readiness for career problem solving and career decision making, and improving career thoughts related to career choice (Osborn et al., 2013). The CTI also helps clients to identify potential dysfunctional career thoughts that allow them to begin to challenge and alter negative thinking, prepares them to fully explore information about themselves, take options under consideration, and make informed career decisions (Osborn et al., 2013).

The Cognitive Information Processing (CIP) approach (Peterson et al., 1996) to career development and services was also designed to be used with clients in career counseling. This approach is concerned with thought and memory processes in solving career problems and making effective career decisions. Key assumptions of the CIP approach require that the process (a) involves emotions and cognition, (b) involves content and process knowledge, (c) necessitates organizational skills to effectively sort through information, and (d) involves a skill that can be acquired (Osborn et al., 2013). As individuals move along a continuum of indecision to the decision stage, people may experience confusion, anxiety, stress, or external locus of control in the indecision stage, whereas they may achieve feelings of hope, internal locus of control, and general well-being in the decision stage. Thus practitioners can help clients who get stuck in career indecision to open up new career ideas and to gain the momentum necessary for change by (a) defining the problem, (b) understanding the etiology of the problem, (c) formulating alternatives, (d) prioritizing alternatives, (e) implementing solutions, and (f) evaluating outcomes (Peterson et al., 1996).

Motivational Interviewing (MI)

MI is a client-centered counseling approach designed to strengthen an individual's motivation and commitment to change (Miller & Rollnick, 1991). Studies have shown that MI is effective in changing health behaviors in various contexts, such as reducing the risk of substance abuse and management of cardiovascular conditions, diabetes, mental health, hypertension, and asthma (Miller & Rose, 2009).

MI has also received increasing attention in the field of career counseling. Its potential benefits for career counseling have been discussed in studies (i.e., Klonek et al., 2016; Rochat & Rossier, 2016) to foster an individual's vocational behavior and development (Rochat, 2018). For instance, the use of MI has been suggested to establish strong working alliances between counselors and clients and to promote clients' engagement in the career planning process, job-seeking behaviors, and return to work behavior change. In particular, MI as a career counseling intervention that has been widely used for individuals from a lower economic status, juvenile offenders who use drugs, and individuals with psychiatric disabilities (i.e., Leukefeld et al., 2003; Lloyd et al., 2008; Muscat, 2005). Clients often have competing interests, values, and conflicts related to their personal, social, psychological, and vocational goals. MI can be a useful tool for counselors to learn how to effectively help clients to explore and resolve ambivalence (Manthey et al., 2015), to make positive decisions and, ultimately, to achieve goals.

MI is consistent with the stages of change by focusing conversation toward recognizing and reducing barriers to change, such as ambivalence and low confidence, and developing and implementing plans to initiate and maintain change. MI involves (a) establishing an empathetic relationship with clients, (b) focusing on a targeted change, (c) evoking and fostering one's own motivation in favor of the change (change talk) while responding empathically to the person's arguments against the change (sustain talk), and (d) planning the change when the person is ready for it. Core principles of MI include (a) expressing empathy through reflective listening, (b) rolling with resistance rather than opposing it directly, (c) developing discrepancies between goals and problem behavior, and (d) supporting self-efficacy for change.

The basic interaction techniques and skills that are used early and often in the MI approach include open questions, affirmations, reflective listening, and summary reflections. During the intake/preliminary assessment process, integrating MI techniques helps counselors to establish better working alliances with clients and enhance the quality of this process. Further, when developing career goals and development plans, MI techniques, such as rules of importance and confidence, exploring the extremes, and determination of barriers and values, can be used to help the client's self-determination process and promote an incremental or transformational approach to change and the counselor's utilization of informed choice and partnership approaches (Torres et al., 2019). When designing these steps, the counselor should ensure that the considered tasks are likely to provide the client with direct evidence that could strengthen his/her beliefs regarding the client's personal capabilities and contextual opportunities and, ultimately, foster vocational behavior and career development (Rochat, 2018).

Implications

Challenges that adults face when seeking employment have and will continue to evolve. As indicated, the economic situation and the overall changes in technology have created roadblocks for traditional blue-collar workers. However, they may also present a new opportunity for advancement. As such, career counselors of the 21st century must be ready to evolve as well. There are several implications at different levels that can improve workforce participation among working-age adults. Although policy or environmental changes may require a higher level of planning and implementation and may not be for the health and allied health professions to address directly; nevertheless, front-line professionals, such as counselors, can have a role. Specifically, they can use their counseling approaches, such as CIP and MI, to assist their clients with identifying personal and environmental barriers and encourage them to take an active approach to problem solving. Counselors can also offer consultative support for their clients and employers to enhance the compatibility of individual workers, as well as employers—for instance, realizing that specific working-age groups may face unique challenges that prohibit them from working because of multiple life roles and other demands. Flexible workplace policies can be suggested to help employees with caregiving responsibilities achieve a satisfactory work-life balance, as well as other reasonable work accommodations. Adult workers must now be equipped with the multiple knowledge and skill sets they need to advance.

Providing opportunities for continuous education and/or on-the-job training will allow workers to be more equipped and competitive in maintaining or being promoted to higher level positions. Having specific programs helps individuals who may struggle with seeking or securing a job (e.g., those with criminal records, immigrant workers, and those with disabilities that may affect their compatibility). With the advancement and expectation of technological savviness, encouraging seasoned workers who may feel less comfortable with the use of technology for job seeking, maintenance, and professional networking and communications to engage in training would better prepare them to be compatible with the current workforce standards. Such approaches to professional development for workers who may want to explore other career options or opportunities can further enhance their visibility and searchability with prospective employers, particularly in the service sectors and specialty areas. However, encouraging workers of all ages to enhance their education and on-the-job training is the best avenue for further skills development (Pew Research Center, 2016). Finally, the vicious and cyclical effect of chronic work stress exposure results in job dissatisfaction, job insecurity, and deteriorating physical and mental health. Subsequently, adult workers who need to seek additional or multiple jobs to make ends meet cannot face the challenges given their less-than-optimal health and the challenge involved in acquiring a secure job. Helping employers to establish a positive work environment will help reduce occupational stress, as well as building positive work relationships between workers and employers to maintain a sense of royalty. As indicated in the findings, employers consistently speak for the impetus for workers to receive additional training, but lack of time and resources remain major barriers to advanced training. The concept of work must be redefined so that investment is shown in both the employers and the workers.

Summary

With global and economic changes and the advancement of technology that result in job insecurity and high job turnover rate, the concerns about job loss and job transition among adults is an important aspect to address. In this chapter, we provided an overview of information that is important to understanding adults' roles from the context within which to view the stages of career development: exploration, establishment, and maintenance. We also described a number of factors and trends affecting career development and growth in adults, including economic and political factors that interact with personal and demographic factors as well as the overall changes in technology. Strategies to support career transition are largely similar to those in the initial career choice, but unique elements need to be taken into account when working with adults considering career change. Counselors should appreciate the breadth of their adult clients' life experiences when exploring job changes, understand their career behaviors, and address their unique needs, challenges, and desires to enhance the career and employment outcomes of adult clients. Therefore, accurate assessment, individualized career counseling, and deliberated job screening that address one's career needs must be done. Lastly, the career decision-making approach and MI were introduced as practical tools that career counselors can use in promoting adult clients' autonomy, career decision-making abilities and successful career pursuit.

Discussion Questions

1. Discuss the unique challenges and issues that working-age adults face.
2. Discuss the implications for career counselors when working with this unique group of working adults considering the challenges mentioned in question #1.
3. Discuss how career counseling interventions/approaches might be uniquely tailored to the career concerns and needs of adults considering a career change.

References

Bogliacino, F., & Pianta, M. (2010). Innovation and employment: A reinvestigation using revised Pavitt classes. *Research Policy, 39*(6), 799–809. https://doi.org/10.1016/j.respol.2010.02.017

Bureau of Labor Statistics (BLS). (2018). *The employment situation—2020*. https://www.bls.gov/news.release/empsit.nr0.htm

Cohen, S., Janicki-Deverts, D., & Doyle, W. J. (2012). Chronic stress, glucocorticoid receptor resistance, inflammation, and disease risk. *Proceedings of the National Academy of Sciences of the United States of America, 109*(16), 5995–5999.

Congressional Budget Office (CBO). (2017). *Factors affecting the labor force participation of people ages 25 to 54*. https://www.cbo.gov/publication/53452

De Sio, S., Cedrone, F., Battagliola, E. T., Buomprisco, G., Perri, R., & Greco, E. (2018). The perception of psychosocial risks and work-related stress in relation to job insecurity and gender differences: A cross-sectional study. *Biomedical Research International*. https://10.1155/2018/7649-85.

Doyle, A. (2019). *Job search strategies for older workers*. The Balance Careers. https://www.thebalancecareers.com/job-search-tips-for-older-job-seekers-2063078.

EU-OSHA-European Agency for Safety and Health at Work. (2001). *Factsheet n.22: Work-related stress*. https://osha.europa.eu/en/publications/factsheet-22-work-related-stress/view

Express Employment Professionals. (2018). Workers want jobs, but seven barriers are in their way. An Express Employment Professionals white paper. https://www.expresspros.com/Newsroom/America-Employed/New-White-Paper-from-Express-Barriers-Between-People-and-Jobs.aspx

Felstead, A. & Gallie, D. (2004). For better or worse? Non-standard jobs and high involvement work systems. *International Journal of Human Resource Management, 15*(7), 1293–1316.

Finn, L. B., Christensen, J. O., & Knardahl, S. (2016). Psychological and social work factors as predictors of mental distress and positive affect: A prospective, multilevel study. *PLoS One, 11*(3), e0152220. https://doi.org/10.1371/j/journal.pone.0152220.

Frey, C. B., & Osborne, M. A. (2017). The future of employment: How susceptible are jobs to computerisation? *Technological Forecasting and Social Change, 114*, 254–280. https://doi.org/10.1016/j.techfore.2016.08.019

Goldin, C., & Katz, L. F. (1998). The origins of technology-skill complementarity. *Quarterly Journal of Economics, 113*(3), 693–732.

Gore, P. A., Jr., Leuwerke, W. C., & Kelly, A. R. (2013). The structure, sources and uses of occupational information In S. D. Brown, & R. W. Lent (Eds.), *Career development and counseling: Putting theory and research to work* (pp. 507–535). Wiley.

Hamer, L. (2016, December 14). *What not to list in your resume skills section.* Retrieved September 14, 2019, from https://www.themuse.com/advice/3-super-basic-resume-skills-you-should-think-twice-before-including

Karamessini, M., Symeonaki, M., & Stamatopoulou, G. (2016). The role of the economic crisis in determining the degree of early job insecurity in Europe (Negotiate working paper 3.3). http://www.negotiate-research.eu

Kim, Y. J., Kim, K., & Lee, S. (2017). The rise of technological unemployment and its implications on the future macroeconomic landscape. *Futures, 87*, 1–9. https://doi.org/10.1016/j.futures.2017.01.003

Klonek, F. E., Wunderlich, E., Spurk, D., & Kauffeld, S. (2016). Career counseling meets motivational interviewing: A sequential analysis of dynamic counselor–client interactions. *Journal of Vocational Behavior, 94*, 28–38. https://dx.doi.org/10.1016/j.jvb.2016.01.008

Kroger, J. (2007). *Identity development: Adolescence through adulthood* (2nd ed.). Sage Publications, Inc.

Lachenmaier, S., & Rottmann, H. (2011). Effects of innovation on employment: A dynamic panel analysis. *International Journal of Industrial Organization, 29*(2), 210–220. https://doi.org/10.1016/j.ijindorg.2010.05.004

Leka, S., Cox, T., & Zwetsloot, G., (2008). *The European framework for psychosocial risk management (PRIMAEF).* I-WHO Publications.

Leka, S., & Jain, A. (2010). *Health impact of psychosocial hazards at work: An overview.* World Health Organization.

Leukefeld, C., McDonald, H. S., Staton, M., & Mateyoke-Scrivner, A. (2003). An employment intervention for abusing offenders. *Fed. Probation, 67*, 27.

Lloyd, C., Tse, S., Waghorn, G., & Hennessy, N. (2008). Motivational interviewing in vocational rehabilitation for people living with mental ill health. *International Journal of Therapy and Rehabilitation, 15*(12), 572–579. https://doi.org/10.12968/ijtr.2008.15.12.31813

Lustig, D. C., Zanskas, S., & Strauser, D. (2012). The relationship between psychological distress and career thoughts. *Journal of Rehabilitation, 78*(4), 3–10.

Manthey, T. J., Brooks, J., Chan, F., Hedenblad, L. E., & Ditchman, N. (2015). Motivational interviewing. In F. Chan, N. L. Berven, & K. R. Thomas (Eds.), *Counseling theories and techniques for rehabilitation and mental health professionals* (pp. 246–277). Springer.

Mauno, S., Kinnunen, U., Makikangas, A., & Natti, J. (2005). Psychological consequences of fixed-term employment and perceived job insecurity among health care staff. *European Journal of Work and Organizational Psychology, 14*(3), 209–237.

Maverick, J. B. (2016). What are the pros and cons of raising the minimum wage? *Investopedia.* https://www.investopedia.com/articles/markets-economy/090516/what-are-pros-and-cons-raising-minimum-wage.asp

Miller, W. R., & Rollnick, S. (1991). *Motivational interviewing: Preparing people to change addictive behavior.* The Guilford Press.

Miller, W. R., & Rose, G. S. (2009). Toward a theory of motivational interviewing. *American Psychologist, 64*, 527–537.

Mucci, N., Giorgi, G., Ceratti, S. D. P., Fiz-Perez, J., Mucci, F., & Arcangeli, G. (2016). Anxiety, stress-related factors, and blood pressure in young adults. *Frontiers in Psychology, 7*, 1–10.

Mucci, N., Giorgi, G., Roncaioli, M., Perez, J. F., & Arcangeli, G. (2016). The correlation between stress and economic crisis: A systematic review. *Neuropsychiatric Disease and Treatment, 12*, 983–993.

Muscat, A. C. (2005). Ready, set, go: The transtheoretical model of change and motivational interviewing for "fringe" clients. *Journal of Employment Counseling, 42*(4), 179–191. https://doi.org/10.1002/j.2161-1920.2005.tb01089.x

Okocha, A. A. (2001). Facilitating career development through Super's life career rainbow. https://files.eric.ed.gov/fulltext/ED462641.pdf

Osborn, D. S., Saunders, D. E., & Wilde, C. (2013). Applying cognitive information processing theory to career decisions of people with disabilities. In D. Strauser (Ed.), *Career development, employment, and disability: From theory to practice* (pp. 125–138). Springer.

Peterson, G. W., Sampson, J. P., Reardon, R. C., & Lenz, J. G. (1996). A cognitive information processing approach to career problem solving and decision making. *Career Choice and Development, 3*, 423–475.

Pew Research Center. (2016). *The state of America (n jobs: How the shifting economic landscape is reshaping work and society and affecting the way people think about the skills and training they need to get ahead.* https://www.pewsocialtrends.org/2016/10/06/the-state-of-american-jobs/

Pew Research Center. (2019, June 12). *Mobile fact sheet.* https://www.pewinternet.org/fact-sheet/mobile/

Reade, N. (2015). *The surprising truth about older workers.* Work & jobs. AARP. https://www.aarp.org/work/job-hunting/info-07-2013/older-workers-more-valuable.html

Reardon, R. C., Lenz, J. G., Sampson, J. P., & Peterson, G. W. (2000). *Career development and planning. A comprehensive approach.* Thomson Learning.

Rochat, S. (2018). Examining motivational interviewing in career counseling from a motivational system theory perspective. *British Journal of Guidance and Counselling, 46*(5), 632–643. https://doi.org/10.1080/03069885.2018.1483005

Rochat, S., & Rossier, J. (2016). Integrating motivational interviewing in career counseling: A case study. *Journal of Vocational Behavior, 93*, 150–162.

Sampson, Jr., J. P., Peterson, G. W., Lenz, J. G., Reardon, R. C., & Saunders, D. E. (1996). *Improving your career thoughts: A workbook for the Career Thoughts Inventory.* Psychological Assessment Resources.

Say, J.-B., & Prinsep, C. R. (2000). *A treatise on political economy; or the production, distribution, and consumption of wealth.* https://ebookcentral.proquest.com/lib/csla/detail.action?docID=3117790

Sharf, R. S. (2014). *Applying career development theory to counseling* (6th ed.). Brooks/Cole.

Silva, H., & Lima, F. (2017). Technology, employment and skills: A look into job duration. *Research Policy, 46*(8), 1519–1530. https://doi.org/10.1016/j.respol.2017.07.007

Super, D. E. (1980). A life-span, life-space approach to career development. *Journal of Vocational Behavior, 16*, 282–298.

Super, D. E. (1990). A life-span, life-space approach to career development. In D. Brown & L. Brooks (Eds.), *Career choice and development: Applying contemporary theories to practice* (2nd ed., pp. 197–261). Jossey-Bass.

Torres, A., Frain, M., & Tansey, T. N. (2019). The impact of motivational interviewing training on rehabilitation counselors: Assessing working alliance and client engagement. A randomized controlled trial. *Rehabilitation Psychology, 64*(3), 328–338. https://dx.doi.org/10.1037/rep0000267

U.S. Census Bureau (2014, November 13). *Computer and internet use in the United States: 2013.* https://www.census.gov/library/publications/2014/acs/acs-28.html.

Vivarelli, M. (2014). Innovation, employment and skills in advanced and developing countries: A survey of economic literature. *Journal of Economic Issues, 48*(1), 123–154. https://doi.org/10.2753/JEI0021-3624480106

Yanchak, K. V., Lease, S. H., & Strauser, D. R. (2005). Relation of disability type and career thoughts to vocational identity. *Rehabilitation Counseling Bulletin, 48*(3), 130–138.

CHAPTER 7

Career Counseling for Older Adults: Retirement and Preretirement

Mary-Anne Joseph and Bernadette Williams York

CHAPTER OVERVIEW

Preretirement, early retirement, and retirement bring with them many benefits but also a significant range of challenges for an aging baby boomer generation (Taylor et al., 2014). This chapter will discuss the change in life roles for older adults as they relate to career counseling and development. Further, considerations in terms of barriers to employment will be discussed in relation to older adults in the career counseling process, specifically what it means to go through the interview and application process after being in the field for many years and how to compete in a competitive job market.

CHAPTER OBJECTIVES

After reading this chapter, the student will be able to complete the following:

1. Discuss the factors that affect continued career development, growth, and engagement among older adults.

2. Discuss life roles and stages for older adult clients.

3. Outline barriers to employment.

4. Discuss strategies for addressing a competitive job market.

For those over the age of 50, it can be difficult to gain employment (Eisenberg, 2018). Job seekers aged 55 and older often face long periods of unemployment, and they frequently experience a significant amount of discrimination in the workplace (Eisenberg, 2018). Job seekers 55 and older tend to be out of work substantially longer than their younger counterparts. Older job seekers usually take 30–34 weeks to find work while younger job seekers typically take approximately 15 weeks (Eisenberg, 2018). It has also been found that the hourly pay for full-time workers starts to decline after 60. Employers begin to compare cost sharing and often conclude that they can hire two younger workers at the cost that they may be paying a worker over the age of 60 (Eisenberg, 2018).

Adults over the age of 55 are often forced to take lower paying jobs to make ends meet (Eisenberg, 2018). Over time, the employment rate of adults over the age of 55 has varied. In 2014, 49% of workers over the age of 55 were unemployed while 29% were unemployed in 2018 (Eisenberg, 2018). In 2000, workers aged 65 and older accounted for 13.1% of the labor force. By 2010, this number grew to 19.5% and fluctuated to 18.9% in 2018. This percentage is projected to reach 25.2% in 2020 (Anderson et al., 2013; Bureau of Labor Statistics, 2019; Toossi & Bureau of Labor Statistics, 2012).

Preretirement, early retirement, and retirement bring with them many benefits but also a significant range of challenges for an aging baby boomer generation (Taylor et al., 2014). In an age of economic uncertainty where the decline of retirement security is of significant concern, older adults have increasingly tried to remain in, or return to, the workforce (Anderson et al., 2013). Unfortunately, a host of factors, such as ageism and changing skill requirements, present challenges for older adults seeking employment. Low-income older adults may lack the necessary education and skills and have limited access to job opportunities and training (Anderson et al., 2013). Let us now turn to a more detailed discussion of these barriers to employment experienced by older adults.

Barriers to Employment for Older Adults

There are a variety of factors that present as barriers to employment for older adults. Such barriers include ageism, workplace discrimination, changing skill requirements, lack of necessary education and skills, and limited access to and preparation for job opportunities and training (Anderson et al., 2013). In this section, we will explore these barriers and discuss effective means of assisting older adults in overcoming these barriers when seeking employment.

Education

From 1997 to 2007, there was an approximate 6% growth in the educational standings of older adults. More older adults were found to have bachelor's degrees or higher in 2007 than in 1997 (Bureau of Labor Statistics, 2008). However, it is maintained that younger adults still hold higher levels of educational attainment than older adults, which poses an additional barrier for older adults. Younger adults continually present as better educated competition for older adults in the workplace, which makes it increasingly difficult for older adults to gain and maintain employment.

It is widely known that educational training expands opportunities for employment and career development. Research has shown that earning rates are correlated with educational training. More specifically, the Census Bureau indicated that workers with high school diplomas earn approximately 50% more than workers without diplomas. Likewise, workers with bachelor's degrees earn approximately 80% more than those with high school diplomas (Census Bureau, 2007).

The issue of educational training and employment can be further compounded when the issue of age is added. When older adults lack educational training, it is often difficult for them to acquire such training. Older adults who are seeking employment are often too financially limited to manage the cost of returning to school or engaging in training. This obstacle to employment is further compounded by the alternative options for employment, which do not require educational training. These alternatives often include physically demanding jobs, such as hotel service and construction, which may be unsuitable for older adults, some of whom may have physical disabilities and limitations (Anderson et al., 2013; Johnson, 2004).

Moreover, employment barriers because of limited or a lack of educational training are more frequently experienced by minorities of color and those who stem from lower socioeconomic backgrounds

(Sum et al., 2011). It has been found that "African American, Hispanic, and less-educated older adults have higher rates of unemployment" (Anderson et al., 2013, p. 321). Therefore, adults over 50, who are also members of a minority group, may encounter three times the marginalization and, potentially, discrimination when seeking employment.

Ageism

Ageism refers to stereotyping, bias, and/or discrimination against individuals based on their chronological age (Butler, 1969). While discrimination based on age is illegal in the United States, ageist attitudes still have a significant effect on the employability of older adults (Anderson et al., 2013; Neumark, 2009). Ageism can manifest itself in employment practices that reflect employers' negative images or perceptions of older adults. For instance, employers may believe that older adults are less flexible, productive, physically able, trainable, and technologically savvy than their younger counterparts (Chiu et al., 2001; Dennis & Thomas, 2007; Henkins, 2005; Loretto & White, 2006; Taylor & Walker, 1998). Such negative perceptions and stereotypes may be internalized by older workers and can adversely affect their sense of worth and their drive to secure employment later in life (Bodner, 2009; Kite & Wagner, 2002).

It is important to note that age discrimination in the workplace may fluctuate with the economy. When unemployment is high, employers may have greater opportunities to discriminate, whereas when unemployment is low and job opportunities are more plentiful, older workers have greater opportunities for employment (Anderson et al., 2013). A tight labor market such as that which was experienced in the United States in 2018–2019 can be most beneficial to workers over the age of 55 (Eisenberg, 2018).

Disability

Research has demonstrated that disability can have an adverse effect on employment and employability. This is of greater concern for older adults, as members of this population are more likely to develop disabling conditions that hamper their ability to become employed and be effective in the workplace. Moreover, disability has been found to be more common among those of lower socioeconomic status. Even their fear of disability "may deter employers from hiring them [older adults] even if they are not disabled at the time of hire, out of a fear that they will subsequently become disabled and impose firing costs" (Neumark, 2009, p. 61).

Socioeconomic Status

Much like education and disability, socioeconomic status can also have an adverse effect on employment and employability (Anderson et al., 2013). However, it is essential to note that the poverty rates for older adults vary across groups. Poverty disproportionately affects minority groups. For instance, approximately 20% of blacks and Hispanics live in poverty, and women are found to be more likely to live in poverty than men. It was found that approximately 10% of female older adults live in poverty as compared to approximately 7% of male older adults.

Many older adults who live in poverty have experienced a lifetime of poverty. Living in poverty for one's entire life can also result in a variety of barriers to employment, which include "reduced access to education and training; fewer job-related resources such as housing, transportation, computer access and diminished social capital" (Anderson et al., 2013, p. 324). In addition, "the social stigma associated with a low-income neighborhood may reduce an applicant's chances of being hired"

(Anderson et al., 2013, p. 524). Employers may hold stereotypes about perceived character flaws of persons living in impoverished neighborhoods (Casciano & Massey, 2008). Affordable housing, access to reliable transportation, accessible environments, and community safety are also factors that limit the employability of older adults who may be living in poverty (Anderson et al., 2013). These issues may pose an even greater barrier for older adults who live in rural areas.

Race and Ethnicity

People of color have historically had higher unemployment rates than those of Caucasian descent (Bureau of Labor Statistics, 2012). It has been found that over the life span, people of color tend to have fewer years of education and less access to health care. This often results in lower earnings, poorer health, fewer resources, and lower lifetime wealth (Burr & Mutchler, 2007; Census Bureau, 2010; Hirschman & Lee, 2005). Race is also associated with job type, and people of color have been found to be significantly more likely to work in physically demanding jobs. As workers age, they may no longer be able to fulfill the job requirements of such physically demanding jobs. This results in fewer job opportunities for those older minority job seekers who lack the education and skills demanded in the fast-moving, technology-driven labor market (Anderson et al., 2013). "For older adults of color, a lifetime of disparities and the pernicious effects of institutional racism constitute two of the greatest barriers to meaningful and rewarding employment in later in life" (Schieman et al., 2005, in Anderson et al., 2013, p. 332).

Technology

The technological skills of older adults may be less advanced and developed than those of their younger counterparts (Anderson et al., 2013). As such, the additional time that older workers may need to develop their skills in this area may have a negative effect on their employability (Charness & Czaja, 2005). Furthermore, it is essential to consider that the availability of and access to training and workforce development opportunities may be limited to older adults because of cost, proximity, and access. In addition, employers who hold negative perceptions of older adults may be reluctant to provide additional training to older workers (Lee, Czaja, & Sharit, 2009; Maurer et al., 2003).

It is, however, essential to note that technology may not be a barrier to employment for all older adults. Some older adults may simply require education and exposure to technology to expand their comfort level in this area. Older adults have the same potential for training as younger adults when it comes to learning how to use technology (Canaff, 1997). It is important to consider that the technological skills of younger adults may become obsolete, which will result in a need for training in this area, which places them on the same playing field as older adults in need of similar training.

It is also essential to note that older adults have the same potential to learn new skills as younger adults. In a study intended to determine whether age differences exist on a configural response learning task, researchers obtained the following results:

> Older adults showed similar rates of learning as indexed by a configural learning score compared to young adults. These results suggest that the ability to acquire knowledge incidentally about configural response relationships is largely unaffected by cognitive aging. The configural response learning task provides insight into the task demands that constrain learning abilities in older adults. (Freedberg et al., 2015, p. 1)

The findings of this study support the notion that older adults provide the same quality of work when it comes to the acquisition of new skills. Essentially, this validates the value of older workers and refutes misnomers that older adults are unable to learn new skills and therefore may not be a good match for today's workforce.

Thusly, on-the-job training can also be provided to assist older adults in learning how to use everyday office technology. Computer-assisted career guidance systems are another form of assessment and information for older workers that can be used to enhance their technological skills in addition to teaching computer literacy. Older adults can also seek training through organizations such as SCORE and the American Association of Retired People (AARP). How technology can also be a barrier for this population is discussed later in this chapter.

Benefits of Hiring Older Workers

Over the years, researchers have produced a wealth of information that supports a positive perception of older workers that should be considered by employers and society at large.

1. *Older workers have been found to have lower absentee and turnover rates than younger workers* (Eisenberg, 2018). This is an essential marketing tool that can be used by career counseling professionals when marketing the skills of older adults.

2. *Older workers tend to possess a strong work ethic.* They have been found to exhibit higher levels of productivity and are less prone to substance abuse when compared to younger workers (Newman, 1995). This is another factor that career counselors can use when highlighting the vocational skills of older adults. It is also a means of highlighting that these workers can directly contribute to the expansion of product and service provision for an employer, which directly affects the company's bottom line.

3. *Older workers are also a good source of labor for employers during the holiday season* (Eisenberg, 2018). Career counseling professionals can also use this factor to help employers boost their service provision and product production. Likewise, career counselors can readily identify companies that actively hire seasonal workers in preparation for serving older adults.

4. *Older workers are valued because of their skills and experience and because they are members of the fastest-growing consumer base* (Eisenberg, 2018). Career counseling professionals should embrace the quality that lies in the experience of their older adult clients and use it as a marketing tool to help their clients become employed by emphasizing to employers that this worker can serve as a resource, a trainer, and a leader to their colleagues, therein enhancing the employer's workforce.

5. *Older adults tend to be more honest, experienced, and dependable* (AARP, 1990; Anderson et al., 2013; Canaff, 1997). This fact goes hand in hand with previous factors, and it too serves as a resource for career counseling professionals to use when marketing their clients who are older adults.

6. *Older adults tend to be more deliberate in their thinking* (AARP, 1990). Career counseling professionals should highlight this when working with these clients by teaching them and employers how to harness these skills. In doing so, they should highlight the idea that these workers tend to base their decisions on sound judgment and experience as opposed to risk (AARP, 1990).

7. *Older workers are often less preoccupied with family problems* (Canaff, 1997). Career counseling professionals should be mindful that employers often seek employees who will be loyal and committed to their companies. Because older adults often do not have young children or overly demanding familial responsibilities, they represent ideal candidates who can be loyal and committed to their company.

8. *Older workers are more grounded and patient, and they are more likely to stay with a job longer than younger workers* (Newman, 1995). This further highlights the strengths discussed in the previous item.

9. *Older workers often gain higher levels of satisfaction in employment, unlike younger workers who may be more focused on title, growth, and work activities* (Carter & Cook, 1995). Career counseling professionals would do well to capitalize on this fact and use it in their marketing of their clients, reminding employers that satisfaction in the workplace is an essential component of a productive worker.

Introduction to Career Counseling for Older Adult Clients

As a career counselor working with older adults, it is important to understand the theories of adult development. Three of the leading theorists are presented next: Donald Super, Robert Havighurst, and Erik Erikson.

Super

Expanding on the work of Eli Ginzberg, Donald Super developed five stages of life and career development. These stages are (1) growth, (2) exploration, (3) establishment, (4) maintenance, and (5) decline (Super, 1957). Stage one is the growth stage, which encompasses human experiences from birth to age 14. This stage is characteristic of the development of self-concept, attitudes, needs, and the general world of work. Stage two is the exploration state, which encompasses human experiences from the ages of 15 to 24. This stage is characteristic of the development of tentative choices and skills.

Stage three is the establishment stage, which encompasses human experiences from age 25 to 44 (Super, 1957). This stage is characteristic of the establishment of entry-level skills and stabilization through work experience. Stage four is the maintenance stage, which encompasses human experiences between the ages of 45 and 64. According to Super, this stage is characteristic of a continued adjustment process to improve position. Finally, stage five is the decline stage, and it encompasses human experiences from the age of 65 years and older. According to Super, this stage is characteristic of reduced output and preparation for retirement.

Super discussed the concept of vocational maturity, which indicates that people cycle through each of the stages when they go through career transitions (Super, 1957). Therefore, when considering the older adult in later adulthood, one may experience characteristics of all five stages: In the decline stage, older adults may reduce their work hours. In the maintenance stage, they may decide to keep doing only the things they enjoy. During the establishment stage, older adults may begin doing things they have wanted to do while finding a good retirement plan in the exploration stage and developing and valuing nonoccupational roles in the growth stage. As you see, these stages are not linear, and they can be reoccurring.

Likewise, in middle adulthood during the decline stage, one may be focused on things that are essential. In the maintenance stage, those in Super's middle adulthood range tend to be focused on holding their own against the competition (Super, 1957). During the establishment stage, they develop new skills; while during the exploration stage, they identify new tasks to work on; and during the growth stage, these middle-aged adults are accepting their own limitations.

Havighurst

Robert Havighurst was the founder of the Havighurst developmental task theory in which he posited that there are six stages of development: (1) infancy, (2) early childhood, (3) middle childhood, (4) adolescence, (5) middle age, and (6) later maturity (Havighurst, 1972). During middle age, Havighurst indicated that adults' activities are focused on the following: achieving adult civic and social responsibility, as well as establishing and maintaining an economic standard of living. They also assist teenagers to become responsible and happy adults while developing adult leisure-time activities and relating to their spouses. In addition, those in this stage of development accept and adjust to the physiologic changes of middle age and aging parents.

During the later maturity stage, Havighurst stated that older adults are generally adjusting to decreasing physical strength and health, as well as retirement and a reduced income (Havighurst, 1972). Some individuals may be coping with the death of a spouse or working to establish an affiliation with their age group while meeting social and civil obligations. In addition, these individuals are believed to be working to establish satisfactory physical living arrangements.

Erikson

Erik Erikson developed eight stages of psychosocial development. These stages are (1) trust versus mistrust, (2) autonomy versus shame/doubt, (3) initiative versus guilt, (4) industry versus inferiority, (5) identity versus role confusion, (6) intimacy versus isolation, (7) generativity versus stagnation, and (8) integrity versus despair. Let us turn our attention to Erikson's later stages of development, which are encompassing of older adults: generativity versus stagnation and integrity versus despair.

According to Erikson, the generativity versus stagnation stage of development covers those in the age range of 40 to 65. The very name of this stage speaks to its meaning. Generativity involves people's ability to find their life's work and contribute to the development of others. This may occur through a person's involvement in volunteering, mentoring, and raising children. During this stage, people are engaged in meaningful and productive work that positively contributes to society. Alternatively, those who do not master this task may experience stagnation. If people are experiencing stagnation, they generally believe they are not leaving a mark on the world and may not be well connected to others; thus, they do not strive for productivity and self-improvement.

According to Erikson, integrity versus despair occurs from age 65 until death. During this stage of development, Erikson stated that people reflect on their lives and feel either a sense of satisfaction or a sense of failure. Those who develop pride in their accomplishments feel a sense of integrity and have few regrets in their lives. Alternatively, those who are not successful at this stage experience despair; their lives tend to be filled with feelings of bitterness, depression, and despair. They often focus on "should haves," "could haves," and "would haves."

The Effect of Life Roles and Developmental Theories on Careers

As illustrated in the previous sections, older adults tend to be perceived as being in somewhat of a downward spiral. Most of these theories of development involve the concept of adjusting to loss and decline. The negative language used in Super's (1957), Havighurst's (1972), and Erikson's (1963) theories of adult development supports negative stereotypes of older adults. "This negative stereotype has permeated our culture and influenced our belief that one is no longer productive after age 65" (Canaff, 1997, p. 81).

Such theoretical perceptions may have also lent a hand to those who have discriminated against older adults in the workplace, as these theories have perpetuated the stereotypes about older adults. However, it must be considered that perceptions of older adults from the 1960s through the 1990s significantly varies from that of the current decade. With the expansion of technological advancements and improvements in the diagnosis and treatment of varying conditions, human beings are living more active, productive, and effective lives in their older years. As such, it is essential that career counselors are prepared to serve this population of clientele, as their needs will be many.

Older Worker Case Study

Ronald is a 61-year-old African American male who is currently unemployed. Ronald is divorced but does not have any children or grandchildren. He is currently living alone with his dog in an apartment he is renting from a friend. Ronald has a long work history of being a car salesman and was very successful in this occupation; however, after 14 years of working at the same car dealership, the owner decided to sell the company. Ronald no longer wants to work as a car salesman because of the physical demands of being on his feet all day and the long work hours, including weekends. He is hoping to find employment in a field that is less physically demanding. Ronald, who has a bachelor's degree in marketing, has been searching for a job for the last 9 months without success. He has started to smoke cigarettes again after quitting 20 years ago and finds himself eating fast food most nights in front of the TV.

Consider the following questions while exploring the subsequent sections:

1. What challenges, specific to older workers, is Ronald facing while seeking new employment?
2. According to Erickson, what stage of development is Ronald experiencing?
3. What steps would you take to assist Ronald in his job search?
4. What referrals, if any, would you make?

Practical Considerations for Working With Older Adults

Finding work after 50 can be critically important to your client's ability to enter retirement financially secure (Eisenberg, 2018). When preparing to work with older adults, career counselors need to assess themselves regarding issues related to ageism age implicit bias, facts on aging, anxiety about aging (Wisdom et al. 2014), and interest in working with older adults.

First and foremost, career counselors are to assess their own attitudes toward older adults and aging (Galinkos, 1979), remembering that they have a professional obligation to ensure that their biases, prejudices, and fears do not interfere with their ability to serve this population in an effective and efficient manner. This is of concern since it has been found that individuals with greater levels of anxiety about aging may exhibit a lower level of interest in working with older adults and higher levels of ageism (Boswell, 2012; Cottle & Glover, 2007; Ferrario et al., 2008; O'Hanlon & Brookover, 2002). Therefore, these professionals should consider focusing their service provision on other populations or enhance their knowledge about aging to lower their anxiety about the subject and dispel stereotypes and prejudices they may hold regarding older adults.

Working with older adults may require some unique considerations at the start of the relationship. Career counselors should be aware of the generational and cultural issues that may pose barriers to this relationship. Some older adults may be hesitant to seek assistance, as this may not be an approved action for members of their generation, and as a result, clients may demonstrate some hesitation to participating in the career counseling process (Anderson et al., 2013 Canaff, 1997).

This hesitation can potentially be alleviated by using the following strategies:

1. The establishment of a strong rapport between the client and the service provider.
2. A clear explanation of the relationship and the roles each of you will play in the service provision process.
3. Discussions about confidentiality and possibly a discussion about age difference if the service provider is significantly younger than the client.
4. In addition, it will be essential for the career counselor to ensure that he/she is accommodating any disability-related needs that the client may have.

Key considerations that career counselors should employ when working with older adults include the following:

1. Emphasize the strengths of your clients, and remind them of the benefits noted earlier that they bring to employers as older workers.
2. Develop a working knowledge of any health conditions that may affect your clients' employability. Gain information regarding the effect of the condition on the body and methods being actively used to treat the condition.
3. Ensure that the career counseling experience is one that is shared and allows clients to openly contribute to the development of their plans.
4. Focus on the here and now (Canaff, 1997). Older adults often reenter the workforce to supplement their income, and they are often seeking stable positions. They are often less concerned about positions with growth opportunities.
5. Consider using a more "hands-on" approach. Older adults may be less knowledgeable about the job market and may require your assistance in identifying suitable positions for which they are qualified (Canaff, 1997).
6. Embrace the use of community services and refer clients to organizations that provide technology training to older adults who want to enhance their technological skills.
7. Assist your older clients with considering alternate working arrangements.

Overcoming Disability-Related Barriers

Career counselors can help their older adult clients overcome disability-related barriers using education. They can educate their clients about their disabilities so that their clients can educate others, such as employers, about their disabilities (Landmark et al., 2017). In addition, career counselors should help clients to be prepared to discuss how their disabilities will not affect their ability to work. While employers cannot ask about this in the interview, it may be beneficial for clients to build employers' confidence in their abilities by being proactive and sharing helpful information but not too much information.

Help clients learn how to promote their disabilities as a strength rather than a weakness. This may be of particular importance when clients' disabilities are visible to those they encounter. When clients are comfortable with themselves and their disabilities, it's easier for others to be comfortable with them (Landmark et al., 2017). Also, clients are to be educated about the legislation that protects their rights in the workplace and during the interview process. Such legislation is discussed later in this chapter.

Overcoming Technological Barriers

When working to help clients overcome employment barriers related to technology, career counselors would do well to teach their clients how to keep up-to-date with technology. This can be done through the identification and use of free technology classes available to older adults at no or reduced cost in the community.

Rehabilitation engineers may be a good resource for those working with older adults with disabilities, particularly for those who are blind and visually impaired. Rehabilitation engineers can be a source of some basic skills training for using assistive technology and computers in the workplace. In addition, rehabilitation engineers serve as good consultants for problem solving when clients run into obstacles in the workplace. Software training may be free through some software companies; generally, the manufacturers tend to offer some level of training on their software. Trainings on office software may be costly at times; however, career counselors would do well to explore free options available in the community to older adults. In addition, career counselors would do well to identify community and federally funded programs that aim to educate older adults about technology.

Another means of developing technology training and resources for older adults is through collaborations with interns. Career counselors can work with their agency interns and employ them to help develop and implement technology training for older adults as part of their internships. Young adults can be a great source for technology training, as some of them tend to be very technologically savvy. Also, connecting with your local universities' computer science programs may be a great source of locating volunteers to help with technology training for older adults.

Overcoming Barriers During the Interview Process

Career counselors are to engage their resources and assist clients in preparing for the interview process (Oursler et al., 2017). Engage in mock interviews with older adult clients. Help clients identify and develop appropriate responses for target questions that may be asked during an interview. In addition, career counselors are to help clients prepare to specifically discuss why they are the best fit for the positions they are interviewing for. They must be prepared to discuss the factors that align them with younger workers without directly comparing themselves to younger workers. Help clients to prepare to discuss factors that will make them a sure fit for jobs that younger workers may not be able to demonstrate.

Aid clients in preparing to demonstrate their skills if requested. During the interview, clients should demonstrate confidence and initiative, as well as organizational skills, timeliness, preparedness, and comfort. Ensure that clients have the appropriate attire for interviews; ensure that they are not dressed out of date. Older adults who have not applied for employment recently may not be familiar with current trends. Yes! Our older adults may need a fashion consultant.

Developing an Effective Resume

Career counselors should be prepared and equipped to help clients design a job-specific resume. Sell employers what they want to buy. If not well versed in this area, career counselors should take the time to obtain resume development training. Students can do this by going through their college's or university's office of career services. Counselors should build these skills so that they can use them to help their clients. Specifically, career counselors should

- know how to help clients draft a job-specific resume;

- know how to help clients solidify their experience so that they are not discarded or disregarded as overqualified applicants;

- know how to help clients develop effective, engaging, and enticing cover letters to accompany their resumes; and

- know how to help clients develop innovative, creative, and exciting portfolios that display their work and ensure that clients have their portfolios in both electronic and hard copy formats.

In addition, career counselors should be prepared to help older adults complete their first couple of job applications. Allow the clients to be the drivers; counselors should be the supportive copilots helping them along the way. It may have been a long time since older adults retired or applied for a job, and they may need some assistance through the process. The job market may have changed; questions on applications may have changed. These are all things we should consider. It is career counselors' responsibility to educate their clients about today's job market. If clients have been working in a field for 10, 20, or even 30-plus years, they may not be familiar with today's job market.

Overcoming Barriers Due to Race/Ethnicity and Socioeconomic Status

Career counselors would do well to educate themselves about the community resources available to older adults. Career counselors should develop a resource list of the free resources available to older adults in their community. Identify resources that can help older adults with transportation, housing, technology training, and other social services that can improve their employability and sustain them in the workplace.

In addition to exploring community resources, career counselors should take the time to develop a strong sense of cultural competence. They should take the time to become knowledgeable about the inequalities oppressed minority groups face. Career counselors have an ethical obligation to ensure that they are not subscribing to or using stereotypical or prejudicial attitudes and behaviors that may exacerbate the marginalization of members of these populations. Also, career counselors should work to actively advocate against the prejudicial treatment of individuals from oppressed populations. In addition, career counselors should take the time to discuss barriers due to race and ethnicity with their clients and talk to them about how they can minimize or eliminate the effects of these barriers. The issue of culture and career is discussed further in the chapter.

Overcoming Work Schedule Barriers

Nontraditional work schedules provide older employees with flexible times and places they can work. Such nontraditional schedules may include part-time work, telework, work at home opportunities, job sharing, and flexible work schedules (Anderson et al., 2013). The flexibility provided in these nontraditional work schedule options can accommodate the caregiving activities and physical limitations that may be central to the lives of some older adults.

Innovation and flexibility may be the keys to helping older adults remain employed and gain employment (Anderson et al., 2013). An example of an innovative program is CVS Pharmacy's snowbird program. This program allows employees to transfer to a different CVS Pharmacy location on a seasonal basis to work at jobs such as greeting-card specialists, cosmetic consultants, photo supervisors, and pharmacists. "Generally, the CVS/Pharmacy employ older workers in northern stores in the summer and southern stores in the winter" (Anderson et al., 2013, p. 327). The inception of this program has led to increased numbers of older adults who are employed at CVS Pharmacy.

Measurement Assessments

When it comes to the use of measurement assessments for older clients, career counselors should consider the use of structured and unstructured interviews as opposed to standardized tests (Canaff, 1997). The use of standardized assessments tends to elicit elevated levels of stress among older adults, which may not produce useful data that accurately measures their skills, interests, or abilities.

Interviews should focus on values assessment, past successes, accomplishments, financial standings, familial needs, and extensive career history. This can aid the career counselor and the client in identifying the client's vocational needs and developing effective strategies for addressing such needs. However, if testing is preferred, the career counselor should work jointly with the client to select the most suitable assessment for the client. According to the Counseling Psychologist Press, assessments such as the *Campbell Interest and Skill Survey* (National Computer Systems, 1994), which examines interests and perceived skills, may be used rather than the more commonly used assessments, such as the *Self-Directed Search* (Psychological Assessment Resources, 1994) or the *Strong Interest Inventory.*

Career counselors can use such assessments to help clients identify suitable job match and explore clients' transitional skills to ensure the best job match (Kelley & Buchanan, 2017). This can aid the career counselor in determining what if any training clients may need before they are deemed job ready. Through community agencies or the career counselor's agency, the career counselor should be able to aid clients in obtaining the vocational training they may need to fulfill the requirements of their desired jobs.

Interview and Job Application Process

Older workers are just as employable as younger workers; however, they may not be as up-to-date on the more recent proactive job-hunting skills and employer trends (Canaff, 1997). Older adults may require assistance with interviewing skills, resume writing, and negotiating. Career counselors should consider using mock interviews to aid older adults in becoming familiar and comfortable with the interview process. In addition, support in the area of resume and cover letter writing would be beneficial to this clientele. Over the years, the acceptable presentation and content of a resume has changed, and there are mild variations across job categories with which the older job seeker may not be familiar.

Advocacy in Career Counseling With Older Adults

While working to serve an older adult population, career counselors will need to take on the role of advocate (Canaff, 1997). As a service provider, the career counselor will actively work with employers and members of the community to eliminate barriers and stereotypes that hamper the employability of the older adults they serve. The previously mentioned benefits of hiring older adults represent valuable information that can be used by employers to both strengthen and diversify their workforces. In addition, career counselors and related service providers can use this information to educate employers about the benefits of hiring older adults and advocate for change.

Legislation and Federal Programs

Legal mandates and social programs have been established to address the employment barriers experienced by older adults. These have included the Equal Employment Opportunity Commission (EEOC), the Age Discrimination in Employment Act, the Older Americans Act, and the Senior Community Service Employment Program, as well as nontraditional work schedules. These programs and the subsequent legislation were implemented to increase the employment of older adults and minimize the effects of barriers to employment for this population.

EEOC

The EEOC was established under the Civil Rights Act of 1964. The EEOC "is responsible for enforcing federal laws that make it illegal to discriminate against a job applicant or employee because of the person's race, color, religion, sex (including pregnancy), national origin, age (40 or older), disability or genetic information" (EEOC, 2013).

The Age Discrimination in Employment Act

The Age Discrimination in Employment Act (ADEA) is used by the EEOC to protect older works from discrimination in the workplace. This legislation protects job applicants and employees who are over the age of 39 from discrimination based on age. The legislation provides protections in hiring, promotion, discharge, compensation, or terms. Approximately 65% of the cases investigated by the EEOC in 2006 were age related.

Criticisms of the EEOC

Some argue that "the effectiveness of the EEOC and enforcement of the ADEA have been mixed" (Anderson et al., 2013, p. 326). This may stem from the challenges the EEOC encounters regarding identifying and proving discrimination in the hiring process (Neumark, 2008). In addition, critics have expressed that the EEOC focuses too intensely on individual cases and does not spend enough time challenging institutional discrimination. It is argued that perhaps the EEOC could more effectively protect vulnerable populations in the workforce if it took an approach that addressed both the cause and effect of discrimination in the workplace (Anderson et al., 2013; Rothenberg & Gardner, 2011).

The Older Americans Act

The Older Americans Act (OAA) was enacted in 1965 by President Lyndon Johnson. This legislation led to the establishment of the National Aging Network, comprising the Administration on Aging on the federal level, State Units on Aging at the state level, and Area Agencies on Aging at the local level (Administration for Community Living, 2019). This piece of legislation supports a range of home- and community-based services such as Meals on Wheels and other nutrition programs, in-home services, transportation, legal services elder abuse prevention, disease prevention/health promotion services, and elder rights programs, as well as the National Family Caregiver Support Program and the Native American Caregiver Support Program.

Founded under the OAA, the Older American Community Service Employment Act (OAA Title V) works with the Department of Labor to provide employment opportunities for seniors. More specifically, this federal program provides subsidized community service and employment training to low-income unemployed individuals aged 55 and older. It is the only nationally mandated workforce training program for seniors.

Senior Community Service Employment Program

Senior Community Service Employment Program (SCSEP) was established in 1965 under Title V of the OAA. The program is funded through the U.S. Department of Labor, and it is designed to assist low-income and unemployed older adults over the age of 55 in gaining employment. Through this program, older adults are matched with part-time training assignments that aid in building their skills and self-confidence (SCSEP, 2018).

SCSEP programs have been found to add significant value to the community by increasing revenue, employing a substantial number of older adults, and serving disadvantaged populations, such as older adults, minorities, and persons with disabilities (Washko, Schack, Goff, & Pudlin, 2011). Despite the success of this program in 2011 and 2012, the recession led to significant cuts to the program's budget, which has resulted in a lower level of service provision to disadvantaged populations. Such programs require great levels of community support and political advocacy to enhance their funding to service lower income older adults who need employment (Gonyea & Hudson, 2011).

Summary

Too many older adults remain poor and disadvantaged (Anderson et al., 2013). It is essential that career counselors and other related professionals work to reduce employment barriers for older adults. It is also imperative that these career counseling professionals gain a thorough understanding of older adults' rationale for remaining in, reentering, or staying out of the workforce. Those serving in the career counseling field working with older adults have an important role to play in expanding the understanding of employment of older adults and advocating for change to expand the employability and employment opportunities for members of this population.

Discussion Questions

1. What barrier to employment does education pose for older adults?
2. What barrier to employment does ageism pose for older adults?
3. What barrier to employment does disability pose for older adults?
4. What barrier to employment does socioeconomic status pose for older adults?
5. What barrier to employment do race and ethnicity pose for older adults?
6. List and describe the benefits of hiring older adults.
7. Compare and contrast the impact of Super's, Havighurst's, and Erikson's career development theories on the career development of older adults.
8. Discuss three strategies for helping older adults to overcoming technological barriers.
9. Discuss three strategies for helping older adults to overcoming barriers during the interview process.
10. Discuss three strategies for helping older adults to overcoming barriers due to race/ethnicity and socioeconomic status.

References

Administration for Community Living. (2019). Older Americans Act. https://acl.gov/about-acl/authorizing-statutes/older-americans-act

American Association of Retired People. (AARP). (1990). Working age, 6, 1–7.

Anderson, K. A., Richardson, V. E., Fields, N. L., & Harootyan, R. A. (2013). Inclusion or exclusion? Exploring barriers to employment for low-income older adults. *Journal of Gerontological Social Work, 56*, 318–334. https://doi.org/10.1080/01634372.2013.777006

Bodner, E. (2009). On the origins of ageism among older and younger adults. *International Psychogeriatrics, 21*, 1003–1014.

Boswell, S. S. (2012). Old people are cranky: Helping professional trainees' knowledge, attitudes, aging anxiety, and interest in working with older adults. *Educational Gerontology, 38*, 465–472. https://doi.org/10.1080/03601277.2011.559864

Bureau of Labor Statistics. (2008). *Older workers.* http://www.bls.gov/spotlight/2008/older workers/

Bureau of Labor Statistics. (2012). *Unemployed persons by age, sex, race, Hispanic or Latino ethnicity, marital status, and duration of unemployment. Table 31: Household data annual averages.* http://www.bls.gov/cps/cpsaat31.pdf

Bureau of Labor Statistics. (2019). *Employment status of the civilian noninstitutional population by age, sex, and race.* https://www.bls.gov/cps/cpsaat03.pdf

Burr, J. A., & Mutchler, J. E. (2007). Employment in later life: A focus on race/ethnicity and gender. *Generations, 31*(1), 37–44.

Butler, R. N. (1969). Age-ism: Another form of bigotry. *Gerontologist, 9,* 243–246.

Canaff, A. L. (1997). Later life career planning: A new challenge for career counselors. *Journal of Employment Counseling, 34,* 85–93.

Carter, M. T., & Cook. K. (1995). Adaptation to retirement: Role changes and psychological resources. *Career Development Quarterly, 44,* 67–82.

Casciano, R., & Massey, D. S. (2008). Neighborhoods, employment, and welfare use: Assessing the influence of neighborhood socioeconomic composition. *Social Science Research, 37,* 544–558.

Census Bureau. (2007). *Educational attainment in 2005.* http://www.census.gov/population/www/pop-profile/files/dynamic/EdAttainment.pdf

Census Bureau. (2010). *2009 annual social and economic supplement.* http://www.census.gov/cps/

Charness, N., & Czaja, S. J. (2005). *Older worker training: What we know and don't know.* AARP. https://www.aarp.org/research/work/issues/2006_22

Chiu, W. C. K., Chan, A. W., Snape, E., & Redman, T. (2001). Age stereotypes and discriminatory attitudes toward older workers: An East–West comparison. *Human Relations, 54,* 629–661.

Cottle, N. R., & Glover, R. J. (2007). Combating ageism: Change in student knowledge and attitudes regarding aging. *Education Gerontology, 33*(6), 501–512.

Dennis, H., & Thomas, K. (2007). Ageism in the workplace. *Generations, 31*(1), 84–89.

Eisenberg, R. (2018). Older job hunters: Powerful good news. *Next Avenue.* https://www.nextavenue.org/older-job-hunters-good-news/

Equal Employment Opportunity Commission. (2013). Overview. Retrieved from http://www.eeoc.gov/eeoc/index.cfm

Erikson, E. H. (1963). *Childhood and society.* W. W. Norton.

Ferrario, C. G., Freeman, F. J., Nellett, G., & Scheel, J. (2008). Changing nursing students' attitudes about aging: An argument for the successful aging paradigm. *Educational Gerontology, 34,* 51–66. https://doi.org/10.1080=03601270701763969

Freedberg, C. R., Hazeltine, M. E., & Voss, M. W. (2015). Are there age-related differences in the ability to learn configural responses? *PLoS ONE, 10*(8), e0137260. https://doi.org/10.1371/journal.pone.0137260

Galinkos, M. (1979). *Counseling the aged.* American Personnel and Guidance Association.

Gonyea, J. G., & Hudson, R. B. (2011). Promoting employment and community service among low-income seniors: The success and challenges of the Senior Community Service Employment Program. *Public Policy & Aging Report, 21*(1), 40–47

Havighurst, R. (1972). *Developmental tasks and education.* Longman.

Henkins, K. (2005). Stereotyping older workers and retirement: The managers' point of view. *Canadian Journal on Aging, 24,* 353–366

Hinkle, J. S. (1992). Computer assisted career guidance and single subject research: A scientist-practitioner approach to accountability. *Journal of Counseling & Development, 70,* 391–396.

Hirschman, C., & Lee, J. C. (2005). Race and ethnic inequality in educational attainment in the United States. In M. Rutter & M. Tienda (Eds.), *Ethnicity and causal mechanisms* (pp. 107–138). Cambridge University Press.

Johnson, R. W. (2004). Trends in job demands among older workers, 1992–2002. *Monthly Labor Review, 127*(7), 48–56.

Kelley, K. R., & Buchanan, S. K. (2017). College to career ready: Innovative practices that lead to integrated employment. *Journal of Vocational Rehabilitation, 46*(3), 327–332. https://doi-org.proxy.library.ohio.edu/10.3233/JVR-170869

Kite, M. E., & Wagner, L. S. (2002). Attitudes toward older adults. In T. D. Nelson (Ed.), *Ageism: Stereotyping and prejudice against older persons* (pp. 129–161). Cambridge, MA: MIT Press.

Landmark, L. J., Zhang, D., Ju, S., McVey, T. C., & Ji, M. Y. (2017). Experiences of disability advocates and self-advocates in Texas. *Journal of Disability Policy Studies*, *27*(4), 203–211. https://doi-org.proxy.library.ohio.edu/10.1177/1044207316657802

Lee, C. C., Czaja, S. J., & Sharit, J. (2009). Training older workers for technology-based employment. *Educational Gerontology*, *35*, 15–31.

Loretto, W., & White, P. (2006). Employers' attitudes, practices and policies towards older workers. *Human Resource Management Journal*, *16*, 313–330.

Maurer, T. J., Weiss, E. M., & Barbeite, F. G. (2003). A model of involvement in work related learning and development activity: The effects of individual, situational, motivational, and age variables. *Journal of Applied Psychology*, *88*, 707–724.

National Computer Systems. (1994). *Campbell interest and SWU survey.*

Neumark, D. (2008). *Reassessing the Age Discrimination in Employment Act.* AARP. http://assets.aarp.org/rgcenter/econ/2008_09_adea.pdf

Neumark, D. (2009). The Age Discrimination in Employment Act and the challenge of population aging. *Research on Aging*, *31*, 41–68.

Newman, B. K. (1995). Career change for those over 40: Critical issues and insights. *Career Development Quarterly*, *44*, 64–67.

O'Hanlon, A. M., & Brookover, B. C. (2002). Assessing changes in attitudes about aging: Personal reflections and a standardized measure. *Educational Gerontology*, *28*(8), 711–725.

Oursler, J., Lu, W., Herrick, S., & Harris, K. (2019). Using direct skills teaching to improve job skills for persons with disabilities. *Journal of Employment Counseling*, *56*(2), 69–84. https://doi-org.proxy.library.ohio.edu/10.1002/joec.12113

Psychological Assessment Resources. (1994). *Self-directed search.*

Rothenberg, J. Z., & Gardner, D. S. (2011). Protecting older workers: The failure of the Age Discrimination in Employment Act of 1967. *Journal of Sociology & Social Welfare*, 38, 9–30.

Senior Community Service Employment Program (SCSEP). (2018). About us. National Council on Aging. https://www.ncoa.org/economic-security/matureworkers/scsep/

Sum, A., Khatiwada, I., & Trubskyy, M. (2011). The labor market experiences and problems of America's low-income older workers in recent years. *Public Policy & Aging Report*, *21*(1), 18–28.

Super, D. E. (1957). *The psychology of careers.* Harper & Row.

Taylor, A. W., Pilkington, R., Feist, H., Dal Grande, E., & Hugo, G. (2014). A survey of retirement intentions of baby boomers: An overview of health, social, and economic determinants. *BMC Public Health*, *14*(355). https://doi.org/10.1186/1471-2458-14-355

Taylor, P., & Walker, A. (1998). Employers and older workers: Attitudes and employment practices. *Ageing and Society*, *18*, 641–658.

Toossi, M., & Bureau of Labor Statistics. (2012). *Labor force projections 2020: A more slowly growing workforce.* http://www.bls.gov/opub/mlr/2012/01/art3full.pdf

Washko, M. M., Schack, R. W., Goff, B. A., & Pudlin, B. (2011). Title V of the Older Americans Act, the Senior Community Service Employment Program: Participant demographics and service to racially/ethnically diverse populations. *Journal of Aging & Social Policy*, 23, 182–197.

Wisdom, N. M., Connor, D., Hogan, L. R., & Callahan, J. L. (2014). The relationship of anxiety and beliefs toward aging in ageism. *Journal of Scientific Psychology*, 10–21.

PART III

Career Counseling for Special Populations

CHAPTER 8

Career Counseling for Multicultural Groups

Myshalae Euring

CHAPTER OVERVIEW

Multicultural groups tend to experience significant levels of disadvantage in the workforce because of their limited access to resources and advantages at earlier points in life (Atkinson, 2004). Factors such as lower socioeconomic status, social class status, and access to premier educational and vocational resources have long affected the career paths of individuals from multicultural backgrounds. This chapter will identify and define culture and cultural differences in work-related activities. Five major cultural groups will be discussed, along with the common mental health issues of each of these cultural groups. Further, this chapter will discuss strategies for working with multicultural groups through the career counseling process.

CHAPTER OBJECTIVES

After reading this chapter, the student will be able to complete the following:

1. Define culture.

2. Identify cultural differences in work-related activities.

3. Discuss and identify mental health issues across cultural groups.

4. Outline strategies for working with multicultural groups.

What Is Culture?

Culture has historically been a difficult concept to define. Historically, there have been several definitions of culture from a complex whole, which includes knowledge, capabilities, and habits (Taylor, 1871) to (Bello, 1991) "the totality of the way of life evolved by a people in their attempts to meet the challenge of living in their environment, which gives order and meaning to their social, political, economic, aesthetic and religious norms thus distinguishing a people from their neighbors" (p. 189). As you can ascertain from those definitions, culture is nuanced and complex. Culture is a variety of things that make people individuals. In essence, culture entails a totality of traits and characteristics that are specific to a people to the extent that it differentiates them from other people and societies (Idang, 2015). Culture also includes social norms, taboos, and values, which are beliefs that are held about what is right and wrong and what is important in life. Simply, culture consists of the shared worldviews, practices, values, and social norms associated with a particular group of people (Hays & Erford, 2018). Culture is the way a group of people do things together, whether voluntarily or involuntarily. There is prison culture, school culture, and organizational culture; culture is not specific to individuals who are a part of the same background. Even within families, each person is a combination of multiple cultural identities.

One can easily say that if you have a group of siblings who are brought up in the same family, with the same parents, not all of them are going to be exactly the same. This is the same with culture. To become a culturally competent counselor, you have to understand the complexities of culture. While it is impossible to know everything about every individual's culture, the competent counselor understands that the journey to cultural competence is an evolving process.

Cultural Competence

Cultural competence is the awareness, knowledge, and skill needed to function effectively with culturally diverse populations (Sue & Sue, 2016). The culturally competent counselor understands that sociopolitical experiences, homophobia, sexism, prejudice, ageism, ableism, and racism affect each client's worldview and overall well-being. It is important that culturally competent counselors understand their cultural identities because their values, beliefs, and attitudes can impede the counseling process. To achieve awareness, the culturally competent counselor must constantly acquire knowledge about diverse groups to eventually develop culturally appropriate interventions and strategies. Developing alternative helping roles is essential to the culturally competent counselor, which can include mentoring, working outside the office, seeing clients as individuals instead of a culmination of "issues" and symptoms, and becoming aware of societal conditions that can affect diverse clients.

Cultural Humility

As previously mentioned, it is impossible for any counselor to possess the understanding, knowledge, and skills necessary to be an expert about all diverse populations. Acquiring cultural competence is an evolving lifelong process and requires that counselors become aware of their limitations. It is imperative that counselors practice with cultural humility, a concept defined by Hook et al. (2013) as

> Culturally humble therapists rarely assume competence (i.e., letting prior experience and even expertness lead to overconfidence) for working with clients just based on their prior experience working with a particular group. Rather, therapists who are more culturally humble approach clients with respectful openness and work collaboratively with clients to understand the unique intersection of clients' various aspects of identities and how that affects the developing therapy alliance. (p. 354)

In other words, never assume that you know everything about a client's personal experiences because you've worked with clients with a similar culture or background. You wouldn't consider yourself fluent in another language after your first lesson, so apply the same rationale to counseling. Aspire to be a culturally competent counselor who practices cultural humility and acknowledges that counselors are limited in their knowledge and understanding of a client's cultural worldview.

Cultural Differences in Work-Related Activities

Diversity in the work environment promotes acceptance, respect, and teamwork despite differences in race, age, gender, native language, political beliefs, religion, sexual orientation, or communication styles among employees. There are many benefits to having a more diverse workplace. Some employers may harbor unfair prejudices and biases that will hinder the hiring process. Culturally competent counselors need to be aware of the various challenges associated with diversity in the workplace so that they can be prevented and addressed.

Employer's Perceptions of Multicultural Groups

Discrimination and harassment in the workplace can come in many forms. And although such misconduct can sometimes be overt, such as the use of racial slurs or denial of advancement opportunities, it can also be subtle or even concealed. Discrimination occurs when a member of a protected class is treated differently than their peers. In an ideal world, every employer would hire the most competent employee regardless of race, ethnicity, age, gender, sexual orientation, gender identification, and disability. Unfortunately, we don't live in an ideal world, and some employers have the same bias and prejudices that hinder culturally competent counselors. As a counselor with an understanding of cultural competence, you have a distinct advantage when helping your clients navigate through their journeys into the careers of their choice. You can serve as a guide and educator for both clients and employers about individual strengths and capabilities and the benefits of a culturally diverse workforce.

Cultural Identity

Every work environment has a distinct culture: the organization's leadership, values, traditions, beliefs, interactions, behaviors, and attitudes that contribute to the emotional, relational, and productive environment of the workplace (Alvesson & Sveningsson, 2015). Having an understanding of your client's cultural worldview will enable you to assist your client's transition into his/her job or career. While cultural identity isn't confined to race, both race and ethnicity are important constructs in cultural identity development. Race in this context is not merely physical appearance but becomes more complex and nuanced as it is constructed, shaped, and reshaped by the lives and experiences of those who live it and as it is described by those observing those authentic experiences (Coleman, 2011). Racial identity development is a process of moving from a state of racial unawareness and nonidentification to one of awareness and self-identification (Hays & Erford, 2018). To understand racial and cultural development, it is important to examine racial identity development models of diverse groups.

Racial/Cultural Identity Development Model

Individual groups will be explored throughout the chapter. The following model outlines five levels of development that many oppressed people experience as they attempt to understand themselves in terms of their culture, the dominant culture, and the oppressive relationship between the two cultures (Sue & Sue, 2016). Atkinson and Hackett (1998) developed the minority identity development model to integrate various racial identity models and their clinical practice. This model was later revised and renamed the racial/cultural identity development model (R/CID) by Sue and Sue (1990, 1999) to include a broader population and eliminate the term "minority." The levels included in the R/CID are conformity, dissonance, resistance, immersion, introspection, and integrative awareness. These levels have corresponding attitudes and beliefs for each stage and level.

Conformity Phase

Conformity in this context is comparing all races and cultures against the white European standards that represent their reference group for cultural values, systems, and lifestyles. While this isn't the case in every country, adherence to traditional European beauty, intelligence, and values is widespread around the world. In this first stage, members of the oppressed group adjust themselves to avoid feeling inferior. A good example is the plethora of skin bleaching products available to "whiten" dark skin since having dark complexion is considered inferior to a pale complexion.

A characteristic of the conformity stage is developing ethnocentric monoculturalism, the belief that your particular cultural heritage is superior but others, especially non-white groups, are inferior. Your own group doesn't have the power to impose its standards on less-dominant groups, so while you believe that your particular culture is superior to other cultures, you are still inferior to the dominant group. Maintaining this stage of conformity can lead to internalized racism or "self-hatred," which is disliking yourself because of your race and ethnicity and because you are not a member of the dominant group.

Dissonance Phase

In the dissonance phase, it is increasingly difficult to deny your cultural heritage when you receive information or experience events that are inconsistent with your culturally held beliefs. You begin to learn how you're perceived by other members of dominant groups and/or how you're perceived in society and begin to question these perceptions. There's a great deal of inner turmoil occurring in this stage because of the constant questioning about the attitudes and beliefs you have about your own culture. This phase is gradual but can be expedited by monumental events, such as an assassination or legislation that effects your cultural group. During the dissonance phase, you can be both self-deprecating and self-appreciating. You come to the realization that you don't have to accept the stereotypes and ideas presented about your culture from the dominant group and attribute them to yourself. This creates a sense of pride but can also create an increase in suspicion and distrust of certain members of the dominant group.

Resistance and Immersion Phase

In this phase, you begin to reject the values of the dominant culture and attempt to eliminate oppression. The resistance and immersion phase is one of self-discovery. You learn as much as you can about your own history and culture, which increases your self-worth. You feel pride in your cultural characteristics and experience connectedness, a sense of family, admiration, and respect for members of your group. You also realize that other groups are being oppressed and discriminated against, so you form alliances with members of other groups and form relationships based on your shared experiences. This is also the stage where you try to convince individuals in the conformity and dissonance stages to reach your level of understanding. You want others to view members of the dominant group as oppressors and share your increased distrust and dislike of members of that group.

Introspection Phase

During the introspection phase, there are sometimes conflicts between the views of your cultural group and your individual views. There may be resentment if you feel pressured to make decisions that are not consistent with your personal beliefs to please the group. An example of this is hearing, "Well, we don't like this group of people, so you can't be friends with them or date them," and you feeling conflicted because you don't feel that way. There are positive aspects to this stage. You have an increased understanding of the difference in oppression that other groups may experience; you become more empathetic and attempt to promote social change. There are decreased feelings of anger and distrust about the dominant group, and you begin to recognize that you can incorporate some characteristics of the dominant group into your cultural identity.

Integrative Awareness Stage

This is the final stage of development. You have developed a strong sense of self, and you can integrate the unique aspects of your own culture and those of the dominant culture. You believe that there are acceptable and unacceptable characteristics of all cultures and the importance of either rejecting or accepting them to suit your beliefs. Since you have undergone a period of introspection, gained knowledge, and experienced the anger and the disappointment from acknowledging oppression, racism, and all of the other "isms," you become committed to eliminating all forms of oppression.

In addition to your new sense of purpose, you have a positive self-image and a strong sense of self-worth. You have pride in your own cultural group and empathy for your own group experience. When it comes to other groups, you form a selective trust and liking for members of the dominant group who also want to help eliminate oppression. In an ideal world, everyone would be in the integrative awareness phase, but that is not realistic. Identity development is an individual journey, and some may never reach the last stage. As a counselor, you feel obligated to "push" clients or loved ones through the stages, but remember, you cannot force anyone into awareness.

Working within a racial identity development framework will help you recognize the differences between the members of the same minority group with respect to cultural identity. This is extremely beneficial for counselors, especially if they haven't been exposed to other cultural groups. Using racial identity models will provide a better understanding of how sociopolitical factors influence and shape a client's identity. It is imperative that counselors recognize and accept the role oppression plays in an individual's development. It's not something that's clients are imagining or embellishing. This is their lived experience.

Challenges to Becoming Culturally Competent

As previously stated, culture consists of all things that people have learned to do, believe, value, and enjoy. It is the totality of the ideas, beliefs, skills, tools, customs, and institutions into which members of society are born (Ratts & Pederson, 2014). Counseling and psychotherapy have traditionally been conceptualized in Western, individualistic terms (i.e., white, male) (Ivey et al., 2005). To become culturally competent is to recognize that traditional theories and interventions must be adapted based on individual lived experiences. Failure to do so can create barriers to cultural competency and the effectiveness of the therapeutic process. Differences in cultural and class-bound values must be taken into account by the culturally competent counselor. While this is not an exclusive list, this section will explore the culturally and class-bound values of individualism versus collectivism, expressiveness, poverty, and language barriers.

Culture-Bound Values

Individualism Versus Collectivism

Most forms of counseling and psychotherapy are individualistic in nature. With individualism, individuals are encouraged to forge their own paths, become their own person, and work to achieve their goals and desires. Individualism is the cornerstone of American culture, emphasizing competition between other individuals for status, recognition, and achievement (Ivey et al., 2014). While individualism is understood and encouraged in American and Western cultures, this is not the case for all cultures. Collectivism, characterized by group orientation or collective society, is the tradition in many non-Western cultures. Clients brought up in a collectivist environment may not embrace counseling that encourages separation from the family unit or denouncement of long-held beliefs of familial pride and responsibility. Counselors need to be cognizant that their cultural beliefs do not hinder the counseling process.

Expressiveness

Counselors rely on clients to display behavioral, emotional, and verbal expressiveness in counseling sessions. The "ideal" client is often an individual who is verbal, articulate, and able to express his/her thoughts and feelings clearly (Sue & Sue, 2016). Many clients will not meet this ideal because of cultural differences. Some cultures may consider silence a mark of respect, while others are taught not to share personal or family details with strangers. To some counselors, silence may indicate a lack of interest or willingness to participate while restraint could be interpreted as inhibition or repression. It is imperative that counselors understand the cultural basis for client behavior and not take silence personally. Try to ask probing questions to get to the root of the issue causing the silence or accept silence as the answer and continue with the session.

Class-Bound Values

Poverty

Classism and social class have been identified as two of the most overlooked topics in psychology and mental health practice (American Psychological Association, Task Force on Socioeconomic Status, 2007). Income inequality is a contributing factor to the lack of mental health care for marginalized groups and individuals living in a low socioeconomic class. Some counselors fail to realize the stress and hardship that occurs with a lack of financial resources when research has proven that living in poverty is related to depression, poor physical health, and exclusion from mainstream society (Reed & Smith, 2014). Counselors, especially from middle- and upper-class backgrounds, should be aware of the reality of living in poverty and not view clients in a negative light, especially if the attitudes and mannerisms of clients fail to measure up to the standards of the "ideal client."

Language Barriers

The use of Standard English in health care delivery may unfairly discriminate against those from a bilingual or lower socioeconomic background and result in devastating consequences (Ratts & Pederson, 2014). Everyone should have access to quality health care and the option to receive care in their primary language. It is often tempting to ask the children of clients to serve as interpreters, but this can be problematic. Parents may not want their children to know about their personal struggles, or the children may not have the vocabulary necessary to accurately communicate with the counselor. When using other interpreters, counselors should find individuals who speak a similar dialect and do not have obvious social/cultural differences. For example, a client who speaks Mandarin Chinese cannot be understood by an interpreter who only speaks Cantonese. Remember to direct your questions and conversations to your client with the interpreter serving as a "bridge." Make sure that you maintain eye contact and speak to your client instead of speaking directly to the interpreter. It is important for your client to know that his/her values are heard, even if you can't speak the client's language.

Counseling Multicultural Groups

In this section, we will examine five cultural groups and explore effective counseling approaches for each group. These five groups are not the only groups you will encounter in a counseling setting, but they will be emphasized for the purpose of this chapter. Also, remember that no culture is monolithic; there will be differences among individuals from the same culture, so counselors will need to adapt to meet individual needs.

African Americans

African Americans have been referred to by many words throughout the history of this country, evolving from derogatory terms, such as negro, to black, Afro-American, and African American. One of the reasons African American was chosen to be an acceptable term is because of Afrocentrism, a mode of thought and action in which the centrality of African interests, values, and perspectives predominate and place African people in the center of any analysis from African phenomena (Asante, 2003). So a little bit more simply, Afrocentrism is the devotion to the idea that what is in the best interest of African consciousness is at the heart of ethical behavior.

Developing cultural identity for African Americans is nuanced because the African American population is becoming increasingly heterogeneous in terms of ethnic and racial identity, social class, educational level, and political orientation. Racial identity is developed through a process in which African Americans transform from a non-Afrocentric identity to one that is Afrocentric.

The African American Family

An unfortunate part of African American cultural identity development is the awareness and recognition of internalized racism. African Americans absorb the racist messages that are omnipresent in our society, which are internalized and made a part of everyday life. Many families are headed by women, and child rearing is usually undertaken by a large number of relatives or extended family members. As a whole, African American males are more accepting of women's work roles and are willing to share responsivity in roles not traditionally handled by women. Spirituality and religion are important for many African Americans because churches provide comfort, economic support, opportunities for self-expression, leadership, and community involvement (Ballard, 1973). Historically, attending Sunday services was the only opportunity for slaves to experience a modicum of autonomy. The church became a safe haven where people could speak freely, worship freely, and join in a community of brothers and sisters. African Americans possess positive ethnic identity, resourcefulness, and coping skills to deal with societal issues, familial and extended kinship relationships, and community support systems. It's very important to recognize that these protective factors and strengths have allowed African Americans to survive in an intolerant society for years.

African Americans and Counseling

Counselors have a tendency to be biased toward African American families, especially those headed by single mothers. Counselors may believe stereotypes that African American parents are neglectful and incompetent, while this could be farthest from the truth. Research proves that even with internalized racism and overt racism and prejudice, African American families instill positive self-esteem in their youth while displaying role flexibility (Sue & Sue, 2016).

Spiritual beliefs remain a protective factor from stressors for African Americans. That can be a benefit and a hindrance to the counseling process because some African Americans feel like seeking counseling instead of just relying on prayer or spiritual assistance is somehow denying Christianity. Guilt and shame often result from seeking outside help. As a result, African Americans are more inclined to turn to churches and pastors for assistance instead of counselors and other mental health professionals.

The counseling environment should be empathetic and understanding and viewed as a smaller part of a larger society that influences African Americans. The counselor may be expected to assume a non-traditional role, not sitting in the role of expert because it often comes across as judgmental. Given the historical mistrust of medical personnel, doctors, and surgeons in the African American community, the counselor may be perceived as a physician-like figure or evaluator. This can hinder rapport and promote distrust, especially if clients feel that they aren't receiving fair or equitable treatment because of their race. Counselors should help African American clients identify goals and appropriate means of obtaining goals. To try to determine the external factors that prevent counseling from being successful, examine but don't dismiss issues regarding racial identity. Please understand that power and privilege can greatly affect the counseling relationship. Those topics need to be discussed.

According to Sue & Sue (2016), existential therapy, cognitive behavioral therapy (CBT), and family systems therapy are effective with African Americans. Using the here-and-now approach of existential therapy emphasizes understanding and can help gain resolutions to issues while in the "present" moment. It is also beneficial for counselors to help clients become aware of the possibilities surrounding them. CBT is effective because it helps counselors and clients recognize and replace negative thinking and patterns of behavior, identify their faulty belief systems, and explore the life that they would like to have. The overall goal of family systems therapy is to help clients see the pattern of troubled relationships and to help create new ways of establishing relationships. In this therapeutic relationship, the counselor is more of a teacher, a coach, a model of behavior, and, sometimes, a consultant who helps families learn ways to detect and solve present and generational issues.

Asian Americans and Pacific Islanders

According to a Pew Research Center analysis of U.S. Census Bureau data, Asian Americans are the fastest-growing major racial or ethnic group in the United States. More than 20 million Asians live in the United States, and almost all trace their origins to 19 groups from East Asia, Southeast Asia, and the Indian subcontinent (U.S. Census Bureau, 2015). The largest Asian groups in the United States include Chinese (4.9 million), Indian (4.0 million), and Filipino (3.9). There are over one million individuals of Vietnamese, Korean, and Japanese ancestry (Pew Research Center, 2017). In U.S. culture, Asian Americans are usually considered to be the "model minorities," which means that Asian Americans achieve universal and unparalleled academic and occupational success (Museus & Kiang, 2009). The "model minority" myth is a harmful stereotype that contributes to the misconception that all Asians are the same and belong to the same social "box." This couldn't be further from the truth. In fact, income inequality in the United States is greatest among Asian Americans, displacing African Americans as the most economically divided racial or ethnic group in the United States (Pew Research Center, 2018). While Asian Americans rank as the highest earning racial and ethnic group in the United States, this status is not shared by the entire Asian American population. Counselors should be aware of differences between groups, which include ethnicity, culture, migration and relocation experiences, degree of assimilation or acculturation, identification with the home country, facility in the native language and English, family composition, educational background, religion, and sexual orientation (Nadal et al., 2012).

The Asian American Family

Asian families tend to be collectivistic with a focus on family and group orientation. Unlike individualistic cultures, there is an expectation for children to work toward what will benefit their families most and not participate in dishonorable behavior. Most families are patriarchal, with males and elders occupying higher status within the family unit. Communication flows downward from parents to children, with the expectation that children will defer to their elders. Children are supposed to adhere to what is "correct," strive for family harmony, and adapt to the needs of family members, especially elders (Sue & Sue, 2016). Instead of working toward independence and autonomy, adolescents are expected to assist, support, and respect their families (Fuligini et al., 1999).

Sons are expected to carry on the family name and tradition, even when married. While there are differences between groups, parenting styles tend to be more authoritarian and directive (Kim, 2011). There is less emphasis on praise and rewards than on the parents giving instruction to children. The criticism that comes from correction is used for behavior modification (Paiva, 2008). Strong emotional displays are normally considered a sign of immaturity or lack of self-control. Many Asian Americans may express emotional difficulties through somatic complaints because it is considered more acceptable to say that they have a backache, headache, and so on than to admit to feeling depressed or anxious (Sue & Sue, 2016). Fathers are frequently distant, authoritative, and not emotionally demonstrative. Mothers are attuned to their children but are usually less nurturing than mothers in other cultures. Unfortunately, the emphasis on goal and academic orientation can result in depression, anxiety, and isolation in Asian American adolescents, along with a sense of failure if families are disappointed (Sue & Sue, 2016).

Asian American cultural values promote resiliency and strength while providing a strong family support system. Individual success and achievement are a source of pride for the entire family, giving each member a sense of responsibility. With the history of racism, oppression, discrimination, and colonization in the case of Pacific Islanders, ethnic identity pride, collectivism, family harmony, and respect for elders can serve as buffers against stress, prejudice, and low self-esteem (Hwang et al., 2010; Vakalahi, 2009).

Asian Americans and Counseling

Asian Americans may not be familiar with the processes and procedures of counseling and will need clinicians to take an active role in structuring the session and providing advice, consultation, and facilitation of family and community support systems (Atkinson et al., 1998). Many counseling theories and techniques, including CBT and solution-focused strategies, may be effective with Asian American clients. Clinicians should adapt to the level of acculturation and racial identity of the client (Sue & Sue, 2016). Clinicians should direct counseling sessions while encouraging full participation from the client. In this way, clients can take ownership of their goals and interventions. Asian Americans view counselors who demonstrate multicultural competence by addressing the cultural beliefs of clients as more competent (Wang & Kim, 2010). Therefore, it is important that culturally competent counselors recognize the individual cultural identities of their clients, as well as the specific challenges of Asian Americans and Pacific Islanders.

Racial Identity Issues

As Asian Americans are progressively exposed to the standards, norms, and values of the wider U.S. society, the result is increasing assimilation and acculturation (Sue & Sue, 2016). Depending on their level of acculturation and identity development, clients may feel as if they are "between two worlds" and not feel comfortable in either one. Clients may present the following questions in a counseling session: "Do I stick to everything that's traditional in my culture to please my family?" "Do I combine my tradition with Western tradition?" "Am I wrong for wanting to do that?" It is not the counselor's job to answer the questions for the client but to understand that the client could experience assimilation, separation/enculturation, integration/biculturalism, or marginalization as a result of the conflict (Hwang et al., 2010).

Assimilation means completely excluding your cultural group just to be a member of the dominant society, for example, only speaking English or forgoing traditional holidays or dress. The opposite is separation or enculturation when clients exclusively identify with Asian culture. Integration or biculturalism consists of retaining Asian values while learning the necessary skills and values to adapt to the dominant culture. Clients experiencing marginalization perceive their own culture as negative and feel inept at adapting to the dominant culture (Sue & Sue, 2016).

Racism

Asian Americans and Pacific Islanders have and continue to face racism and discrimination (Hwang et al., 2010). Negative stereotypes about this group are still perpetuated in the media and popular culture. In addition to negative stereotypes, language, socioeconomic status, and immigration history can greatly affect the lived experiences of Asian clients. Clinicians must recognize the effects of racism on the mental health of Asian Americans and Pacific Islanders. Depending on the level of acculturation, some clients may dismiss or minimize racist behavior, but the effects of racism are detrimental to mental health (Sue & Sue, 2016). For both Asian Americans and Pacific Islanders, experiencing racial discrimination could result in depression, alienation, and intergenerational conflicts (Chang et al., 2015). It is important that clinicians are cognizant that discrimination and racism exist for this group and provide assistance with dealing with racism and changing the environment.

The Latinx Community

I want to begin this section by correcting common misconceptions about the Latinx community. Look at the definitions for Latinx and Hispanic.

- Latinx (gender-neutral term): Someone whose heritage can be traced to at least one of 33 countries in Latin America and the Caribbean, including Portuguese-speaking Brazil. This identity is tied to geography and excludes Spain.

- Hispanic: Someone whose heritage includes Spanish-speaking people—from anywhere, including Spain. This identity is tied to language and excludes Brazil. For some, this term further emphasizes the colonization of Spain in Latin America.

Hispanic and Latinx are ethnicities, not races. Often, when people incorrectly refer to Latinx and Hispanic as a race, they're referring to "mestizos," or mixed-race people of both indigenous and European ancestry. In Mexico, the majority of the population identifies as "mestizos." Please understand that clients can be from any background and be Latinx or Hispanic. You cannot look at someone and determine if they are Latinx or Hispanic. Afro-Latinx people are of African descent and are from Latin America, such as Cardi B (Dominican) or Tyson Beckford (Panamanian). Some have Middle Eastern heritage, like Salma Hayek and Shakira (both part Lebanese). Peru even had a president of Japanese ancestry: Alberto Fujimori (Bupara, 2019).

As mentioned with other groups, determining your client's level of acculturation is integral to the counseling process. Individuals with minimum acculturation may have a hard time being open, self-disclosing, and building trust and rapport, so the clinician must probe carefully (Sue & Sue, 2016). Instead of being overly intrusive, asking about background, generational status, residential history, immigration information, primary language, religion, sexual orientation, strength of religious beliefs, and support from the extended family will usually determine the level of acculturation (Lopez-Baez, 2006).

Counseling the Latinx Community

Techniques and interventions used with the Latinx community should be culturally adapted reflections of the client's level of acculturation, familiarity with mental health practices, linguistic issues, cultural identity, and environmental experiences (racism/discrimination) (Sue & Sue, 2016). The Latinx community does not always make the same Western distinctions between mental and physical health. So nonphysical health problems might be regulated to a physician, a priest, or a minister instead of a counselor or a psychologist (Ai et al., 2014). You could be working with someone who has a fear of deportation, so he/she may not want to give any kind of personal information. Counselors should always be aware of linguistic barriers because they can't assist a client if they have no idea what the client is saying. Cultural values and traditions are the cornerstones of the Latinx family (*falisimo*). According to Lopez-Baez (2006), in traditional Latinx culture, men are expected to be strong, dominant, and providers for the family (*machismo*). Women are expected to be nurturing, modest, virtuous, submissive, and self-sacrificing (*marianismo*). *Personalismo* is the cultural orientation in which personal relationships are valued over institutional obligations and responsibilities. *Fatalismo* is the idea that life's misfortunes are inevitable, and people feel resigned to their fate. *Simpatico*, the relationship style displayed by many individuals from the Latinx community, emphasizes social harmony in a gracious, hospitable, and personable atmosphere.

There is a negative stigma surrounding mental illness in the Latinx community. This is true for both the American-born and Latinx immigrants who are more likely to fear embarrassment or social discrimination if they acknowledge symptoms of mental illness than members of the dominant group (Sue & Sue, 2016). The traditional family structure can contribute to the reluctance of seeking mental health services. Men are expected to be strong, dominant, and providers. There's not a whole lot of confidence in authority figures who don't meet that expectation (Lopez-Baez, 2006). As a result, clients can experience feelings of isolation and depression because of the constant need to be strong, and that comes with a reluctance to seek counseling. With *marianismo*, women are expected to be nurturing, modest, virtuous, submissive, and self-sacrificing (Baumann et al., 2010). The inability to express feelings of anger or experiencing guilt about any kind of self-care can result in anxiety and depression (Sue & Sue, 2016).

The traditional family structure can also hinder the counseling process with children, or teenagers, or even young adults who are still living in the home. Traditional-oriented families can have a strict hierarchy, with special authority given to parents, older family members, and males. Gender roles are clearly delineated. In most families, the father typically is the primary figure of authority. Children are expected to be obedient and are not usually involved in making family decisions. Parents may expect adolescents to work to help with family financial obligations. Parents reciprocate by providing for their children through young adulthood, and even after marriage. Older children are generally expected to care for and protect their younger siblings. Older sisters often function as surrogate mothers, and children are raised to respect elders and other authority figures (Sue & Sue, 2016). Counselors need to be mindful of these cultural differences. Suggestions of assertiveness or independence could come across as the counselor telling a client to be disrespectful.

Stressors such as racism, discrimination, and fear of deportation can lead to a plethora of emotional issues, especially if combined with identity and acculturation conflicts. Latinx adolescents are particularly vulnerable to the effects of acculturation conflict and societal racism (Sue & Sue, 2016). Counselors should be aware of their cultural biases and refrain from generalizing members of the Latinx community into one group. It is also important that counselors be cognizant of the strengths of the Latinx community. The idea of *simpatico* is a cultural strength because it helps to incorporate that sense of family and comfort into the community, events, and relationships, so it really brings about a sense of belonging. Spirituality can bring about stress relief by promoting a deeper sense of purpose, meaning, and belonging, so it can also be a source of deep strength when dealing with personal or family issues. *Familismo* can be a huge and significant social and emotional support for individuals and families, while *personalismo* promotes respect, interdependence, and cooperation.

Native Americans

Millions of Americans who identify as either black or white have some Native American ancestry. Native Americans have intermixed with different tribes and other races as well. So now some tribes include at least 60% of Native Americans who have mixed heritage, along with black, white, and Latinx backgrounds. Unfortunately, some tribes have decided to push back against mixed-race members, especially those with African American blood. Some tribes have even gone so far as to reject individuals who meet the 25% Indian quantum of Native blood simply because they're African American or the descendants of Native and slave heritage.

Statistically, out of the 175 Native American languages once spoken in the United States, there are only about 20 of those that are passed on to younger generations now. There are about 566 active and distinct tribes in the United States, but the majority of Native Americans do not live on reservations. Many are returning to reservations because of the emergence of casinos and to engage in a more nurturing environment than reservations provided in the past. Over half of Native Americans live in metropolitan areas, and Native Americans have the highest national poverty rate of any other group. There are also fewer Native American high school graduates compared to the rest of the U.S. population. It is also very important for potential counselors to be aware that Native Americans have distinct health issues. Death by any cause is 50% higher compared to white individuals, and these reasons can be anything from car accidents to being poisoned or other injuries. The alcoholism mortality rate is over twice as high for Native Americans compared to the U.S. population as a whole. Seventy-five percent of all Native Americans experience injuries and violence between the ages of 1 and 19; this population also suffers severely from depression, anxiety, and substance abuse.

Native Americans have endured racism the longest compared to other ethnic minorities in the United States. Some common stereotypes that Native Americans have to deal with are that all Native Americans have so-called Indian names that have to do with nature or animals or anything like that and that all Native Americans look a certain way. They have to have black hair, tan skin, and brown eyes, and if they don't, then they're not Native American, or if they're darker, they can't be Native American; if they are lighter, they are not Native American. Other stereotypes include all Native Americans are alcoholics, get an automatic free ride from the government (which if anyone knows anything about history, you know that is completely untrue), and are confined to reservations, live in teepees, wear braids, and ride horses.

In addition to stereotypes and discrimination, there are also lots of microaggressions and themes of microaggressions that are associated with Native Americans, such as the very popular, "My grandmother was a Cherokee princess." There's no such thing as a Cherokee princess; the tribal system was not built like that. Do not assume that every Native American tribe is the same. Do not ask Native Americans what their totem animal is or if they live in a teepee. Other reoccurring narratives are that Native Americans are primitive, lazy, and undeserving of assistance since they are unfamiliar with modern technology and technological constructs.

As with other groups, counselors should be aware of their client's level of acculturation. Acculturation can be a source of great conflict within families. Individuals can be traditional, so they speak little English, and they try to practice their traditional tribal customs and methods of worship. Individuals who are marginal may be bilingual but have lost touch with their cultural heritage and are not fully accepted within mainstream society. When individuals are bicultural, they are conversant in values from both cultures and can kind of communicate in a variety of contexts. The assimilated individual is all about the mainstream culture's values, behaviors, and expectations. There's no connection with traditional culture. Pan-traditional individuals have been exposed to and adopted mainstream values but are trying to return to a traditional life.

In addition to acculturation, there are several cultural implications involved when counseling Native Americans, with the most important being historical background.

Counselors should be aware of the generational effects of loss of land, language, identity, acculturation issues, alcohol and substance abuse, suicide, domestic violence, and a negative outlook on formal (white) education. Seizure of Native American land by the U.S. government began in 1776, leaving only small pockets of land for reservations. Native American children were separated from their parents and extended families by state child welfare and private adoption agencies. In that time, 25%–35% of all Native American children were being removed from their homes, and 85% of those children were placed outside of their families and communities, even when they had willing relatives ready to take them in. This course of events led to enacting the Child Welfare Act of 1978 to stop the separation and complete upheaval of Native American families.

Substance abuse is one of the greatest issues in the Native American population, and it is associated with low self-esteem, cultural identity conflicts, lack of positive role models, social pressure, and a break-down within the family. Suicide is another big issue with the Native American population. Between the ages of 15 and 34, the suicide rate is 250% higher than the general population, and it is the second leading cause of death among that age group. Males are at the greatest risk for suicide, but the entire group is at very high risk. Youth have twice the rate of attempted or completed suicide compared to other members of their community. All of the suicide attempts, ideations, and completions are associated with alcohol abuse, poverty, boredom, family breakdown, and disconnect from culture and community. Domestic violence is another issue that's prevalent in the Native American population. Physical and sexual abuse are often experienced in the early stages of life for women, especially if they are members of the lesbian, gay, bisexual, transgender, queer, or questioning population. Possible causes for this are substance abuse and social and economic stressors, as well as marginalization and role and identity changes for men and women from traditional ways of life.

Native Americans and Counseling

There are some strategies and interventions that are culturally appropriate and tend to be effective. Most comprehensive services are provided to Native Americans through the Indian Health Service and Tribal Mental Health and Substance Abuse Services. Person-centered therapy and CBT are very good intervention-wise. The Substance Abuse and Mental Health Services Administration created the Gathering of Native Americans, which is a curriculum that was developed to specifically work with the Native American population. Counselors should do their best to communicate with tribal leaders and to build relationships in the community and learn how they can be of assistance so that they can build rapport and trust, which will make it easier to work with individuals and tight-knit communities.

Counselors should be aware that to many Native Americans honor and respect are gained by sharing in the accumulation of material goods. In other words, once the money is earned, Native Americans tend to stop working and enjoy what they have in the present. Cooperation is a huge cultural value, so having a strong relationship with family members is definitely a priority. Native American children tend to avoid confrontation and do not engage in activities that do not benefit the entire group. Noninterference is important because the rights of others are respected by others. To many Native Americans, it is more important to observe than to act, even in parenting. Time orientation is also important because many Native Americans believe life should be lived in the present without worrying about the future. Counselors should remain in the "here and now," helping clients develop strategies or negotiate conflicts as they arise.

Native Americans believe that the mind, spirit, and body are all interconnected and illness refers to an imbalance between these elements. They believe that healing can be achieved by something as simple as talking to a friend or doing something that is peaceful, such as watching children play or the sunset. It's best if counselors do not try to get too scientific or too vague and just attempt to help their clients identify solutions with respect to curative events, behaviors, and feelings. Native Americans believe that learning occurs by listening and not talking, and they tend not to ask direct questions and avoid direct eye contact. It is important for counselors to determine the difference between behaviors based on cultural values and those resulting from actual issues with communication.

Cultural Appropriation

Cultural appropriation is a polarizing topic but needs to be discussed in relation to cultural competence. Cultural appropriation is defined as the unauthorized use by members of one group of the cultural expressions and resources of another (Riley & Carpenter, 2016). Simply, someone from one group is adopting cultural/traditional dress or appearance as a costume or statement. Someone from that group is offended and calls it cultural appropriation. If you don't understand why that would be offensive, imagine the person from the cultural group saying, "Okay, you can dress up in my skin or cultural attire and be praised for being 'woke' or fashionable, but I live in my skin and culture every day. These are things that I'm judged for. I don't get praised for being myself, and I can't take my own skin on and off like a costume."

White Racial Identity

Unfortunately, there's chronic exposure to ethnocentric monoculturalism that's manifested in white supremacy in this country and many others. Racism is a part of our lives in the United States. It exists in all aspects of our culture. Period. It's not something that's exaggerated, and it's not something that can be pushed under the rug by saying, "Well, that was a long time ago." It's every day, all day. It's important that white counselors understand their racial identity development and how it affects their relationships. Your stage of white racial identity development affects your relationships with people of different races and ethnicities. The way that white people perceive themselves as racial beings can be linear or nonlinear. It can be, "I am just going to believe about other people how I have been raised, or the people around me, or according to my environment, social economic level" or "I am going to change these things, as I learn and grow, and are actually exposed to different kinds of people" (Sue & Sue, 2016). The most desirable goal of white racial identity development is for a white person to accept his/her whiteness in a way that is defined in a nonracist manner. The process of white identity development can be broken down into seven phases: (1) naivete, (2) conformity, (3) dissonance, (4) resistance and immersion, (5) introspective, (6) integrative awareness, and (7) commitment to anti-racist action (Sue & Sue, 2016).

Naivete is the "I don't see color" phase. It's having an apparently neutral stance in regard to racial and cultural differences and kind of naïve curiosity about race; racial awareness is minimal or nonexistent. Conformity results from misinformation and socialization that causes an individual to accept negative attitudes and ideas toward people of other races and ethnicities. This is the stage where if even if you declare that you're not racist, you still may have stereotypical views about other races or ethnicities. Your information about other ethnic groups and races is based solely based on social stereotypes. The dissonance phase is very different. This is a stage where personal experiences cause individuals to become aware of their prejudices and biases. A major event allows them to realize that, yes, racism does exist, and it's a big deal. Some of the feelings that can go along with this stage are guilt, shame, anger, and depression. The guilt and shame may come from not speaking up or taking action when and recalling that things happened that weren't necessarily right or just. The next stage is resistance and immersion. This is when an individual questions and challenges racism. There is an increased awareness of how racism operates in the U.S. culture and institutions around the world. The individual also recognizes how being white grants advantages that may be inaccessible or denied to minorities, which is white privilege. This is also the stage where an individual discovers that overidentification is not appreciated and experiences rejection from the minority group the person is trying to identify with.

The introspective phase and integrative awareness phase come next. This is when individuals accept participation in oppression and the benefits of white privilege, as well as racism being a part of U.S. society. They accept their whiteness and begin to redefine their self-identity based on all the knowledge and awareness they've gained during the other stages. There's a feeling of disconnectedness, isolation, confusion, and loss sometimes when they realize that the people around them, especially family and loved ones, aren't where they are developmentally and might not ever be. There is also the time when an individual appreciates racial diversity in a healthy and positive way. The next phase is the commitment to anti-racist action. This starts with social action and an increased commitment to eradicate oppression. There's moral fortitude, observing wrong and actively trying to make it right. Individuals take direct action, which means things such as not allowing racist jokes and educating significant individuals in their lives about racial issues. In this phase, white people are often isolated from family and friends who don't understand their desired change. For some, this kind of isolation and rejection may cause them to go back to an earlier phase in development so they can be more comfortable with the people around them.

To achieve cultural competence, increase your understanding by supplementing factual knowledge with experienced reality. That means do the things that you're learning about, apply the principles, and find someone willing to help you understand his/her minority group. Be aware of your biases and the biases of people around you. Become comfortable asking sensitive racial questions from a sincere and well-meaning place. Most minorities are willing to respond and share if concerns are motivated by a desire to learn and not a microaggression.

Lastly, become committed to personal action against racism. That means take action. Use your white privilege to help others. Interrupt other white people when they make racist remarks, speak out against bias and discrimination, advocate for multicultural curriculums in schools, ensure that minority candidates are fairly considered for job positions, take on multicultural tasks in organizations, and continue to work on developing a white, nonracist identity. It is important that white counselors understand that this country was built on white supremacy and the oppression for people of color. For minorities, living in a society that was designed for them *not* to succeed deeply affects mental health, physical health, and standard of living. While you're on your journey to white racial identity development, try to educate yourself about the lived experiences of other groups and seek to change your circle of influence with multicultural awareness.

Summary

Your understanding of your own cultural values and biases, histories of prejudice, cultural stereotyping and discrimination, and awareness of other worldviews, as well as your clients' worldviews, will enhance or hinder the counseling process. The journey to multicultural competence is a marathon, not a sprint. It's an evolving process that you are not expected to master. Consider this chapter as a guide and not a blueprint for understanding everything about different cultural groups and do your best to provide culturally appropriate services to all groups in our society.

Discussion Questions

1. How can a counselor use awareness, knowledge, and skill to function effectively with culturally diverse populations?
2. What are characteristics of the "ideal client"?
3. What can counselors do to continuously assess their cultural competence?

References

Ai, A.L., Aisenberg, E., Weiss, S.I. et al. Racial/ethnic identity and subjective physical and mental health of Latino Americans: An asset within? *American Journal of Community Psychology, 53,* 173–184 (2014). https://doi.org/10.1007/s10464-014-9635-5

Alvesson, M., & Sveningsson, S. (2015). *Changing organizational culture: Cultural change work in progress* (2nd ed.). Routledge.

American Psychological Association. (2007). *Task force on socioeconomic status. Report of the APA Task Force on Socioeconomic Status.*

Asante, M. K. (2003). *Erasing racism: The survival of the American nation.* Prometheus Books.

Atkinson, D. R. (2004). *Counseling American minorities: A cross-cultural perspective* (6th ed.). McGraw-Hill.

Atkinson, D. R., & Hackett, G. (1998). *Counseling diverse populations* (2nd ed.). McGraw-Hill.

Ballard, A. B. (1973). *The education of black folk: The Afro-American struggle for knowledge in white America.* Harper and Row.

Baumann, A. A., Kuhlberg, J. A., & Zayas, L. H. (2010). Familism, mother-daughter mutuality, and suicide attempts of adolescent Latinas. *Journal of Family Psychology, 24*, 616–624.

Bello, S. 1991. *Culture and decision making in Nigeria.* National Council for Arts And Culture.

Bupara, A. (2019). Anti-colonial action in real time: Mestizx Latinx people, place, cisheteropatriarchy, and our way forward," *sprinkle: an undergraduate journal of feminist and queer studies*, *12*(15).

Chang, H.-L., Han, E.-J., Lee J.-S., & Qin, D. B (2015). Korean American adolescent ethnic-identity pride and psychological adjustment: Moderating effects of parental support and school environment. *Asian American Journal of Psychology, 6*, 190–199.

Coleman, S. (2011). Addressing the puzzle of race. *Journal of Social Work Education, 47*, 91–108.

Fuligini, A. J., Burton, L., Marshall, S., Perez-Febles, A., Yarrington, J., Kirsh, L. B., & Merriweather-DeVries, C. (1999). Attitudes toward family obligations among American adolescents with Asian, Latin American, and European backgrounds. *Child Development, 70*, 1030–1044.

Hays, D. G., & Erford, B. T. (2018). *Developing multicultural counseling competence: A systems approach.* Pearson Education.

Hook, J. N., Davis, D. E., Owen, J., Worthington, E. L., & Utsey, S. O. (2013). Cultural humility: Measuring openness to culturally diverse clients. *Journal of Counseling Psychology, 60*, 353–366.

Hwang, W.-C., Woods, J. J., & Fujimoto, K. (2010). Acculturative family distancing (AFD) and depression in Chinese American Families. *Journal of Consulting and Clinical Psychology, 78*, 655–667.

Idang, Gabriel E. (2015). African culture and values. *Phronimon, 16*(2), 97–111. Retrieved November 22, 2019, from http://www.scielo.org.za/scielo.php?script=sci_arttext&pid=S1561-40182015000200006&lng=en&tlng=en.

Ivey, A. E., Ivey, M., Myers, J., & Sweeney, T. (2005). *Developmental counseling and therapy.* Lahaska.

Ivey, A. E., Ivey, M. B., & Zalaquett, C. P. (2014). *Intentional interviewing and counseling* (8th ed.). Brooks/Cole.

Kim, B. S. K. (2011). *Counseling Asian Americans.* Cengage.

Lopez-Baez, S. I. (2006). Counseling Latinas: Culturally responsive interventions. In C. C Lee (Ed.), *Multicultural issues in counseling* (3rd ed., pp. 187–194). American Counseling Association.

Museus, S. D., & Kiang, P. N. (2009). Deconstructing the model minority myth and how it contributes to the invisible minority reality in higher education research. *New Direction for Institutional Research, 2009*(142), 1–15.

Nadal, K. L., Escobar, K. M., Prado, G., David, E.J.R., & Haynes, K. (2012). Racial microaggressions and the Filipino American experience: Recommendations for counseling and development. *Journal of Multicultural Counseling and Development, 40*, 156–173.

Paiva, N. D. (2008). South Asian parents' constructions of praising their children. *Clinical Child Psychology and Psychiatry, 13*, 191–207.

Pew Research Center. (2017). *Key facts about Asian Americans, a diverse and growing population.* https://www.pewresearch.org/fact-tank/2017/09/08/key-facts-about-asian-americans/

Pew Research Center. (2018). *Income inequality in the U.S. is rising most rapidly among Asians.* https://www.pewsocialtrends.org/2018/07/12/income-inequality-in-the-u-s-is-rising-most-rapidly-among-asians/

Ratts, M. J., & Pedersen, P. B (2014). *Counseling for multiculturalism and social justice.* American Counseling Association.

Reed, R., & Smith, L. (2014). A social justice perspective on counseling and poverty. In M. J. Ratts & P. B. Pederson (Eds.), *Counseling for multiculturalism and social justice* (pp. 259–273). American Counseling Association.

Riley, A., & Carpenter, K. (2016). Owning red: A theory of Indian (cultural) appropriation. *Texas Law Review, 94,* 859–861.

Sue, D. W., & Sue, D. (1990). *Counseling the culturally different: Theory and practice.* Wiley.

Sue, D. W., & Sue, D. (1999). *Counseling the culturally different: Theory and practice.* Wiley.

Sue, D. W., & Sue, D. (2016). *Counseling the culturally diverse: Theory and practice.* Wiley.

Taylor, E. B. (1871). *Primitive culture: Researches into the development of mythology, philosophy, religion, language, art and custom* (2nd ed.). John Murray.

Vakalahi, H.F.O. (2009). Pacific Islander American students: Caught between a rock and a hard place? *Children and Youth Services Review, 31*, 1258–1263.

Wang, S., & Kim, B.S.K. (2010). Therapist multicultural competence, Asian-American participants' cultural values, and counseling process. *Journal of Counseling Psychology, 57*, 394–401.

CHAPTER 9

Career Counseling for Gender Differences and Dual Careers

Roxanna Pebdani, Serene Lin-Stephens, and Erin Fearn-Smith

CHAPTER OVERVIEW

Patriarchal values have long affected the career paths of men and women alike throughout history. While society has seen a major shift in the vocational roles played by men and women over the last five decades, women are still working to overcome barriers in the workplace, and men are still judged for assuming significant roles in the household (Perrone et al., 2005). In an age where most families consist of two working parents, gender roles remain imbalanced in the home and the workplace. This chapter will provide an overview of gender differences in the workplace and issues that dual-career families face that should be addressed by career counselors.

CHAPTER OBJECTIVES

After reading this chapter, the student will be able to complete the following:

1. Outline gender differences in the workplace.

2. Discuss the gender role challenges experienced by men and women in the workplace.

3. Discuss the gender role challenges experienced by men and women in the household.

4. Identify and address challenges that dual-career families face.

5. Discuss and implement strategies for helping dual-career families overcome the challenges they encounter.

Context

There are many aspects of life in which gender differences exist, and careers are no exception. Young children learn about gender differences in potential career options from a young age, and those messages continue into adulthood, where they then encounter workplace issues, such as pay inequality, sexual harassment, and disparities at home that affect work lives. In addition, career progression and development can be affected by maternity and paternity leaves, childcare, and household duties. This chapter addresses gender differences in the workplace through the themes of inequality and difference. We will address career issues such as income disparities, the influence of gender stereotypes on a person's career decision making and career opportunities, and the presence and prevalence of sexual harassment in the workplace. We will also discuss issues that face both dual- and single-income families and the effect of maternity and paternity leave, childcare, and household duties on a person's opportunities for career progression.

Financial Inequities in the Workplace

In 1963, a U.S. labor law was passed called the Equal Pay Act of 1963. The passage of this law made it illegal to discriminate based on a person's sex by paying men and women in equal roles different salaries. Despite this, there continues to be a gap in wages between men and women in the United States. According to the Pew Research Center, as recently as 2018, women still earned only 85% of what men earn in the United States. This means that for every $1 a man earns, a woman earns $0.85. This wage gap is consistent across every state in the United States (Chapman & Benis, 2017), as well as Australia (Kennedy et al., 2017), China (Hare, 2018), Canada, Sweden, the United Kingdom (Fortin et al., 2017), Japan (Hara, 2018), and many other countries around the world. This wage gap widens when we look through an intersectional lens. A recent study found that white women make $0.76 to each dollar a man makes, but African American women make $0.63 to each dollar, and Latina/xs make a staggering $0.54 to every dollar a male counterpart makes (Chapman & Benis, 2017).

Many explanations have been made for this wage gap. Some researchers argue that women are more likely to experience interruptions in their career paths, work shorter hours, and work part time (Blau & Kahn, 2017). However, some argue that differences in occupation (often called occupational segregation) represent one of the biggest contributors to the wage gap worldwide (Hegewisch et al., 2010).

Occupational Segregation in Career Counseling

A review of the history of career counseling and vocational guidance reveals a deep-rooted bias toward males (Savickas & Baker, 2005). The influential trait-and-factor (Parsons, 1909) and personality type–occupational fit approaches (Holland, 1966) propose an objective match between personal qualities and suitable jobs that centralize around interest and skills but are relatively free from social constraints. However, the privilege of choice is not equally given to everyone, especially women (Correll, 2001) and individuals from minority backgrounds (Hirsh & Cha, 2008). Similarly, when illustrating career decision making, often males are the default example, a notable one being Krumbotlz's career theory (Krumboltz et al., 1976). The narrow scope of career counseling is accentuated by Tyler's (1967) early observation that "much of what we know about the stages through which an individual passes as he prepares to find his place in the world of work might appropriately be labeled the vocational development of white middle class males" (p. 61). To address the problems of basing career development on the norm of white middle-class males and treating other cohorts as sub or special groups (Brown & Brown, 2012; Sharf, 1997), researchers have begun to reconceive career development by studying gender stereotypes. This bears important implications for occupational opportunities for women.

Gender Stereotypes

Gender stereotypes are oversimplified ideas of individuals based on gender attributes. The profound effects of gender stereotypes are seen in many areas, including career preferences and occupational choices (Gadassi & Gati, 2009; He et al., 2019), family and work roles (Marks et al., 2018; Perrone et al., 2005; Perrone et al.,

2009), perception of career success (Frear et al., 2019), and workplace gender equality (Hardacre & Subasic, 2018). The first prominent theory that factored into productive contributions of people from different genders, particularly women, was Super's life-span, life-space approach (Super, 1980).

Super maintains that career development encompasses most, or all, of an individual's life roles as a child, student, leisurite, citizen, worker, spouse, homemaker, parent, and pensioner. By positioning homemaking as one of the nine life roles that individuals play, women can now receive the long-overdue recognition of their significant roles and potential career patterns. Paradoxically, although Super contributed to a more inclusive career theory by acknowledging a large part of women's productive activities, this recognition is simultaneously symptomatic of the gender stereotypes women face. Despite the theoretical assumption that the homemaking life role can be assumed by both males and females, women continue to dominate in the homemaking space and domestic activities while occupying comparatively lower level positions to males in the workspace to maintain work-life balance for family priorities (Frear et al., 2019; Zaikman & Marks, 2017).

Women are considerably underrepresented in management; professional fields, such as science, technology, engineering, and mathematics (STEM); and entrepreneurial careers (Hüttges & Fay, 2015; Padovez-Cualheta et al., 2019), and they are perceived as inferior in performance in comparison to their male counterparts (Buchanan & Milnes, 2019). Males continue to be perceived as more effective leaders (Hardacre & Subasic, 2018), stronger in abstract and numeric thinking, and less suitable for "warm" jobs, such as childcare worker, nurse, or secretary (He et al., 2019), compared to women. The effects of gender stereotypes on career preferences were reported as more pronounced in women than men (Gadassi & Gati, 2009).

Gottfredson's Theory of Circumscription and Compromise

The effect of gender stereotypes on career choice begins early. Linda Gottfredson's theory of circumscription and compromise (Gottfredson, 1981) specifically addresses gender and occupational stereotypes by relating them to stages of child development. According to Gottfredson, gender is the most protected core element of self-concept, and occupations are the most important determinants of social class.

The development of self-concepts and vocational preferences are inseparable because occupational stereotypes are sex-typed, shared by all cohorts of a society, and observed by young children as significant differentiators of people. Because gender self-labeling occurs as early as ages 2 to 3 (Kohlberg as cited in Gottfredson, 1981), when youngsters develop self-concepts, they make judgments of adult gender and occupational roles based on their compatibility with their own self-images. As self-concepts become more complex, vocational preferences also become more delineated and concrete, yet narrow. Vocational decision making embodies a process of circumscription. In this process, occupational choices are simplified based on a person's perceived fit between a career option and the person's self-concept. Choices incompatible with one's self-concepts or images (including gender) are eliminated. As a result, children may prematurely rule out nontraditional vocational options.

In addition to the compatibility between vocational image and self-image, as early as ages 9–13, children can already distinguish aspirations that are tolerable, realistic, and idealistic, guided by a sense of levels of effort required for reasonable rewards. By the end of junior high school, youngsters are already sophisticated enough to sensibly display gendered occupational understanding. By adolescence, the perceptions young people hold about job accessibility and reality determine how they make career choice decisions and compromises. Gottfredson's principles of compromise state that such compromises are based on an alignment between gender self-concepts and occupational goals, a tendency to settle on a job option that is acceptable rather than optimal, and psychological accommodations people made toward their choices (Gottfredson, 1981). The perceptions of gender-specific occupations and how they relate to a person's self-concept continue into adulthood.

Gender Stereotypes in Careers

Many studies affirm that gender stereotypes affect women profoundly from the onset of childhood. In a 10-year longitudinal study, Helwig (2001) reported that children's conception of suitable occupations supported Gottfredson's hypothesis of gendered occupational aspirations based on children's developmental stages. They found that a higher percentage of boys have more "fantasy" occupational aspirations than girls, and in contrast, girls have more "realistic" occupational aspirations (Helwig, 2001). Although girls' choices may seem to be more "mature," this may indicate a higher level of social constraint imposed on how they perceive their potential. Boys, on the other hand, seem to enjoy more liberty in defining who they want to be and can become. This gap is amplified in adulthood.

Even in Super's relatively gender-neutral life-role approach, in which the life roles can be played by both males and females, gender stereotypes based on biological and social attributes continue to shape the relationship between gender and socially appropriate work roles. According to Super, "When positions are defined more precisely, roles may be linked to sex, as in the biologically determined parental role of mother and in the socially determined (and therefore socially alterable) work roles of engineer, police officer, secretary, and nurse" (Super, 1980, p. 284). Family ideologies, such as marriage and motherhood, present significant challenges to women's participation in public life, paid work, and professional activities (Evetts, 1996). Women are vulnerable to stereotype threat (Steele & Aronson, 1995), a phenomenon in which members of a marginalized social group are at risk of confirming a negative expectation about their group. Women are penalized for displaying non-gender-conforming behavior and emotions, such as dominance and pride, thus harming their chances of obtaining success (Brescoll, 2016). Gender stereotypes interfere with women's participation and performance in many areas, most notably education (C. S. Smith & Hung, 2008), athleticism (Hively & El-Alayli, 2014), STEM careers (Evetts, 1996), and leadership and management (Hoyt & Murphy, 2016).

By the same token, just as gender stereotypes affect women, they also affect men. In Hardie's (2015) study using data taken from the U.S. National Study of Youth and Religion, the researcher found that close to 66.98% of young men aspire to a job that is male dominated (job composition of < 40% female), 18.52% aspire to gender-neutral jobs, and only 14.52% aspired to jobs with more than 60% female composition. While gender self-concept (manhood) may play an important role in young men's reluctance to enter female-dominated occupations, studies have reported that other barriers, such as income and perception of competency, deter men from taking up work traditionally occupied by women.

Hardie also found that the median income of female-dominated careers was statistically lower than that of male-dominated occupations. In another study, He et al. (2019) showed that female jobs were perceived to require less competency. Such findings illuminate the consequences of gender stereotypes in the job market beyond a person's interests and skills. Moreover, the gender stereotypes in the job market, as Gaucher et al. (2011) contended, are sustained by gendered wording embedded in job descriptions. Job advertisements for male-dominated work used more masculine wording (such as assertive, competitive, leader) than for female-dominated work. They tested the consequences of highly masculine wording in three experimental studies and found that the more masculine words used in a job advertisement, the more participants perceived more men within those occupations and the less women found those jobs appealing. They highlighted that it was the perception of belongingness—rather than skills—that mediated the effects of gendered stereotyping on job appeal. In another study, Calanca et al. (2019) examined skills requirements in job advertisements and found that skills stereotypically associated with females attracted wage penalties, lending further support to the gendered barrier to making career choices flexible.

There are many influences on male and female career choices at the individual, organizational, and societal levels. Reid's (2018) study on how males construct their identities in relation to their wives' work allows us to better understand how a more equal gender self-concept is possible. Reid found that men in dual-career relationships can define themselves in different ways. Men who define themselves as what Reid called "breadwinners" in their families accord little status or financial value to the employment that their wives hold. On the other hand, men who consider themselves to be "breadsharers" accord high status and/or financial value to the work of their wives. In short, men who value the work their wives do tend to be part of more egalitarian households that value men and women equally. At an organizational level, it is necessary to have formal workplace support and human resource policies that ensure gender quality in the workplace. Human resource policies, supervisor and organizational support, and perceived meaningfulness of work can increase career success for female managers, which can, in turn, influence their ability to assert themselves in the workplace (Lee & Lee, 2019).

It is commonly understood that women receive more negative attributes in work evaluations (Smith et al., 2019). Despite this, formal human resources practices, such as performance-based evaluations, are still an important channel to give women, especially mothers, a legitimate way to gain recognition through making claims about their work contributions (Luekemann & Abendroth, 2018). On a societal level, the prestige ascribed to nontraditional careers is widening work options for both men and women. The growing entrepreneurial careers, for example, are found to give individuals more job and family satisfaction (Padovez-Cualheta et al., 2019). The emerging experience economy, coined by Pine and Gilmore (1998) as the next economy following the industrial and service economies, has created income sources without institutional gendered pay gaps, as well as social value and meaning that are achievable regardless of the gender hierarchy or glass ceilings. Online marketplaces and experience brokers, such as Airbnb, have been quick to claim the sharing and gig economy afforded by their women hosts, who dominate the hosting community globally and generated more than $20 billion in income within 10 years of the establishment of the platform (Airbnb, 2017, 2018). The new social meanings attached to nontraditional careers will be an important consideration in career decision making for individuals in the future.

Gender stereotypes are a complex phenomenon in cisgender terms (male, female), yet the complexity of the phenomenon cannot be fully comprehended without the inclusion of individuals who are transgender and/or gender nonconforming persons who have been the subject of significant gender prejudice (Pflum et al., 2015). People who are transgender and/or gender nonconforming have experienced high social stigma through negative gender stereotypes that identify them as deviant, confused, and mentally ill (Howansky et al., 2019). They also experience discrimination in the forms of microaggressions and horizontal oppression (discrimination by peer members of the lesbian, gay, bisexual, transgender, queer, or questioning (LGBTQ) community) in employment and other support systems, such as health care, education, policy and legislation, and social settings (Dispenza et al., 2012). Having a nontraditional gender identity can also affect a person's career and academic choices (Schneider & Dimito, 2010). Given these consequences of nonconforming gender identities, research and theory development on people who are transgender and/or gender nonconforming are a glaring weakness in career counseling literature (Prince, 2013). This is discussed in depth in Chapter 10.

Career counselors should be conscious of gender diversity. By being gender aware, counselors can take into consideration multiple challenges that clients face in career decision making, which does not happen in gender-blind environments. The American Counseling Association provides guidelines for counselors to develop competencies and form counseling strategies that are gender accommodating in respect to human growth and development, social and cultural diversity, helping relationships, group work, professional orientation and ethical practice, career and lifestyle development, assessment, research, and program evaluation (Harper et al., 2013).

Gender-Based Violence

Violence against women and other forms of gender-based violence have a significant effect on health and work. Although women are particularly vulnerable (European Institute for Gender Equality, 2019b; García-Moreno et al., 2013), gender-based violence affects all people who deviate from socially determined gender roles and can be perpetrated by both men and women (Carpenter, 2006). Definitions of gender-based violence include physical, sexual, or psychological abuse in the family, community, work, or other institutions; violence related to traditional marital customs; exploitation; trafficking and forced prostitution; violence condoned by a state; sexual slavery; forced or coercive contraception, sterilization, pregnancy, termination, or infanticide; and workplace violence, including bullying and harassment related to personal family or living arrangements, preferences or beliefs, language, or racial, cultural, social, or political origins or orientations (Cruz & Klinger, 2011).

Gender-Based Violence in the Workplace

One in 4 women and 1 in 10 men in the United States have reported physical or sexual violence and/or stalking at some point in their lives (Smith et al., 2018). Domestic violence includes physical assault, sexual violence, threats of violence, stalking, and psychological abuse, such as emotional aggression and coercive control over behavior, money, and support networks (Ridley et al., 2005). In the United States, 31.5% of women and 27.5% of men have experienced some form of intimate partner violence (Sumner et al., 2015), with black women (Pearlman et al., 2016), Latinas (Pearlman et al., 2016; Zadnik et al., 2016) and women with disabilities at particular risk (Breiding & Armour, 2015). In addition, members of the LGBTQ community, especially transgender persons, are at very high risk of intimate partner violence (Langenderfer-Magruder et al., 2016).

The effects of this violence on workplace experiences are rarely discussed (Ridley et al., 2005). These issues—both when the abusive relationship is active and long after the relationship has ended (McLean & Bocinski, 2017)—affect workers' health and productivity, creating an economic case, as well as a human rights case (Bonomi et al., 2009), for bringing family and intimate partner violence into the common workplace discourse. Given the prevalence and severity of these issues, career counselors must be cognizant of this context within their work with clients (Brown et al., 2005). This can be done by offering sensitivity to power dynamics, trauma, and a range of potentially unfamiliar barriers to employment, as well as resourcefulness through linking people with practical supports, assisting with identifying and building personal social capital, and undertaking advocacy roles with employers and community resources where necessary.

A study jointly conducted by the Maine Department of Labor and Family Crisis Services (Ridley et al., 2005) in which survivors of domestic violence were interviewed identified a number of work-related issues arising from intimate partner violence, including safety risks, reduced productivity, and disruptions to attendance. This study also identified disruption to family and social supports, child relationships and safety, school continuity, and housing security, all of which have secondary effects on work and health. These researchers found that 60% of participants either had to leave their jobs or had been fired from their jobs as a direct consequence of the abuse.

Sexual Harassment in the Workplace

Gender stereotypes and discrimination in aggressive forms can manifest in sexual harassment. Like sexual discrimination, sexual harassment is associated with a high degree of job dissatisfaction (Antecol et al., 2009). In addition, it is associated with reduced organizational commitment, poor physical and mental health, and behaviors of withdrawal (Willness et al., 2007), as well as negative economic outcomes for affected individuals and organizations (McLaughlin et al., 2017). The effects of sexual harassment and assault have lasting effects on career and life goal setting (Fineran & Gruber, 2009).

Sexual harassment takes the form of gender harassment (verbal and nonverbal behaviors that convey offensive, degrading gendered attitudes), unwanted sexual attention, and sexual coercion (sexual imposition or extortion of sexual cooperation) (Fitzgerald et al., 1995). Contributing factors to sexual harassment include organizational factors, such as workplace climate and gender imbalance (Fitzgerald et al., 1997; Willness et al., 2007), as well as social-cultural factors by which gender is inherently a personal vulnerability characteristic (Bergman & Henning, 2008). The prevalence of sexual harassment is documented in many studies. These contextual factors are supported by findings from studies of women in male-dominated work environments. In one study, 80% of women working in STEM fields and mostly male workplaces reported experiencing gender discrimination at work (Ansley, 2018).

The recent #MeToo movement demonstrates the prevalence and severity of sexual harassment in many workplaces. Originally coined by Tarana Burke to empower victims of sexual abuse in 2006, a decade later, following the Harvey Weinstein sexual allegations in 2017, actress Alyssa Milano initiated the use of the hashtag. Her use amassed more than 12 million tweets with the hashtag within 24 hours, with effects rippling across industries, politics, and the legislative arena (Tippett, 2018). However, while the #MeToo movement reignites public attention of sexual harassment, its implications for individuals' career development are yet to be clarified. Sixty-eight percent of 2,900 respondents surveyed by Ansley feared that the #MeToo movement will lead to unfair dismissals or negative consequences at their jobs (Ansley, 2018). Others cautioned that the push for broad harassment policies might inadvertently produce avoidance behaviors that lead to sidelining underrepresented groups. For example, some who are overly cautious may avoid contact with females, thus leading to unintentional discrimination or segregation and, consequently, disadvantaging the career progression of the women around them (Tippett, 2018). The #MeToo movement is paving the way for workplaces that do not accept or normalize sexual harassment. However, the unintended negative side effects of #MeToo highlight the need to revisit workplace equality fundamentals, including principles of fairness, transparency, trust, mutual respect, and equal participation in decision making. Recent research also recommended specific training to minimize workplace sexism and promote character building, such as courage (Atwater et al., 2019).

Issues Facing Families

More families today than ever before are concurrently participating in employment and caring for children under 18 years (U.S. Census Bureau, 2018b). While women's participation in employment and contribution to household income has evolved considerably over the past century or so (Harkness, 2010), changes regarding domestic responsibilities have been far more subtle. Studies have found that women often undertake a far greater role in the performance of household and family labor tasks than men (Bartley et al., 2005; Kulik & Rayyan, 2003; Perrone et al., 2005; Rosenbluth et al., 1998). Daminger (2019) explored this issue further by examining the cognitive aspect of domestic labor: the "mental load" (Daminger, 2019). This cognitive dimension (the "mental load"), which is predominantly carried by women, includes anticipating, planning, organizing, and monitoring domestic and family material and social arrangements, and it constitutes an invisible and often discounted psychological burden. This additional load, coupled with potentially inflated perceptions of contributions from men (Dex et al., 2012) and relationship conflicts arising from perceptions of inequity (Newkirk et al., 2017), may contribute to increased experiences of stress (Zuzanek, 1998) and even increased rates of divorce (Craig & Sawrikar, 2007).

Women are also more likely than men to undertake informal caring roles for other family members, including spouses or parents (Arber & Ginn, 1995). A study conducted by Cannuscio et al. (2002) found that people undertaking 36 or more caring hours per week experienced significantly more symptoms of anxiety and depression than those without the caring responsibility. Similarly, researchers analyzed data from the U.K. Household Longitudinal Study and found that nearly one fourth of families surveyed included informal careers and that women undertaking informal caring roles experienced higher rates of psychological distress than both women who were not undertaking a career role and men who were in a career role (Lacey et al., 2019).

As family dynamics and social expectations adjust to shifting families and work obligations, challenges for families must be considered in contemporary career counseling. This includes ongoing gender disparities in income and employment security, as well as identity pressures from lingering norms and traditional gender role expectations (Cruz & Klinger, 2011). In addition, limitations in access to social and structural supports for men and women to facilitate increasing employment or domestic responsibilities and relationship management and negotiation should also be addressed (Newkirk et al., 2017).

Maternity and Paternity Leave

The United States lags behind other countries in the provision of maternity and paternity leave. As the only Organization for Economic Co-operation and Development country without statutory parental leave arrangements (Organization for Economic Co-operation and Development, 2019), the arrival of a new family member can be highly disruptive to workers' careers and, potentially, their livelihoods. The Family and Medical Leave Act (FMLA) provides eligible employees of covered employers with entitlement to a period of up to 12 weeks of unpaid leave from work (U. S. Department of Labor, 2012). However, accessing this leave can still be difficult for eligible employees because of financial constraints (Klerman et al., 2012). While there is no federal provision for paid maternity or paternity leave, California, New Jersey, Rhode Island,

and, most recently, New York have laws allowing for a leave period of between 4 and 6 weeks with partial payment (Burtle & Bezruchka, 2016).

Childcare

Access to childcare support is another indicator of family roles and employment outcomes in the experience of dual-income families, and this is influenced by geographic location, income status, and personal access to informal support networks. Three distinct childcare structures are described by Presser (2003): (1) formal childcare arrangements through early childhood education resources in the community; (2) informal childcare arrangements through personal networks, such as grandparents or shared care with other families; and (3) split-shift parenting, each potentially employed independently or in combination with one or more of the other childcare structures (Presser, 2003). Each of these childcare options can have a differing effect on career options and opportunities and should be addressed in career counseling as necessary.

In addition, the cost of childcare can be prohibitive for some workers. The cost of childcare in the United States varies widely by state. In 2019, annual infant care fees ranged from $5,436 in Mississippi (11.7% median family income or 36.1% of minimum wage income) all the way up to $24,243 in Washington, DC (28.6% of median family income or 83.3% of minimum wage income) (European Institute for Gender Equality, 2019a). Career counselors will benefit from this insight; they should be sensitive to the reality that formal childcare is not a certainty for all workers and is likely to be influenced by home location, income, and resource access. Supporting people to explore and build on existing capital with their personal social networks can be of significant value in establishing informal arrangements (Dominguez & Watkins, 2003)

Single-Parent Families

Balancing employment and parenting are challenging tasks for many people, and single parenting increases that challenge exponentially. Single parents experience reduced access to income, less flexible work schedules, and limited access to childcare, and they currently represent 15.5% of all parents living with children under the age of 18 years in the United States (U. S. Census Bureau, 2018). Single-parent families have reduced access to income and a greater risk of poverty. Although measures vary, poverty in single-parent families in the United States is consistently high and often underrepresented in the data. Data from the LIS Cross-National Data Center in Luxembourg shows that in 2016, almost half (48.45%) of children in single-parent families in the United States lived in poverty (LIS, 2019), compared with 13.61% of children living in two-parent families (LIS, 2009). The data presented by the U.S. Census Bureau for the same period reflects 8.4% of children in a household with married parents living below the poverty threshold, compared to 42.1% of children living with a female householder without a husband, and 19.9% of children living with a male householder without a wife.

Poverty compounds the challenge of being a single parent, and it limits access to employment. Single-parent households are less likely to have an employed parent than partnered-parent households. A recent study found that 97% of two-parent households comprised an employed parent, compared with 77% of single-parent households. Single men, however, are still more likely to be employed (84%) than single women (74%) (U. S. Census Bureau, 2018a).

Single parents may be more challenged in accessing employment, as work schedules are often less flexible as a consequence of limited formal childcare arrangements (Enchautegui, 2013). Single parents are also less likely to share childcare or transport responsibilities (Enchautegui, 2013). Although the single-parent population includes both women and men, women comprise more than 8 in 10 single parents (13% of the total parenting population cohabiting with children under 18), while less than 2 in 10 are men (2.5% of the total parenting population cohabiting with children under 18) (U. S. Census Bureau, 2018). As such, remaining abreast of the local, practical, and social resources, as well as the policy frameworks and services, prioritizing this group is critical in providing the support that drives successful outcomes for this group.

Opposite-Sex Couples

Recent decades have seen the rate of father-only earning families decrease and mother-only earning families increase (although this cohort is still small). However, in families with children under the age of 18, dual-earning couples are the most common (U.S. Census Bureau, 2018b). As such, support is most effective in career counseling when consideration is given to the influences of family responsibilities, relationship dynamics, and household support and agreements.

Dual-income families consisting of married opposite-sex couples are generally well-placed financially. The U.S. Census Bureau (2017) reported that, compared to dual-income, opposite-sex couples, unmarried couples earn on average less than 74% of that of the married population (U. S. Census Bureau, 2017). Domestic support, however, has not increased with the rate of earning expectation, and dual-income families are more challenged with issues of well-being and satisfaction. Research has found that work and family roles both influence and are influenced by mental health and personal satisfaction with life (Barnett et al., 1995; Salvatore & Sastre, 2001).

A counselor's role in career counseling may include developing support to negotiate decision making around work and family responsibilities within the context of the household dynamic. Studies investigating spousal decision-making strategies identified the importance of communication on relationship satisfaction (Jackson & Scharman, 2002; Weigel et al., 2006). Communication strategies that facilitate greater satisfaction in spousal relationships include "direct influence" communication, such as bargaining rather than refusing communication; constructive decision making that allows for negotiating short-term support (such as taking time off from work to care for sick children); and long-term support (such as negotiating career commitments to support a partner's pursuits) (Weigel et al., 2006).

Negotiating the division of labor in domestic environments can be challenging for dual-earning families, and a role exists for career counselors to support the process of navigating equity. Bittman et al. (2003) found that relational expectations regarding domestic contributions increased as income earning decreased, and vice versa (Bittman et al., 2003). With consideration of the potential disparity in earning power, however, the traditional "exchange theory," which determines that the partner bringing the greater financial resource to the relationship be responsible for the smaller domestic contribution is disrupted in contemporary relationships.

Navigating parenting responsibilities offers a further challenge for dual-income, opposite-sex families. While women most often maintain the primary parenting role (McBride & Mills, 1993; Offer & Schneider, 2011), research suggests that when fathers undertake primary care responsibilities, they are less likely to have active social support or to be connected with community resources (Zimmerman, 2000), which may be the consequence of enduring stigma connected to traditional social expectations of men's roles in family constructs (Lee & Lee, 2018).

Same-Sex Couples

Although some progress has been made in recent years, same-sex couples are disadvantaged through social, structural, and personal stigmas and discrimination in relation to employment (Wall, 2013). Pollack (1987) warned against presuming that same-sex parents are just the same as other parents or comparing same-sex parents to heterosexual parents, as this heterosexist lens reinforces existing oppression and discounts their experience of social discrimination in both public and private life (Wall, 2013). According to a 2017 U.S. Census report, all-female couples are more likely to have children (23.8%) than all-male couples (8.5%) and less likely than opposite-sex couples (38–39%) (U. S. Census Bureau, 2017). However, same-sex couples are often unable to access the same health insurance benefits as their heterosexual colleagues and are less likely to have the same access to parental leave (Hack, 2010).

Wall (2013) reported that gay family structures were commonly dismissed and shaped into heteronormative structures in not only employment but also school and childcare environments, including assumptions about a parent's partner being a sibling or grandparent rather than a partner or co-parent (Erwin, 2007). Families are also oppressed through lingering myths in social discourse regarding harm to the development of children of gay parents; this stigma can have psychological and social effects on same-sex couples and their families.

U.S. data, however, indicates that gay and lesbian couples are more likely than opposite-sex couples to be employed, to be educated to at least a bachelor's degree level, and to live in a home that they own (U.S. Census Bureau, 2017). This same data shows that all-male couples are the highest earning households, followed by married opposite-sex couples, then all-female couples, and, finally, unmarried opposite-sex couples. Rothblum (2017) draws attention to the working hours undertaken by same-sex couples, speculating that paternalistic values, social discrimination, and anti-maternity sentiments may account for gay men working more part-time roles than heterosexual men and lesbian women working longer hours than heterosexual women (Rothblum, 2017).

Counselors working with people in same-sex relationships will benefit from being sensitive to choices around disclosure, creating an affirmative space, being sensitive to applying a heteronormative lens to family structures, and using inclusive language (Wall, 2013). Further information about the LGBTQ community and career counseling is presented in Chapter 10.

Other Family Compositions

Although the normative U.S. family structure in the common discourse is the nuclear family (Allen & Farnsworth, 1993), that family structure does not reflect the majority of contemporary U.S. families. More common are blended families comprising biological and stepparents, single-parent families, adoptive and fostering relationships, and extended family groups (Sabourin, 2003). The normative family construct; however, is often the foundation for workplace policy and employee benefit frameworks, such as access to leave and health insurance. Griffin (2018) described significant barriers to accessing leave entitlements under the FMLA for grandparents, even as primary caretakers for their new grandchildren (Griffin, 2018).

Informal caring arrangements in nontraditional family structures are also a consideration in career counseling. Research shows significant variations between children participating in formal versus informal childcare. Children in formal childcare centers demonstrate higher achievement in "basic concepts development, problem-solving, mathematical concepts and constructing ability" (Del Boca, 2015), while children in informal (grandparent) childcare perform better in vocabulary tests. In addition, studies highlight positive outcomes regarding family financial safeguarding with informal care arrangements with grandparents and others (Del Boca, 2015; Geurts et al., 2015; Low & Goh, 2015). Informal caring roles have also been found to be undertaken primarily by women (Lacey et al., 2019). Maintaining sensitivity to the potential effect on personal time and economic resources associated with informal or unrecognized family caring relationships and offering time to thoroughly explore the breadth of available options in community resources, appropriate childcare, employment location, and potential hours of employment may enhance the working alliance that career counselors build with the people they are supporting.

Summary

The effect of gender on career counseling is wide reaching and lifelong. The process of circumscription, which often leads individuals to choose careers within familiar gender stereotypes, happens at a very young age and is often maintained throughout the lifetime. Similarly, occupational segregation affects both women and men. This means that often women are underrepresented in management positions and STEM fields. Men also experience occupational segregation, being more likely to be employed as mechanics, plumbers, pilots, and in other stereotypically male fields. There is little research on occupational segregation for individuals who are transgender or gender nonconforming; however, research shows that individuals who are transgender and/or gender nonconforming experience discrimination in the workplace. As such, career counselors must be aware of these differences and their effects on clients.

In addition, issues such as gender-based violence and sexual harassment can also be present in the workplace and at home. Although these issues more commonly affect women, they can also affect men. Any instance of gender-based violence or sexual harassment can have a negative effect on work experience and work productivity. As such, career counselors must have an understanding of the effect of gender-based violence on the lived experiences of their clients.

Finally, the effect of family life on an individual's work life is an important consideration in career counseling. From the limited maternity and paternity leave policies in the United States to the high cost of childcare around the country, some parents may experience significant barriers to employment and career development. These experiences vary depending on family composition—with dual-income couples having different experiences than single-income couples and with single-parent households having higher rates of poverty and increased rigidity in childcare arrangements. Career counselors will benefit from exploring a client's familial and childcare situation to provide further context to their client's life. Ultimately, career counseling should be undertaken with an understanding of the different workplace and home situations that can affect men and women, and they should take gender into account as they counsel their clients.

Discussion Questions

1. Discuss Linda Gottfredson's theory of circumscription and compromise. How will this influence your work with clients?
2. What familial issues affect dual-career couples? How should a career counselor address these issues when working with clients? Is this different for opposite-sex and same-sex, dual-career couples? Why?

3. What familial issues do single parents face, and how can a career counselor support a single parent in his/her career decision-making processes?

4. What issues do individuals who are transgender or gender nonconforming face in the workplace? How will this affect your work as a career counselor?

References

Airbnb. (2017). *Women hosts and Airbnb: Building a global community.* https://www.airbnbcitizen.com/wp-content/uploads/2017/03/Women-Hosts-and-Airbnb_Building-a-Global-Community.pdf

Airbnb. (2018). *Women hosts have earned nearly $20 billion on Airbnb.* https://press.airbnb.com/women-hosts-have-earned-nearly-20-billion-on-airbnb/

Allen, K. R., & Farnsworth, E. B. (1993). Reflexivity in teaching about families. *Family Relations, 42(3),* 351–356.

Ansley, D. (2018). Has the law been unsuccessful in curtailing sexual harassment in organizations? *Contemporary Readings in Law and Social Justice, 10*(2), 79–85.

Antecol, H., Barcus, V. E., & Cobb-Clark, D. (2009). Gender-biased behavior at work: Exploring the relationship between sexual harassment and sex discrimination. *Journal of Economic Psychology, 30*(5), 782–792.

Arber, S., & Ginn, J. (1995). Gender differences in informal caring. *Health & Social Care in the Community, 3*(1), 19–31.

Atwater, L. E., Tringale, A. M., Sturm, R. E., Taylor, S. N., & Braddy, P. W. (2019). Looking ahead: How what we know about sexual harassment now informs us of the future. *Organizational Dynamics, 48*(4), 1–9.

Barnett, R. C., Raudenbush, S. W., Brennan, R. T., Pleck, J. H., & Marshall, N. L. (1995). Change in job and marital experiences and change in psychological distress: A longitudinal study of dual-earner couples. *Journal of Personality and Social Psychology, 69*(5), 839.

Bartley, S. J., Blanton, P. W., & Gilliard, J. L. (2005). Husbands and wives in dual-earner marriages: Decision-making, gender role attitudes, division of household labor, and equity. *Marriage & Family Review, 37*(4), 69–94.

Bergman, M. E., & Henning, J. B. (2008). Sex and ethnicity as moderators in the sexual harassment phenomenon: A revision and test of Fitzgerald et al. (1994). *Journal of Occupational Health Psychology, 13*(2), 152.

Bittman, M., England, P., Sayer, L., Folbre, N., & Matheson, G. (2003). When does gender trump money? Bargaining and time in household work. *American Journal of Sociology, 109*(1), 186–214.

Blau, F. D., & Kahn, L. M. (2017). The gender wage gap: Extent, trends, and explanations. *Journal of Economic Literature, 55*(3), 789–865. https//:doi.org/0.1257/jel.20160995

Bonomi, A. E., Anderson, M. L., Rivara, F. P., & Thompson, R. S. (2009). Health care utilization and costs associated with physical and nonphysical-only intimate partner violence. *Health Services Research, 44*(3), 1052–1067.

Breiding, M. J., & Armour, B. S. (2015). The association between disability and intimate partner violence in the United States. *Annals of Epidemiology, 25*(6), 455–457.

Brescoll, V. L. (2016). Leading with their hearts? How gender stereotypes of emotion lead to biased evaluations of female leaders. *Leadership Quarterly, 27*(3), 415–428.

Brown, C., Linnemeyer, R. M., Dougherty, W. L., Coulson, J. C., Transgrud, H. B., & Farnsworth, I. S. (2005). Battered women's process of leaving: Implications for career counseling. *Journal of Career Assessment, 13*(4), 452–475.

Brown, D., & Brown, D. (2012). *Career information, career counseling, and career development.* Pearson.

Buchanan, T., & Milnes, T. (2019). Pre-career perceptions of gendered work performance: The impact of same-gender referents and work experience on men's evaluation bias. *Gender Issues, 36*(1), 89–112.

Burtle, A., & Bezruchka, S. (2016). Population health and paid parental leave: What the United States can learn from two decades of research. *Healthcare (Basel, Switzerland), 4*(2). https://doi.org/10.3390/healthcare4020030.

Calanca, F., Sayfullina, L., Minkus, L., Wagner, C., & Malmi, E. (2019). Responsible team players wanted: An analysis of soft skill requirements in job advertisements. *EPJ Data Science, 8*(1), 13.

Cannuscio, C. C., Jones, C., Kawachi, I., Colditz, G. A., Berkman, L., & Rimm, E. (2002). Reverberations of family illness: A longitudinal assessment of informal caregiving and mental health status in the Nurses' Health Study. *American Journal of Public Health, 92*(8), 1305–1311.

Carpenter, R. C. (2006). Recognizing gender-based violence against civilian men and boys in conflict situations. *Security Dialogue, 37*(1), 83–103.

Chapman, S. J., & Benis, N. (2017). Ceteris non paribus: The intersectionality of gender, race, and region in the gender wage gap. *Women's Studies International Forum, 65*, 78–86. https://doi.org/https://doi.org/10.1016/j.wsif.2017.10.001

Correll, S. J. (2001). Gender and the career choice process: The role of biased self-assessments. *American Journal of Sociology, 106*(6), 1691–1730. https://doi.org/10.1086/321299

Craig, L., & Sawrikar, P. (2007). *Housework and divorce: The division of domestic labour and relationship breakdown in Australia.* HILDA Conference, University of Melbourne, Australia, 19–20 July 2007. pp. 1–22.

Cruz, A., & Klinger, S. (2011). *Gender-based violence in the world of work: Overview and selected annotated bibliography.* International Labour Office.

Daminger, A. (2019). The cognitive dimension of household labor. *American Sociological Review, 84*(4), 609–633.

Del Boca, D. (2015). *Child care arrangements and labor supply* (Vol. 88074). Inter-American Development Bank.

Dex, S., Scott, J. L., & Plagnol, A. (2012). *Gendered lives: Gender inequalities in production and reproduction.* Edward Elgar Publishing.

Dispenza, F., Watson, L. B., Chung, Y. B., & Brack, G. (2012). Experience of career-related discrimination for female-to-male transgender persons: A qualitative study. *Career Development Quarterly, 60*(1), 65–81.

Dominguez, S., & Watkins, C. (2003). Creating networks for survival and mobility: Social capital among African-American and Latin-American low-income mothers. *Social Problems, 50*(1), 111–135.

Enchautegui, M. E. (2013). *Nonstandard work schedules and the well-being of low-income families.* Washington, DC: Urban Institute. Retrieved from: https://www.urban.org/sites/default/files/publication/32696/412877-Nonstandard-Work-Schedules-and-the-Well-being-of-Low-Income-Families.PDF

Erwin, T. M. (2007). Two moms and a baby: Counseling lesbian couples choosing motherhood. *Women & Therapy, 30*(1–2), 99–149.

European Institute for Gender Equality. (2019a). *The cost of child care in the United States.* https://www.epi.org/child-care-costs-in-the-united-states/

European Institute for Gender Equality. (2019b). *What is gender based violence?* https://eige.europa.eu/gender-based-violence/what-is-gender-based-violence

Evetts, J. (1996). *Gender and career in science and engineering* (Vol. 2). CRC Press.

Fineran, S., & Gruber, J. E. (2009). Youth at work: Adolescent employment and sexual harassment. *Child Abuse & Neglect, 33*(8), 550–559.

Fitzgerald, L. F., Drasgow, F., Hulin, C. L., Gelfand, M. J., & Magley, V. J. (1997). Antecedents and consequences of sexual harassment in organizations: A test of an integrated model. *Journal of Applied Psychology, 82*(4), 578.

Fitzgerald, L. F., Gelfand, M. J., & Drasgow, F. (1995). Measuring sexual harassment: Theoretical and psychometric advances. *Basic and Applied Social Psychology, 17*(4), 425–445.

Fortin, N. M., Bell, B., & Böhm, M. (2017). Top earnings inequality and the gender pay gap: Canada, Sweden, and the United Kingdom. *Labour Economics, 47*, 107–123. https://doi.org/10.1016/j.labeco.2017.05.010

Frear, K. A., Paustian-Underdahl, S. C., Heggestad, E. D., & Walker, L. S. (2019). Gender and career success: A typology and analysis of dual paradigms. *Journal of Organizational Behavior, 40*(4), 400–416.

Gadassi, R., & Gati, I. (2009). The effect of gender stereotypes on explicit and implicit career preferences. *Counseling Psychologist, 37*(6), 902–922.

García-Moreno, C., Pallitto, C., Devries, K., Stöckl, H., Watts, C., & Abrahams, N. (2013). *Global and regional estimates of violence against women: Prevalence and health effects of intimate partner violence and non-partner sexual violence.* World Health Organization.

Gaucher, D., Friesen, J., & Kay, A. C. (2011). Evidence that gendered wording in job advertisements exists and sustains gender inequality. *Journal of Personality and Social Psychology, 101*(1), 109.

Geurts, T., Van Tilburg, T., Poortman, A.-R., & Dykstra, P. A. (2015). Child care by grandparents: Changes between 1992 and 2006. *Ageing & Society, 35*(6), 1318–1334.

Gottfredson, L. S. (1981). Circumscription and compromise: A developmental theory of occupational aspirations. *Journal of Counseling Psychology, 28*(6), 545.

Griffin, J. (2018). *FMLA leave for the birth of a grandchild?* HR Resource. https://www.hrsource.org/maimis/Members/Articles/2018/10/October_23/FMLA_Leave_for_the_Birth_of_a_Grandchild_.aspx

Hack, S. (2010). Domestic partner benefits: Where does your workplace stand? *American Water Works Association, 102*(9), 42.

Hara, H. (2018). The gender wage gap across the wage distribution in Japan: Within-and between-establishment effects. *Labour Economics, 53*, 213–229. https://doi.org/10.1016/j.labeco.2018.04.007

Hardacre, S. L., & Subasic, E. (2018). Whose issue is it anyway? The effects of leader gender and equality message framing on men's and women's mobilisation towards workplace gender equality. *Frontiers in Psychology, 9*, 2497.

Hardie, J. H. (2015). Women's work? Predictors of young men's aspirations for entering traditionally female-dominated occupations. *Sex Roles, 72*: 349–362. doi: 10.1007/s11199-015-0449-1

Hare, D. (2018). Decomposing growth in the gender wage gap in urban China: 1989–2011. *Economics of Transition and Institutional Change, 27*(4). https://doi.org/10.1111/ecot.12222

Harkness, S. (2010). *The contribution of women's employment and earnings to household income inequality: A cross-country analysis.* Retrieved from: https://www.lisdatacenter.org/conference/papers/harkness.pdf

Harper, A., Finnerty, P., Martinez, M., Brace, A., Crethar, H., & Loos, B. ALGBTIC LGBQQIA Competencies Taskforce. (2013). Association for lesbian, gay, bisexual, and transgender issues in counseling competencies for counseling with lesbian, gay, bisexual, queer, questioning, intersex, and ally individuals. *Journal of LGBT Issues in Counseling, 7*(1), 2–43.

He, J. C., Kang, S. K., Tse, K., & Toh, S. M. (2019). Stereotypes at work: Occupational stereotypes predict race and gender segregation in the workforce. *Journal of Vocational Behavior, 115*(103318), 1–17. https://doi.org/10.1016/j.jvb.2019.103318

Hegewisch, A., Liepmann, H., Hayes, J., & Hartmann, H. (2010). Separate and not equal? Gender segregation in the labor market and the gender wage gap. *IWPR Briefing Paper, 377.*

Helwig, A. A. (2001). A test of Gottfredson's theory using a ten-year longitudinal study. *Journal of Career Development, 28*(2), 77–95.

Hirsh, C. E., & Cha, Y. (2008). Understanding employment discrimination: A multilevel approach. *Sociology Compass, 2*(6), 1989–2007. https://doi.org/10.1111/j.1751-9020.2008.00157.x

Hively, K., & El-Alayli, A. (2014). "You throw like a girl": The effect of stereotype threat on women's athletic performance and gender stereotypes. *Psychology of Sport and Exercise, 15*(1), 48–55.

Holland, J. L. (1966). *The psychology of vocational choice: A theory of personality types and model environments.* Blaisdell.

Howansky, K., Wilton, L. S., Young, D. M., Abrams, S., & Clapham, R. (2019). (Trans) gender stereotypes and the self: Content and consequences of gender identity stereotypes. *Self and Identity*, DOI: 10.1080/15298868.2019.1617191.

Hoyt, C. L., & Murphy, S. E. (2016). Managing to clear the air: Stereotype threat, women, and leadership. *Leadership Quarterly, 27*(3), 387–399.

Hüttges, A., & Fay, D. (2015). *Gender influences on career development.* Hogrefe Publishing.

Jackson, A. P., & Scharman, J. S. (2002). Constructing family-friendly careers: Mothers' experiences. *Journal of Counseling & Development, 80*(2), 180–187.

Kennedy, T., Rae, M., Sheridan, A., & Valadkhani, A. (2017). Reducing gender wage inequality increases economic prosperity for all: Insights from Australia. *Economic Analysis and Policy, 55*, 14–24. https://doi.org/10.1016/j.eap.2017.04.003

Klerman, J. A., Daley, K., & Pozniak, A. (2012). *Family and medical leave in 2012: Executive summary.* Abt Associates Inc.

Krumboltz, J. D., Mitchell, A. M., & Jones, G. B. (1976). A social learning theory of career selection. *Counseling Psychologist, 6*(1), 71–81. https://doi.org/10.1177/001100007600600117

Kulik, L., & Rayyan, F. (2003). Wage-earning patterns, perceived division of domestic labor, and social support: A comparative analysis of educated Jewish and Arab-Muslim Israelis. *Sex Roles, 48*(1–2), 53–66.

Lacey, R. E., McMunn, A., & Webb, E. (2019). Informal caregiving patterns and trajectories of psychological distress in the UK Household Longitudinal Study. *Psychological Medicine, 49*(10), 1652–1660.

Langenderfer-Magruder, L., Whitfield, D. L., Walls, N. E., Kattari, S. K., & Ramos, D. (2016). Experiences of intimate partner violence and subsequent police reporting among lesbian, gay, bisexual, transgender, and queer adults in Colorado: Comparing rates of cisgender and transgender victimization. *Journal of Interpersonal Violence, 31*(5), 855–871.

Lee, J. Y., & Lee, S. J. (2018). Caring is masculine: Stay-at-home fathers and masculine identity. *Psychology of Men & Masculinity, 19*(1), 47.

Lee, Y., & Lee, J. Y. (2019). Mediating effects of the meaningfulness of work between organizational support and subjective career success. *International Journal for Educational and Vocational Guidance, 19*(1), 151–172.

LIS. (2009). *Inequality and poverty key figures.* http://www.lisdatacenter.org/

Low, S. S. H., & Goh, E. C. L. (2015). Granny as nanny: Positive outcomes for grandparents providing childcare for dual-Income families. Fact or myth? *Journal of Intergenerational Relationships, 13*(4), 302–319. https://doi.org/10.1080/15350770.2015.1111003

Luekemann, L., & Abendroth, A.-K. (2018). Women in the German workplace: What facilitates or constrains their claims-making for career advancement? *Social Sciences, 7*(11), 214.

Marks, L. R., Harrell-Williams, L. M., Tate, K. A., Coleman, M. L., & Moore, K. (2018). Family influence, critical consciousness, and career calling in women of color. *Career Development Quarterly, 66*(4), 329–343.

McBride, B. A., & Mills, G. (1993). A comparison of mother and father involvement with their preschool age children. *Early Childhood Research Quarterly, 8*(4), 457–477.

McLaughlin, H., Uggen, C., & Blackstone, A. (2017). The economic and career effects of sexual harassment on working women. *Gender & Society, 31*(3), 333–358.

McLean, G., & Bocinski, S. G. (2017). *The economic cost of intimate partner violence, sexual assault, and stalking.* Institute for Women's Policy Research. https://iwpr.org/publications/economic-cost-intimate-partner-violence-sexual-assault-stalking/

Newkirk, K., Perry-Jenkins, M., & Sayer, A. G. (2017). Division of household and childcare labor and relationship conflict among low-income new parents. *Sex Roles, 76*(5–6), 319–333.

Offer, S., & Schneider, B. (2011). Revisiting the gender gap in time-use patterns: Multitasking and well-being among mothers and fathers in dual-earner families. *American Sociological Review, 76*(6), 809–833.

Organization for Economic Co-operation and Development. (2019). *PF2.1 Parental leave systems.* OECD Family Database. http://www.oecd.org/els/family/database.htm

Padovez-Cualheta, L., Borges, C., Camargo, A., & Tavares, L. (2019). An entrepreneurial career impacts on job and family satisfaction. *RAUSP Management Journal, 54*(2), 125–140.

Parsons, F. (1909). *Choosing a vocation.* Houghton, Mifflin and Company.

Pearlman, D. N., Zierler, S., Gjelsvik, A., & Verhoek-Oftedahl, W. (2016). Neighborhood environment, racial position, and risk of police-reported domestic violence: A contextual analysis. *Public Health Reports, 118*(1), 44–58.

Perrone, K. M., Webb, L. K., & Blalock, R. H. (2005). The effects of role congruence and role conflict on work, marital, and life satisfaction. *Journal of Career Development, 31*(4), 225–238.

Perrone, K. M., Wright, S. L., & Jackson, Z. V. (2009). Traditional and nontraditional gender roles and work–family interface for men and women. *Journal of Career Development, 36*(1), 8–24.

Pflum, S. R., Testa, R. J., Balsam, K. F., Goldblum, P. B., & Bongar, B. (2015). Social support, trans community connectedness, and mental health symptoms among transgender and gender nonconforming adults. *Psychology of Sexual Orientation and Gender Diversity, 2*(3), 281.

Pine, B. J., & Gilmore, J. H. (1998). Welcome to the experience economy. *Harvard Business Review, 76*, 97–105.

Pollack, S. (1987). Lesbian mothers: A lesbian-feminist perspective on research. In S. Pollack, & J. Vaughn (ed.s) *Politics of the heart: A lesbian parenting anthology.* Firebrand Books.

Presser, H. B. (2003). Race-ethnic and gender differences in nonstandard work shifts. *Work and Occupations*, *30*(4), 412–439.

Prince, J. P. (2013). Career development of lesbian, gay, bisexual, and transgender individuals. In *Career development and counseling: Putting theory and research to work*, 275–298.

Reid, E. M. (2018). Straying from breadwinning: Status and money in men's interpretations of their wives' work arrangements. *Gender, Work & Organization*, *25*(6), 718–733.

Ridley, E., Rioux, J., Lim, K. C., Mason, D., Houghton, K. F., Luppi, F., & Melody, T. (2005). *Domestic violence survivors at work: How perpetrators impact employment*. Maine Department of Labor & Family Crisis Services.

Rosenbluth, S. C., Steil, J. M., & Whitcomb, J. H. (1998). Marital equality: What does it mean? *Journal of Family Issues*, *19*(3), 227–244.

Rothblum, E. D. (2017). Division of workforce and domestic labor among same-sex couples. In R. Connelly & E. Kongar (Eds.), *Gender and time use in a global context* (pp. 283–303). Springer.

Sabourin, T. C. (2003). *The contemporary American family: A dialectical perspective on communication and relationships*. Sage Publications.

Salvatore, N., & Sastre, M. T. M. (2001). Appraisal of life: "Area" versus "dimension" conceptualizations. *Social Indicators Research*, *53*(3), 229–255.

Savickas, M. L., & Baker, D. B. (2005). The history of vocational psychology: Antecedents, origin, and early development. In W. B. Walsh, M. L. Savickas, & P. J. Hartung (Eds.), In *Handbook of vocational psychology: Theory, research, and practice* (3rd ed., pp. 15–50). Lawrence Erlbaum Associates Publishers.

Schneider, M. S., & Dimito, A. (2010). Factors influencing the career and academic choices of lesbian, gay, bisexual, and transgender people. *Journal of Homosexuality*, *57*(10), 1355–1369.

Sharf, R. S. (1997). *Applying career development theory to counseling*. Brooks.

Smith, C. S., & Hung, L.-C. (2008). Stereotype threat: Effects on education. *Social Psychology of Education*, *11*(3), 243–257.

Smith, D. G., Rosenstein, J. E., Nikolov, M. C., & Chaney, D. A. (2019). The power of language: Gender, status, and agency in performance evaluations. *Sex Roles*, *80*(3–4), 159–171.

Smith, S. G., Zhang, X., Basile, K. C., Merrick, M. T., Wang, J., Kresnow, M.-J., & Chen, J. (2018). *The national intimate partner and sexual violence survey: 2015 data brief–updated release*. National Center for Injury Prevention and Control, Centers for Disease Control and Prevention.

Steele, C. M., & Aronson, J. (1995). Stereotype threat and the intellectual test performance of African Americans. *Journal of Personality and Social Psychology*, *69*(5), 797.

Sumner, S. A., Mercy, J. A., Dahlberg, L. L., Hillis, S. D., Klevens, J., & Houry, D. (2015). Violence in the United States: Status, challenges, and opportunities. *JAMA*, *314*(5), 478–488. https://doi.org/:10.1001/jama.2015.8371

Super, D. E. (1980). A life-span, life-space approach to career development. *Journal of Vocational Behavior*, *16*(3), 282–298.

Tippett, E. C. (2018). The legal implications of the MeToo movement. *Minnesota Law Review*, *103*, 229.

Tyler, L.E. (1977). *Individuality*. Jossey-Bass.

U. S. Census Bureau. (2017). *Household characteristics of opposite-sex and same-sex couple households: 2017 American Community Survey*. https://www2.census.gov/programs-surveys/demo/tables/same-sex/time-series/ssc-house-characteristics/ssex-tables-2017.xlsx

U.S. Census Bureau. (2018a). *Current population survey, March and annual social and economic supplements, 2018 and earlier*. https://www2.census.gov/programs-surveys/demo/tables/families/2018/cps-2018/taba3.xls

U. S. Census Bureau. (2018b). *Current population survey, 2018 annual social and economic supplement: Table A3. Parents with coresident children under 18, by living arrangement, sex, and selected characteristics: 2018*. https://www2.census.gov/programs-surveys/demo/tables/families/2018/cps-2018/taba3.xls

U. S. Department of Labor. (2012). *Fact sheet #28: The Family and Medical Leave Act*. https://www.dol.gov/whd/regs/compliance/whdfs28.pdf

Wall, M. L. (2013). Working with lesbian-headed families: What social workers need to know. *Advances in Social Work*, *14*(2), 433–441.

Weigel, D. J., Bennett, K. K., & Ballard-Reisch, D. S. (2006). Roles and influence in marriages: Both spouses' perceptions contribute to marital commitment. *Family and Consumer Sciences Research Journal, 35*(1), 74–92.

Willness, C. R., Steel, P., & Lee, K. (2007). A meta-analysis of the antecedents and consequences of workplace sexual harassment. *Personnel Psychology, 60*(1), 127–162.

Zadnik, E., Sabina, C., & Cuevas, C. A. (2016). Violence against Latinas: The effects of undocumented status on rates of victimization and help-seeking. *Journal of Interpersonal Violence, 31*(6), 1141–1153.

Zaikman, Y., & Marks, M. J. (2017). Promoting theory-based perspectives in sexual double standard research. *Sex Roles, 76*(7–8), 407–420.

Zimmerman, T. S. (2000). Marital equality and satisfaction in stay-at-home mother and stay-at-home father families. *Contemporary Family Therapy, 22*(3), 337–354.

Zuzanek, J. (1998). Time use, time pressure, personal stress, mental health, and life satisfaction from a life cycle perspective. *Journal of Occupational Science, 5*(1), 26–39.

CHAPTER 10

Career Counseling for LGBT+ Clients

Erica L. Wondolowski, Michelle McKnight-Lizotte, and Emily Lund

CHAPTER OVERVIEW

The changes in legislation and community support over recent decades have improved the rights of members of the LGBT community. However, these individuals still face just as significant an amount of discrimination and mistreatment in today's workforce (Datti, 2009). This chapter will provide an overview of factors that may influence the career counseling process when working with gay, lesbian, bisexual, and transgender clients. Further, this chapter will touch on cultural differences in sexual orientation among multicultural groups, and strategies for counseling gay, lesbian, bisexual, and transgender youth.

CHAPTER OBJECTIVES

After reading this chapter, the student will be able to complete the following:

1. Outline factors general counseling issues for LGBT clients.

2. Discuss ways in which discrimination of sexual minorities in the workplace may occur.

3. Identify cultural differences in sexual orientation among multicultural groups.

4. Identify strategies for counseling LGBT youth.

Sexual orientation and gender identity play a significant role in vocational success and, therefore, should be a consideration for the career counselor, as most employment settings in the United States are characterized by heterosexual ubiquitousness (Gedro, 2009). Heterosexism refers to the predominant worldview where heterosexual (one male and one female) relationships are the "norm" and any other type of intimate relationship or sexual/gender expression is outside the norm (Herek, 2007). U.S. society/culture, the public education system, and the legal system are rooted in heterosexist norms and ideals. For individuals identifying with a sexual orientation/gender identity outside of heterosexuality and cisgenderism (lesbian, gay, bisexual, transgender (LGBT+)), living in a heterosexist society can result in feelings of insignificance, oddness, or invisibility (Majied, 2010). The tension that occurs when one identifies as LGBT+ and lives within a heteronormative society is coined "minority stress" (Meyer, 1995) and has been shown to affect people across their life span (Chen et al., 2010). Minority stress includes experiencing ongoing stressors related to social processes, such as discrimination, bias, and harassment (Meyer, 2003).

Discrimination and ongoing microaggressions within the workplace are common experiences for LGBT+ adults. Microaggressions are "brief and commonplace daily verbal, behavioral, or environmental indignities, whether intentional or unintentional, that communicate hostile, derogatory, or negative slights and insults toward members of oppressed groups" (Nadal, 2008, p. 23). Specific to LGBT+ populations, microaggressions can include the use of incorrect pronouns, heteronormative comments and assumptions, and societal invalidation of experiences of marginalization (Chang & Chung, 2015).

Employees identifying as LGBT+ have been fired, failed to be promoted, harassed, and endured verbal, physical, and emotional abuse in the workplace as a direct result of their orientation/identity (Resnick & Galupo, 2018; Sue et al., 2019). Routinely, gay men face higher levels of discrimination in traditionally male-oriented fields, and lesbians face greater discrimination in traditionally female occupations (Ahmed et al., 2013).

It is reported that 4.5% or approximately 11.3 million individuals in the United States identify as LGBT+ (The Williams Institute, 2019). Further, those identifying as transgender are 6% of the approximately 1.4 million U.S. adults. Specific to vocation, 9% of qualified individuals who identify as LGBT+ are unemployed, 25% make less than $24,000 annually, 15% are uninsured, and 27% are food insecure in comparison to those who do not identify as LGBT+ whose rates are 5%, 18%, 12%, and 27%, respectively (The Williams Institute, 2019).

For those who identify as being LGBT+ and feeling unwelcome at their jobs, approximately 10% report having left a job, while 1 in 5 indicate that they have or are currently searching for a new employer (HRC, 2014). Many work cultures begin with, and are subsequently defined by, those informal communications between colleagues and peers that occur in common areas, such as employee lounges ("water cooler talk"/"the grapevine"). These exchanges serve to provide sources to satisfy relational, social, and support needs within the career realm (Fay, 2011). In an effort to escape the tasks before them at work, employees often discuss their personal lives, including their relationships, social life, and dating. Reportedly, 80% of individuals who do not identify as LGBT+ speak openly about their relationships, social life, and dating weekly, if not daily, at work, while 53% of those who identify as LGBT+ nationwide report intentionally hiding this part of their identities (HRC, 2014). The reasons reported for this intentional nondisclosure include the statement, "It's nobody's business" (64%), as well as fear of making colleagues uncomfortable (38%), the potential for being stereotyped (36%), and the loss of connections or relationships with coworkers (31%) (HRC, 2014, p. 10). It is the overarching workplace culture, however, that dictates these fears and the level to which they are experienced. Indicative of what is found to be acceptable behavior, jokes are also "fair indicators of culture and climate" and may reveal unspoken and symbolic prejudice (HRC, 2014, p. 15)

Legislative History/Current Legislation

Historically, federal and state laws have reflected and furthered heteronormative discrimination and prejudice. With regard to rights for persons who identify as LGBT+, it wasn't until the mid-1960s that the first piece of legislation to even acknowledge a facet of LGBT+ rights (discrimination based on sex) was passed. Although many statutes and laws have been creatively applied, most federal civil rights laws do not currently include explicit protections on the basis of sexual orientation or gender identity. What follows is an abbreviated time line of key legislation and court cases to affect the LGBT+ community.

Title VII of the Civil Rights Act of 1964

The Civil Rights Act (1964) was the first piece of legislation to outlaw discrimination as it pertained to civil rights and labor law on the basis of race, color, religion, sex, or national origin. Title VII applies to all private sector and state/local government employers with 15 or more employees, as well as applicants and civilian employees of federal government agencies. All of these individuals are entitled to rights listed under Title VII but also Executive Order 11478 (2014) as amended, which outlines protections to those in the federal civilian workforce as it pertains to discrimination and harassment on the basis of race, color, religion, sex, national origin, disability, age, sexual orientation (added in 1998), status of a parent (added in 2000), and gender identity (added in 2014; U.S. Equal Employment Opportunity Commission, 2019).

Lawrence v. Texas (2003)

On June 26, 2003, the U.S. Supreme Court deemed American laws prohibiting homosexual activity between consenting adults unconstitutional based on the concepts of personal autonomy and noninterference between consenting adults. The Court further held that consensual sexual conduct was, indeed, protected within substantive due process, as outlined under the 14th Amendment to the U.S. Constitution (U.S. Const. amend. XIV). In doing so, the Court also invalidated sodomy laws in 13 additional states, subsequently making sexual activity between persons of the same-sex legal within every U.S. state and territory.

Obergefell v. Hodges (2015)

Twelve years after the *Lawrence v. Texas* (2003) ruling, the U. S. Supreme Court ruled that the 14th Amendment (U.S. Const. amend. XIV) requires all states and territories to allow for the marriage licensing and recognition of same-sex couples in the landmark *Obergefell v. Hodges* (2015) case. Prior to this ruling, only 37 states and the District of Columbia had legalized gay marriage. Many of the states that resisted same-sex marriage had also gone so far as to enact bans or "Defense of Marriage" Acts. Not only did *Obergefell v. Hodges* (2015) acknowledge the right to same-sex marriage, but it also subsequently opened up the discussion for dependent and spousal benefits as it pertained to health insurance and adoption, among other topics.

Federal Agency Policy

Several federal agencies have also adopted policies that specifically provide protections to those identifying as LGBT+. Agencies such as the Departments of Labor, Education, Justice, and the Office of Personnel Management all invoked policies that directly affected programs such as housing assistance (Equal Access to Housing in HUD Programs Regardless of Sexual Orientation or Gender Identity, 2012), access to health care, and the development of grants solely focused on benefiting the LGBT+ community (HRC, 2019d). Specifically, the Patient Protection and Affordable Care Act (2010) prohibits discrimination on the basis of sex and subsequently has implemented regulations that declare state discrimination against individuals who identify as transgender as per se sex discrimination. The U.S. Department of Health and Human Services has followed suit and implemented regulations interpreting the protection against sex discrimination, including gender identity and sex stereotyping (Nondiscrimination in Health Programs and Activities, 2016). As such, health care providers and health plans cannot adopt categorical exclusions of transition-related care or exclude patients from care based on their gender identity; in addition, they are required to treat individuals consistent with their gender identity, including the use of proper pronouns and access to single-sex facilities.

Title IX of the 1972 Patsy T. Mink Equal Opportunity in Education Act

In education, institutions and educational programs/activities that receive federal financial assistance from the U.S. Department of Education are held to, among others, Title IX of the 1972 Patsy T. Mink Equal Opportunity in Education Act (formally known as the Education Amendments of 1972). Title IX protects individuals from exclusion or discrimination from educational programs or activities on the basis of sex, although exemptions exist for those institutions and programs/activities that are specific to single-sex or the religiously affiliated. In 2010, a "Dear Colleague Letter" (U.S. Department of Education, 2010) was released by the U.S. Department of Education, outlining the protections against gender-based harassment of students, to include same-sex harassment, harassment for "failing to conform" to gender stereotypes or norms, discrimination/harassment against those who identify as transgender or gender nonconforming, and failing to respect the student's gender identity as it pertains to same-sex classes, bathroom access, and pronoun use. Four years later, the U.S. Department of Education (2014) provided guidance during the Obama administration, further explaining that

> Title IX protects all students at recipient institutions from sex discrimination, including sexual violence. Any student can experience sexual violence: from elementary to professional school students; male and female students; straight, gay, lesbian, bisexual and transgender students; part-time and full-time students; students with and without disabilities; and students of different races and national origins. (p. 5)

On February 22, 2017, Battle and Wheeler (2017), acting assistant secretary for civil rights within the U.S. Department of Education and acting assistant attorney general for civil rights for the U.S. Department of Justice, respectively, coauthored a "Dear Colleague Letter" in which Obama-era protections outlined for individuals who identify as transgender and gender nonconforming were rescinded. Citing a failure to contain extensive legal analysis, opportunity for public process, or thorough explanation of how protection of persons who identify as transgender aligns with the expressed language of Title IX, the authors and agencies they represent arguably left those identifying as transgender and gender nonconforming vulnerable to bullying and other violence.

The Equality Act

In the spring of 2019, Representative David N. Cicilline (D-RI-1) introduced H.R. 5 in the U.S. Senate under the name Equality Act (2019). In it, the proposal seeks to provide a nationwide array of protections for individuals who identify as LGBT+ regardless of state law by incorporating the protections into existing federal civil rights laws (e.g., Civil Rights Act of 1964, Fair Housing Act of 1968, Jury Selection and Services Act of 1968, and Equal Credit Opportunity Act of 1974), explicitly including sexual orientation and gender identity as protected characteristics, and expanding protections for other disenfranchised groups and members of all protected classes by further defining key terms (Tran, 2019). One term that is proposed to be more clearly defined is that of public accommodations. Should the Equality Act (2019) be passed, the law would then include public spaces and services, such as retail stores, banks and legal services, and transportation services. While court decisions have generally favored the protection of individuals who identify as LGBT+

under the protected characteristic of sex as outlined in Title VII (Civil Rights Act, 1964), over the years, it has remained that "judicially crafted protections cannot replace explicit federal statutes prohibiting discrimination on the basis of sexual orientation and gender identity" (HRC, 2019d, p. 18).

It remains that individuals who identify as LGBT+ in addition to other members of disenfranchised and marginalized groups cannot feel protected because there is no federal law explicitly outlining under what conditions these individuals are within their rights or that conveys the sentiment that it is safe for them to be wholly true to who they are. As of this writing, although all but five states have laws addressing hate crimes, the variation on who and to what extent they are protected is great (HRC, 2019g). This variation provides little solace to individuals as they change jobs, cross state lines during travel, or move to a different state. Individuals who identify as LGBT+ have no unequivocal protections as they transition from one place of employment to the next. Policies, protections, benefits, and overall work culture can vary drastically between employers and even between positions for the same employer. For individuals who have wed their same-sex spouse, moving may require relinquishing rights afforded to them in one state but not in the one they are moving to.

Discrimination of Sexual Minorities in the Workplace

As of 2019, sexual orientation and gender identity are not federally protected classes; thus, legal protection for LGBT+ individuals in employment varies from state to state or even city to city. In addition, 17 states offer no employment discrimination protection on the basis of sexual orientation or gender identity, 21 states and Washington, DC, forbid employment discrimination on the basis of sexual orientation or gender identity, one state forbids employment discrimination on the basis of sexual orientation but not gender identity, and the remaining seven forbid discrimination for public (government) employees only (HRC, 2019f). Thus the rights of LGBT+ individuals who are seeking employment may vary considerably depending on the location or the sector in which they are seeking employment. This may be a factor in some LGBT+ individuals' career or educational decisions, as they may wish to work in areas of the country in which they have greater legal protections.

In addition to blatant employment discrimination (i.e., being explicitly fired for one's sexual orientation or gender identity), LGBT+ individuals may face more subtle discrimination when applying for jobs. Tilcsik (2011) sent out 3,538 fictitious resumes to 1,769 job postings in 2005. Resumes were either coded as "gay" (i.e., documenting relevant experience in an LGBT+-related organization) or "not gay" (i.e., documenting relevant experience in a non-LGBT+-related but socially or politically progressive organization) but were otherwise of near-identical quality. Resumes that were coded as "not gay" received callbacks at a rate of 11.5% as compared to a 7.2% call back rate for resumes coded as "gay" (Tilcsik, 2011). Furthermore, these significant differences in callback rates were even higher when a job required what could be considered stereotypically "masculine" traits (i.e., aggressiveness, assertiveness, decisiveness, ambition), with resumes coded as "not gay" receiving callbacks at almost 3 times the rate of resumes coded as "gay." Although resumes coded as "gay" still received significantly fewer callbacks when employers were located in a city, county, or state with sexual orientation–related antidiscrimination ordnances, there did appear to be a geographic difference in results. Specifically, states in more historically conservative parts of the country, such as the South and Midwest, had great differences in callback rates between resumes coded as "gay" and "not gay," whereas states located in the eastern and western United States had more equal callback rates for both sets of resumes. Although dated, these findings strongly support that there is tangible discrimination against openly gay job seekers, even in areas with formal antidiscrimination ordinances.

Even if an applicant conceals sexual orientation or gender identity on a resume, there is still the potential for discrimination during or after a job interview. This may be especially true if an individual presents as visibly transgender, stereotypically nonheterosexual, or gender nonconforming. In 2008, Make the Road New York (2010) sent out 24 pairs of equally qualified and trained individuals to interview for retail jobs in Manhattan. Each pair consisted of a gender nonconforming and a gender-confirming individual. In 11 of 24 cases, only the gender-conforming individual was offered a job; in one case, both were offered jobs; in one case, only the gender nonconforming individual was offered a job. These results highlight a clear preferential hiring pattern for gender-conforming individuals that may work against applicants who are likely to be perceived by employers as gender nonconforming and thus potentially LGBT+.

Despite having high rates of postsecondary education, LGBT+ individuals are more likely than heterosexual and cisgender individuals to be unemployed, uninsured, food insecure, and low-income (The Williams Institute, 2019). These differences are even more pronounced for lesbians, LGBT+ people of color, and transgender individuals (Sears & Badgett, 2012), often as a result of experiencing multiple axes of discrimination. Career counselors should remain up-to-date on discrimination laws in their locales and advise clients of their legal rights, if any, as they apply for jobs. They should also provide emotional support to clients who are or have been experiencing employment discrimination, as these experiences can increase isolation, self-stigma, and overall minority stress and thus worsen general well-being (Meyer, 2003).

The Intersectionality of Cultural Differences to Sexual Orientation

Much of the existing research about the experiences of LGBT+ individuals' centers on Caucasian/white people. There is a dearth of research regarding the experiences of LGBT+ individuals from other multicultural groups. The intersection of an individual's cultural identity and sexual orientation is unique for each person, and promoting broad overgeneralizations of specific groups would be a disservice for both the counselor and client; even so, it is imperative that career counselors are introduced to at least some of the cultural characteristics of the following multicultural groups. Research specific to the intersection of one's racial identity and sexual orientation/gender identity/gender expression is very limited at this time. There is evidence that racial minorities experience more discrimination based on their sexual orientation or gender identity that LGBT+ individuals who are white experience (Whitfield et al., 2014). One must be careful not to overemphasize the influence of cultural norms, as it can reinforce harmful stereotypes and place the onus on those within that culture rather than acknowledging the role of systemic racism and marginalization.

The topic of sexual orientation within the context of vocational counseling is only further confounded by the intersectionality of the experiences individuals have within their given culture(s)—that is, how particular cultural backgrounds and customs guide loved ones' receipt of information of nonheteronormative status. Areas such as predominant religious or spiritual affiliations, media and other representation within society, history of successes and failures within the LGBT+ community and a particular culture, and prevalence of health and behavior concerns can all shape the way individuals who identify as LGBT+ are received within their given culture(s). They are, therefore, not only navigating their LGBT+ identity within the workplace but also what it means to be an LGBT+ person within their particular cultural context.

The management of multiple identities may be further complicated if individuals are living in a nation where they are identified as a cultural and/or sexual minority. Pachankis and Bränström (2018) reported that the national laws, policies, and attitudes affecting sexual minorities can affect upward of 60% of country-level variation in life satisfaction and more that 70% of country-level variation in sexual orientation concealment. For individuals within the LGBT+ community who reside within countries that attach a high negative stigma to nonheteronormative behavior, choosing to conceal their sexual orientation served as a protective factor and resulted in greater life satisfaction ratings than those who chose to disclose. It should be expressly stated that the forthcoming information should inform how counselors navigate their relationships and interactions with their clients but that each client should be treated as an individual who may or may not prescribe to all or even certain cultural standards and expectations.

African American/Black Cultures

Roughly 4.6% of the LGBT+ population identifies as African American (AA)/black, with approximately 62% identifying as female and 38% male (The Williams Institute, 2019). LGBT+ AA/black individuals have often experienced discrimination and prejudice continuously over the course of their entire lives. The experience of discrimination and bias often starts in childhood with black children being judged as older than they are, dehumanized, and accused of committing a crime more often than their white peers (Goff et al., 2014). AA/black LGBT+ youth must contend with discrimination and implicit bias on multiple fronts, including their racial identity, sexual orientation, and gender identity and expression.

Homophobia in general is prominent within the AA/black culture and is driven by both political and religious messaging (Barnes, 2013; Kennamer et al., 2000). Religion and spirituality are noted as major sources of social support, personal affirmation, and emotional well-being for AA/black individuals (Miller, 2008). However, overall, AA/black churches are not open and affirming of LGBT+ individuals. LGBT+ AA/black individuals may choose not to come out to avoid rejection by their ethnic and racial communities, as this can cause significant physical and social harm (Wilson & Miller, 2002). To avoid cultural repercussions caused by "coming out," AA/black LGBT+ individuals may avoid seeking mental health care or medical treatment for sexually transmitted diseases. This is especially concerning as AA/black individuals are disproportionately affected by new human immunodeficiency virus (HIV) diagnoses, with AA/black men involved in same-sex relationships having the highest new diagnosis rates (CDC, 2017).

LGBT+ AA/black individuals experience economic disadvantages because of ongoing discrimination, housing insecurity, lack of quality affordable health care, and limited educational opportunities (CDC, 2017). Rates of unemployment (11% vs. 9% non-LGBT+), lack of medical insurance (17% vs. 13% non-LGBT+), and food insecurity (37% vs. 26% non-LGBT+) differ drastically from heterosexual individuals who identify as AA/black (The Williams Institute, 2019). In addition, 36% of the AA/black LGBT+ population makes less than $24,000, whereas of their heterosexual peers, only 29% earn this much. Same-sex couples who identify as AA/black also make approximately $1,500 less than their heterosexual peers (The Williams Institute, 2019).

Latinx Cultures

Of the LGBT+ population that identifies as Latinx, approximately 54% identify as female and 46% male (The Williams Institute, 2019). LGBT+ Latinx individuals also experience economic disadvantages because of ongoing discrimination. Rates of unemployment (9% vs. 8% non-LGBT+) and food insecurity (31% vs. 23% non-LGBT+) differ drastically from heterosexual individuals who identify as Latinx (The Williams Institute, 2019).

The Latino culture of *marianismo* typically encompasses traditional gender-role attitudes for Latinx women in which virginity, fidelity, and family are central (Castillo et al., 2010; Sue et al., 2019). These traditional gender roles, expectations, and norms can cause significant internal discord for gender nonconforming Latinx individuals, especially for Latinx males considering the prominent *machismo* culture (Estrada et al., 2011). *Machismo* is the Latinx culture conceptualization of male gender roles as being strong, dominant, and leading family providers (Sue et al., 2019). Higher levels of *machismo* are correlated with higher levels of prejudice toward LGBT+ individuals and internalized homophobia (Hirai et al., 2014). The Latinx culture can view men who are gay or bisexual as "less than" a man.

In addition to strict cultural expectations regarding gender roles, language can also create difficulties when trying to convey LGBT+ identities or access resources for individuals who do not speak English (HRC, 2018b). For example, direct translations for terms such as *queer* and *genderqueer* are not available for Spanish or Spanish-derived languages, and terms that may be appropriate and respectful in one language may be deemed derogatory or pejorative in another (HRC, 2018b). This can prove to be such a barrier that the Human Rights Campaign Foundation (HRC, 2019e) suggests avoiding LGBT+ terminology altogether, whether negative or positive in connotation.

With over 379,000 Latinx immigrants in the United States identifying as LGBT+, many may face complex barriers as a result of the intersection between ethnic minority status, sexual minority status, and immigration status (Gates, 2013). For example, immigrants face additional barriers seeking health care and obtaining employment, which can result in a lack of testing and treatment of sexually transmitted diseases. Research credits traditional religious beliefs, language barriers, low educational attainment, and traditional gender roles in culture as reasons that expressing an LGBT+ identity as Latinx is difficult (Akerlund & Cheung, 2000). It is important to also consider that those identifying as LGBT+ who are immigrants may have come from a country where identifying as such is considered criminal or the political climate is less accepting than in the United States. As such, risk for those who may have come to the United States without the proper paperwork or on asylum status, facing possible deportation to these countries is particularly dangerous. Immigration status and subsequently an individual's level of acculturation can further affect the beliefs of the family regarding whether sexual orientation is a choice (HRC, 2018b). This should be considered when working with LGBT+ clients who are also in families that have immigrated within recent generations.

Asian Cultures

As with all broad racial and ethnic categories, Asian Americans are a diverse, multicultural group in and of themselves. Asian Americans have ancestry and roots in a wide number of countries, such as Japan, China, India, Laos, Thailand, Malaysia, and the Philippines, and each country has one—and often several—distinct languages and cultures. In addition, people indigenous to the Pacific Islands, such as Samoans, Tongans, and Native Hawaiians, are often categorized under the broader "Asian American and Pacific Islander (API)" label, adding even more diversity of culture, language, and experience to an already diverse label.

Many Asian Americans are immigrants or descendants of recent immigrants. Asian Americans often make up the largest proportion of new U.S. citizens and permanent residents in a given year (Department of Homeland Security, 2018). Thus immigration issues are of key concern to many Asian Americans, including Asian Americans who are LGBT+ (Dang & Hu, 2005), and, as with Latinos, they may experience additional minority stress as a result. Approximately 15% of undocumented and 35% of documented LGBT+ adults are Asian or Pacific Islander (Gates, 2013).

In the United States, individuals who are both API and LGBT+ comprise 4.4% of the population, with 52% identifying as female and 48% identifying as male (The Williams Institute, 2019). In addition, over half of LGBT+ Asian American respondents report that homophobia, transphobia, or both were "a problem" within the Asian American community, although they reported a wide range of experiences with heterosexual and cisgender members of the community, with responses ranging from very negative to mixed to very positive" (Dang & Hu, 2005; HRC, 2019c). Ethnocentrism and racism from other LGBT+ Asian Americans were also reported to be issues by many respondents (Dang & Hu, 2005), again reflecting the fact that the Asian identity label encompasses a wide range of ethnicities, cultures, and experiences.

Those within the United States often have to contend with families and cultural traditions that are not entirely embracing of their identities (HRC, 2019b). Asian traditions are often highly conservative in nature, with high regard for the family line and good name, as well as relatives in their country of origin (if they immigrated to the United States; HRC, 2019a). In addition, the family structure is hierarchical and patriarchal in nature with a strong emphasis on collectivism and allegiance, and strong displays of emotion are looked down upon (Sue et al., 2019). For these reasons, the idea of being shunned or disowned by their families, thrown out of their homes, or having no financial support may prevent LGBT+ API individuals from sharing their sexual orientation or gender identity with family members. Family members may feel guilt or shame regarding their LGBT+ loved ones as a result of an overall lack of knowledge and education on the subject (HRC, 2019a).

Many API individuals who identify as LGBT+ are raised as Buddhist, Christian, Confucian, Hindu, Islamic, or Sikh, each of which has its own evaluation as to what degree identifying as LGBT+ is accepted and affirmed (HRC, 2019a). In addition, as those who comprised the category of API are highly diverse, so too are the languages spoken. Depending on the language spoken, there may not be LGBT+ terminology or concepts available. Several of these cultures have had long-standing terms for individuals who may not fit within Western or otherwise traditionally binary gender structures, such as "*phet thi sam* in Thailand, *meti* in Nepal, the *khanith* in the Arabian Peninsula, *bakla* in the Philippines, and *mak nyah* in Malasia" (HRC, 2019a, p. 52). Some languages, such as Korean, Chinese, and Japanese, do not use gender pronouns, which can prove challenging to individuals who are trying to express that they are gender nonconforming on nonbinary (HRC, 2019a).

Individuals who identify as Asian and LGBT+ are affected by economic insecurity, HIV and health inequity, immigration concerns, and stigma/persecution (HRC, 2019b). Rates of unemployment (7% vs. 5% non-LGBT+), lack of medical insurance (9% vs. 7% non-LGBT+), and food insecurity (8% vs. 6% non-LGBT+) differ drastically from heterosexual individuals who identify as Asian (The Williams Institute, 2019).

Although there is an overall lack in individuals who are API and identify as LGBT+ represented in the media, entertainment, and politics, it has increased in recent years. Often, in dramatized media, API men who are LGBT+ are depicted as sexual or effeminate and the women are depicted as hypersexual (Hamamoto, 1994). Treatment and perception of API individuals who identify as LGBT+ may also stem from morals and values conveyed from the country of origin. For example, recently, the Communist government in China under President Xi Jinping banned the portrayal of same-sex relationships, going so far as to censor television and online access (Griffiths, 2019). In March of 2019, most mentions of homosexuality were removed from the biodrama *Bohemian Rhapsody*, which follows the life of Queen lead singer Freddie Mercury, who is known to have been gay (Griffiths, 2019).

Native American/First Nations Peoples

Native American cultures often have a complex and multilayered relationship with sexual orientation and gender identity because of the mixing of colonial influences and cultural and human oppression with traditional beliefs and practices. First, it should be acknowledged that Native American cultures are far from a monolith and that even individuals from the same tribal background may have differing views on sexual orientation and gender identity. That being said, there are some current and common pan-Indian issues related to sexual orientation and gender identity that are worth discussing. Chief among them is the term/concept of "two spirit." The two-spirit term was coined by Native American activists in the 1990s as an affirming pan-Indian term to describe Native American individuals who are nonheterosexual, noncisgender, non-gender-confirming, or some combination thereof, as well as to recognize the traditional issue of nonbinary (i.e., beyond male and female) gender and sex classifications and identities in some traditional tribal cultures (Jacobs et al., 1997).

The term nonbinary is anti-colonialist in nature and meant to encompass the unique experience of being both Native American and LGBT+ (Jacobs et al., 1997), addressing both discrimination from within and outside of tribal culture. The term has become popular in Native American LGBT+ communities and may be used in addition to or in lieu of another Western LGBT+ identity, such as "gay," "lesbian," "bisexual," or "transgender." Often, the decision to use this term reflects a strong pride and sense of identification with both one's sexual orientation or gender identity and one's identity as a Native American or a member of a specific tribe or tribes (Jacobs et al., 1997). Despite the embracing of the two-spirit identity by many Native American LGBT+ individuals, they may still face unwelcoming or discriminatory attitudes and behaviors from within or outside their culture, and these feelings of rejection may be heightened by alienation from family members who are members of nonaffirming religious institutions, as well as overall racism and erasure from nonindigenous communities.

Native Americans make up only about 1% to 2% of the U.S. population (National Congress of American Indian, n.d.; U.S. Census Bureau, 2018) and have faced significant historical trauma that continues to affect Native American communities today (Balsam et al., 2004). In addition, Native American individuals experience high rates of current trauma (e.g., childhood physical and sexual abuse), often resulting in a combination of both personal and historical trauma that increases the risk of substance abuse, depression, and post-traumatic stress disorder among Native Americans (Balsam et al., 2004). Two-spirit or LGBT+ youth may face additional victimization because of their sexual orientation, gender identity, or gender expression, which may compound already-present historical and interpersonal trauma. Thus it is vital that counselors working with LGBT+ Native American youth be aware of the potential effects of both interpersonal and historical trauma and use a trauma-informed and culturally aware counseling model when possible. Because both tribal cultural norms and individual levels of acculturation and identification differ greatly among Native American youth, any culturally responsive intervention modification should be done after gaining a thorough understanding of the client's specific tribal background and identity.

In the United States, Native Americans who identify as LGBT+ comprise 5.6% of the population (The Williams Institute, 2019). Individuals who are both Native American and LGBT+, much like other disenfranchised cultures, are affected by economic insecurity and health inequity. Rates of unemployment (14% vs. 8% non-LGBT+), lack of medical insurance (23% vs. 17% non-LGBT+), and food insecurity (31% vs. 29% non-LGBT+) differ drastically from heterosexual individuals who identify as Native American and are greater overall than those of other marginalized cultures (The Williams Institute, 2019). In popular media, entertainment, and politics, representation of Native Americans who identify as LGBT+ is near nonexistent. Historically, Native Americans are portrayed as heterosexual, cisgender, shamans, wise men, sidekicks, princesses, and matriarchs (White, 2012). It is important that if a counselor is working with a large Native American population, such as on or near a reservation, they incorporate suggestions and guidance from tribal leaders and counseling professionals who are also members of that tribal as one method of culturally adapting interventions to better align with that community's cultural norms and beliefs (Morsette et al., 2009).

Counseling LGBT+ Youth

Many career decisions are finalized in late adolescence or early adulthood. Because of the heterosexism in society, LGBT+ youth do not have the same identity development process as heterosexual youth (Gedro, 2009). Because of societal heterosexism, LGBT+ youth experiencing same-sex attraction or not identifying with their biological sex can feel embarrassed or alienated from their peers. When compared to their heterosexual peers, LGBT+ students are more likely to be victimized, bullied, and report their school environment as "unsupportive" (Kann et al., 2016). In a national school climate survey, 81.9% of LGBT+ students reported being verbally harassed and 38.3% reported being physically harassed as a result of their sexual orientation (Kosciw et al., 2012).

In general, elevated rates of victimization among LGBT+ individuals continue across the life span (Katz-Wise & Hyde, 2012). These continuous experiences of both subtle and blatant stigma, discrimination, victimization, and harassment have been shown to be strongly linked to greater depression, suicidality, and substance use in LGBT+ individuals (Burton et al., 2013; Lea et al., 2014; Plöderl et al., 2014). If not adequately addressed, these conditions could negatively affect the ability of LGBT+ youth to perform to their highest potential in postsecondary education and employment. Thus when considering the amount of minority stress experienced by LGBT+ youth, a career counselor may need to guide them in developing coping strategies and identifying support within the family, school, peer, and community (Dispenza et al., 2016).

LGBT+ youth experience higher levels of career indecision and decreased career maturity, often because of the fact that their energy must be more focused on their status as a sexual minority, as well as a lack of social support (Schmidt & Nilsson, 2006). LGBT+ youth may struggle to balance their career interests with their sexual identities and may feel unsafe discussing this conflict openly (Chen & Keats, 2016). LGBT+ youth may also stereotype occupations as being either LGBT+-friendly or unfriendly, thereby limiting their actual career interests to those they perceive as being open and affirming, thus choosing a career they feel is "safe" over one they may be interested and talented in (Pope et al., 2004). In describing the effect of the social process on individuals who identify as LGBT+, Lindley (2006) stated, "Beyond the direct negative consequences of discrimination, LGB individuals must devote considerable energy to issues not faced by heterosexuals, such as how to manage their sexual identity at work and how to react to societal messages regarding what are and what are not 'acceptable' occupations for lesbians or gay men" (p. 152). Career counselors must be aware that interest inventories may not be (and are very likely not) normed for LGBT+ youth and may have a heterosexist testing bias. For example, the Meyers–Briggs Type Indicator and the Self-Directed Search have been criticized for emphasizing and reinforcing sex-role and sex-orientation stereotypes (Pope et al., 2004). Thus the results of standardized measures that have not been specifically normed for LGBT+ youth should be taken with caution and combined with other sources of information (e.g., interviews, observations, work samples).

Evidence-Based Practices for the LGBT+ Community

Research indicates that counselors who work with the LGBT+ community benefit from the following: the ability to appraise prejudices/biases and identify risk factors, awareness of the many forms of internalized oppression; possession of adequate medical knowledge; provision of advocacy in the forms of community and social support; acting in an ethical manner; awareness of federal and state laws; consideration of the political, social, and physical environments in which clients live; rational insight into one's own stereotypes and biases; familiarity with LGBT+ resources; and provision of validation to their clients (Dispenza et al., 2012; Dispenza et al., 2017; Levitt et al., 2009). Specific to individuals who identify as transgender or gender nonconforming, counselors often established stronger rapport and saw greater success rates when they were aware of the effect of the current stage of transition a client was in regarding career development (dickey et al., 2016; Sangganjanavanich, 2009); didn't equate the client's experiences to those who identify as lesbian, gay, or bisexual (McCullough et al., 2017); and used appropriate language and terminology, including preferred gender pronouns and names (ACA, 2010).

Disclosure

For heterosexual, cisgender workers, it is often commonplace to discuss families, spouses, and external social lives while at work in efforts to create collegial relationships. For employees who identify as LGBT+, discussing any of these topical issues may inadvertently disclose their sexual orientation and/or gender identity, subsequently positioning them as possible targets of discrimination and prejudice. A split between the private and public self is consequently created as a survival tactic and coping mechanism for many LGBT+ workers (Ferfolja & Hopkin, 2013; Köllen, 2015). Not discussing them, however, can create feelings of isolation and stress while also decreasing overall workplace satisfaction (Cole, 2006; Velez et al., 2013).

When working with this population, it is recommended that counselors assist their clients in exploring the various outcomes that could result following potential disclosure, whether it be during the pre-employment interview or following employment (Dalgin & Bellini, 2008; Dispenza et al., 2018). Once outcomes are identified, the counselor can then aid the client in developing ways of coping in the event that the disclosure brings about negative or adverse responses in the workplace. Using role play within the counseling environment to practice disclosure, as well as responding to outcomes following disclosure, is recommended (Dalgin & Bellini, 2008; Dispenza et al., 2018).

Coping Strategies

Counselors should use a strengths-based approach with LGBT+ clients, while also acknowledging the potential challenges they may face and establish coping strategies that integrate them (Dispenza & Pullman, 2017). Such strengths may include actively defining themselves, being aware of oppression, maintaining social supports, embracing self-worth, and cultivating hope for the future (Singh et al., 2011). Specifically, clients should be encouraged to examine their choice of vocation, determine identity management techniques, and establish coping strategies by which they can address discrimination that may occur in the workplace. Furthermore, clients should be assisted in identifying resources specific to the LGBT+ community, which may be offered through their employers and/or the greater community (Chung et al., 2009). Empowerment techniques and interventions might also prove useful in examining how heteronormative influences permeate their lives, recognizing the internalization of heterosexism, and coping with the subsequent effect on their overall well-being (Dispenza & Pullman, 2017).

Considering the high impact of prejudice, stigma, and heterosexism, it is essential that counselors aid clients in identifying, implementing, and enriching their coping and self-regulation resources (Dispenza et al., 2016). Research cautions counselors from insisting that clients employ overly self-affirming or assertive coping strategies and, instead, encourages counselors to assist clients in establishing an awareness of, and balance between, healthy activism and healthy withdrawal/replenishing (Chung et al., 2009; Levitt et al., 2009). If a client is pushed to be assertive and active for the cause beyond their comfort level, it could render the client emotionally and physically vulnerable and be viewed as the counselor's insensitivity toward individual identity development and cultural teachings.

Theories

Historically, theoretical approaches, such as the systems theory framework (McMahon, 2011), life-span, life-space approach (Super, et al., 1996), and theory of work adjustment (Dawis & Lofquist, 1984) have been broadly applied to clients seeking career counseling. Although each of these maintain aspects that are helpful with marginalized populations, none are specifically developed for direct application to these groups. When working with individuals who identify as LGBT+, counselors should choose and use interventions in a methodical and intentional manner that addresses clients' functioning within social and interpersonal relationships, emotional regulation, and cognitive frameworks (Dispenza & Pullman, 2017). More recently, research has indicated efficacy with a number of career counseling approaches when applied to clients who identify as LGBT+.

Social Justice Counseling

The social justice counseling approach encourages counselors to consider the client holistically, looking at the macro-, micro-, and mesolevels when conducting assessments, diagnosing, and engaging in treatment (Sue et al., 2019). Acknowledging the significant role that the system can play as a determinate in the client's life, social justice counseling finds that failure to consider systemic and sociopolitical influences often results in attribution error. Furthermore, this approach concedes that organizations are quite powerful and often steadfast in their positions; any challenge to the status quo could result in stern punitive actions. This approach is advocacy focused, seeking to produce "conditions that allow for equal access and opportunity; reducing or eliminating disparities in education, health care, employment, and other areas that lower the quality of life for affected populations," and as such, the counselor has several additional roles, such as consultant, change agent, and community worker (Sue et al., 2019, p. 90). For counselors to be considered culturally competent, Sue et al. (2019) posited that they should be able to intervene effectively with the client, professional procedural and ethical codes, institutional procedures, and social policy.

Relational Approach

Schultheiss's (2003) relational approach to career counseling is founded on the premise that career development is directly affected by the client's relational context. Specifically, the counselor seeks to assist clients in drawing from relationships with others as a source of experience and strength to apply this to the career development process. Fisher et al. (2011) report that when applied to women who identify as sexual minorities, family and career supports positively related to individual career aspirations. The working alliance within the counseling relationship may further serve as a proxy for strong and secure social relationships by which the client develops confidence and personal strength (Speciale & Scholl, 2019).

When counselors support clients as they develop greater insight into relational goals and the effect these goals have within multiple areas of their lives, clients subsequently develop a more expansive repertoire of resources to be accessed in the event of obstacles. Counselors should facilitate the connecting of clients with supportive communities so as to combat any feelings of isolation that may arise in relation to their sexual identities within a heteronormative society (Prince, 2013).

Minority Stress Framework

The minority stress framework is based on the knowledge that stigma, prejudice, and subsequent discrimination experienced by the client cultivates a social environment that is both hostile and stressful. As a direct result, the client's mental health is negatively affected (Meyer, 2003). With applications for multiple marginalized populations, this model works to examine the client's experience of prejudice, expectations within the context of rejection, motivations for hiding and concealment, and the process of internalized homophobia. This information can then be used to identify the direct effect on the client's career development process and overall emotional and physical well-being (Chan, 2019).

Dispenza (2015) emphasized the importance of developing techniques geared at navigating minority stress-related issues at work; enacting coping resources when addressing a client's perception of anxiety and stigmatization; identifying and acknowledging the effect of outside influences, such as the family, on the client; and exploring how each of the identities the client aligns with has shaped not only their career trajectory but also their life overall (Dispenza, 2011; Dispenza, 2015; Dispenza et al., 2016).

Career Assessment Tools

Currently, there are hundreds of assessment instruments available to aid in career counseling: interest and personality inventories, ability and aptitude tests, environmental assessments, and state and trait measures, among others (Gysbers et al., 2014). In the development phase of these various tests and measures, developers subject the assessments to stringent validity and reliability trials whereby ensuring that the assessment examines what it is meant to and that it does so consistently over time. Specific to the LGBT+ community, counselors must be made aware that "often the norming and psychometric development research indicates that the assessment measures have not been used with significant numbers of individuals who belong to underrepresented groups" (Gysbers et al., 2014, p. 226). Subsequently, there is little known regarding the validity of these instruments when used with individuals who identify as LGBT+, for example. Counselors should proceed with caution when interpreting results, seek to confirm results of one assessment with the results of another, and remain open to finding new measures or approaches to employ with clients. Furthermore, assessment tools and the given results are meant to guide further exploratory conversations with our clients rather than be prescriptive, and results should be interpreted within the context of the client's worldview.

Summary

When working with clients who identify as LGBT+, it is essential that the counselor/professional acknowledge the role of this characteristic in seeking, applying for, and maintaining employment. Historical oppression and current discrimination can significantly affect the client, often resulting in lowered engagement and perceived support within the workplace. Only within the last 60 years have individuals who identify as LGBT+ received protections through government policy and legislation. For those who identify as transgender or gender nonconforming, protections have only been enacted since 2010 where those who identify as transgender received protections based on *per se* sex discrimination with the passage of the Patient Protection and Affordable Care Act (2010).

Despite government initiatives to institute equality, these directives were, and continue to be, met with significant resistance. As of 2019, 15+ states offer no employment discrimination protection on the basis of sexual orientation or gender identity. As individuals who identify as LGBT+ seek job opportunities, they must consider that policies, protections, benefits, and overall work culture will vary not only from state to state, but from employer to employer, simply due to their sexual orientation/gender identity. Research indicates that employers tend to hire those individuals who present as gender nonconforming (Make the Road New York, 2010) and homosexual (Tilcsik, 2011) at significantly lower levels than their heterosexual and cisgender counterparts. Subsequently, LGBT+ individuals are more likely than heterosexual and cisgender individuals to be unemployed, uninsured, food insecure, and low-income (The Williams Institute, 2019).

For the career counselor, it is also imperative that an appreciation for the intersectionality between the client's cultural identity and sexual orientation/gender identity be cultivated. While broad overgeneralizations could prove detrimental to the rapport building and service-delivery processes, knowledge pertaining to the differing worldview of individuals based upon this intersectionality can provide substantial insight into their lived experience and related concerns and fears. Intersectionality can also extend to LGBT+ youth who are often navigating their sexual/gender identities in addition to their vocational aspirations.

In addition to having a basic foundation of the sociopolitical environment in which the client exists, it is essential that the career counselor employ an established theory to ensure that evidence-based practices are implemented correctly and effectively. Theories such as social justice counseling (Sue et al., 2019), Schultheiss's (2003) relational approach, and the minority stress framework (Meyer, 2003) are three such theories. The career counselor also needs be wary when administering and interpreting assessments and other standardized measures as these tools often are not specifically normed for LGBT+ individuals and could provide inaccurate results due to the uniqueness of the group. It is reported that interventions pertaining to exploring the various outcomes that could occur following potential identity or orientation disclosure (Dalgin & Bellini, 2008; Dispenza et al., 2018), role playing conversations where the client communicates their sexual orientation/gender identity, assisting in the examination of vocational decision making, identifying identity management techniques, and establishing effective and healthy coping mechanisms (Chung et al., 2009) are all evidence-based methods that have shown to be helpful with this particular population. It is imperative, however, that counselors select and implement interventions in a methodical and intentional manner where clients' functioning within social and interpersonal relationships, emotional regulation, and cognitive frameworks are considered (Dispenza & Pullman, 2017).

Discussion Questions

1. You have a new client who discloses to you that they are gay. They would like your advice about being "out" as they search for a new job. What factors might you discuss with them in this counseling relationship?
2. One facet to being considered a culturally competent clinician (whether it be for the LGBT+ culture, racial/ethnic cultures, or otherwise) is staying current regarding significant issues that may affect them. Using the information provided in the chapter, explore and provide examples of how interventions with clients who identify as LGBT+ in the United States may have differed and evolved over the past several decades.

References

Ahmed, A. M., Anderson, L., & Hammarstedt, M. (2013). Are gay men and lesbians discriminated against in the hiring process? *Southern Economic Journal, 79*(3), 565–85. https://doi.org/10.4284/0038-4038-2011.317

Akerlund, M., & Cheung, M. (2000). Teaching beyond the deficit model: Gay and lesbian issues among African Americans, Latinos, and gay Asian Americans. *Journal of Social Work Education, 36*(2), 279–93. https://doi.org/10.1080/10437797.2000.10779008

American Counseling Association (ACA). (2010). Competencies for counseling with transgender clients. *Journal of LGBT Issues in Counseling, 4*, 135–159. https://doi.org/10.1080/15538605.2010.524839

Balsam, K. F., Huang, B., Fieland, K. C., Simoni, J. M., & Walters, K. L. (2004). Culture, trauma, and wellness: A comparison of heterosexual and lesbian, gay, bisexual, and two-spirit Native Americans. *Cultural Diversity and Ethnic Minority Psychology, 10*(3), 287–301. https://doi.org/10.1037/1099-9809.10.3.287

Barnes, S. L. (2013). To welcome or affirm: Black clergy views about homosexuality, inclusivity, and church leadership. *Journal of Homosexuality, 60*, 1409–1433. https://doi.org/10.1080/00918369.2013.819204

Battle, S., & Wheeler, II, T. E. (2017). *Dear colleague letter.* https://assets.documentcloud.org/documents/3473560/Departments-of-Education-and-Justice-roll-back.pdf

Burton, C. M., Marshal, M. P., Chisolm, D. J., Sucato, G. S., & Friedman, M. S. (2013). Sexual minority-related victimization as a mediator of mental health disparities in sexual minority youth: A longitudinal analysis. *Journal of Youth and Adolescence, 42*(3), 394–402. https://doi.org/10.1007/s10964-012-9901-5

Castillo, L. G., Perez, F. V., Castillo, R., & Ghosheh, M. R. (2010). Construction and initial validation of the marianismo beliefs scale. *Counselling Psychology Quarterly, 23*(2), 163–175. https://doi.org/10.1080/09515071003776036

Centers for Disease Control [CDC]. (2017, February). *HIV among African Americans* [Fact Sheet]. https://www.cdc.gov/nchhstp/newsroom/docs/factsheets/cdc-hiv-aa-508.pdf

Chan, C. D. (2019). Broadening the scope of affirmative practices for LGBTQ+ communities in career services: Applications from a systems theory framework. *Career Planning and Adult Development Journal, 35*(1), 6–21.

Chang, T. K., & Chung, Y.B. (2015). Transgender microaggressions: Complexity of the heterogeneity of transgender identities. *Journal of LGBT Issues in Counseling, 9*(3), 217–234. https://doi.org/10.1080/15538605.2015.1068146

Chen, C. P., & Keats, A. (2016). Career development and counselling needs of LGBTQ high school students. *British Journal of Guidance & Counselling, 44*(5), 576–588. https://doi.org/ 10.1080/03069885.2016.1187709

Chen, E. C., Androsiglio, R., & Ng, V. (2010). Minority stress and health of lesbian, gay, and bisexual individuals: A developmental-contextual perspective. In J. G. Ponterotto, J. Manuel Casas, L. A. Suzuki, & C. M. Alexander (Eds.), *Handbook of multicultural counseling* (3rd ed., pp. 531–544). Sage.

Chung, Y. B., Williams, W., & Dispenza, F. (2009). Validating work discrimination and coping strategy models for sexual minorities. *Career Development Quarterly, 58(2)*, 162–170. https://doi.org/10.1002/j.2161-0045.2009.tb00053.x

Civil Rights Act of 1964, 42 U.S.C. § 7, § 2000e *et seq* (1964). https://www.eeoc.gov/laws/statutes/titlevii.cfm.

Cole, S. W. (2006). Social threat, personal identity, and physical health in closeted gay men. In A. M. Omoto, H. S. Kurtzman, & S. Howard (Eds.), *Sexual orientation and mental health* (pp. 245–267). American Psychological Association. https://doi.org/10.1037/11261-012

Dalgin, R. S., & Bellini, J. (2008). Invisible disability disclosure in an employment interview: Impact on employers' hiring decisions and views of employability. *Rehabilitation Counseling Bulletin, 52(1)*, 6–15. https://doi.org/10.1177/0034355207311311

Dang, A., & Hu, M. (2005). *Asian Pacific American lesbian, gay, bisexual and transgender people: A community portrait. A report from New York's Queer Asian Pacific Legacy Conference* [Paper presentation]. National Gay and Lesbian Task Force Policy Institute, New York, NY, United States. http://aapidata.com/wp-content/uploads/2015/05/lgbt-2004-apa-portrait.pdf

Dawis, R. V., & Lofquist, L. H. (1984). *Psychological theory of work adjustment. An individual-differences model and its applications.* University of Minnesota Press.

Department of Homeland Security (2018). *2017 yearbook of immigration statistics.* Author. https://www.dhs.gov/immigration-statistics/yearbook/2017

dickey, l. m., Walinsky, D., Rofkahr, C., Richardson-Cline, K., & Juntunen, C. (2016). Career decision self-efficacy of transgender people: Pre-and post-transition. *Career Development Quarterly, 64*(4), 360–372. https://doi.org/10.1002/cdq.12071

Dispenza, F. (2011). *Minority stress and life role saliency among sexual minorities* [Doctoral dissertation, Georgia State University]. ProQuest Dissertations and Theses.

Dispenza, F. (2015). An exploratory model of proximal minority stress and the work-life interface for men in same-sex, dual-earner relationships. *Journal of Counseling and Development, 93*, 321–332. https://doi.org/10.1002/jcad.12030

Dispenza, F., Brown, C., & Chastain, T. E. (2016). Minority stress across the career-lifespan trajectory. *Journal of Career Development, 43*(2), 103–115. https://doi.org/0.1177/0894845315580643

Dispenza, F., Kumar, A., Standish, J., Norris, S., & Procter, J. (2018). Disability and sexual orientation disclosure on employment interview ratings: An analogue study. *Rehabilitation Counseling Bulletin, 61*(4), 244–255. https://doi.org/10.1177/0034355217725888

Dispenza, F., & Pulliam, N. (2017). Career development. In C. B. Roland & L. D. Burlew (Eds.), *Counseling LGBTQ adults through the lifespan* [pp. 36–39]. https://www.counseling.org/docs/default-source/default-document-library/counselinglgbtq-adults-throughout-the-life-span-final.pdf?sfvrsn=2

Dispenza, F., Varney, M., & Golubovic, N. (2017). Counseling and psychological practices with sexual and gender minority persons living with chronic illnesses/disabilities (CID). *Psychology of Sexual Orientation and Gender Diversity, 4*(1), 137–142. https://doi.org/10.1037/sgd0000212

Dispenza, F., Watson, L. B., Chung, Y. B., & Brack, G. (2012). Experience of career-related discrimination for female-to-male transgender persons: A qualitative study. *Career Development Quarterly, 60*(1), 65–81. https://doi.org/10.1002/j.2161-0045.2012.00006.x

Equal Access to Housing in HUD Programs Regardless of Sexual Orientation or Gender Identity, 77 FR 5661 (2012).

Equal Credit Opportunity Act of 1974, 15 U.S.C. § 1691 *et seq.* (1974).

Equality Act, H.R. 5, 116 Cong. (2019).

Estrada, F., Rigali-Oiler, M., Arciniega, G. M., & Tracey, T. J. (2011). Machismo and Mexican American men: An empirical understanding using a gay sample. *Journal of Counseling Psychology, 58*, 358. https://doi.org/10.1037/a0023122

Exec. Order No. 11478, 79 FR 42971 (2014).

Fair Housing Act of 1968, 42 U.S.C. 3601 (1968).

Fay, M. J. (2011). Informal communication of co-workers: A thematic analysis of messages. *Journal of Qualitative Research in Organizations and Management, 6*(3), 212–229. https://doi.org/10.1108/17465641111188394

Ferfolja, T., & Hopkin, L. (2013). The complexities of workplace experience for lesbian and gay teachers. *Critical Studies in Education, 54*(3), 311–324. https://doi.org/10.1080/17508487.2013.794743

Fisher, L. D., Gushue, G. V., & Cerrone, M. T. (2011). The influences of career support and sexual identity on sexual minority women's career aspirations. *Career Development Quarterly, 59*(5), 441–454. https://doi.org/10.1002/j.2161-0045.2011.tb00970.x

Gates, G. J. (2013*). LGBT adult immigrants in the United States.* The Williams Institute.

Gedro, J. (2009). LGBT career development. *Advances in Developing Human Resources, 11*(1), 54–66. https://doi.org/10.1177/1523422308328396

Goff, P. A., Jackson, M. C., Di Leone, B.A.L., Culotta, C. M., & DiTomasso, N. A. (2014). The essence of innocence: Consequences of dehumanizing black children. *Journal of Personality and Social Psychology, 106*, 526–545. https://doi.org/10.1037/a0035663

Griffiths, J. (2019). *Can you be gay online in China? Social media companies aren't sure.* CNN.com. https://www.cnn.com/2019/04/17/tech/weibo-china-censorship-lgbtintl/index.html

Gysbers, N. C., Heppner, M. J., & Johnston, J. A. (Eds.). (2014). *Career counseling: Holism, diversity, and strengths* (4th ed.). American Counseling Association.

Hamamoto, D. (1994). *Monitored peril: Asian Americans and the politics of TV representation.* University of Minnesota Press. https//doi.org/0.2307/2760917

Herek, G. M. (2007). Confronting sexual stigma and prejudice: Theory and practice. *Journal of Social Issues, 63*(4), 905–925. https://doi.org/10.1111/josi.2007.63.issue-4

Hirai, M., Winkel, M., & Popan, J. (2014). The role of machismo in prejudice toward lesbians and gay men: Personality traits as moderators. *Personality and Individual Differences, 70*, 105–110. https://doi.org/10.1016/j.paid.2014.06.028

Human Rights Campaign Foundation (HRC). (2014). *The cost of the closet and the rewards of inclusion: Why the workplace environment for LGBT people matters to employers.* https://assets2.hrc.org/files/assets/resources/Cost_of_the_Closet_May2014.pdf?_ga=2.1872049.1094148138.1567376294-1372065148.1567376294

Human Rights Campaign Foundation (HRC). (2018a). *Coming out: Living authentically as LGBTQ Asian and Pacific Islander Americans.* https://assets2.hrc.org/files/assets/resources/HRC-Coming_Out-API-FINAL-web-2018.pdf?_ga=2.235190273.1014635541.1568513778-1372065148.1567376294

Human Rights Campaign Foundation (HRC). (2018b). *Coming out: Living authentically as LGBTQ Latinx Americans.* https://assets2.hrc.org/files/assets/resources/HRC_Coming_Out_Latinx.pdf?_ga=2.28714812.1400074442.1567527260-1372065148.1567376294

Human Rights Campaign Foundation (HRC). (2018c). *LGBTQ working people of color need paid leave.* https://assets2.hrc.org/files/assets/resources/HRC-PaidLeave-POCReport-FINAL.pdf?_ga=2.70926992.1207782396.1567441179-440475687.1563979797

Human Rights Campaign Foundation (HRC). (2019a). *2019 LGBTQ Asian and Pacific Islander youth report.* https://assets2.hrc.org/files/assets/resources/FINAL-API-LGBTQ-YOUTHREPORT.pdf?_ga=2.54375592.1014635541.1568513778-1372065148.1567376294

Human Rights Campaign Foundation (HRC). (2019b). *Being Asian/Pacific Islander & LGBTQ.* https://www.hrc.org/resources/being-asian-pacific-islander-lgbtq-an-introduction

Human Rights Campaign Foundation (HRC). (2019c). *Coming out issues for Asian Pacific Americans.* https://www.hrc.org/resources/coming-out-issues-for-asian-pacific-americans

Human Rights Campaign Foundation (HRC). (2019d). *Inclusive interpretations of sex discrimination law.* https://assets2.hrc.org/files/assets/resources/HRC-SexDiscriminationReport-Final.pdf?_ga=2.83882067.4954558.1568476021-440475687.1563979797

Human Rights Campaign Foundation (HRC). (2019e). *Language and coming out issues for Latinxs.* https://www.hrc.org/resources/language-and-coming-out-issues-for-latinas-and-latinos

Human Rights Campaign Foundation (HRC). (2019f). *State maps of laws and policies: Employment.* https://www.hrc.org/state-maps/employment

Human Rights Campaign Foundation (HRC). (2019g). *Ten people breaking barriers for LGBTQ API representation.* https://www.hrc.org/blog/ten-people-breaking-barriers-for-lgbtq-api-representation

Jacobs, S. E., Thomas, W., & Lang, S. (Eds.). (1997). *Two-spirit people: Native American gender identity, sexuality, and spirituality.* University of Illinois Press.

Jury Selection and Services Act of 1968, 28 U.S.C. § 1861 *et seq.* (1968).

Kann, L., Olsen, O.E., McManus, T., Harris, W.A., Shanklin, S.L., Flint, K.H., Queen, B., Lowry, R., Chyen, D., Whittle, L., Thornton, J., Lim, C., Yamakawa, Y., Brener, N., & Zaza, S. (2016). Sexual identity, sex of sexual contacts, and health-related behaviors among students in grades 9–12: United States and selected sites, 2015. *Morbidity and Mortality Weekly Report, 65*(9), 1–208. https://doi.org/ 10.15585/mmwr.ss6509a1

Katz-Wise, S. L., & Hyde, J. S. (2012). Victimization experiences of lesbian, gay, and bisexual individuals: A meta-analysis. *Journal of Sex Research, 49*(2–3), 142–167. https://doi.org/10.1080/00224499.2011.637247

Kennamer, J. D., Honnold, J., Bradford, J., & Hendricks, M. (2000). Differences in disclosure of sexuality among African American and white gay/bisexual men: Implications for HIV/AIDS prevention. *AIDS Education and Prevention, 12*, 519–531.

Köllen, T. (2015). The impact of demographic factors on the way lesbian and gay employees manage their sexual orientation at work: An intersectional perspective. *Management Research Review, 38*(9), 992–1015. https://doi.org/10.1108/MRR-.5-2014-0099

Kosciw, J. G., Greytak, E. A., Bartkiewicz, M. J., Boesen, M. J., & Palmer, N.A. (2012). *The 2011 national school climate survey: The experiences of lesbian, gay, bisexual and transgender youth in our nation's schools.* Gay Lesbian and Straight Education Network.

Lea, T., de Wit, J., & Reynolds, R. (2014). Minority stress in lesbian, gay, and bisexual young adults in Australia: Associations with psychological distress, suicidality, and substance use. *Archives of Sexual Behavior, 43,* 1571–1578. https://doi.org/10.1007/s10508014-0266-6

Levitt, H. M., Ovrebo, E., Anderson-Cleveland, M. B., Leone, C., Jeong, J. Y., Arm, J. R., Bonin, B. P., Cicala, J., Coleman, R., Laurie, A., Vardaman, J. M., & Horne, S. G. (2009). Balancing dangers: GLBT experience in a time of anti-GLBT legislation. *Journal of Counseling Psychology, 56*(1), 67–81. https://doi.org/10.1037/a0012988

Lindley, L. (2006). The paradox of self-efficacy: Research with diverse populations. *Journal of Career Assessment, 14,* 143–160. https://doi.org/10.1177/1069072705281371

Majied, K. (2010). The impact of sexual of orientation and gender expression bias on African American students. *Journal of Negro Education, 79*(2), 151–165.

Make the Road New York. (2010). *Transgender need not apply: A report on gender identity job discrimination.* http://www.maketheroadny.org/pix_reports/TransNeedNotApplyReport_05.10.pdf

McCullough, R., Dispenza, F., Parker, L. K., Viehl, C. J., Chang, C. Y., & Murphy, T. M. (2017). The counseling experiences of transgender and gender nonconforming clients. *Journal of Counseling and Development, 95,* 423–434. https://doi.org/10.1002/jcad.12157

McMahon, M. (2011). The systems theory framework of career counseling. *Journal of Employment Counseling, 48*(4), 170–172.

Meyer, I. H. (1995). Minority stress and mental health in gay men. *Journal of Health and Social Behavior, 36,* 38–56. https://doi.org/10.2307/2137286.

Meyer, I. H. (2003). Prejudice, social stress, and mental health in lesbian, gay, and bisexual populations: Conceptual issues and research evidence. *Psychological Bulletin, 129,* 674–697. https://doi.org/10.1037/033-2909

Miller, R. L. (2008). The church and gay men: A spiritual opportunity in the wake of the clergy sexual crisis. *Journal of Religion & Abuse, 5,* 87–102. https://doi.org/10.1300/J154v05n03_13

Morsette, A., Swaney, G., Stolle, D., Schuldberg, D., van den Pol, R., & Young, M. (2009). Cognitive behavioral intervention for trauma in schools (CBITS): School-based treatment on a rural American Indian reservation. *Journal of Behavior Therapy and Experimental Psychiatry, 40*(1), 169–178. https://doi.org/10.1016/j.jbtep.2008.07.006

Nadal, K. L. (2008). Preventing racial, ethnic, gender, sexual minority, disability, and religious microaggressions: Recommendations for promoting positive mental health. *Prevention in Counseling Psychology: Theory, Research, Practice and Training, 2,* 22–27.

National Congress of American Indians (n.d.). *Indian country demographics.* http://www.ncai.org/about-tribes/demographics#R1

Nondiscrimination in Health Programs and Activities, 81 Fed. Reg. 31375 (2016).

Obergefell v. Hodges, 576 US (2015).

Pachankis, J. E., & Bränström, R. (2018). Hidden from happiness: Structural stigma, sexual orientation concealment, and life satisfaction across 28 countries. *Journal of Consulting and Clinical Psychology, 86*(5), 403–415. https://doi.org/10.1037/ccp0000299

Patient Protection and Affordable Care Act, 42 U.S.C. § 18001 *et seq.* (2010).

Plöderl, M., Sellmeier, M., Fartacek, C., Pichler, E., Fartacek, R., & Kralovec, K. (2014). Explaining the suicide risk of sexual minority individuals by contrasting the minority stress model with suicide models. *Archives of Sexual Behavior, 43,* 1559–1570. https://doi.org/10.1007/s10508-014-0268-4

Pope, M. Barrett, B., Szymanski, D. M., Chung, Y. B., Singaravelu, H., McLean, R., & Sanabria, S. (2004). Culturally appropriate career counseling with gay and lesbian clients. *Career Development Quarterly, 53,* 158–177. https://doi.org/10.1002/j.2161-0045.2004.tb00987.x

Prince, J. P. (2013). Career development of lesbian, gay, bisexual, and transgender individuals. In S. D. Brown & R. W. Lent (Eds.), *Career development and counseling: Putting theory and research to work* (pp. 275–297). John Wiley & Sons, Inc.

Resnick, C. A., & Galupo, M. P. (2018). Assessing experiences with LGBT microaggressions in the workplace: Development and validation of the microaggression experiences at work scale. *Journal of Homosexuality, 66*(10), 1380–1403.

Sangganjanavanich, V. F. (2009). Career development practitioners as advocates for transgender individuals: Understanding gender transition. *Journal of Employment Counseling, 46*, 128–135. https://doi.org/10.1002/j.2161-1920.2009.tb00075.x

Schmidt, C. K., & Nilsson, J. E. (2006). The effects of simultaneous developmental processes: Factors relating to the career development of lesbian, gay and bi-sexual youth. *Career Development Quarterly, 55*(1), 22–37. https://doi.org/10.1002/j.2161-0045.2006.tb00002.x

Schultheiss, D. E. P. (2003). A relational approach to career counseling: Theoretical integration and practical application. *Journal of Counseling and Development, 81*(3), 301–310. https://doi.org/10.1002/j.1556-6678.2003.tb00257.x

Sears, B., & Badgett, L. (2012). *Beyond the stereotypes: Poverty in the LGBT community*. The Williams Institute. UCLA School of Law. https://williamsinstitute.law.ucla.edu/williams-in-the-news/beyond-stereotypes-poverty-in-the-lgbt-community/

Singh, A. A., Hays, D. G., & Watson, L. D. (2011). Strength in the face of adversity: Resilience strategies of transgender individuals. *Journal of Counseling and Development, 89*, 20–27. https://doi.org/10.1002/j.1556-6678.2011.tb00057.x

Speciale, M., & Scholl, M. B. (2019). LGBTQ affirmative career counseling: An intersectional perspective. *Career Development Network Journal, 35*(1), 22–35.

Sue, D. W., Sue, D., Neville, H. A., & Smith, L. (2019). *Counseling the culturally diverse: Theory and practice* (8th ed.). John Wiley & Sons, Inc.

Super, D. E., Savickas, M. L., & Super, C. M. (1996). A lifespan, life-space approach to career development. In D. Brown, L. Brooks, & Associates (Eds.), *Career choice and development* (pp. 121–128). Jossey-Bass.

Tilcsik, A. (2011). Pride and prejudice: Employment discrimination against openly gay men in the United States. *American Journal of Sociology, 117*(2), 586–626. https://doi.org/10.1086/661653

Tran, V. (2019). *HRC releases sex discrimination report*. https://www.hrc.org/blog/hrc-publishes-sex-discrimination-report

U.S. Census Bureau (2018). *Quick facts*. https://www.census.gov/quickfacts/fact/table/US/PST045218

U.S. Const. amend. XIV.

U.S. Department of Education. (2010). *Dear colleague letter*. https://www2.ed.gov/about/offices/list/ocr/letters/colleague-201010.html

U.S. Department of Education. (2014). *Questions and answers on Title IX and sexual violence*. https://www2.ed.gov/about/offices/list/ocr/docs/qa-201404-title-ix.pdf

U.S. Equal Employment Opportunity Commission. (2019). *Preventing employment discrimination against lesbian, gay, bisexual or transgender workers*. https://www.eeoc.gov/eeoc/publications/brochure-gender_stereotyping.cfm

Velez, B. L., Moradi, B., & Brewster, M. E. (2013). Testing the tenets of minority stress theory in workplace contexts. *Journal of Counseling Psychology, 60*, 532–542. https://doi.org/10.1037/a0033346

White, F. (2012). Ubiquitous American Indian stereotypes in television. In E. DeLaney Hoffman (Ed.), *American Indians and popular culture: Media sports, and politics* (pp. 135–150). ABC-CLIO.

Whitfield, D. R., Walls, N. E., Langenderfer-Magruder, L., & Clark, B. (2014). Queer is the new black? Not so much: Racial disparities in anti-LGBTQ discrimination. *Journal of Gay & Lesbian Social Services, 26*, 426–440. https://doi.org/10.1080/10538720.2014.955556

The Williams Institute. (January 2019). *LGBT demographic data interactive*. https://williamsinstitute.law.ucla.edu/visualization/lgbt-stats/?topic=LGBT

Wilson, B., & Miller, R. (2002). Strategies for managing heterosexism used among African American gay and bisexual men. *Journal of Black Psychology, 28*, 371–391. https://doi.org/10.1177/009579802237543

CHAPTER 11

Career Counseling for Individuals With Disabilities

Michelle McKnight-Lizotte, Trenton Landon, and Emily Lund

CHAPTER OVERVIEW

Legislative and civil action over the past century has significantly affected the lives of individuals with disabilities. While legislation against discrimination in the workplace has expanded, the civil rights of people with disabilities (PWDs) have improved, and PWDs have gained a major presence in the workforce, they still encounter challenges in the area of career development and growth (Maroto & Pettinicchio, 2015). This chapter will explore factors affecting career development and employment of people with a wide range of disabilities. This chapter will also discuss the implications for career counseling for individuals with disabilities and private and public rehabilitation agencies that are available to assist individuals with disabilities entering into or transitioning in the world of work.

CHAPTER OBJECTIVES

After reading this chapter, the student will be able to complete the following:

1. Identify, implement, and recommend reasonable accommodations in the workplace for individuals with a wide range of disabilities.

2. Identify factors affecting successful job placement for individuals with a wide range of disabilities.

3. Outline implications for career counseling for individuals with disabilities.

4. Identify and outline private and public rehabilitation agencies that can enhance the career success of individuals with disabilities.

Factors Affecting Career Development and Placement

The importance of work and its positive effect on people's mental and physical health cannot be understated. Work is fundamental in allowing individuals to survive and obtain social power (Bluestein, 2006). However, access to this incredibly vital activity is not universally available to all people, especially not to the largest minority group in the United States: PWDs. As of 2016, it was estimated that 12.8% of the U.S. population reported living with a disability (U.S. Census Bureau, 2016). In the United States, individuals with disabilities report a 19.3% labor force participation rate compared to the 66.3% labor force participation rate of individuals without disabilities (U.S. Bureau of Labor Statistics, 2020). In addition to lower employment rates, PWDs work fewer hours and make less money when compared to people without disabilities (Houtenville et al., 2014). In 2016, individuals aged 16 and over with disabilities had median earnings of $22,047, whereas individuals aged 16 and over without disabilities had median earnings of $32,479, resulting in a disparity of over $10,000 a year in income (Kraus et al., 2018). This chapter will use the definition of disability provided by the UN Convention on the Rights of Persons with Disabilities, which is "those who have long-term physical, mental, intellectual or sensory impairments which in interaction with various barriers may hinder their full and effective participation in society on an equal basis with others" (United Nations, 2006, Article 1—Purpose, para. 2).

PWDs experience major social barriers to employment, including stigma, lowered expectations, and negative attitudes of employers (Erickson et al., 2014a). Some employers report feeling that hiring PWDs is a "risk" and that they worry about legal implications, loss of income, and having to pay for expensive workplace accommodations (Erickson et al, 2014b; Schur et al., 2014). Individuals with disabilities endure major repercussions when economic downturns occur. For example, during the "Great Recession" of 2007–2009, PWDs were unemployed at 5 times the rate of people without disabilities (Bureau of Labor Statistics, 2012; Kaye, 2010; Mitra & Kruse, 2016). Federal legislation, such as the Americans with Disability Act (ADA) of 1990 [P. L. 101-336] and the Workforce Investment Opportunity Act of 2014 [P. L. 113-128], were enacted to decrease the barriers faced by PWDs seeking employment; they have failed to eliminate discrimination in hiring, wage disparity, and firing of PWDs in the United States (Fabian & Pebdani, 2013; Syzmanski et al., 2010).

Onset of Disability

The time period that PWDs experience disability can affect their career trajectories and outcomes. People who acquire a disabling condition later in their lives and careers may struggle to identify their new interests and abilities or to find useful accommodations or other appropriate employment options. As an illustration, a person who was born with a missing limb, such as a leg, will have developed and matured through life, having always figured out a way to accommodate their physical difference (think prosthetics, assistive technology for driving), whereas a person who is 40 years old and loses a leg in an industrial accident where they work in construction may have difficulty relearning their job or exploring new careers given the recent change.

When considering the time of onset of disability, it is also necessary to understand how the age the person was at the time they acquired their disability may affect their career choice because of expectations and exposure to careers. The effect of the onset of disability may be moderated by factors such as age, gender, race, culture cognitive ability, educational attainment, social support, financial hardship, migrant status, and social class. The time period between ages 14 and 26, considered to be a vital time period for youth with disabilities, is covered in-depth in Chapter 5.

Social Security Benefits

The Social Security Disability Insurance (SSDI) program was established by Title II of the Social Security Act of 1954 to provide eligible PWDs with monthly income benefits and Medicare health insurance. SSDI can be provided to individuals with disabilities who can demonstrate that they are unable to work in "substantial gainful activity" because of their physical or mental impairments that are expected to last more than 12 months or result in death. The process individuals go through to "prove" their disability affects their ability to work is often tedious, exhaustive, and slow, typically lasting several years, which can serve as a barrier to applying for SSDI. Once someone is deemed eligible for participation in SSDI, they still have a 24-month waiting period to obtain health benefits. Career counselors need to be aware that alcoholism and drug addiction are not included as disabilities covered by SSDI (Brew & Gleason, 2014).

PWDs who are receiving SSDI may not seek to return to the world of work because they may be uncertain of their abilities and wary of losing the financial and medical benefits associated with SSDI (Burkhauser & Houtenville, 2010). Likely, because of these concerns, only very few PWDs receiving SSDI return to work and leave SSDI (Hawleya et al., 2009). As a result of this lack of incentive to return to work, the Social Security Administration created specific incentives in the Social Security Disability Amendments of 1980, 1986, 1989, 1990, and then with the Ticket to Work and Work Incentives Improvement Act of 1999 [Public Law 106-170]. These pieces of legislation encouraged individuals receiving SSDI by providing employment preparation and job placement services and allowing SSDI recipients to continue to receive Medicare (federally provided health insurance).

Accommodations Used by PWDs

The ADA requires that employers provide "reasonable accommodations" to employees when needed. Reasonable accommodations have been defined as "any change to the application or hiring process, to the job, to the way the job is done, or the work environment that allows a person with a disability who is qualified for the job to perform the essential functions of that job and enjoy equal employment opportunities " (ADA National Network, 2018). The language in the ADA mandates the provision of accommodations, except in situations in which such accommodations cause "undue hardship" for the employer. ADA defines undue hardship as accommodations that create "significant difficulty or expense" for the employer (U.S. EEOC, 1992, pp. 111–112), while the reality is that the majority of workplace accommodations are often low cost or no cost. For instance, Loy (2015) found that 58% of employee accommodations cost nothing, and the other 42% cost $500 or less. The most frequently requested and used work-site accommodation is flexible work arrangements; this can include flexible start and end times, more breaks, and the ability to work from home (Sundar et al., 2018).

Depending on the extent of functional limitations caused by a disability, some individuals with physical disabilities may have difficulty meeting the technical standards required for certain jobs or careers; in addition, employers and educational programs may not realize that they can accommodate someone's physical disability via assistive technology or reasonable accommodations and thus may be unwilling to work with the person to do so (Andrews et al., 2013; Lund et al., 2016). This may result in individuals being shut out of a career or job because of employer prejudice and ignorance, even if they could indeed perform the essential tasks with reasonable accommodations. Thus individuals with visible disabilities may readily disclose to potential employers to assure the employer that they can perform the essential functions of the position while those with invisible disabilities may choose not to disclose or may wait to disclose so as not to have their qualifications or abilities doubted (Lund et al., 2016). Career counselors may wish to work with clients with disabilities to discuss how to most advantageously navigate disability disclosure and requests for reasonable accommodations

Physical Disabilities

Physical disability, which can also be called orthopedic disability or mobility impairment, typically encompasses those disabilities that affect mobility, balance, dexterity, or limb use. Examples may also include limb loss or congenital limb difference, paralysis (e.g., paraplegia, quadriplegia), arthritis, cerebral palsy, muscular dystrophy, post-polio syndrome, or stroke (Smart, 2012). Depending on the origin, physical disabilities may be stable or episodic in nature and can be visible or invisible. Physical disabilities may be congenital or acquired. Congenital physical disabilities may occur because of genetic conditions, birth defects, or trauma at or shortly after birth. Acquired physical disabilities may occur as a result of acute or chronic illness because of treatment for another condition (e.g., limb amputation because of bone cancer), accidents (e.g., spinal cord injury from a car accident), or other trauma (Smart, 2012).

Many of the conditions that cause physical disability may also result in other co-occurring impairments. For example, someone with mobility impairment caused by a stroke may also have cognitive impairments from the same event; similarly, someone with cerebral palsy may also have co-occurring learning or cognitive impairments as a result of the cerebral trauma that caused the cerebral palsy. Physical disabilities may also result from broader chronic health conditions; for instance, an individual with multiple sclerosis may have difficulty with balance or walking in addition to fatigue, cognitive confusion, or sensory limitations. Still, other people may have a physical disability with no other co-occurring conditions; thus, physical disability may occur on its own or need to be considered within a broader context of functional limitations and abilities.

Many of the accommodations required by people with physical disabilities in the workplace require changes to the physical environment. For example, an individual who uses a wheelchair may need to have preferential use of an office with a wider door or shelves lowered for greater ease of access. Other accommodations may include things like reassignment of nonessential physical work duties (e.g., lifting boxes) or flexible scheduling (e.g., for workers with fatigue).

Sensory Disabilities

Sensory disabilities are described as a disability of the senses (e.g., sight, hearing, smell, touch, taste). This section will describe autism spectrum disorders (ASDs), vision loss, and hearing loss. The Americans with Disabilities Amendments Act of 2008 [P.L. 110-325] expanded the "major life activities" covered under the ADA to include hearing, seeing, speaking, communicating, and learning, as well as other major life activities.

ASD

ASDs are included in the category of sensory disabilities because they affect individuals' sensory experiences (sensitivity to sound, light, and touch). ASD is a complex neurodevelopmental diagnosis that affects individuals of all ethnic backgrounds and socioeconomic status. Males are affected 4 times more than females (Baio et al., 2018). The Centers for Disease Control (CDC) estimates 1:59 individuals are diagnosed with ASD (CDC, 2018). An individual diagnosed with ASD will have persistent deficits in communication and social interactions that may include difficulty with reciprocal conversations, a lack of eye contact, resistance to change, highly focused interests, and difficulty maintaining relationships (APA, 2013). It is commonly believed that all individuals with ASD have a comorbid cognitive impairment; this is false, as over half of individuals with an ASD diagnosis have average to above-average intellectual capabilities (Baio et al., 2018; Mayes & Calhoun, 2003). However, research indicates that adults with ASD and an average-range intelligence quotient (IQ) were 3 times more likely to be unengaged in any form of employment or postsecondary education following high school when compared to their peers with ASD who also have an intellectual disability (Taylor & Seltzer, 2011).

Individuals with ASD experience greater difficulty obtaining and maintaining employment when compared to individuals with other types of disabilities often because of the social skill difficulties innate to the diagnosis (Hedley et al., 2016). Individuals with ASD are also less likely to attend postsecondary education than their peers without disabilities, as well as those with other types of disabilities (Cederlund et al., 2008). The social and communication deficits experienced by individuals with ASD can affect employment and postsecondary success (Beardona & Edmonds, 2007). For example, individuals with ASD enrolled in postsecondary education have reported difficulty engaging with peers in general, and this can become a major concern in group assignments (Lizotte, 2018).

In terms of employment, individuals with ASD may need additional coaching and preparation (such as scripting or role playing) to present well during the job interview process (McKnight-Lizotte, 2018). Once they are on the job, common workplace accommodations for individuals with ASD include a consistent work schedule, limited unstructured time, and modified work environment as needed (to address sensory sensitivities). In addition, advance notice regarding scheduling changes or meeting topics, as well as allowing an employee with ASD to respond in writing rather than verbally, could be accommodations necessary for individuals with ASD (Prince, 2017). Some people with ASD may benefit from having their employer and coworkers educated about ASD to better understand communication differences. Research shows that supportive coworkers and organizational support are helpful for an individual with ASD to maintain employment (Hendricks, 2010). Accommodations can include a job coach who may shadow them and help assist in explaining social situations and setting up natural supports on the job. As far as strengths in employment, research shows that people on the spectrum can demonstrate more productivity, as they can be more focused on their work than employees without ASD (Cowen, 2011).

Vision Loss and Blindness

Blindness is considered to have the least stigma attached to it of any disability (Smart, 2012). However, even without social stigma, this disability group is still negatively affected by and sparingly represented in employment. In 2016, only 32.2% of Americans who were blind or experiencing vision loss were working, with 10.7% unemployed and the other 63.8% were not active in the labor force (Bureau of Labor Statistics, 2016). Individuals using glasses or contacts are not considered to have a "visual impairment" and therefore are not protected by the ADA since their glasses/contacts restore their sight fully (Smart, 2012, p. 158).

Transportation is a major barrier for people experiencing vision loss, especially in rural areas without any form of public transportation. One study found that one third of people who were blind or vusally impaired had turned down a job because of transportation difficulties (Crudden et al., 2015). A career counselor could explore alternative forms of transportation for a client experiencing transportation difficulties such as ride share apps or hiring a driver. For those unable to find acceptable transportation opens, self-employment may be a more sustainable alternative (Ibsen & Swicegood, 2017). Another barrier for obtaining appropriate employment for people that are blind or visually impaired has been documented to be negative employer attitudes (Coffey et al., 2014). Employers with a negative attitude report feeling like there are very few jobs in their company a person who is blind or visually impaired could do, or that it would be expensive to employ a blind or visually impaired person (Lynch, 2013).

Beyond transportation and employer attitudes, effective accommodations and assistive technology should be considered for someone who is blind or visually impaired to meet the demands of their job. Obviously, this would vary greatly depending on the individual and on the job. For example, if someone who is visually impaired were hired to be a cashier, there may be several accessibility barriers to be addressed. Is the cash register equipped with braille on the keys? Does the employee need a cash-reading machine to identify the numeral amount of cash a customer is paying with? There are many forms of assistive technology that can be used to assist individuals who are low vision or blind.

Deaf or Hearing Impairment

With approximately 3.9 million working-age adults in the United States experiencing hearing loss, it is one of the most common disabilities a career counselor will encounter. People of all ages, races, educational backgrounds, and socioeconomic statuses experience hearing loss and deafness. People who are deaf or experience severe hearing loss use visual methods, such as American Sign Language, to communicate. Because of this method of communication, individuals may struggle to find employment, as employers may perceive this communication difficulty as too big of a barrier to overcome because of the high cost of sign language interpreters (Haynes & Linden, 2012).

The two primary barriers to employment for people who are deaf or hard of hearing are communication difficulties and discrimination (Perkins-Dock et al., 2015). Workplace accommodations for individuals with hearing loss can include assistive listening devices, alerting devices, video relay services, captioned tele- phones, and sign language interpreters. One study identified telephone technology aids and assistance from coworkers as the top-two accommodations used by deaf employees (Haynes & Linden, 2012). Natural supports are methods used to accommodate an individual with a disability that are naturally occurring in the workforce; they can include coworkers, policies, tools, etc. Natural supports can occur spontaneously (e.g., a coworker notices an area the PWD is struggling in and offers to assist) or be planned (e.g., an employer asks an employee to take meeting notes for the employee who is deaf because they must watch the interpreter during the meeting).

Dual Sensory Loss

While it is a low-incidence disability category, there are individuals diagnosed with dual sensory loss, meaning they are both vision and hearing impaired (Smart, 2012). People often call this "deafblindness." Research indicated that 79% of individuals experiencing dual sensory loss are unemployed (American Foundation for the Blind, 2017). Much of the individual's specific functional abilities would be related to the time at which they lost each of their sensory abilities. For example, if someone was a "hearing" person for a time before they became deaf, they likely are a person who uses speech. Whereas someone who is born both deaf and blind would have a difficult time learning to speak verbally. Individuals who are deafblind are often socially isolated and vulnerable to abuse and neglect (Simcock & Manthorpe, 2014). Participation in the community, including employment, plays a significant role in one's physical and mental health, increase someone's self-worth and self-esteem, and should therefore be a priority for those with dual sensory loss (Shadrick & Etlen, 2019).

Learning Disabilities

In the United States, "learning disabilities" (often referred to as "specific learning disabilities" or "SLDs") refers to a group of conditions that interfere with one's ability to perform basic linguistic or mathematical tasks (e.g., spelling, reading, writing, mathematical computation) in the absence of a generalized intellectual impairment (Smart, 2012). In addition, federal law (Individuals with Disabilities Education and Improvement Act [IDEA], 2004) and clinical diagnostic guidelines found in the *Diagnostic and Statistical Manual of Mental Health Disorders, 5th Edition* (*DSM-5*) (APA, 2013) both specify that the individual's unexpectedly poor performance in one or more academic domains cannot be better explained by factors such as lack of instruction; untreated or inadequately treated emotional, psychiatric, vision, or hearing concerns; or environmental, cultural, or socioeconomic disadvantage. In other words, SLDs are present when an individual without a general intellectual disability performs unexpectedly poorly at certain academic tasks (e.g., word decoding in reading, basic calculation in math) despite having received adequate instruction in an adequate environment.

Traditionally, SLDs were diagnosed via a discrepancy model wherein a certain gap between an individual's cognitive (intellectual) testing and achievement (academic) testing was required (Boat & Wu, 2015); however, this method has fallen out of favor in many places and is no longer required by either federal or clinical guidelines (APA, 2013; IDEA, 2004). A popular alternative diagnostic model is the Response to Intervention or Response to Treatment Intervention, which bases diagnosis of SLD on an individual's inability to adequately respond (i.e., show academic growth) when provided with high-quality instructional intervention. Specific learning disabilities have been traditionally defined by the subtypes of skills that are impaired; for example, "dyslexia" has been traditionally used to refer to SLDs in the areas of reading, "dysgraphia" for SLDs in the area of written expression, and "dyscalculia" for SLDs in the area of mathematics (Boat & Wu, 2015). However, such terms no longer appear in either the *DSM-5* (APA, 2013) or IDEA (2004).

Because SLDs affect academic achievement, research on and accommodations for SLDs have generally focused on school-based interventions and accommodations. A variety of evidence-based interventions are used to instruct students with SLD, particularly in elementary schools, and often to great effect (Boat & Wu, 2015). In addition to increasing academic achievement, early identification and intervention with students with SLDs can lessen the emotional, social, and behavioral consequences that may result from chronic academic frustration and help maintain or improve student enjoyment of and engagement in school (Boat & Wu, 2015). For students with continued impairments as a result of SLD, specific academic accommodations, such as speech-to-text or text-to-speech technology or audiobooks, may be helpful and can be used in secondary and postsecondary education and employment settings (Boat & Wu, 2015).

Because the effects of SLD are primarily academic in nature, many individuals with SLD may not disclose their disability or seek accommodations in the workplace (Price et al., 2003). Rather, SLD may affect career development by affecting educational and career choices themselves (Gerber & Price, 2003; Lindstorm & Benz, 2002). For example, an individual with an SLD that affects math computation may choose a college major with minimal to no math requirements, or an individual with an SLD that affects reading comprehension and written expression may choose a technical career or major as opposed to a traditional liberal arts degree with many courses that require heavy reading and writing loads. This is not to say that individuals with SLDs cannot complete higher education; indeed, many do so quite successfully. However, they may gravitate toward educational and career paths that emphasize their academic and vocational strengths and minimize any remaining academic or functional weaknesses (Gerber & Price, 2003; Lindstorm & Benz, 2002). Career counselors may be able to assist students and adults with SLDs to determine appropriate career and educational paths that capitalize on both their interests and their strengths (Lindstorm & Benz, 2002). Schools, vocational rehabilitation, and career counselors, as well as potential employers, may also be helpful in securing testing accommodations for required entrance exams, licensing, or employment testing (Gerber & Price, 2003; Lindstorm & Benz, 2002). Individuals with SLDs may avoid asking employers for any sort of accommodations because of the stigma attributed to the label of "learning disability" (Gerber & Price; Price et al., 2003), which may further guide them into educational and career paths where these accommodations are less likely to be necessary.

Emotional Disabilities

Emotional disabilities—also referred to as "emotional disturbance," "emotional and behavioral disabilities," and other similar terms depending on state law and regulations—are defined by IDEA (2004) as

> a condition exhibiting one or more of the following characteristics over a long period of time and to a marked degree that adversely affects a child's educational performance:
>> (A) An inability to learn that cannot be explained by intellectual, sensory, or health factors.
>> (B) An inability to build or maintain satisfactory interpersonal relationships with peers and teachers.
>> (C) Inappropriate types of behavior or feelings under normal circumstances.
>> (D) A general pervasive mood of unhappiness or depression.
>> (E) A tendency to develop physical symptoms or fears associated with personal or school problems. (Sec 300.8.c.4)

This category also includes schizophrenia but excludes students who are determined to be "socially maladjusted" (e.g., antisocial or delinquent) unless they also meet the criteria for an emotional disturbance in addition to having social maladjustment (IDEA, 2004). This social maladjustment exclusion criterion has been criticized for being poorly defined and difficult to consistently apply and separate out from qualifying emotional disabilities (Merrell & Walker, 2004).

The IDEA criteria for emotional disturbance may overlap significantly with the criteria for many psychiatric disorders, such as depression and other mood disorders, anxiety disorders, and schizophrenia and other psychotic disorders (APA, 2013). Although schools do not formally diagnose these disorders for special education classification purposes, students with these conditions may receive both clinical diagnoses to access outside medical and psychotherapeutic services and other resources and special education classification to access special education services for assistance within the elementary and secondary school system, including transition services. Given the extremely high rate of unemployment among adults with mental illness, particularly more severe mental illness (Luciano & Meara, 2014), these students may benefit from intensive transition services that include supported education, supported employment, or both, as well as both professional and peer support regarding symptom management, disclosure strategies, or reasonable accommodations (Ellison & Mullen, 2018). This process can also include supported career exploration and development that takes into account the individual's abilities, interests, needs, and functional limitations. Given the generally episodic nature of many of these conditions, careers that provide for flexibility in scheduling may be good fits for many young adults with emotional disabilities. Professional support, either on or off the job site, may be important in assisting with acclimation to the job and job-site culture and expectations, managing the stress inherent with working, addressing interpersonal conflict at the job site, and determining and requesting reasonable accommodations (Koletsi et al., 2009).

Intellectual Disabilities

The *DSM-5* defines intellectual disability (IDD) as a "deficit in general mental ability, such as reasoning, problem solving, planning, abstract thinking, judgment, academic learning, and learning from experience" (APA, 2013, p. 31). The three essential features of this disorder are (a) general deficits in mental abilities; (b) impairment in adaptive functioning based on comparison to peers of the same age, gender, and sociocultural background; and (c) onset in the developmental period; the severity (mild, moderate, severe) is also typically specified (APA, 2013). Measurements of IQ have historically been correlated to IDD diagnostic procedures (Smart, 2012), but more recent developments focus on adaptive functioning, particularly given the questionable validity of lower end IQ scores (APA, 2013). It should be noted that the historical distinction for IDD was mental retardation (Mackelprang & Salsgiver, 2015); however, this term carries significant negative connotations and is highly offensive. As such, disability rights groups sought to change the term, leading to the present intellectual disability terminology (Mackelprang & Salsgiver, 2015).

Given the media portrayal of persons with IDD as slow or lacking the capacity to understand, social stigma regarding IDD is high and can lead to co-occurring depression (Porter & Kaplan, 2011). Human services professionals, teachers, and other providers may at times fail to fully include individuals with IDD in the planning process, instead bypassing the individual in favor of parents/guardians or simply making the decision for the person (Mackelprang & Salsgiver, 2015). Individuals with IDD often face difficulties with personal independence, social participation, and academic and/or occupational functioning in a variety of home and community-based settings (APA, 2013; Wehman et al., 2014). Work-based barriers experienced by those with IDD primarily center on difficulties with social integration within the work setting (Argan et al., 2016; Butterworth & Strauch, 1994; Chadsey, 2007).

While policy shifts have represented a "commitment to integrated employment for individuals with IDD" (Timmons et al., 2011, p. 285), participation rates for individuals with IDD in facility-based or sheltered employment have steadily grown (Mank, 2003; Winsor & Butterworth, 2008). Individuals with IDD employed in workshop-type settings are at times reluctant to leave for community-based employment because of the existing social relationships they have and the familiarity with their current work setting (Timmons et al., 2011). Given the description of social relationships as a fundamental human need (Andersen et al., 2000; Ryan & Deci, 2000), it may not be surprising to see individuals with IDD electing to remain in familiar surroundings with familiar friends and coworkers rather than venture into the community. Increasing social connections for individuals with IDD may help to increase their interest in external employment, and career counselors should be working to increase the social capital of those they serve through community integration and inclusion. Shortages of social capital (the economic advantage one enjoys as a result of one's social relationships) may be the result of social isolation or deprivation and have the ability to adversely affect the wages of PWDs (Phillips et al., 2014).

Early work experiences have been shown beneficial for PWDs (Certo & Leuking, 2006; Haber et al., 2016), but early work experiences for individuals with IDD are limited. Riesen and Oertle (2019) examined employer perspectives and their concerns regarding work-based learning for individuals with IDD in secondary school settings. Employers' concerns were stigma related: "Fear, attitudinal barriers of managers and co-workers" and a general perception that employers had no place for persons with IDD were prevalent (Riesen and Oertle, 2019, p. 31). Recent legislative developments, such as the Workforce Innovation and Opportunity Act (WIOA; 2014) have placed a greater emphasis on work readiness for all PWDs. Greater collaboration between service providers in rehabilitation practice settings (e.g., state/federal vocational rehabilitation (VR), community rehabilitation programs) and professionals in secondary schools (e.g., high school transition specialists, special education teachers) is needed (Riesen & Oertle, 2019).

Despite some of the employment challenges experienced by individuals with IDD, evidence-based practices do exist, substantiating their ability to sustain work. Supported employment is characterized by employment in a competitive and community-based setting with ongoing support provided by a job coach or other service provider (Wehman et al., 2014). This approach to job development and placement is an empirically validated intervention for people with intellectual disabilities and severe mental illness

(Wehman et al., 2014). Such an individualized approach embodies principles of empowerment and informed choice by establishing the person with the disability as the primary decision maker and ensuring their placement in the community. The individual placement and support model has also been shown to improve employment outcomes for those with severe mental illness (Bond et al., 2008; Campbell et al., 2011), and preliminary research extrapolating this approach to those with IDD is promising (Wehman et al., 2014).

Persons with IDD have been found to have talents that drive successful business outcomes; they represent a willing group of ideal workers, often exceed employer and supervisor expectations, and present fewer challenges than employers expect (Institute for Corporate Productivity, 2014). Job restructuring, assistive technology, and adjusted work schedule may be beneficial accommodation practices. Accessible training sites, visual depictions of work functions and expectations (as opposed to written manuals or logs), and modification of some policies may be needed to allow an individual with IDD to thrive in the work setting.

Employer's Perceptions of Hiring Individuals With Disabilities

There remains a prominent disconnect between the perspectives of potential employers regarding the abilities of PWDs and the reality of their employment-related strengths (Baker et al., 2018). Employers discriminating against PWDs in the workforce is a long-standing problem. Even with the ADA, which federally prohibits employment discrimination against PWDs, discrimination in hiring and employment decisions has not ended (Marini, 2012). Employers report that they are fearful of hiring PWDs because they feel that such employees put them at risk of lawsuits if they have to discipline or fire them (Kaye et al., 2011). In addition, employers report that they worry about hiring PWDs because they may not know how to handle their needs on the job and are concerned that other employees will have to spend extra time assisting them (Kaye et al., 2011).

While employment discrimination is a cross-disability issue, research has shown that the more obvious a disability is, the more likely the individual will experience prejudice in their search for employment (Gouvier et al., 1991). Employers have reported feeling that workers with disabilities are undereducated, unproductive, unqualified, and expensive to hire (U.S. Department of Labor, 2014a). Certain disabilities are shown to have lower employer prejudice than others. For example, employers state that they would rather hire an individual with a physical disability than a mental or emotional disability (Khalema & Shankar, 2014). Which brings up an interesting point: Unless an employee discloses their disability before being hired or after, the employer may never know which of his employees have an invisible disability (such as an emotional or mental disability).

Following hiring, an individual with a disability must disclose their disability to their employer to request a workplace accommodation. However, in fear of discrimination, many employees, especially those with psychological disabilities, often do not disclose their disabilities or ask their employers for accommodations (Jans et al., 2012). Having an organizational culture that is supportive and accessible may encourage disclosure from PWDs. An employer could ask employees, "Do you have any special requirements?" in annual reviews and during the hiring processes (Prince, 2017, p. 81). The size of employers' businesses can also affect the likelihood that they will implement accommodations; typically, larger organizations are more open and willing to accommodate PWDs whereas small businesses are less likely (Bruyere et al., 2006). When employers do provide accommodations, they report that the requested accommodations typically cost little, are effective, assist productivity, and allow PWDs to maintain their employment (Solovieva et al., 2011).

Once employers have employed individuals with disabilities, they are more positive toward the future hiring of PWDs (Hernandez et al., 2000). This is not surprising, as PWDs can be excellent employees.

Private and Public Rehabilitation Agencies

A variety of service providers exist that focus on improving employment outcomes for PWDs, including those with the disabilities described in this chapter. These agencies represent a variety of public and private not-for-profit and private for-profit entities. The collaborative efforts of these public and private agencies have helped to drive service provision to PWDs. Service provision of rehabilitation counselors should reflect efforts to improve vocational independence, independent living opportunities, and higher rates of social and community-based inclusion (CRCC, 2019). While rehabilitation counselors are employed in a variety of settings (Fabian & MacDonald-Wilson, 2012; Saunders et al., 2009), some of the primary service providers include the state/federal vocational rehabilitation system, community rehabilitation programs, and for-profit rehabilitation.

State/Federal VR

The U.S. state/federal VR system is the oldest and most widely recognized service provider for PWDs. Dating back to the early 1900s and legislation focused on service provision to injured veterans (and later civilians), the state/federal VR program has a long history of successful placement of PWDs. This practice setting serves over one million PWDs on an annual basis (Martin et al., 2010) and operates in all 50 states, the District of Colombia, and many territories of the United States (Fabian & MacDonald-Wilson, 2012). Many states have a general vocational rehabilitation agency, although some operate a separate VR agency specific to serving individuals who are blind or have visual impairments.

State/federal VR agencies are mandated by the Rehabilitation Act (1973) and its subsequent amendments. These agencies are tasked with assisting individuals with a wide range of disabilities to find and secure employment, and recent efforts have focused on providing services to those with the most significant disabilities (Rehabilitation Services Administration (RSA), 2005). Relying on a mixture of state and federal funds, these agencies spend more than $2.5 billion annually to assist PWDs in finding, obtaining, and maintaining employment (Martin et al., 2010; U.S. Government Accountability Office, 2005). Vocational rehabilitation services are not entitlement based but rather eligibility is based on applicants' demonstrating the presence of a documented physical or mental impairment, having a substantial impediment to employment as a result of their disability, requiring VR services to become employable, and being able to participate in employment (Rehabilitation Act, 1973). Participants range from 14 years of age to adulthood, and the rehabilitation counselor is tasked with reviewing documentation to determine eligibility.

This eligibility determination is part of a relatively standard process across all state/federal VR agencies. The VR process consists of the application, eligibility determination, development of the individual plan for employment (IPE), service provision, job placement and related services, and service termination after the successful attainment of employment (Ditchman et al., 2013). The types of services included in the IPE and delivered to the eligible participant are individualized to the specific need and identified vocational goal of service recipients. This can include vocational training (e.g., welding, plumbing, cosmetology), postsecondary education (e.g., associate's and bachelor's degrees), or assistance in securing employment based on existing transferable skills. Other services designed to maximize employability may be related to assistive technology needs, provision of counseling and guidance (including mental health therapies), transportation assistance, and benefits and planning assistance for those receiving social security benefits (e.g., Supplemental Security Income; SSDI). The goal is to maximize the individual's "employment, independence, and integration into the community and the competitive labor market" (RSA, 2005).

Community-Based Rehabilitation Programs

The state/federal VR system does serve a significant number of PWDs, but the estimated 1.5 million served are a mere fraction of the estimated 51 million Americans with disabilities (Fabian & MacDonald-Wilson, 2012). Community rehabilitation programs (CRPs) that are housed in local communities play an important role in the provision of services to PWDs. These agencies are typically accredited as service providers through organizations such as the Commission on Accreditation of Rehabilitation Facilities (CARF). To the public, accreditation represents competence in many areas of service provision, which may include employment, behavioral health, aging services, and child and youth services (CARF, 2019). Service providers working specifically with employment-related pursuits may be required to be certified through training sponsored by the Association of Community Rehabilitation Educators (ACRE). The ACRE certification is designed to represent competency-based endorsement in employment services and customized employment (ACRE, 2013).

The vast majority of CRPs work in collaboration with state/federal VR agencies, and funding for community-based rehabilitation programs comes from a variety of state and federal sources. Private donations from donors and agency-sponsored fundraisers may also help with funding concerns. The role of these agencies has grown over time and will likely continue to evolve. The types of services provided, and their expected outcomes have been affected by WIOA (2014), as it has a greater emphasis on community-based rather than workshop-style provision of services. Rehabilitation counselors employed in these settings may work with a specific population (e.g., substance abuse, psychiatric disorders) or specialize in conducting specific assessments, work with employers through supported employment programs, and direct employer consultation and recommendation of accommodations, among other services (Fabian & MacDonald-Wilson, 2012).

For-Profit Rehabilitation

Private-sector rehabilitation counselors may perform vocational evaluations, assessments, and other services designed to measure work capacity, barriers to work, and overall return-to-work capabilities. Life care planning and expert witness testimony in litigation procedures are growing fields and typically offer higher rates of compensation. It should be noted that while the knowledge and skill of rehabilitation counselors working in for-profit settings closely mirror that required of rehabilitation counselors working in public settings, the relationship these individuals have with service recipients can be quite different (Fabian & MacDonald-Wilson, 2012). As these relationships are often for short periods of time to conduct evaluations, even the terminology used to identify changes from client/consumer/customer to "evaluee" (CRCC, 2017). Regardless of the terminology or practice setting, the "primary responsibility of rehabilitation counselors is to respect the dignity of clients and to promote their welfare" (CRCC, 2017, p. 4), with clients being defined as the "individuals with or directly affected by a disability, who receive services from rehabilitation counselors" (CRCC, 2017, p. 2).

Implications for Career Counseling

Career counselors must be considerate and competent regarding their clients' potential intersectionality. The effect of disability on employment intersects with other characteristics, such as age, race, gender, sexual orientation, marital status, and educational attainment level (Sevak et al., 2015). For example, Cichy et al. (2015) found that older PWDs were more likely to be discriminated against in hiring and denied work-site accommodations. Furthermore, the prevalence rates of disability are statistically greater for individuals identifying as lesbian, gay, or bisexual (Fredriksen-Goldsen et al., 2013). Therefore, career counselors need to be aware of all potential areas of intersectionality in their clients. Multiple areas of cultural oppression within an individual absolutely affect the person's career development journey as they cope with discrimination and stigma on multiple fronts (Fabian & Pebdani, 2013; Kosciulek, 2014).

Career counselors must empower their clients to be self-advocates potentially using psychoeducational techniques to educate PWDs about their legal protections and rights. Practitioners may need to assist clients with effective communication strategies and assertiveness skills to prepare clients to potentially disclose their disabilities and request accommodations from their employers (Ebener et al., 2016). At the community level, career counselors can work to educate employers and the general public about disability-related issues through community organizations and events (Ebener et al., 2016), as disability awareness and programs designed to educate others about the benefits and strengths of hiring PWDs are able to reduce negative attitudes and biases (Martinez, 2013).

As a career counselor working with PWDs, it is vital to remember that you should not work in isolation. Collaborate with organizations that provide employment services to PWDs such as vocational rehabilitations, independent living organizations, and CRPs. These agencies and organizations may have resources and information that you do not, such as funding for assistive technology or postsecondary education.

Summary

When considering career counseling with PWDs, it is imperative that the counselor recognizes each individual as a whole person, not just a disability. Counselors must recognize the unique strengths, talents, and interests of each individual rather than solely focusing on the person's employment limitations and barriers. Career counseling for PWDs must be an empowering, creative, and individualized process to be effective (Kosciulek, 2014). It is imperative that career counseling be individualized for each PWD in order to best match their specialized abilities, interests, and skills. Most career counseling theories were not created to be used with PWDs; therefore, their applicability to PWDs varies and must be considered (Fabian & Pebdani, 2013). The same must be considered when evaluating results from career interest inventories that were not created or normed for PWDs.

Case Study

John is a 25-year-old man who was diagnosed with autism in childhood. He is coming to see a career counselor because he is unsure how to move forward in looking for the "right" job. John explains that he dropped out of college the first time when he was 19 because he struggled with the social interactions he was forced to have as part of college coursework (group work, discussion groups, etc.). After dropping out, he moved back home and enrolled in online coursework specific to his interest in graphic design, as his job goal at that time was video game design. John became overwhelmed with the coursework and felt very socially isolated, which led to him going into a deep depression. For the past few years, John has been living with his parents. He is no longer taking college courses, rarely leaves his home, and no longer wishes to be a video game designer. John wants guidance on how he should proceed from here. He wants to work but is unsure what that will look like, and he has no idea what type of work he is qualified to do.

Discussion Questions

1. You are working with a client with a disability who is debating whether to apply for SSDI. How might you explain the process, as well as the benefits and barriers they may encounter in the SSDI process?
2. You are working with a client who is a minor; their parents are very worried about the lack of services available to adults with disabilities. What type of services would you tell the parents about to educate them about adult service providers?
3. You are working with a client who is newly employed and recently disclosed their physical disability to their employer. The employer is resistant to providing any type of accommodations to your client. How could you educate your client about their legal rights and assist them in advocating for their needs?

References

ADA National Network. (2018). Reasonable accommodations in the workplace. https://adata.org/sites/adata.org/files/files/Reasonable_Accom_Workplace_final2018(2).pdf

American Foundation for the Blind. (2017). Statistical snapshots from the American foundation for the blind. Retrieved from http://www.afb.org/info/blindness-statistics/2

American Psychiatric Association (APA). (2013). *Diagnostic and statistical manual of mental health disorders* (5th ed.).

Americans With Disabilities Act of 1990. Pub. L. 101–336. 26 July 1990. 104 Stat. 328.

Americans With Disabilities Act Amendments Act of 2008. Pub. L. 110–325. 25 September 2008. 122 Stat. 3553.

Andersen, S. M., Chen, S., & Carter, C. (2000). Fundamental human needs: Making social cognition relevant. *Psychological Inquiry, 11,* 269–275.

Andrews, E. E., Kuemmel, A., Williams, J. L., Pilarski, C., Dunn, M., & Lund, E. M. (2013). Providing culturally competent supervision to trainees with disabilities in rehabilitation settings. *Rehabilitation Psychology, 58,* 233–244.

Argan, M., Hughes, C., Thoma, C. A., & Scott, L. A. (2016). Employment social skills: What skills are really valued? *Career Development and Transition for Exceptional Individuals, 39*(2), 111–120.

Association of Community Rehabilitation Educators (ACRE). (2013). *Types of certificates.* http://www.acreducators.org/certificates.

Baio, J., Wiggins, L., Christensen, D.L., et al. (2018). Prevalence of autism spectrum disorder among children aged 8 years. Autism and Developmental Disabilities Monitoring Network, 11 sites, United States, 2014. *Morbidity and Mortality Weekly Report Surveillance Summaries, 67* (No. SS-6), 1–23.

Baker, P.M.A., Linden, M. A., LaForce, S. S., Rutledge, J., & Goughnour, K. P. (2018). Barriers to employment participation of individuals with disabilities: Addressing the impact of employer (mis)perception and policy. *American Behavioral Scientist, 62*(5), 657–675.

Beardona, L., & Edmonds, G. (2007). ASPECT consultancy report: A national report on the needs of adults with Asperger's syndrome. The Autism Centre, Sheffield Hallam University.

Bluestein, D. L. (2006). *The psychology of working: A new perspective for career development, counseling, and public policy.* Routledge.

Boat, T. F., & Wu, J. T. (2015). In T. F. Boat & J. T. Wu (Eds.), *Mental disorders and disabilities among low-income children* (pp. 179–188). National Academies Press.

Bond, G., Drake. R., & Becker, D. (2008). An update on randomized controlled trials of evidence-based supported employment. *Psychiatric Rehabilitation Journal, 31,* 280–290.

Brew, K., & Gleason, R. P. (2014). Incentive to remain ill? How disability benefits affect health status. *The Journal for Nurse Practitioners, 10*(2), 107–112.

Bruyere, S. M., Erickson, W. A., & VanLooy, S. A. (2006). The impact of business size on employer ADA response. *Rehabilitation Counseling Bulletin, 49*(4), 194.

Bureau of Labor Statistics. (2012). *News release: The employment situation-December 2011*. U.S. Department of Labor. http://www.bls.gov/news.release/archives/empsit 01062012.pdf

Bureau of Labor Statistics. (2016). [Unpublished data tables of specific disability questions in the Current Population Survey, 2015 Annual Averages]. Author.

Burkhauser, R. V., & Houtenville, A. J. (2010). Employment among working-age people with disabilities: What the latest data will tell us. In E. M. Szymanski & R. M. Parker (Eds.), *Work and disability: Contexts, issues, and strategies for enhancing employment outcomes for people with disabilities* (3rd ed., pp. 49–86). Pro-Ed.

Butterworth, J., & Strauch, J. D. (1994). The relationship between social competence and success in competitive work place for persons with mental retardation. *Education and Training in Mental Retardation and Developmental Disabilities, 29*, 118–133.

Campbell, K., Bond, G. R., & Drake, R. E. (2011). Who benefits from supported employment: A meta-analytic study? *Schizophrenia Bulletin, 37*(2), 370–380.

Cederlund, M., Hagberg, B., Billstedt, E., Gillberg, I.C., & Gillberg, C. (2008). Asperger syndrome and autism: A comparative longitudinal follow-up study more than 5 years after original diagnosis. *Journal of Autism and Developmental Disorders, 38*(1), 72–85.

Certo, N. J., & Leuking, R. G. (2006). Service integration and school to work transition: Customized employment as an outcome for youth with significant disabilities. *Journal of Applied Rehabilitation Counseling, 37*(4), 29–35.

Chadsey, J. (2007). Adult social relationships. In S. L. Odom, R. H. Horner, M. E. Snell, & J. Blacker (Eds.), *Handbook of developmental disabilities* (pp. 449–466). Guilford Press.

Cichy, K. E., Li, J., McMahon, B. T., & Rumrill, P. D. (2015). The workplace discrimination experiences of older workers with disabilities: Results from the national EEOC ADA research project. *Journal of Vocational Rehabilitation, 43*, 137–148. https://doi.org/10.3233/JVR-150763

Coffey, M., Coufopoulos, A., & Kinghom, K. (2014). Barriers to employment for visually impaired women. *International Journal of Workplace Health Management, 7*(3), 171–185.

Commission on Accreditation of Rehabilitation Facilities (CARF). (2019). *Who we are*. http://www.carf.org/About/WhoWeAre/.

Commission on Rehabilitation Counselor Certification (CRCC). (2017). *Code of professional ethics for rehabilitation counselors*. https://www.crccertification.com/code-of-ethics-4

Commission on Rehabilitation Counselor Certification. (2019). *CRC/CRCC scope of practice statement*. https://www.crccertification.com/crc-crcc-scope-of-practice

Cowen, T. (2011). *An economic and rational choice approach to the autism spectrum and human neurodiversity* (Working Paper in Economics No. 11–58). George Mason University.

Crudden, A., McDonnall, M. C., & Hierholzer, A. L. (2015). Transportation: An electronic survey of persons who are legally blind. *Journal of Visual Impairment and Blindness, 109*(6), 445–456.

Ditchman, N., Wu, M., Chan, F., Fitzgerald, S., Lin, C., & Tu, W. (2013). Vocational rehabilitation. In D. Strauser (Ed.), *Career development, employment, and disability in rehabilitation* (pp. 343–360). Springer Publishing Company.

Ebener, D. J., Fioramonti, D. L., & Smedema, S. M. (2016). Career development in men with disabilities: A psychosocial perspective. *Career Planning, 32*(1), 120–129.

Ellison, M., & Mullen, M. (2018). *Issues in employment for young adults with mental health conditions*. University of Massachusetts Medical School, Department of Psychiatry, Systems and Psychosocial Advances Research Center. https://escholarship.umassmed.edu/cgi/viewcontent.cgi?article=1130&context=pib

Erickson, W. A., von Schrader, S., Bruyere, S. M., & VanLooy, S. A. (2014a). The employment environment: Employer perspectives, policies, and practices regarding the employment of persons with disabilities. *Rehabilitation Counseling Bulletin, 57*, 195-208. doi: 10.1177/0034355213509841

Erickson, W. A., von Schrader, S., Bruyere, M., VanLooy, S. A., & Matteson, S. (2014b). Disability-inclusive employer practices and hiring of individuals with disabilities. *Rehabilitation Research, Policy, and Education, 28*, 309–328. https://doi.org/10.1891/2168-6653.28.4.309

Fabian, E. S., & MacDonald-Wilson, K. L. (2012). Professional practice in rehabilitation service delivery systems and related system resources. In R. M. Parker & J. B. Patterson (Eds.), *Rehabilitation counseling, basics and beyond* (5th ed., pp. 55–84). PRO-ED Inc.

Fabian, E. S., & Pebdani, R. (2013). The career development of youth and young adults with disabilities. In S. Brown & R. W. Lent (Eds.), *Career development and counseling: Putting theory and research to work* (2nd ed., pp. 357–486). Wiley.

Fredriksen-Goldsen, K. I., Kim, H. J., Barkan, S. E., Muraco, A., & Hoy-Ellis, C. P. (2013). Health disparities among lesbian, gay, and bisexual older adults: Results from a population-based study. *American Journal of Public Health, 103*, 1802–1809. https://doi.org/10.2105/AJPH.2012.301110

Gerber, P. J., & Price, L. A. (2003). Persons with learning disabilities in the workplace: What we know so far in the Americans with Disabilities Act era. *Learning Disabilities Research & Practice, 18*(2), 132–136.

Gouvier, W. D., Steiner, D. D., Jackson, W. T., Schlater, D., & Rain, J. S. (1991). Employment discrimination against handicapped job candidates: An analog study of the effects of neurological causation, visibility of handicap, and public contact. *Rehabilitation Psychology, 36*(2), 121–129. https://doi.org/10.1037/h0079077

Haber, M. G., Mazzotti, V. L., Mustian, A. L., Rowe, D. A., Bartholomew, A. L., Test, D. W., & Fowler, C. H. (2016). What works, when, for whom and with whom: A meta-analytic review of predictors of postsecondary success for students with disabilities? *Review of Educational Research, 86*(1), 123–162.

Hawleya, C., Diaza, S., & Reid, C. (2009). Healthcare employees' progression through disability benefits. *Work, 34*, 53–66.

Haynes, S., & Linden, M. (2012). Workplace accommodations and unmet needs specific to individuals who are deaf or hard of hearing. *Disability and Rehabilitation: Assistive Technology, 7*(5), 408–415.

Hedley, D., Uljarević, M., & Cameron, L. (2016) Employment programmes and interventions targeting adults with autism spectrum disorder: A systematic review of the literature. *Autism, 21*, 929–941.

Hendricks, D. (2010). Employment and adults with autism spectrum disorders: Challenges and strategies for success. *Journal of Vocational Rehabilitation, 32*, 125–134. https://doi.org/10.3233/JVR-2010-0502

Hernandez, B., Keys, C., & Balcazar, F. (2000). Employer attitudes toward workers with disabilities and their ADA employment rights: A literature review. *Journal of Rehabilitation, 66*(4), 4–16.

Houtenville, A. J., Brucker, D. L., & Lauer, E. A. (2014). *Annual compendium of disability statistics: 2014*. Institute on Disability, University of New Hampshire

Individuals with Disabilities Education Act (IDEA), 20 U.S.C. § 1400 (2004).

Institute for Corporate Productivity. (2014). *Employing people with intellectual and developmental disabilities: A report for the Institute for Corporate Productivity*. https://ohioemploymentfirst.org/up_doc/Employing_People_With_Intellectual_and_Developmental_Disabilities.pdf

Ipsen, C. & Swicegood, G. (2017). Rural and urban vocational rehabilitation self-employment outcomes. *Journal of Vocational Rehabilitation, 46*, 97–105.

Jans, L. H., Kaye, H. S., & Jones, E. C. (2012). Getting hired: Successfully employed people with disabilities offer advice on disclosure, interviewing, and job search. *Journal of Occupational Rehabilitation, 22*(2), 155–165.

Kaye, H. S. (2010). The impact of the 2007–09 recession on workers with disabilities. *Monthly Labor Review, 133*(10), 19–30.

Kaye, S. H., Jans, L. H., & Jones, E. C. (2011). Why don't employers hire and retain workers with disabilities? *Journal of Occupational Rehabilitation, 21*, 526–536.

Khalema, N., & Shankar, J. (2014). Perspectives on employment integration, mental illness and disability, and workplace health. *Advances in Public Health, 2014*, https://doi.org/10.1155/2014/258614

Koletsi, M., Niersman, A., van Busschbach, J. T., Catty, J., Becker, T., Burns, T., Fioritti, A., Kalkan, R., Lauber, C., Rössler, W., Tomov, T., Wiersma, D., & EQOLISE Group. (2009). Working with mental health problems: Clients' experiences of IPS, vocational rehabilitation and employment. *Social Psychiatry and Psychiatric Epidemiology, 44*(11), 961–970.

Kosciulek, J. F. (2014). Facilitating the career development of individuals with disabilities through empowering career counseling. In N. C. Gysbers, M. J. Heppner, & J. A. Johnston (Eds.), *Career counseling: Holism, diversity, and strengths* (4th ed., pp. 129–139). American Counseling Association.

Kraus, L., Lauer, E., Coleman, R., & Houtenville, A. (2018). *2017 Disability statistics annual report*. University of New Hampshire.

Lindstrom, L. E., & Benz, M. R. (2002). Phases of career development: Case studies of young women with learning disabilities. *Exceptional Children, 69*(1), 67–83.

Lizotte, M. (2018). I am a college graduate: Postsecondary experiences as described by adults with autism spectrum disorders. *International Journal of Education and Practice, 6*(4), 179–191.

Loy, B. (2015). *Accommodation and compliance series workplace accommodations: Low cost, high impact.* Job Accommodation Network.

Luciano, A., & Meara, E. (2014). Employment status of people with mental illness: National survey data from 2009 and 2010. *Psychiatric Services, 65*(10), 1201–1209.

Lund, E. M., Andrews, E. E., & Holt, J. M. (2016). A qualitative analysis of the reflections of professional psychology trainees with disabilities. *Training and Education in Professional Psychology, 10,* 206–213.

Lynch, K. A. (2013). Survey reveals myths and misconceptions abundant among hiring managers about the capabilities of people who are visually impaired. *Journal Of Visual Impairment & Blindness, 107*(6), 408–410

Mackelprang, R. W., & Salsgiver, R. O. (2015). *Disability: A diversity model approach in human service practice* (3rd ed.). Lyceum Books, Inc.

Mank, D. (2003). Supported employment outcomes across a decade: Is there evidence of improvement in the quality of implementation? *Mental Retardation, 41,* 188–197.

Marini, I. (2012). Theories of adjustment and adaptation to disability. In I. Marini, N. M. Glover-Graf, & M. J. Millington (Eds.), *Psychosocial aspects of disability: Insider perspectives and strategies for counselors* (pp. 133–168). Springer.

Maroto, M., & Pettinicchio, D. (2015). Twenty-five years after the ADA: Situating disability in America's system of stratification. Disability Studies Quarterly, *35*(3). Retrieved from http://dsq-sds.org/article/view/4927/4024

Martin, R. West-Evans, K., & Connelly, J. (2010). Vocational rehabilitation: Celebrating 90 years of careers and independence. *American Rehabilitation, 34*(1), 15–18.

Martinez, K. (2013). Integrated employment, employment first, and US federal policy. *Journal of Vocational Rehabilitation, 38,* 165–168.

Mayes, S. D., & Calhoun, S. L. (2003). Ability profiles in children with autism: Influence of age and IQ. *Autism, 7*(1), 65–80.

McKnight-Lizotte, M. (2018). Work-related communication barriers for individuals with autism: A pilot qualitative study. *Australian Journal of Rehabilitation Counselling, 24*(1), 12–26.

Merrell, K. W., & Walker, H. M. (2004). Deconstructing a definition: Social maladjustment versus emotional disturbance and moving the EBD field forward. *Psychology in the Schools, 41*(8), 899–910.

Mitra, S., & Kruse, D. (2016). Are workers with disabilities more likely to be displaced? *International Journal of Human Resource Management, 27,* 1550–1579. https://doi.org/10.1080/09585192.2015.1137616

Perkins-Dock, R. E., Battle, T. R., Edgerton, J. M., & McNeill, J. N. (2015). A survey of barriers to employment for individuals who are deaf. *Journal of the American Deafness & Rehabilitation Association, 49*(2), 66–85.

Phillips, B. N., Robison, L. J., & Kosciulek, J. F. (2014). The influence of social capital on starting wage for people with and without disabilities. *Rehabilitation Counseling Bulletin, 58*(1), 37–45.

Porter, R. S., & Kaplan, J. L. (Eds.). (2011). The Merck manual of diagnosis and therapy (19th ed.). Merck Sharp & Dohme Corp.

Price, L., Gerber, P. J., & Mulligan, R. (2003). The Americans with Disabilities Act and adults with learning disabilities as employees: The realities of the workplace. *Remedial and Special Education, 24*(6), 350–358.

Prince, M. J. (2017). Persons with invisible disabilities and workplace accommodation: Findings from a scoping literature review. *Journal of Vocational Rehabilitation, 46,* 75–86.

Rehabilitation Act of 1973, Pub. L. 93–112. 26, U.S.C. 29 ss. 791 (1973).

Rehabilitation Services Administration. (2005). *Annual report.* Office of Special Education and Rehabilitation Services. https://www2.ed.gov/about/reports/annual/rsa/2005/rsa-2005-annual-report.pdf

Riesen, T., & Oertle, K. M. (2019). Developing work-based learning experience for students with intellectual and developmental disabilities: A preliminary study of employers' perspectives. *Journal of Rehabilitation, 85*(2), 27–36.

Ryan, R. M., & Deci, E. L. (2000). Self-determination theory and the facilitation of intrinsic motivation, social development, and well-being. *American Psychologist, 55,* 68–78.

Saunders, J. L., Barros-Bailey, M., Chapman, C., & Nunez, P. (2009). Rehabilitation counselor certification: Moving forward. *Rehabilitation Counseling Bulletin, 52*(2), 77–84.

Schur, L., Nishii, L., Adya, M., Kruse, D., Bruyere, S. M., & Blanck, P. (2014). Accommodating employees with and without disabilities. *Human Resource Management, 53,* 593–621. https://doi.org/10.1002/hrm.21607

Sevak, P., Houtenville, A. J., Brucker, D. L., & O'Neill, J. (2015). Individual characteristics and the disability employment gap. *Journal of Disability Policy Studies, 26,* 80–88 https://doi.org/1044207315585823

Shadrick, I., & Etlen, C. (2019). Predictors of competitive employment of adults with deaf-blindness following vocational rehabilitation. *Journal of Applied Rehabilitation Counseling, 50*(2), 148–159.

Simcock, P., & Manthorpe, J. (2014). Deafblind and neglected or deafblindness neglected? Revisiting the case of Beverley Lewis. *Journal of Social Work, 44*(8), 2325–2341.

Smart, J. (2012). *Disability across the developmental lifespan for the rehabilitation counselor.* Springer Publishing Company.

Solovieva, T. I., Dowler, D. L., & Walls, R. T. (2011). Employer benefits from making workplace accommodations. *Disability and Health Journal, 4*(1), 39–45.

Sundar, V., O'Neill, J., Houtenville, A. J., Phillips, K. G., Keirns, T., Smith, A., & Katz, E. E. (2018). Striving to work and overcoming barriers: Employment strategies and successes of people with disabilities. *Journal of Vocational Rehabilitation, 48,* 93–109. https://doi.org/10.3233/JVR170918

Taylor, J. L., & Seltzer, M. M. (2011). Employment and post-secondary educational activities for young adults with autism spectrum disorders during the transition to adulthood. *Journal of Autism and Developmental Disorders, 41*(5), 566–574.

Ticket to Work and Work Incentives Act of 199. Pub. L. 106-170. 17 December 1999. U. S. C. 113 Stat. 1860.

Timmons, J. C., Hall, A. C., Bose, J., Wolfe, A., & Winsor, J. (2011). Choosing employment: Factors that impact employment decision for individuals with intellectual disability. *Intellectual and Developmental Disabilities, 49*(4), 285–299.

United Nations. (2006). United Nations Convention on the Rights of Persons with Disabilities. *Treaty Series, 2515,* 3. Retrieved from: https://www.un.org/development/desa/disabilities/convention-on-the-rights-of-persons-with-disabilities/convention-on-the-rights-of-persons-with-disabilities-2.html

U.S. Bureau of Labor Statistics. (2020). Persons with a disability: Labor force characteristics summary. U.S. Department of Labor. https://www.bls.gov/news.release/pdf/disabl.pdf

U.S. Census Bureau. (2016). *American community survey.* https://www.census.gov/acs/www/data/data-tables-and-tools/data-profiles/2016/

U.S. Department of Labor (2014a). *Office of Disability Employment Policy—Current disability employment statistics.* http://www.dol.gov/odep/

U.S. Department of Labor. (2014b). *Persons with a disability: Labor force characteristics–2013.* http://www.bls.gov/news.release/disabl.nr0.htm

U.S. Government Accountability Office. (2005). *Vocational rehabilitation—Better measures and monitoring could improve the performance of the VR program* (Report No. GAO-05-865).

Wehman, P., Chan, F., Ditchman, N., & Kang, H. J. (2014). Effect of supported employment on vocational rehabilitation outcomes of transition-age youth with intellectual and developmental disabilities: A case control study. *Intellectual and Developmental Disabilities, 52*(4), 296–310.

Winsor, J., & Butterworth, J. (2008). Trends & milestones: Participation in integrated employment and community-based non-work services for individuals supported by state intellectual/developmental disabilities agencies. *Intellectual and Developmental Disabilities, 46,* 166–168.

Workforce Innovation and Opportunity Act of 2014. Pub. L. 113–128. 22 July 2014. U.S.C. 29 ss. 3101, et. seq.

CHAPTER 12

Career Counseling for Veterans

Rebecca R. Sametz and Tyler A. Riddle

CHAPTER OVERVIEW

After war, many veterans return home with a significant amount of life challenges that hamper their potential for vocational success (Elnitsky et al., 2018). The challenges faced by veterans warrant the immediate and appropriate implementation of career services to aid them in their transition to civilian life. This chapter will address and identify the challenges facing veterans, including reintegrating into the community, reconnecting with family, reorienting to the less-structured character of civilian life, and adjusting to life with a disability. Further, this chapter will provide an overview of specific veteran's benefits and programs and employment. This includes campus transitions, academic success, and the role of various entities in supporting veterans returning to academic settings.

CHAPTER OBJECTIVES

After reading this chapter, the student will be able to complete the following:

1. Outline the effects of multiple and extended deployments on veterans and their families.

2. Describe the challenges veterans reintegrating into the community and reconnecting with their families are facing. This is also known as the military-civilian gap.

3. Identify benefits and programs available for assisting veterans with transitioning into the world of work.

4. Implement strategies for working with veterans who are reintegrating into the civilian workforce.

Introduction

After war, many veterans return home with a significant number of life challenges that hamper their potential for vocational success (Elnitsky et al., 2018). The challenges faced by veterans warrant the immediate and appropriate implementation of career services to aid them in their transition into civilian life. This chapter will address and identify the challenges veterans face, including reintegrating into the community, reconnecting with family, reorienting to the less-structured character of civilian life, and adjusting to life with a disability. Further, this chapter will provide an overview of specific veterans' benefits, programs, and employment. This includes campus transitions, academic success, and various entities that support veterans who return to academic settings.

What Does It Mean to Be a Veteran?

The first question that needs to be answered is, what does it mean to be a veteran? Title 38 of the Code of Federal Regulations defines a veteran as "a person who served in the active military, naval, or air service and who was discharged or released under conditions other than dishonorable" (Veteran Affairs, 2018). Therefore, anyone who has completed service for any branch of the armed forces is classified as a veteran as long as they were not dishonorably discharged.

There are three different types of military service that can be coded as actively serving in the military: full-time, part-time, and reserves. Someone who is serving full-time is an *active-duty* service member (Veteran Affairs, 2018). Simply, the person is available for duty 24 hours per day, 7 days a week unless on leave (e.g., vacation) or pass (e.g., authorized time off). Someone who serves part-time performs duties one weekend per month, plus 2 weeks of training per year. Members of the Reserves and National Guard are considered part-time, although since the Gulf War in 1990, they've spent approximately more time called to full-time active duty (Veteran Affairs, 2018). Lastly, someone who is on *reserve* is available to deliver supplementary support to active-duty forces when obligated. All of the different military services have a reserve branch under the patronage of the Department of Defense (DoD; e.g., Army Reserve, Air Force Reserve, Navy Reserve, Marine Corps Reserve, and Coast Guard Reserve; Veteran Affairs, 2018).

Reasons for Joining the Military

Rozanova et al. (2016) reviewed qualitative articles that examined reasons individuals joined the military, which included pragmatic and career-oriented reasons, as well as the search for certainty in the military culture, either as a life perspective or as a life leading to opportunities elsewhere. For instance, one pragmatic reason for joining the military was to establish a pathway to socioeconomic achievement related to the post-Second World War introduction of the G.I. Bill for training and educational opportunities (Sampson & Laub, 1996). Many people wanted to have the opportunity to go back to college and obtain a degree for free or to be able to provide that opportunity to family members (e.g., children).

Nowadays, young people in poor communities similarly view military service as a career-building strategy, but their outcomes are very different. For example, there are many veterans who return from serving who are at or below the poverty line or homeless (Masten, 2013). This is partly because the removal of troops from Iraq and Afghanistan coincided with an economic recession (Rozanova et al., 2016). Further, many veterans struggle with identifying with a career that matches the duties they were performing while serving.

Individuals also join the military because they want to serve their country and protect its liberty and freedom. However, reasons for serving include opportunities to travel the world and to improve or learn new skills that they could not necessarily learn if they did not serve.

Effects of Multiple Deployments

With the line of work that individuals in the military are exposed to, there comes "baggage" that they bring back with them when returning from deployments, whether it is for leave or because they are exiting the military. Being in the military is a learning curve for not only the individual serving but also for the person's family and children. In this section, we will discuss some of the family dynamics that must be considered when working with veterans and their families, including struggles reintegrating into the community after serving for an extended period of time and adjusting to life with a disability.

Family

Military families face very unique challenges and hardships, such as the deployment of a parent or sibling into a war zone (Masten, 2013). However, one must remember that these are in addition to the hardships that families already have that are not specifically related to the military (e.g., struggling to find childcare, making ends meet financially, and educating and disciplining their children).

Moving and Mobility

Moving is something that goes hand in hand with having a spouse or family member in the military. Military families are known to move every 2 to 3 years, which is considerably more often than nonmilitary families (Lester & Flake, 2013). While reports and studies on military families have indicated that moving can provide opportunities to explore the world and experience other cultures, there are also issues of separation from loved ones, changes in daycare and school, disruptions to relationships or other social ties, and disruptions in health care, as well as the stress of adapting to a new environment (Cozza & Lerner, 2013; Lester & Flake, 2013; Masten, 2013). One area where there is limited research and focus is the burden that frequent moves place on spouses in terms of their careers. Many spouses who have a significant other in the military struggle with maintaining employment and, more importantly, growing within their career fields. Career counselors who do not have an understanding of the deployment cycle will struggle with recognizing the unique needs and challenges to service members and their families and the overall culture of the military.

Separation and Reunification

Being in the military is all about a series of separations and reunifications with family and loved ones. This cycle of separation and reunification is not as common among civilian families (Cozza & Lerner, 2013), which is why it is important to note here. There are several factors that are important to note when it comes to judging the effect that deployment has on a child, including age and length of separation. Multiple and prolonged deployments have a greater effect on a family than short deployments (Masten, 2013). What is important to note is that families that already have financial, relationship, and/or emotional issues are more affected than families who function well before deployment. However, this cycle does mean that when a spouse or family member returns from deployment and is reunited with the family, there is a period of adjustment. This is also true for when the family member deploys. For instance, deployment can come at a bad time for a family, and it could mean missing or disrupting developmental milestones that happen only once in a child's life (i.e., first word, walking, confirmation, graduation, marriage).

Injury, Death, and Disability

There is always the risk of physical and mental harm for those who serve in the military, which can ultimately have devastating effects on children and families (Masten, 2013). In their 2011 report, the DoD stated that approximately 56% of all members of the military are exposed to some level of combat (DoD, 2013). During Operation Enduring Free (Afghanistan, 2001), Operation Iraqi Freedom (Iraq, 2003), and

Operation New Dawn (Iraq, 2010), about two million troops were deployed overseas with up to 100,000 injuries in about 6,825 fatalities.

Injuries and disabilities can change the way parenting is done, depending on the disability. The entire family dynamic can change if a parent is unable to perform certain activities, and the other parent is responsible for not only caring for the child(ren) but also the spouse. The signature injuries of the current conflict are traumatic brain injury (TBI) and blast wounds, which affect 13%–25% of military personnel (Wolfe et al., 2009). High rates of mental health conditions are also associated with TBI, such as post-traumatic stress (15%–60%), depression (23%), anxiety (43%), and substance use disorders (10%–34%) (Rozanova et al., 2016). Suicide ideations, threats, attempts, and completions are also of critical importance, as they are the result of a preventable mental health condition (Gallaway et al., 2015). Therefore, it is not only a time when the individual serving in the military needs to make adjustments to ways of living but also the family must do the same. This can cause additional stress, as well as financial difficulties (Masten, 2013).

Adjusting to Life With a Disability

There is an estimation that more than 54 million Americans struggle with chronic illness and disabilities. With the high amount of stress and exposure to combat, veterans are at higher risk for developing chronic illnesses and being disabled (Marini & Stebnicki, 2012; Stebnicki, 2016). Many veterans who experience permanent illness and disabling conditions endure a complex level of psychosocial adjustment related to their residual functional capacity and overall well-being. One thing that career counselors should take into account is that it is important to bring the family into the process to ensure that all involved are supportive of the individual returning to work. One thing that can limit the individual is the family's willingness to support the veteran, whether it be to return to work or seek additional education.

Reintegration Into the Community

Military members face a number of challenges as they leave active duty and reenter the civilian world. One of the unmistakable cultural differences between military and civilian occupations is that in the armed forces, men and women are trained for engaging in combatants. They learn how to survive, adapt, and avoid being killed and how to respond to critical incidents, caring for their wounded brothers and sisters. They are in occupations where they may witness death and injury (Adler & Castro, 2013). There are frequent geographic relocations; separation from family, friends, and loved ones; and required availability on a 24-hour basis. It is within this culture that service members' lives, health, and safety depend on each of them being mentally and physically fit for duty. There is no job as a civilian that makes these types of demands. Therefore, many active-duty personnel who transition to civilian life feel unprepared to work in civilian occupations.

Many of today's veterans have been deployed to combat areas around the world in the Global War on Terror (GWoT). The political disagreement with the GWoT is often most easily expressed by the veterans of today's all-volunteer force. In U. S. history, no other conflict as large or as long has been fought with an all-volunteer force.

The military-civilian gap has seldom been greater than it is today. In fact, in the most recent statistics from 2017, only 15% of America's youth had a parent who served in the military, while 40% had a parent who had served in 1995 (Garamone, 2019).

According to DoD official Anthony Kurta, "Today, when asked how likely it is they will be serving in the military in the next few years, 87% responded 'definitely not' or 'probably not,'" he said. "While the American public has faith in the efficacy of our military, they feel little to no personal connection with it" (Garamone, 2019). These factors combined with misperceptions of the military and its veterans leads to a lack of knowledge and creates a general inability for civilians and military members to identify with one another.

It is important to note and recognize that it is natural for veterans and their family members to respond with some level of reluctance, resistance, and defensiveness as they motivate themselves for the reintegration process. This is particularly true when there are mental and physical injuries that were sustained while on deployment. Further, what most career counselors need to understand when working with veterans is that these lingering effects of deployment may interfere with the career counseling process. However, there are community organizations that exist to assist with breaking down those barriers so that the counseling process can be successful.

Veterans' Benefits and Programs

Veterans have access to benefits that civilians may not that can assist them in transitioning to civilian life, locating work, and seeking educational opportunities to be more qualified for particular careers. While this section does not discuss all the benefits and programs that veterans have access to, the ones discussed are the most common.

Veterans Affairs Vocational Rehabilitation and Employment

State vocational rehabilitation (VR) programs are widely recognized as "one of the largest providers of employment services and supports for individuals with disabilities" (Nye-Lengerman, 2017, p. 40). For veterans and service members, the Veterans Affairs (VA) Vocational Rehabilitation and Employment (VR&E) program provides services to help with job training, employment accommodations, resume development, and job-seeking skills coaching for free for those who are eligible. Veterans of the U.S. Armed Forces are eligible for benefits upon discharge from active military service under other than dishonorable conditions (U.S. Department of Veteran Affairs, 2019b). There are even opportunities for VR&E to assist veterans in starting their own businesses or independent living services for those who have severe disabilities and are unable to work at competitive employment work sites. VR&E is staffed with vocational rehabilitation counselors who are equipped to assist veterans with service-connected disabilities to obtain suitable employment and/or achieve independent living goals (U.S. Department of Veteran Affairs, 2019b).

As a career counselor, it is important to note that not all veterans are comfortable with returning to the VA to receive services. Many may seek services outside of the VA system before going back because of the stigma associated with the VA (Wyse et al., 2018). Some veterans have reported the long wait times for receiving services or even to complete an intake as not a good use of their time. Further, research does exist that reports veterans have stated that the VA system is too complex to navigate, and it is difficult to see the positives in the services that they could receive because of the lengthy application process (Wyse et al., 2018). On the other hand, there are veterans who have reported not knowing about the VR&E. What is clear for career counselors is that understanding and knowing that this program exists for veterans is important in terms of another community agency that can provide additional support to veterans transitioning into civilian life and the world of work.

G.I. Bill

The G.I Bill refers to any VA education benefit earned by members of active duty, selected reserve, and National Guard Armed Forces and their families (Military.com, 2019). The benefit is designed to help service members and eligible veterans cover the costs associated with getting an education and training. The G.I Bill has several programs, and each is administrated differently, depending on a person's eligibility and duty status. There are several types of training a veteran can receive with the G.I Bill. The following is a list of those services:

- College degree programs, including associate's, bachelor's, and advanced degree programs
- Vocational/technical training, including noncollege degree programs
- On-the-job/apprenticeship training
- Licensing and certification reimbursement
- National testing programs, such as Scholastic Assessment Test (SAT), and Advanced Placement Exam (AP)
- Flight training
- Correspondence training
- Work-study programs
- Tuition assistance top-up
- Tutorial assistance

This program has been assisting qualified veterans and their family members since 1944 by providing money to cover all or some of the costs for school or training (U.S. Department of Veterans Affairs, 2019a).

Roles and Strategies for Career Counselors

The truth is that developing a career is difficult for most everyone, whether you are a soldier or a civilian. Research suggests that many veterans are relegated to unskilled or semiskilled positions, such as fast-food worker, retail sales clerk, construction worker, truck driver, security guard, janitorial cleaning services, landscape groundskeeper, or material handler working in a warehouse (Stebnicki, 2016). This is not saying that these are the only jobs that veterans are capable of doing, but that they are drawn to these types of positions because they are plentiful and readily available within today's economy. The biggest thing that veterans report when it comes to speaking about work is that they would prefer to have a career rather than just a job (Elnitsky et al., 2018).

Professional counselors who work in the area of career counseling and development serve in many different roles to assist their clients with career goals, educational opportunities, job-seeking skills training, resume and cover letter development, workplace stress, and maintaining employment (Stebnicki, 2016). A good place to begin when working with veterans is to get a better idea of what they did prior to the military and the jobs they held while in the service (Wyse et al., 2018).

Another technique that can be used by career counselors for veterans is to have them write a personal life story or testimonial that is educational, work, and career related. Writing engages a different part of the bran and allows individuals to communicate deeper thoughts and insights as opposed to answering yes/no questions in a structured interview or on various career assessments. The personal life story or testimonial should include, at a minimum, work or professional experiences, interests, aptitudes, special skills and abilities, hobbies, personal experiences, and peak insights that evolved, which prompted clients to pursue their educational or career paths (Syzmanski, 1999). To build a strong working relationship and understanding of the client, a career counselor may also ask the veteran about any significant life events that helped cultivate who they are and where they see themselves going in the future. This gives the career counselor a chance to build rapport with their client and to have a better understanding of the client's mindset and reasoning for choosing a particular career or line of work.

Career Theory and Approaches

There are various career theory approaches that can be useful when working with this particular population. However, research suggests that a cognitive approach, known as CIP, is most effective with this population. CIP empowers individuals to become effective decision makers and problem solvers (Hayden et al., 2013). The structure of the intervention with its focus on the knowledge domains of self and options, the process of decision making, and the associated thoughts an individual may be having related to this process appears to offer a structure in which to work with this population on their career development. Career counselors should remind themselves that many veterans enter into the military just after high school and have not learned the skills necessary to engage the civilian job market successfully. Therefore, it is important through CIP that career counselors are sensitive to information that may seem obvious to some but may not be for this population.

CIP can assist veterans in making an appropriate current career choice and in the process, learn improved problem-solving and decision-making skills, which can be used in future choices. The goal of career counselors is not to only assist their clients in obtaining a job but also to assist them in developing skills that can be used when they are no longer working with that client. CIP can assist veterans in making an appropriate career choice by focusing on career problem-solving and decision-making processes. It forces the veteran to examine the problem and explore different scenarios in which decisions must be made and to examine those decisions as they relate to a career.

Strength-based counseling coupled with CIP may also be useful for those veterans who struggle with understanding and recognizing their own personal strengths. Strength-based counseling focuses on individual strength, community, and societal factors (Hayden et al., 2013), which has shown to be another approach that is useful with this population. This approach allows veterans to recognize their own personal strengths as it relates to work, as well as community and societal factors that could affect or support them in the career counseling process. Addressing career issues with this population often reduces depression, likelihood of substance abuse, and other secondary deleterious outcomes.

Summary

As a specialized population, veterans often require assistance integrating into the civilian workforce. Career counselors would do well to ensure that they are knowledgeable about the myriad of challenges faced by this population and develop a dynamic tool belt of skills and resources that can aid them in overcoming barriers that may be limiting their ability to return to the workforce and to once again engage in a meaningful career.

Discussion Questions

1. What types of strategies and techniques would you use with veterans?
2. How can families be incorporated into the career counseling process for veterans?
3. What other struggles may exist for veterans that this chapter did not touch on?

References

Adler, A. B., & Castro, C. A. (2013). An occupational mental health model for the military. *Military Behavioral Health, 1,* 41–51.

Cozza, S. J., & Lerner, R. M. (2013). Military children and families: Introducing the issue. *The Future of Children, 23*(2), 3–11.

Department of Defense (DoD). (2013, February). *Department of Defense health related behaviors survey of active duty military personnel.* Retrieved August 25, 2019, from file:///Users/rebeccasametz/Downloads/Final%202011%20HRB%20 Active%20Duty%20Survey%20Exec%20Summary_2.pdf

Elnitsky, C. A., Fisher, M. P., & Blevins, C. L. (2018). Military service member and veteran reintegration: A conceptual analysis, unified definition, ad key domains. *Frontiers in Psychology, 8*(369). https://doi.org/10.3389/fpsyg.2017.00369

Gallaway, M. S., Lagana-Riordan, C., Dabs, C. R., Bell, A. A., Bender, D. S., Fink, K., Forys-Donahue, J. A., Pecko, S. C., Schmissrauter, R., Perales, M. A., Coombs, M. R., Rattigan, M. R., Milliken, A. M. (2015). A mixed methods epidemiological investigation of preventable deaths among U.S. Army soldiers assigned to a rehabilitative warrior transition unit. *Work, 50,* 21–36.

Garamone, J. (2019). *DOD official cites widening military-civilian gap.* U.S. Department of Defense. Retrieved August 25, 2019, from https://www.defense.gov/explore/story/Article/1850344/dod-official-cites-widening-military-civilian-gap/

Hayden, S. C., Green, L., & Dorsett, K. (2013). Perseverance and progress: Career counseling for military personnel with traumatic brain injury. *VISTAS Online,* 1–8.

Lester, P., & Flake, E. (2013). How wartime military service affects children and families. *The Future of Children, 23*(3), 121–134.

Marini, I., & Stebnicki, M. A. (2012). *The psychological and social impact of illness and disability* (6th ed.). Springer Publishing.

Masten, A. S. (2013). Afterword: What we can learn from military children and families. *The Future of Children, 23*(2), 199–212.

Military.com. (2019). *GI Bill overview.* Military.com. Retrieved August 25, 2019, from https://www.military.com/education/gi-bill/learn-to-use-your-gi-bill.html

Nye-Lengerman, K. (2017). Vocational rehabilitation service usage and outcomes for individuals with autism spectrum disorder. *Research in Autism Spectrum Disorder, 41,* 39–50.

Rozanova, J., Noulas, P., Smart, K., Roy, A., Southwick, S. M., Davidson, L., & Harpaz-Rotem, I. (2016). "I'm coming home, tell the world I'm coming home." The long homecoming and mental health treatment of Iraq and Afghanistan war veterans. *Psychiatry Quarterly, 87*(3), 427–443.

Sampson, R., & Laub, J. (1996). Socioeconomic achievement in the life course of disadvantaged men: Military service as a turning point, circa 1940–1965. *American Sociological Review, 61*(3), 347–367.

Stebnicki, M. A. (2016). In I. Marini, & M. A. Stebnick (Eds.), *The professional counselor's desk reference* (2nd ed., pp. 499–506). Springer Publishing Company.

Syzmanski, E. M. (1999). Disability, job stress, the changing nature of careers, and the career resilency portfolio. *Rehabilitation Counseling Bulletin, 42*(4), 279–289.

U.S. Department of Veterans Affairs. (2019a). *About GI Bill benefits*. VA Benefits and Healthcare. Retrieved August 25, 2019, from https://www.va.gov/education/about-gi-bill-benefits

U.S. Department of Veteran Affairs. (2019b). *Vocational rehabilitation and employment (VR&E)*. VA Benefits and Healthcare. Retrieved August 25, 2019, from https://www.benefits.va.gov/VOCREHAB/VRE_Process.asp

Veteran Affairs. (2018). *What is a veteran? The legal definition*. VA.org. https://va.org/what-is-a-veteran-the-legal-definition/

Wolfe, S. J., Bebarta, V. S., Bonnett, C. J., Pons, P. T., & Cantrill, S. V. (2009). Blast injuries. *Lancet, 374*, 405–415.

Wyse, J. J., Pogoda, T. K., Mastarone, G. L., Gilbert, T., & Carlson, K. F. (2018). Employment and vocational rehabilitation experiences among veterans with polytrauma/traumatic brain injury history. *Psychological Services, 17*(1), 65–74.

CHAPTER 13

Career Counseling for Individuals Recovering From Substance Abuse

Sara P. Johnston and Susan Lingle

CHAPTER OVERVIEW

Substance abuse is often a lifelong challenge that may have an adverse effect on one's career development and growth (Rieckman et al., 2012). From the "Just Say No" campaign to the opioid epidemic, society has long sought to minimize the negative effects that substances may have on the lives of individuals and families. This chapter will address challenges individuals recovering from substance abuse may face when transitioning back into the community, such as family connections, job loss, and the struggle to remain clean. Further, this chapter will address barriers to employment, such as criminal records and childcare challenges, lack of work-readiness skills, soft skills, and interpersonal skills.

CHAPTER OBJECTIVES

After reading this chapter, the student will be able to complete the following:

1. Discuss the effect that substance abuse has on career development.

2. Discuss challenges individuals recovering from substance abuse may face when transitioning back into the community.

3. Outline strategies to remain clean when returning to the world of work.

4. Identify strategies to overcome barriers to employment.

This chapter provides the counselor with an overview of the issues facing clients recovering from substance abuse who want to enter or return to the workforce. Substance abuse disorders (SUDs) are a common and costly problem for employers and employees alike. In the United States, the use and abuse of alcohol, tobacco, illegal drugs, and prescription drugs costs over $740 billion per year, including higher crime rates, lower productivity at work, and higher health care costs (National Institute on Drug Abuse, 2017). Work is an essential component of quality of life; employees in recovery from substance abuse want to return to work (Szymanski & Parker, 2010). Employee turnover is costly, and employers want to retain employees who are in recovery from substance abuse (Batiste, n.d.). In addition, there is a benefit to society as a whole when employees in recovery from substance abuse return to work not only because of the economic benefits to the employee and employer but also because employees who return to work have lower relapse rates (Laudet, 2012). Thus it is essential that career counselors have the knowledge and skills needed to work with clients who are in recovery from substance abuse.

Introduction to Substance Abuse

Clients who are in recovery from substance abuse have a chronic and relapsing condition that is treatable. Substance abuse is not a defect in character or a weakness; rather, substance abuse is a medical disease that is believed to be connected to the reward center of the brain (Arella et al., 1990; Doweiko, 2015; Job Accommodation Network, n.d.). All individuals make choices about whether to use particular substances. Most individuals who use substances do not develop an SUD. However, some individuals become dependent on a substance or substances and may be diagnosed with an SUD (Doweiko, 2015) as defined by the *Diagnostic and Statistical Manual, Fifth Edition* (*DSM-5*) (American Psychiatric Association, 2013). According to the *DSM-5*, SUDs exist on a continuum. This means that *DSM-5* categorizes each type of SUD by severity. Severity is measured from mild to severe. Prior editions of the *DSM* divided substance abuse and addiction into two categories: substance abuse and substance dependence. In the *DSM-5*, the two categories are combined into one, which is SUDs. For individuals with an SUD, substance use ceases to be a choice that they can take or leave; rather, it becomes a physical and psychological need. Changes occur in their brains that cause them to experience cravings for the substance, withdrawal symptoms if they do not have regular access to the substance, and the inability to quit using the substance on their own (Doweiko, 2015; Job Accommodation, n.d.). Many of the clients career counselors work with have received a diagnosis of SUD from another health care provider. However, in some cases, a career counselor may work with a person who is having difficulty finding a job or keeping a job because of an undiagnosed SUD. When casual, voluntary use becomes compulsive substance abuse, clients may begin to experience difficulty at home and at work. The following are some of the behaviors that may occur with substance abuse:

- Unplanned and unexpected absences without supervisor notification or approval

- Excessive use of sick days

- Difficulty in maintaining a schedule and meeting deadlines

- Productivity and quality of work is erratic

- Exhibits inattention, poor judgment, and bad decisions

- Difficulty concentrating and/or poor memory

- Interpersonal conflicts

- Blames others for mistakes

- Change in appearance or hygiene

- Personality changes (e.g., depression, anxiety, anger, impulsiveness)

- Money problems

- Social isolation (Job Accommodation Network, n.d.)

It's important to note that many of these behaviors may be the result of something other than substance abuse, including illness, family difficulties, or other stressors. However, counselors who observe any of the aforementioned behaviors in a client should rule out substance abuse as a cause. There are many brief screening assessments for alcohol abuse, such as CAGE (Cut, Annoyed, Guilty, Eye-opener), that counselors can use to screen for potential SUDs. The CAGE assessment consists of just four questions:

1. Have you ever felt you ought to Cut down on your drinking or drug use?
2. Have people Annoyed you by criticizing your drinking or drug use?
3. Have you felt bad or Guilty about your drinking or drug use?
4. Have you ever had a drink or used drugs first thing in the morning to steady your nerves or to get rid of a hangover (Eye-opener)?

A counselor administering the CAGE would score one point for each yes and zero for each no. High scores mean that the person is at higher risk of having an SUD. Counselors should refer anyone scoring above two to an SUD specialist (Ewing, 1984). Clients who are experiencing difficulties in the workplace because of substance abuse or addiction may be referred to appropriate services, such as the employee assistance program or counseling. Clients with SUDs may experience stigma and discrimination in the workplace because of their addiction. Clients with SUDs may have rights under ADA (1990).

Legal Protections in the Workplace for Clients With Substance Abuse

One of the first questions career counselors may have about working with clients who are in recovery from substance abuse is whether these clients are considered disabled under the ADA (1990). The answer is yes—depending on the particular circumstances. To understand how and when a client may be covered under the ADA, it may be helpful to review a brief history of the ADA with regard to the protections it provides for individuals with disabilities in the workplace.

The ADA of 1990 and Employment Protections

The ADA (1990) has been described as "the most progressive and aggressive piece of legislation passed since the Civil Rights Act of 1964" (Bauer, 1993, p. 40). The ADA was signed into law on July 26, 1990, and was based on previous civil rights legislation, including the Civil Rights Act of 1964, the Rehabilitation Act of 1973, and the Architectural Barriers Act of 1968. However, the ADA expanded the scope of the preceding legislation by including private business entities. The new law was significant in that it represented the first time that the United States had one comprehensive overarching policy addressing the civil rights of people with disabilities (Johnston, 2015).

The ADA's passage culminated decades of work by disability rights advocates in their struggle to convince policy makers to view people with disabilities as citizens entitled to full civil rights. The ADA was unprecedented in that not only did it incorporate the concept of nondiscrimination, or formal equality, contained in earlier civil rights statutes, but it also included the additional requirement of structural equality, or the accommodation of difference because of disability (Colker, 2001, 2005, 2009). This meant that in addition to requiring that people with disabilities be treated equally to people without disabilities, the ADA required, in some cases, that people with disabilities be treated differently than people without disabilities to achieve equality. Civil rights advocates hoped that the structural equality provisions in the ADA would prove more effective than formal equality had been in addressing discrimination (Colker, 2009). Further, the drafters intended that the ADA be interpreted broadly to cover not only people with visible disabilities, such as mobility, vision, and hearing impairments, but also people with invisible and stigmatized disabilities (e.g., substance abuse); people with a record of a disability (e.g., cancer); and, finally, people who may be perceived as having a disability (e.g., genetic predisposition) (Colker, 2009). In sum, although largely based on traditional civil rights statutes, the ADA as enacted went much further in scope than the civil rights legislation that preceded it (Johnston, 2015).

The ADA has five sections: Title I, Employment; Title II, Public Entities; Title III, Public Accommodations and Services Operated by Private Entities; Title IV, Telecommunications; and Title V, Miscellaneous. To be protected under the ADA, a person must fall within one of the three definitions of disability (also referred to as the three-prong test): (a) has a physical or mental impairment that substantially limits one or more life activities, (b) has a record of such impairment, or (c) be regarded as having such an impairment (Colker, 2001, 2009; United States Equal Employment Opportunity Commission, n.d.). Of the five titles of the ADA, Title I is the section most salient to the practice of career counseling.

Title I of the ADA and Substance Abuse

Clients in recovery from a diagnosed SUD have the legal right under Title I of the ADA to be protected from discrimination by private employers. However, the protection extends only to employees in recovery from diagnosed SUDs. Employees who are currently abusing substances are not generally protected under the ADA (Strauser et al., 2018).

Title I of the ADA (1990) allows private employers with more than 15 employees to ensure that employees are not working under the influence of illegal drugs or alcohol. Title I protects employees who are in recovery from substance abuse from workplace discrimination based on a previous diagnosis of SUD. The law states that an individual who is currently engaging in the illegal use of substances is not an individual with a disability. The key is the words "currently engaging." Title I clearly states that private employers may not discriminate against an employee who has a history of substance abuse but who is not currently abusing substances and who has been rehabilitated.

The ADA further states that a job applicant or employee who is currently using illegal drugs is not a "qualified individual with a disability." An employee who is using illegal drugs—whether the use rises to the level of abuse or not—is not protected under the ADA. In contrast, "qualified individuals" under the ADA include job applicants or employees who have successfully completed a rehabilitation program and no longer use illegal drugs. The ADA also considers job applicants or employees who are currently completing a rehabilitation program and no longer using illegal drugs, as well as individuals who are erroneously identified as using illegal drugs, to be "qualified individuals" (U.S. Commission on Civil Rights, 2000). It is important to note that a diagnosis of an SUD is required for an individual to be protected under the ADA. This is because an SUD is considered a substantially limiting impairment under the ADA. An individual who is a former casual user of illegal substances is not protected under the ADA.

It's important to realize that some types of discrimination against clients who use substances are legal. For example, over the past 20 years, employers have become increasingly aware of the costs of employing employees who are tobacco users. Clients who use tobacco may face additional barriers to employment. Many companies legally prohibit smoking on their premises, and more and more companies are taking the additional step of refusing to hire tobacco users or charging them more for their health insurance. In addition, career counselors should be aware of the following provisions in the ADA regarding job applicants or employees who are in recovery from substance abuse: (1) An employer may prohibit the illegal use of drugs and the use of alcohol at the workplace. (2) It is not a violation of the ADA for an employer to give tests for the illegal use of drugs. (3) An employer may discharge or deny employment to persons who currently engage in the illegal use of drugs. It may be helpful to consider a brief case scenario:

> You are a career counselor who has been working with a client who is in recovery for an alcohol abuse disorder. Your client had been employed as an administrative assistant for 60 days and has just completed her probationary period at work. During your most recent meeting, your client disclosed that she was feeling stressed by the high pace of the job and was concerned about relapsing. She asked for your help. How would you respond to this client if she told you that she did relapse, requested a leave of absence to receive treatment, and was fired by the company? Describe any ADA or other legal matters that may be at issue in this case scenario.

The first thing to consider is that Title I of the ADA applies to businesses that have 15 or more employees. Assuming that the client works for such a business entity, the counselor must determine if the client would be considered a "qualified individual" under the ADA. Based on the ADA description of a disability, the client could be qualified because she has a physical or mental impairment that limits one or more major life activities. It is unclear if the client was terminated simply because she asked for leave or if she may have been terminated for alcohol use on the job. If the former is the case, then she may have a case of discrimination under the ADA because employers cannot deny reasonable accommodations, such as time off for rehabilitation. However, if the latter is the case, then the employer may have had grounds to terminate the client if her conduct was such that any other employee would have also been discharged (ADA, 1990). If she does qualify for protection under the ADA, the client may be entitled to job accommodations, such as additional time to complete tasks, time off to receive treatment, and other measures to reduce stress on the job.

Job Accommodations

Career counselors may work with clients who need accommodations for SUDs. The Job Accommodation Network (www.jan.org) is a web-based resource that has information on "accommodating employees with drug addiction" (Job Accommodation Network, n.d.). Job accommodations may include the use of paid or unpaid leave for inpatient medical treatment or flexible scheduling for counseling or to attend support meetings. If an individual is employed in a setting, such as a hospital or clinic, where employees are exposed to drugs in the course of their jobs, employers may need to provide additional supervision or reassign the employee to a job that will not expose the employee to drugs. Other accommodations include reassignment to light duty, a change in duties, transfer to another position, or the services of a job coach (Job Accommodation Network, n.d.).

Employee turnover is costly for employers; therefore, whenever possible, employers choose to work with employees who are having difficulty on the job rather than dismiss them outright (National Safety Council, 2019). In the case of employees who are at risk of losing their employment because of substance abuse or addiction, employers have the option to provide the employee with a "firm choice" or "last chance" agreement. The ADA does not require an employer to provide such an agreement to an employee who has engaged in conduct that warrants dismissal. If, however, the employer does decide to offer an employee a last chance agreement, the employer will agree not to dismiss the employee if the employee agrees to receive treatment for substance abuse, refrain from using alcohol or drugs, and demonstrate improved work performance. If the employee violates any part of the agreement, the employee may be dismissed because of failure to meet the conditions of the agreement. Last chance agreements typically contain the following components: basis for agreement, expectations, time frame for meeting expectations, consequences of violating the agreement, agreement expiration date, and signatures (Batiste, n.d.).

Challenges for Individuals Recovering From Substance Abuse

Clients reentering life from a diagnosis of substance abuse and who have successfully completed a rehabilitation program may have had some time sober, but it can be difficult to manage without support. Stress, family changes, lack of opportunities, no income, restrictions on where they can live, and child support arrears are just some of the examples of barriers for clients trying to restart their lives. Beyond the barriers to employment, there may also be lingering physical and emotional consequences from the substance abuse. Clients might not realize that their mental health has been significantly affected or that it is something they should discuss with a counselor. Career counselors should ensure that their assessment covers psychosocial issues. Later in the chapter, we cover the challenges that clients with SUDs face when they decide to quit using. Topics in the section include family issues, treatment options, grief and resentment, job loss, sobriety, post-acute withdrawal syndrome, "get-well job," barriers to employment, and strategies for success.

Addiction and its aftermath take a toll on families. Counselors should be prepared to assess any family dynamics related to a family member's SUD. Most families require the services of a substance abuse counselor to assist them with issues related to trust, financial stress, and, in some cases, feelings of grief and loss related to the breakup of the family. It is important for career counselors to note that a happier home life is associated with maintaining employment. In addition, family members might attend Al-Anon meetings, which are 12-step meetings for families, children, and others affected by a family member who has an SUD. Career counselors should ensure that their assessment covers psychosocial issues.

Treatment Options

There are several options for individuals diagnosed with an SUD. Options vary in length and intensity. The next section describes a variety of treatment options for clients with SUD.

Residential

In a residential program, clients stay at the treatment facility for a set number of days. Clients should receive lectures, group therapy, and individual counseling. The rules of the facility and the treatment design may vary depending on the payer source to the facility. States require a minimum standard of care, but not all facilities take state-funded clients. Clients can be state funded, insurance, or private pay while in residential treatment. For working clients, FMLA is usually part of the process of working with that client. Clients will also be dealing with and processing worries about possible job or career loss because of their actions while active in their addiction.

Outpatient

In an outpatient program, clients attend treatment a few days out of the week for group therapy, lectures, and individual counseling. Clients who do not qualify for residential treatment may often qualify for outpatient treatment. Outpatient treatment often has a more flexible schedule so that clients can work and attend other meetings. It will be important to help provide support to clients regarding finding a balance between work and all the obligations they might have at this point. For clients who are trying to juggle all the obligations they now have, such as work, 12-step meetings, outpatient treatment, counseling, and probation, it can be overwhelming. Support, encouragement, and help with problem solving will help them to be successful and keep working.

Peer Coaches

A peer coach is a person in recovery who has received training to work with individuals who are working to become sober and in recovery. Peer coaches have flexible hours and can help clients with a number of issues that arise. Peer coaches are different from a counselor or a sponsor, but clients can become confused when they are experiencing stress or crisis. With regard to employment, peer coaches can be partners. They often know who is hiring and have working relationships with employers, so encouraging clients to use this resource can be important in getting them back to work.

Sober Coach

A sober coach is for clients who have the resources to pay someone to be with them 24/7. Oftentimes, musicians, actors, and business executives will have a sober coach to help them. It is important to understand that insurance does not pay for this, so it would be the client's responsibility to private pay for this service.

12-Step Meetings

Twelve-step meetings include Alcoholics Anonymous, Narcotics Anonymous, and Overeaters Anonymous. These meetings work on the 12-step format to help clients admit that they have a problem and find support and acceptance with fellow peers who are or who have dealt with the same issue. (National Institute on Drug Abuse, 2018). Some clients are required to attend meetings because of their legal status, while others choose to attend to support their recovery. Attendance in meetings should not be a barrier to employment since there are a variety of times offered.

Medication Assistance Treatment

This treatment option has both strong advocates and critics. Through the monitored use of low amounts of specific drugs, medication assistance treatment (MAT) can help clients with opioid addiction function in their lives. It can be difficult for clients to MAT because it is not considered abstinence. When working with clients who are considering the program or who are on the program, there can be several things to keep in mind, including time spent at the clinic, how often they have to go to the clinic, where the clinic is located, and what other requirements the clinic has for the client (U.S. Department of Health and Human Services, 2020). MAT can be a barrier to employment if the employer is not supportive or will not allow the client the time to attend the clinic.

Harm Reduction

This option allows clients to stay safe while they are exhibiting risky behaviors. It can be controversial, but, ultimately, it is about meeting clients where they are and lowering risks of exposure. Some examples include needle exchanges, helping clients understand safety strategies when using, safe sex education with access to condoms, and other protective factors.

Job Loss

When discussing job loss with clients who have an SUD, there are several factors to keep in mind. There are a number of reasons for job loss or losses, but often it comes down to the client's substance use—either the use itself, the behaviors associated with the use, or the stress of trying to keep everything managed but not being successful. Job loss for anyone can be stressful, embarrassing, and hard to overcome. However, for clients with SUD, job loss compounds other existing problems, such as financial instability, trouble with the law, and family stress. Clients who have experienced job loss because of an SUD may often go for long periods without work; have multiple job changes, along with short tenures at these jobs; and a variety of different work duties and work environments (Arella et al., 1990). All of these factors can be red flags when human resources or hiring managers review a client's resume or application. Career counselors who work with individuals who have an SUD should address specific job-related issues, such as client perceptions and expectations of a professional work environment. For example, does the client understand soft skills? Does the client understand social norms and healthy boundaries? What does the client's family or social support view as healthy employment behavior? Does anyone in the client's family of origin work? What does the client say about previous job loss? How much blame is the client putting on others regarding the loss of employment? Once a counselor is able to find answers to these questions, a more realistic treatment plan can be established. Taking the time upfront to determine the factors affecting a client's employment is key to being able to address the pertinent issues in counseling. A counselor can ask these questions any time it appears that a reassessment is needed. Depending on the client's answers, the counselor and client can revise the treatment plan to address the new issues.

Grief

A factor related to work that affects clients but often receives a smaller percentage of time in session is the grief related to employment and career loss. There are many components to grief and its effects on a client's ability to return to work or to start looking for a new job or career. Whether the loss was because of disability, mistakes, substance abuse, or other factors, the pain of that loss can be overwhelming. Grief related to unemployment, loss of time, lost income, or loss of stature is significant. Allowing clients the space to discuss and fully process this grief will help them move more successfully into new employment. To provide support to the client, the counselor should explain the grief process and then return to the topic from time to time during future sessions to check in with the client on how the client is coping with any feelings of grief. The validation that occurs when clients understand how this loss has affected them is important to the recovery process. And the validation may extend beyond the effects of substance abuse on a client's employment and may motivate clients to work on other issues related to grief, such as broken promises, regrets, and failed relationships. The counselor may need to assist clients in understanding that feelings of grief may not just "go away" on their own and that managing and coping with grief is a painful but necessary process in moving forward with life.

Resentment

Resentment is another issue related to the past that may affect a client's current employment options. Similar to grief, resentment may be related to multiple issues, such as employment, education, or relationships. Resentments will often increase once a client has started to work. Resentments are a central piece of a person's work in recovery through the AA Big Book (W., Bill, 1976). Understanding and releasing resentments are themes AA sponsors touch on repeatedly. These resentments will directly affect how clients view their new employment and how they will interact with management and other employees. Examples of resentments are frustration over being fired or laid off, feelings of being passed over for opportunities or promotions, a belief that stress or pressure at work caused the drug use and subsequent job loss, and reactions to difficult professions with primary or secondary trauma. When these resentments are not addressed, clients will often bring them out in their new or current work environments. Clients who carry resentments into the workplace may be perceived as unstable, aggressive, bitter, and difficult to work with. It is important for counselors to identify, acknowledge, and help the client process these resentments to prevent resentments from becoming barriers to employment.

Sobriety

Working with clients who have SUD or addiction can be challenging for a number of reasons. For example, many factors affect clients' sobriety, and clients put a lot of pressure on themselves to remain sober, especially when they are new in their recovery. Career counselors who work with this population should understand the subtle but important difference in terminology—that is, persons with addiction mostly refer to themselves as "in recovery" or "sober"; the term "being clean" is used less frequently. Counselors have an important role to play in sobriety.

Counselors first need to discuss the client's history of substance use and abuse. For example, how did the client start using? Did work or fellow employees have a part in the use? Did the client use at work or use to keep working? Did the client make large amounts of money, especially in cash? Did the environment encourage a "party" atmosphere after work was over? Is the client planning on returning to an environment where drugs and/or alcohol are common on the work site? Counselors should take time to learn about possible drug or alcohol issues in career fields. Some of the most common fields with the potential for substance use and abuse are oil fields, construction, day labor, and the service industry (e.g., bartending or restaurant work).

In addition to concerns about a safe environment, other factors should be evaluated in the process of making an appropriate job placement. Clients who are recently out of treatment might have multiple new activities that require their participation, such as outpatient treatment, 12-step meetings, and working with a sponsor. Other requirements that may need to be addressed during business hours include reporting to probation or parole, working with Child Protection Services regarding a client's children, and completing community service hours. If stress or work pressure played a role in the client's substance use, it is important for that counselor to discuss less stressful employment options with the client.

Post-Acute Withdrawal Syndrome

Post-acute withdrawal syndrome (PAWS) can affect clients long after they have stopped using and are in recovery. PAWS manifests as difficult symptoms that persons in recovery experience after detoxing and being sober for a period of time. PAWS is believed to be caused by changes to the brain during the time a person is using. Once sober, physical and emotional healing begins; however, at times, clients find the symptoms of PAWS difficult to manage. Some of the common symptoms include problems with cognition, anxiety, depression, cravings, aches, and disrupted sleep. It is important that clients understand what PAWS is so that they can better manage the symptoms. Career counselors should encourage clients to speak with their primary care providers regarding the symptoms (Addictions and Recovery Organization, 2010).

"Get-Well Job"

Within the recovery and 12-step communities, the concept of a "get-well job" is discussed with some frequency. A get-well job is work that has lower stress, flexibility of schedule, and may be easier to obtain. Considering a get-well job may be a hard decision for clients, in particular for those clients who have held professional positions, but it is worth discussing with the client. The get-well job provides many benefits, including time for commitments, ability to ease into work, possible part-time schedule, and flexibility. It is important in conversations about returning to work via a get-well job to discuss with clients whether they will be able at a later time to return to the career they had before. Sometimes it is harder for clients to accept a "never," but they might be willing to look at a "just for now" scenario.

Barriers to Employment

Clients who have SUDs often have multiple issues affecting their ability to successfully return to work. As discussed earlier, the neurological effects of PAWS could be present and may create barriers to returning to work that will need to be addressed by the counselor and client. In addition, many clients may have other physical or mental health challenges related to their previous substance use, such as heart and lung conditions, post-traumatic stress disorder, and impaired memory or cognition. Some of these issues may resolve in time; others may result in permanent, lifelong disabilities for which the client may need workplace accommodations.

Criminal Records

Clients with criminal records or upcoming court cases will face additional challenges as they seek to return to work. It is important for counselors to understand the ethical requirements of specific professions when assisting clients in their employment search. For example, certain vocations and professions restrict people from obtaining education or employment in the field if they have a criminal history. Certain crimes, such as assault charges, may prevent an individual from being admitted to a nursing program or from obtaining a nursing license. Another issue is that because of a previous criminal record, clients may be unable to meet employer insurance requirements for the job. Counselors should contact the state licensure board for a given profession or the professional organization governing ethics and practice in a particular field to learn more about how a previous criminal history may prohibit entry or employment in the field. This is particularly important before recommending an educational track to a client that would require time, money, and resources only to later find out that the profession was not a career field the client was eligible for because of a criminal record.

Transportation

Another potential barrier to employment is transportation. Limited access to transportation is common among those who have sought addiction treatment. For example, clients involved in the court system might have had a license revoked, unpaid tickets and fines, are unable to drive, or have other possible travel restrictions, such as being prohibited from traveling outside specific geographic boundaries because of a court order or probation requirement. Clients who have lost their licenses or who do not have access to a vehicle may have lower motivation to seek employment because of their unwillingness or inability to use public transportation. Clients may admit to being embarrassed and ashamed because of not being able to drive and/or having to rely on public transportation. Counselors should be familiar with the public transportation system to help educate clients about their options. Some job opportunities may not be feasible for clients who do not live on a bus or subway line, or if the employment site is in an area that is not served by public transportation. Additional barriers to using public transportation include rural locations, lack of funds to purchase tickets, and limited hours or routes. A crucial role for career counselors is assisting clients with budgeting for work-related expenses, including transportation. In addition, it is important for the counselor to discuss the steps the client needs to take to regain a driver's license, pay fines or fees, or attend mandatory driving rehabilitation courses because an inability to drive may affect the type of work the client is able to apply for. Another area career counselors may need to assist clients with is identifying resources that can help remove barriers to employment, such as obtaining housing, setting up a bank account, managing money, and resolving any remaining legal issues.

Strategies for Success

Substance abuse and addiction affect people of all ages, genders, race and ethnicity, religion, and socioeconomic status. Career counselors who develop a relationship with a client that is focused on understanding the client's life and employment experiences play a vital role in the client's successful return to work. Counselors should focus on the client's education and work experiences, both pre- and postaddiction. For example, the counselor will need to determine if the client has ever worked, and if so, in what types of jobs or careers, as well as how many years of education the client has and what degrees or certifications the client holds. Career counseling skills, such as conducting labor market surveys, administering interest and skill inventories and other assessments, and determining transferable skills are especially important for clients who may need to switch careers or obtain additional education or training to remain competitive or to move out of a current job or career into a new field.

Job Search Skills

Career counselors must ensure that the client has the emotional maturity and required knowledge and skills to work in a desired job, career, or field of employment. Persons with SUDs who started using at an early age may have delayed or stunted emotional growth. While this is a common topic within treatment programs and 12-step meetings, it is also important for counselors to address this issue with clients. As an example, a counselor may be working with a 35-year-old male client; however, because this client started using methamphetamine at age 14, the client did not mature at the same rate as his peers and still has the emotional maturity of a 14-year-old. If the client's lack of maturity is not addressed by the counselor, the client may struggle in a job environment that requires interacting with individuals or dealing with situations that require a high level of emotional maturity.

Another factor to assess with a client is what type of resume would be most appropriate. Often, a skills-based resume can help a client who has had multiple jobs, obtained a variety of work skills, or has traveled a long distance between jobs because of substance and addiction, legal trouble or incarceration, or illness.

Although a skills-based resume does not change the client's work history, the focus on skills rather than on dates of employment may assist a client in presenting his/her knowledge, skills, and experience in the best possible light. Counselors and clients can find many articles on and templates for skills-based resumes online. In addition, local workforce offices can provide assistance in putting together a resume.

Interview skills and preparing for an interview can be vitally important for clients, especially for those who have been out of the workforce for some time. An interview can be a stressful experience, and most clients will fare better with some practice. Encouraging clients to get help from the workforce office, their sponsor, or peer coach is a good way to assist clients in becoming comfortable with the interview process.

Additional tips for clients in the interview process include the following:

- Dress one level above the position.

- Make sure clothes are clean, ironed, and appropriate for the work site.

- Be mindful that many people are sensitive to cologne and tobacco smoke; refrain from using either before the interview.

- Complete a resume.

- Compile a job list, which is simply a notebook or document listing all jobs held—include addresses, phone numbers, dates worked, salaries, supervisors' names, and duties.

- Bring copies of your resume and the job list to the interview.

- Understand legal rights under the ADA, including when and how to disclose a disability and the right to accommodations.

- Be prepared to address questions about gaps in work history by practicing answers for inquiries related to criminal history, gaps between jobs, multiple jobs, and short tenure at jobs.

- Set up email and voice mail prior to applying for work. Choose an email address that is professional, such as John-P-Jones@domain.com rather than Hot-Surfer@domain.com.

- Check email and voice mail at least once a day (make sure voice mail is professional and easy to understand).

- Send a thank-you note or email after every phone, web-based, or in-person interview.

Summary

Substance abuse affects all types of people and may interfere with career planning and employment options for many of those individuals. Counselors who work with individuals who have SUDs may be initially overwhelmed by the terminology, multiple treatment programs, and variety and scope of issues experienced by those clients. Addiction and addiction treatment are now more commonly discussed within the health care profession and the workplace; therefore, it is important for counselors to view substance abuse and addiction as a cultural competency and as a specialty population that has specific needs and faces many challenges, including barriers to employment. Because of the heartache, grief, and resentment that may accompany substance abuse and addiction, it is imperative that career counselors develop knowledge and skills to assist clients who have a history of substance abuse and addiction in meeting their career and employment goals. It is imperative that counselors convey to their clients that returning to work is not only possible but also an essential component of recovery. In addition to assisting clients in recovery for substance abuse and addiction, career counselors may also work with clients who are struggling at work because of undiagnosed issues related to abuse of both legal and illegal substances. A basic knowledge of substance abuse and addiction screening tools can assist the counselor in identifying any employment issues related to a client's use of substances. Depending on the results of the screening tools, career counselors can refer clients at risk for an SUD for further assessment and treatment. Early identification of issues related to substance use or abuse may make the difference in the client's ability to keep a job, obtain education or licensure in a profession, or avoid a criminal record.

Case Study

John is a 36-year-old white male who has been referred to a career counselor by his outpatient counselor, Sarah. He will be completing his 90-day treatment for his addiction to alcohol and Ambien. Per his outpatient counselor, he has done well, participated, and not had any failed urinalysis tests while in the program. Sarah advises that John has a pending driving while under the influence (DWI) charge, and she has helped him contact his attorney, but he will need to continue to follow up with the attorney, and the attorney wants to be able to speak with the counselor as needed. John said that at the worst of it, he was drinking a liter of vodka a day. John was using Ambien every night to go to sleep and often took more than prescribed. When asked what made him seek help, John said the DWI and then tearfully added that his girlfriend of 3 years left him after that. He said that he missed a week of work, and it all became unmanageable.

John arrives for his scheduled appointment on time and has fair grooming and dress. It is apparent that John has seen counselors in the past, even before outpatient treatment, and often answers a question before the counselor can finish it. He states that he works at a construction company as an accountant. He is out in the field often completing inventories and helping get deliveries of supplies to the job sites. John states that he was told that he needed inpatient residential treatment but that he didn't think that his employer would let him be gone that long and that he was able to "make it work" by going to outpatient treatment after work. John does have a sponsor whom he speaks with several times a week. John isn't sure if the 12-step approach is for him, but he is "giving it a try." John reports that he goes to AA meetings a "couple of times a week" but does not have an established home group. John says that he does not want to go back to drinking and his addiction; he says that he is getting older and wants to have a family and start his own business at some point.

John says that he never drank at work and denies that his drinking had any negative effects on his job performance. He does say that prior to treatment, after work on job sites, he did drink with his boss and coworkers. John says that this was common, and everyone joined in. John reports that they all knew he was sober now, and they were supportive of it. When asked why he was in counseling, John admits that he was scared he was going to have to do time in prison for the pending DWI. The counselor asks John about depression, and John gets defensive, "Why does everyone keep asking me that?"

Discussion Questions

1. Identify four key issues or barriers for the client in achieving his goals.
2. Discuss additional questions you would ask if you were working with John.
3. List any legal issues (or legal protections) that might be important to consider in this case.
4. Identify five key areas to address on the client's treatment plan. What strengths would you list for the client?

References

Addictions and Recovery Organization. (2010). *Post-acute withdrawal (PAWS)*. https://www.addictionsandrecovery.org/post-acute-withdrawal.htm

American Psychiatric Association (2013). *Diagnostic and Statistical Manual of Mental Disorders* (5th ed.).

Americans With Disabilities Act of 1990, 42 U.S.C., § 12101-12113 (1990).

Arella, L. R., Deren, S., Randell, J., & Brewington, V. (1990). Vocational functioning of clients in drug treatment: Exploring some myths and realities. *Journal of Applied Rehabilitation Counseling, 21*(2), 7–18.

Batiste, L.C. (n.d.). *Last chance agreements for employees with drug and alcohol addictions. Consultants Corner.* Job Accommodations Network. https://askjan.org/publications/consultants-corner/Last-Chance-Agreements-for-Employees-with-Drug-and-Alcohol-Addictions.cfm

Bauer, L. (1993). Trying to comply with the ADA. *State Legislatures, 19*, 40–46.

Colker, R. (2001). Winning and losing under the Americans With Disabilities Act. *Ohio State Law Journal, 62*, 239–283.

Colker, R. (2005). *The disability pendulum: The first decade of the Americans With Disabilities Act.* University Press.

Colker, R. (2009). *When is separate unequal? A disability perspective.* Cambridge University Press.

Doweiko, H. E. (2015). *Concepts of chemical dependency* (9th ed.). Cengage Learning.

Ewing, J. A. (1984). Detecting alcoholism: The CAGE questionnaire. *Journal of American Medical Association, 252*, 1905–1907.

Job Accommodation Network. (n.d.). *Drug addiction.* https://askjan.org/disabilities/Drug-Addiction.cfm?cssearch=2460145_1

Johnston, S. P. (2015). Unequal treatment or uneven consequence: A content analysis of Americans With Disabilities Act Title I disparate impact cases from 1992–2012. *Disability Studies Quarterly, 35*(3). http://dsq-sds.org/article/view/4938/4027

Laudet, A.B. (2012). Rate and predictors of employment among formerly polysubstance dependent urban individuals in recovery. *Journal of Addiction Disorders, 31*, 288–302.

National Institute on Drug Abuse. (2018). Evidence-based approaches to drug addiction treatment. *Principles of Drug Addiction Treatment: A Research-Based Guide* (3rd ed.). https://www.drugabuse.gov/publications/principles-drug-addiction-treatment-research-based-guide-third-edition/evidence-based-approaches-to-drug-addiction-treatment

National Institute on Drug Abuse. (2017). *Tests and statistics.* https://www.drugabuse.gov/related-topics/trends-statistics

National Safety Council. (2019). *What is the cost of substance abuse disorder?* https://www.nsc.org/work-safety/safety-topics/drugs-at-work/costs-for-employers

Rieckman, T., Farentinos, C., Tillotson, C. J., Jonathan, K., & McCarty, D. (2012). The substance abuse counseling workforce: Education, preparation, and certification. *Substance Abuse, 32*(4), 180–190. https://doi.org/10.1080/08897077.2011.600122

Strauser, D. R., O'Sullivan, D., & Wong, A.W.K. (2018). Career development and employment of people with disabilities. In V. M. Tarvydas and M. T. Hartley (Eds.), *The professional practice of rehabilitation counseling* (2nd ed., pp. 273–296). Springer.

Szymanski, E. M., & Parker, R. M. (2010). Work and disability: Basic concepts. In E. M. Szymanski & R. M. Parker (Eds.), *Work and disability: Contexts, issues, and strategies for enhancing employment outcomes for people wtih disabilities* (pp. 1–15). Pro-Ed, Inc

U.S. Commission on Civil Rights. (2000). *Sharing the dream: Is the ADA covering all?* https://www.usccr.gov/pubs/ada/main. htm

U.S. Department of Health and Human Services (2020). *Medication and counseling treatment.* Substance Abuse and Mental Health Services Administration (SAMHSA). https://www.samhsa.gov/medication-assisted-treatment/treatment

U.S. Equal Employment Opportunity Commission. (n.d.). *Disability discrimination.* https://www.eeoc.gov/laws/types/ disability.cfm#resources

W., Bill. (1976). *Alcoholics Anonymous: The story of how many thousands of men and women have recovered from alcoholism.* Alcoholics Anonymous World Services.

CHAPTER 14

Career Counseling for Individuals With Mental Health Disorders

Allison Levine and Catherine Troop

CHAPTER OVERVIEW

Mental health is a lifelong challenge that can put counselors in a position of attempting to understand the mental health aspects of the individual and career concerns (Zunker, 2008). This chapter will discuss the barriers impeding the career development of individuals with mental health, as well as considerations for career development. Further, strategies for assisting individuals with mental health issues in managing their mental health and accommodations that can be used on employment sites will also be provided.

CHAPTER OBJECTIVES

After reading this chapter, the student will be able to complete the following:

1. Discuss mental health and, by extension, mental health disorders.

2. Apply an understanding of mental health disorders to career development in the identification of specific considerations for career development for individuals with mental health disorders.

3. Identify best practices for working with individuals with mental illnesses in obtaining and maintaining employment goals.

4. Understand the unique issue of disability disclosure at work as it pertains to invisible disabilities, such as mental health disorders.

What Is Mental Health?

It is important to establish what mental health is before any discussion of mental illness is carried out. There are a number of definitions of mental health available, but this chapter will use the definition published by the World Health Organization (WHO) in 2014: "Mental health is defined as a state of well-being in which every individual realizes their own potential, can cope with the normal stresses of life, can work productively and fruitfully, and is able to make a contribution to their society." By extension, the WHO includes mental health as a critical component of overall health: "Health is a state of complete physical, mental and social well-being and not merely the absence of disease or infirmity" (WHO, 2014). In striving toward the most appropriate treatment of individuals with mental health disorders, it is essential to remain aware that mental health is an inseparable component of health.

Furthermore, the American Psychiatric Association (2018) stipulates that mental health involves "effective" functioning in specific areas of daily living, including productive activities (school, work, etc.), interpersonal relationships, and the ability to adapt and cope with changes. Of note, for any and all future practitioners working with individuals who may have mental health disorders, the concept of "effective functioning" is not a universal one. This is a subjective value statement—one that often serves to negatively affect individuals who do not have the same experiences, thoughts, or feelings as the majority of the population. A further discussion of this issue can be found later in this chapter.

Mental health is one of the more misunderstood components of rehabilitation counseling given that there is not typically a formula of cause and effect as with other medical ailments. For instance, neuropsychologists (psychologists with specialized training in assessing brain injury or cognitive dysfunction) are not even certain exactly how some mental illnesses form and affect the brain's chemistry. There are not simple medical tests that can be given to determine if a person does, in fact, have bipolar disorder, or schizophrenia, or post-traumatic stress disorder in the way that we as a society have become used to (e.g., blood panels or scans). If I have a sore throat, I can go to the doctor and get tested for streptococcus. If, on the other hand, I am feeling more "down" than I usually do, and I don't feel like leaving my bed for several days in a row, my parent/partner/roommate might think I'm being lazy and tell me to get over it.

In practice, the lack of understanding of specific biological markers for mental health disorders can lead to practitioners making inconsistent diagnoses throughout someone's life. The primary evidence of a disorder is self-report by a client. This requires (1) an individual to seek help, (2) for that individual to be able to express what he/she is experiencing, and (3) for a practitioner to translate this information into a diagnosis and treatment plan. The *Diagnostic and Statistical Manual of Mental Disorders, 5th Edition (DSM-5* (American Psychiatric Association, 2013) has been developed to standardize diagnoses of mental health disorders. This is useful in mental health treatment for many reasons; for example, it provides a standardized nomenclature, reports prevalence and mortality rates, and documents public health information. However, even the introduction to the *DSM-5* warns that "many symptoms assigned to a single disorder may occur, at varying levels of severity, in many other disorders" (American Psychiatric Association, 2013, p. 5). In other words, while a more standardized approach is available, this is still not an exact science, and oftentimes, one presenting symptom may look a lot like a different disorder altogether.

Mental Health Disorders

Now that we've talked through mental health, we can move into understanding when mental health is *not* optimal. Humans naturally have mental states that fluctuate with hormonal, environmental, situational, or even dietary changes. What is defined as a mental health disorder, or a mental illness, is distinctly different from those natural ebbs and flows. Again, we can look to the *DSM-5* for clarity. The *DSM-5* defines a mental disorder as "a syndrome characterized by clinically significant disturbance in an individual's cognition, emotion regulation, or behavior that reflects a dysfunction in the psychological, biological, or developmental processes underlying mental functioning" (American Psychological Association, 2013, p. 20).

At this point, we will revisit the concept of "effective functioning" from earlier in the chapter as it relates to "clinically significant disturbances." Effective functioning looks differently for different people and can be affected by culture, geographic region, age, experiences, and so on. What is problematic is that effective functioning is not a given norm, and to assume that our perspective of what effective functioning should look like is the same across all other people can lead to inadequate diagnoses and stigma against people with mental health disorders. Consider for a moment how you would define "effective functioning" for yourself. On a given day, what does that entail? Going to work or school; completing assignments; interacting with friends, partners, and family; and eating healthily and working out are some common examples that probably came to mind. These came to mind because our society has represented these things to us as valuable and necessary to be a productive member of society. What is most important when identifying whether an individual may or may not be operating in an "effective" way is the context within which they are operating. When something becomes a "clinically significant disturbance," it should be clinically significant in comparison to *that person's* baseline, not compared to another individual with the same diagnosis, the representation of that diagnosis in a TV show or movie, or any other notion about how someone should operate on a day-to-day basis.

Types of Mental Health Disorders

There are several different types of mental health disorders that a person might be living with, and these are often co-occurring, meaning that someone may likely have multiple diagnoses that influence the way their symptoms may present. As such, the *DSM-5* includes codes for subtypes, as well as specifiers affording a more explicit diagnosis, which allows any other practitioner reading the diagnosis to understand the features of that person's mental health disorder. There are a wide variety of mental health disorders, and most commonly, they are grouped by disorders with common features. The groups this chapter will talk about specifically are neurodevelopmental disorders, psychiatric disorders, and personality disorders.

Neurodevelopmental Disorders

Disorders in this category have an onset period during development (i.e., during childhood). They are "characterized by a delay or disturbance in the acquisition of skills in a variety of developmental domains, including motor, social, language, and cognition" (Jeste, 2015, p. 690). Examples of neurodevelopmental disorders include autism spectrum disorder, which affects 5% of children (Baio et al., 2018), attention deficit hyperactivity disorder (ADHD), which affects 7% of children (Visser et al., 2014), and intellectual disability (also known as global developmental delay), which affects 7% of children (Boyle et al., 2011). Practitioners working with transition-age students will most likely encounter individuals with these diagnoses.

Psychiatric and Mood Disorders

Psychiatric illnesses and mood disorders are commonly combined in the same group. Psychiatric illnesses often go by a number of other names, including severe mental illness and psychotic disorders. This group includes schizophrenia spectrum and psychotic disorders with key features, such as delusions, hallucinations, disorganized thinking, and abnormal motor behavior (American Psychiatric Association, 2013). Bipolar and related disorders are considered mood disorders in that they include components of both mania and depression.

Personality Disorders

The *DSM-5* defines personality disorder as follows:

An enduring pattern of inner experience and behavior that deviates markedly from the expectations of the individual's culture, is pervasive and inflexible, has an onset in adolescence or early adulthood, is stable over time, and leads to distress or impairment. (American Psychiatric Association, 2013, p. 645)

There are 11 distinct personality disorders, as well as an "other" category for personality types that do not fit within the other categories. Some of the more common personality disorders are antisocial, borderline, narcissistic, and dependent. Personality disorders are particularly challenging given that they are more behavioral in nature and may present as a person being difficult rather than a disorder. Personality disorders are commonly misdiagnosed and misunderstood, leading to difficult and unsuccessful treatment and work success for this population (Shedler & Westen, 2004).

Negative Attitudes, Stigma, and Discrimination

In general, people with disabilities (PWDs) have been, and continue to be, stigmatized and discriminated against in our society. This stems back millennia: separating those who are "different" can be traced back as far as ancient Greece and Roman times when babies born with visible disabilities were killed or left to die, and adults were made to be jesters in the courts. Moving forward in time, in the United States, the first "Institution for Idiots" was established in Massachusetts in 1848. Involuntary institutionalization of people with mental illnesses persisted into the 1960s until the Community Mental Health Act of 1963, which included much more strict regulations for admitting an individual to inpatient psychiatric hospitals. Given the history of isolation, removal, pity, and ridicule of people with varying types of disabilities from mainstream society, there has rarely been an opportunity for the mainstream to engage regularly with PWDs. This dynamic sets the stage for systemic oppression, discrimination, and stigma experienced by people living with disabilities and certainly those living with mental health disorders.

Livneh (1982) posited several comprehensive classifications for explaining the origins of negative attitudes toward PWDs. Several of these include the following:

- Sociocultural conditioning

- Childhood influences

- Disability as a punishment for sin

- Aesthetic aversion

- Threats to body image integrity

Negative attitudes are then compounded by disability characteristics. For instance, the origin of the disability affects the perception of the person with the disability (e.g., losing a limb as a result of a car accident that was not your fault vs. losing a limb as a result of a car accident you caused while intoxicated). This perception extends to a person's functionality. Negative attitudes toward PWDs decreases as their perceived level of functionality by members of society increases (Livneh, 1982).

Systemically, when laws, policies, and institutions are created with the intention to exclude, or completely disregard, a particular group of people, oppression ensues. It is common knowledge in academic and advocacy-oriented spaces that legislation intended to help PWDs has often had unintended consequences as a result of being created without the input of PWDs. For example, while individuals have indicated strong motivations to work, research suggests that there is an uncertainty about vocational abilities and the potential loss of benefits (Olney, 2007).

Kosciulek (1999) posited the consumer-directed theory of empowerment (CDTE) as a result, following the mantra of many disability advocates: "Nothing about us without us." CDTE was developed with the intention of improving the experiences of PWDs receiving rehabilitation services. If the CDTE and its mantra were considered by policy makers and legislators, then laws targeted at improving experiences for individuals with disabilities would likely be more effective. CDTE emphasizes consumer direction and consumer choice in the development of all services and policies intended to support individuals with disabilities. When individuals experience the opportunity to choose, to have autonomy over their own lives, this contributes to self-efficacy development, as well as feelings of empowerment. Unfortunately, because of long-standing systemic barriers, CDTE is still not the approach that has been taken in the development of services and policies for PWDs.

Discrimination against people with mental health disorders is prevalent in narratives throughout our society. From blaming mass shootings on (unproven) mental illnesses, to representing individuals with bipolar disorder and schizophrenia as criminals and murderers on many television shows, there is a narrative of fear around this group. This is specific to individuals with psychiatric disorders. On the other hand, stigma and discrimination around individuals with neurodevelopmental disorders leads to treating members of this population like perpetual children. Regardless of the setting or group, we all have preconceived notions of what different diagnoses mean, and as a result, we have both explicit and implicit biases about people living with those diagnoses. It is the responsibility of practitioners to reflect on their own preconceived notions and to challenge themselves to look inward in countering such biases.

Mental Health Disorders and Employment

The persistence of negative attitudes about mental health disorders, compounded by the economic situation in the United States, leads to increased unemployment and underemployment of people living with these disorders. People with mental health disorders are less likely to work than those without mental health disorders, and those who do work are more likely to be paid less (Levinson, et al., 2010; Mechanic et al., 2002). In addition, a link between the severity of mental illness and employment status is also likely (Luciano & Meara, 2014). As such, people with mental illnesses are the fastest growing group of individuals in the United States to receive Social Security Disability Insurance (SSDI); approximately 35% of all individuals who receive SSDI qualify as a result of their mental illness (Drake et al., 2012; Social Security Administration, 2013).

People with mental health disorders are underemployed and unemployed at significant rates; the national unemployment rate for individuals with mental illnesses is approximately 80% (National Alliance on Mental Illness, 2014). An emphasis on work for individuals with mental health disorders is imperative given the connection between quality of life and satisfying work experiences (Buntinx & Schalock, 2010; Fleming et al., 2013). A "vocational drive" is believed to be largely inherent across individuals, regardless of the presence of a disability. Employment can play an important role in recovery and overall health; for example, it has been found that work can enhance many areas of a person's life, including self-esteem and the formation of positive relationships with colleagues (Dunn et al., 2011). The sense of empowerment that often comes with employment can help an individual with various aspects of disability, including the development of coping skills and providing a stable routine (Fleming et al., 2013).

Supported Employment

While there is a clear link to the ways in which employment improves recovery and quality of life for individuals with myriad disability types, services that have been demonstrated as leading to successful employment are not widely available. For instance, 30% of people served by the mental health system want to work, but only 2% of that group were found to be receiving supported employment services (Sherman et al., 2017). Supported employment is an evidence-based practice in vocational rehabilitation (VR) for individuals with mental health disorders that has an emphasis on competitive integrated employment in the community. The philosophy of supported employment (SAMHSA, 2009) is that

> every person with a serious mental illness is capable of working competitively in the community if the right kind of job and work environment can be found. Rather than trying to sculpt consumers into becoming "perfect workers" ... consumers are offered help finding and keeping jobs that capitalize on their personal strengths and motivation. (p. 3)

It has been demonstrated that individuals working with rehabilitation services and supported employment have a greater likelihood of obtaining employment (McDowell & Fossey, 2015). This is considered a result of the integrated nature of services with on-the-job support and an emphasis on individualized services and long-term support.

Employer's Perceptions

Employers are trained in managing their particular work settings and most likely have an expertise that is outside of human services. This means that people living with disabilities and their counselors must be prepared to advocate for their needs. Contact and experiences with PWDs have been established as one of the most effective forms of mitigating bias (Devine et al., 2012; Hand & Tryssenaar, 2006). The long history of separating and excluding PWDs from the mainstream resulted in employers lacking exposure to many individuals with mental health disorders and, therefore, a hesitancy in hiring them.

Perceptions of competence of people with mental health disorders are not the primary concern reported by employers; work personalities are the primary concern, with "becoming violent" as a top concern of employers (Hand & Tryssenaar, 2006). There are many more reported negative beliefs about people with mental health disorders, including motivation, quality of work, likelihood of injury, and following directions (Cook et al., 1994). These preconceived notions often lead to a lack of opportunities for individuals with mental health disorders who are seeking work if they disclose their diagnosis during the hiring process.

Accommodations

As a result of misunderstandings, implicit biases, and stigmas, employers may be less likely to want to provide accommodations for people with mental health disorders as compared to individuals with physical disabilities (McAlpine & Warner, 2002; McDowell & Fossey, 2015). This is likely because of the fact that accommodations for people with mental health disorders are less concrete than accommodations for individuals with physical disabilities. Some of the most commonly used accommodations for people with mental health disorders include flexible schedule/reduced hours, modified training and supervision, and modified jobs/duties (McDowell & Fosey, 2015). While adhering to laws that protect individuals with disabilities from discrimination (namely, the Americans With Disabilities Act of 1990), employers may grant these accommodations but cannot control if coworkers will expect similar or the same treatment.

Advocacy

As stigma and misunderstanding are so prevalent in our society and greatly contribute to the employment disparity we have discussed, it is important for professionals in the counseling field to advocate for their clients. Counselors must work under an "anti-stigma" agenda and work actively in the stigma change movement—a movement that one can argue has gained significant attention recently. The dismantling of the long-held beliefs many have about mental illness is the first step in creating a culture where accommodations are made without hesitation or question and, as a result, our clients can seamlessly integrate into work settings. Counselors can do this both in their immediate communities by advocating for employers to hire individuals with mental health disorders. Leveraging relationships will allow employers to gain positive experiences with individuals with mental health disorders and in the broader society by joining professional organizations, lobbying, and writing letters to representatives in legislative positions when needed. To be a counselor of any kind is to believe in the rights and dignity of all people, and that extends beyond what happens inside the walls of our practice settings.

Career Development

Career development for individuals across disability types is multifaceted. It is impossible to presume a similar career development pattern simply because two individuals have similar characteristics or diagnoses. Mental health disorders are especially complicated because the symptomology of certain disorders may change over time and is often unpredictable. As stated earlier in this chapter, and in the academic literature, individuals with mental health disorders who receive supported employment are more likely to be successful in obtaining and maintaining work (McDowell & Fossey, 2015). However, before we discuss employment, it is important to remember that education is a crucial part of career development. Students with mental health disorders are much more likely to drop out of high school than their peers. Students with "emotional disturbances" are more likely to drop out when compared to students with neurodevelopmental disorders, learning disabilities, or those who are deaf/blind (National Center for Education Statistics, 2019). If additional demographic factors are considered, such as race, then we can clearly see that students of color (i.e., black, American Indian, or Hispanic) are at an even greater risk of exiting high school without a diploma or alternative certificate (National Center for Education Statistics, 2019). It has been identified that the onset of mental health issues (specifically, psychiatric or mood disorders) coincides with the prime education years (e.g., adolescence), and we can make a clear connection from symptomatic onset to future adult unemployment.

Exiting high school with a diploma or an alternative certificate is related to future success in employment. If individuals with mental health disorders are dropping out of high school, then they significantly increase their likelihood of future unemployment and poverty. These are concepts that a teenager may not be able to understand. As such, the career development pattern for people with mental health disorders should be addressed in a case-by-case fashion: it is not a linear process. Similarly, the onset of a mental illness is a gradual process and likely will not happen all at once. This complicates the process further, as clients may experience new symptoms over time, especially those in the transition years (i.e., 14 to 24 years old).

Individuals with psychiatric diagnoses are also much more likely to have a VR case closed prior to successful completion of the program. oftentimes as a result of not being able to complete a recommended treatment plan (Tschopp et al., 2001). The combination of stigma, lack of training for counselors working with this population, and missing information on the intersectional issues for individuals in this population contribute to significant challenges in effective career counseling and understanding of career development.

Counselors must have a context from which to work to develop insights into clients' interests, strengths, and disability implications. Part of this framework involves counselor competency with career development theories and the application of these theories in clinical settings.

Social Cognitive Career Theory

Social cognitive career theory (SCCT) has been suggested as one of the more useful career development theories for conceptualizing and understanding career development for people with psychiatric diagnoses (Smith & Milson, 2011). SCCT merges one's introspective and internalized thoughts with social processes as they affect human behavior. More specifically, using Bandura's social cognitive theory (1986) as a starting point, SCCT then bridges Bandura's concept of self-efficacy (1997) with Krumboltz's social learning theory (1979). With regard to individuals with mental health disorders, SCCT is particularly appropriate given its unique take on the person-environment interaction. SCCT affords a more dynamic approach to understanding the person by environmental fit in career development. In other words, SCCT acknowledges the interaction between an individual's personal characteristics, environment, and overt behavior (Lent et al., 2002).

For individuals with mental health disorders, an individualistic and flexible approach to career development is particularly important for long-term success. Symptoms of mental health disorders are known to be acute at times and often exacerbated by one's environment. Understanding this in the context of career development for people with mental health disorders is especially important. In addition, SCCT incorporates a lot of assessment points, which contribute to its more individualized approach. For example, information about clients' interests, values, and personal attributes can be used to promote and support self-efficacy and set reasonable outcome expectancies (Lent et al., 2000).

Summary

Mental health disorders are complicated and multifaceted. Any career counseling approach to assisting people living with these diagnoses should be thoughtful, cautious, and thorough. It is especially important when working with this population that counselors meet their clients where they are and are careful not to project their beliefs about behavior, employment, and functioning onto their clients. This requires personal reflection on your own attitudes about mental illnesses and a pragmatic consideration about how those beliefs may affect the dynamics of a counseling session. Individuals with mental health disorders represent a group of people who need better services and support in attaining their goals for independence and employment. The capability of this group is minimized as a result of long-standing biases and unnecessary fear of the unknown. Career counselors and other human service professionals have an ethical obligation to work toward minimizing the presence of such obstacles for this population.

Understanding your clients and the situations in which they thrive, as well as the situations that may exacerbate symptoms, is imperative for successful career counseling. Further, clients need to be able to develop an introspective understanding of these same situations. Working with individuals who have mental illnesses may require a trial-and-error approach that allows clients the freedom to try different settings without feeling judged or as if though they are failing (i.e., build their self-efficacy). SCCT is a career development theory that is particularly appropriate for this population; however, this chapter outlines considerations to be made when using any career development theory in conceptualizing individuals' trajectories and needs.

Case Study

The client is a 28-year-old African American male diagnosed with bipolar I, polysubstance dependence, and nicotine dependence. The onset of symptoms began during his late teenage years; however, the client has reported that he felt he had ADHD throughout his early education, but this was not diagnosed until his late teenage years. The client was referred by the hospital after being brought to the mental health emergency room for bringing a BB gun into his day program. The client was referred for severe depression and anger issues. The client stated that he would like to obtain part-time work to help relieve financial stressors.

The client attended Riverdale High School and received a general high school diploma. He reports having emergency medical technician (EMT) first responder certification; however, it is currently expired, and he was unclear about whether he will pursue recertification. As mentioned earlier, the client reported that he believes he always had ADHD as a child (before it was diagnosed), and this was a significant barrier to his education; therefore, he is hesitant about furthering his education. When asked about barriers to additional EMT education, the client's answer suggested that he is nervous about possible failure.

The client has worked previously at several places but none for more than a month or so because of losing jobs as a result of drinking or drugging at work. The client currently volunteers with the SB Ambulance Company as a first responder and assists in the maintenance of their vehicles. He reported that he occasionally receives payment for doing certain jobs for this company; however, he stated that this was inconsistent and was unclear on the tasks that are payable. The client's most significant employment history was a job held at a golf club concession stand several years ago. This employment was significant because it was the basis for his drug and alcohol use. The client has an interest in working with and helping people, and he has skills in doing so through his work with the ambulance company and in the peer mentoring group program. The client stated that he has never worked without having a mental illness or substance addiction. He feels now that he is no longer using, he will be able to maintain employment, as he will be able to be more reliable and more competent. The client's main form of transportation is his bicycle, which he frequently works on and has developed a strong working knowledge of mechanics and mechanical skills in doing so. This, in combination with working on the ambulances, has given this client significant knowledge of cars, bicycles, and several mechanical devices used for these processes. Working on the ambulance has given the client a general knowledge of medical terminology, the human body, and how to work in a high-stress environment. The client exhibited poor memory during individual sessions; therefore, these skills may be fleeting or limited without being continually developed.

The client used alcohol, marijuana, and other drugs from the ages of 16–26 but stated that he was addicted only to alcohol. The client reported that he has been sober from all substances for 18 months. The client's mental health is unstable, as his moods cycle frequently, and he is unable to identify that his mood swings are related to his mental health. The client has reported suicidal thoughts, racing thoughts, mania, depression, and anxiety. When feeling good, the client reported that these are all manageable during work time, and as long as he is not using substances, they will not affect his work. The client reported taking Seroquel, Vistaril, and lithium to manage his mental health and attending a psychiatric rehabilitation program to help develop the skills necessary to manage his mental health himself.

Discussion Questions

1. Considering the intense discrimination and stigma surrounding mental health disorders, think for a moment about your own preconceived notions of mental health disorders. How would you feel if you learned that someone close to you was diagnosed with schizophrenia?
2. Employers need to hire people based on their qualifications and are not trained to work specifically with PWDs or mental health disorders. How would you describe a mental health disorder to an employer?
3. Consider disclosing a disability to an employer. What are the pros and cons? How would you have this conversation with a client? What if the client did not want to disclose?

References

American Psychiatric Association. (2013). *Diagnostic and statistical manual of mental disorders: DSM-5*. (5th ed.).

American Psychiatric Association. (2018). *What is mental illness?* https://www.psychiatry.org/patients-families/what-is-mental-illness

Baio, J., Wiggins, L., Christensen, D., Maenner, M., Daniels, J., Warren, Z., Kurzius-Spencer, M., Zahorodny, W., Rosenberg, C. R., White, T., Durkin, M. S., Imm, P., Nikolaou, L., Yeargin-Allsopp, M., Lee, L., Harrington, R., Lopez, M., Fitzgerald, R. T., Hewitt, A., ... Dowling, N. (2018). Prevalence of autism spectrum disorder among children aged 8 years—Autism and Developmental Disabilities Monitoring Network, 11 sites, United States, 2014. *MMWR Surveillance Summaries, 67*(6), 1–23.

Bandura, A. (1986). *Social foundations to thought and action: A social cognitive theory*. Prentice-Hall.

Boyle, C., Boulet, S., Schieve, L., Cohen, R., Blumberg, S., Yeargin-Allsopp, M., Visser, S., & Kogan, M. (2011). Trends in the prevalence of developmental disabilities in US children, 1997–2008. *Pediatrics, 127*(6), 1034–1042.

Buntinx, W. H. E., & Schalock, R. L. (2010). Models of disability, quality of life, and individualized supports: Implications for professional practice in intellectual disability. *Journal of Policy and Practice in Intellectual Disabilities, 7*(4), 283–294.

Cook, J. A., Razzano, L. A., Straiton, D. M., & Ross, Y. (1994). Cultivation and maintenance of relationships with employers of people with psychiatric disabilities. *Psychosocial Rehabilitation Journal, 17*(3), 103–116.

Devine, P. G., Forscher, P. S., Austin, A. J., & Cox, W. T. L. (2012). Long-term reduction in implicit race bias: A prejudice habit-breaking intervention. *Journal of Experimental Social Psychology, 48*(6), 1267–1278.

Drake, R. E., Bond, G. R., Thornicroft, G., Knapp, M., & Goldman, H. H. (2012). Mental health disability: An international perspective. *Journal of Disability Policy Studies, 23*(2), 110–120. https://doi.org/10.1177/1044207311427403

Dunn, C., Wewiorski, N., Rogers, E. (2008). The meaning and importance of employment to people in recovery from serious mental illness: Results of a qualitative study. *Psychiatric Rehabilitation Journal, 32*(1), 59–62.

Fleming, A. R., Fairweather, J. S., & Leahy, M. J. (2013). Quality of life as a potential rehabilitation service outcome the relationship between employment, quality of life, and other life areas. *Rehabilitation Counseling Bulletin, 57*(1), 9–22.

Hand, C., & Tryssenaar, J. (2006). Small business employers' views on hiring individuals with mental illness. *Psychiatric Rehabilitation Journal, 29*(3), 166–173.

Jeste, S. S. (2015). Neurodevelopmental behavioral and cognitive disorders. *CONTINUUM: Lifelong Learning in Neurology, 21*(3), 690–714.

Kosciulek, J. F. (1999). The consumer-directed theory of empowerment. *Rehabilitation Counseling Bulletin, 42*(3), 196–213.

Krumboltz, J. D. (1979). A social learning theory of career decision making. Revised and reprinted in A. M. Mitchell, G. B. Jones, & J. D. Krumboltz (Eds.), *Social learning and career decision making* (pp. 19–49). Carroll Press.

Lent, R., Brown, S., & Hackett, G. (2000). Contextual supports and barriers to career choice: A social cognitive analysis. *Journal of Counseling Psychology, 47*, 36–49.

Lent, R. W., Brown, S. D., & Hackett, G. (2002). Social cognitive career theory. In D. Brown and Associates (Eds.), *Career choice and development* (pp. 255–311). Jossey-Bass.

Levinson, D., Lakoma, M. D., Petukhova, M., Schoenbaum, M., Zaslavsky, A. M., Angermeyer, M., Borges, G., Bruffaerts, R., de Girolamo, G., de Graaf, R., Gureje, O., Haro, J. M., Hu, C., Karam, A. N., Kawakami, N., Lee, S., Lepine, J. P., Browne, M. O., Okoliyski, M., ... Kessler, R. C. (2010). Associations of serious mental illness with earnings: Results from the WHO World Mental Health surveys. *British Journal of Psychiatry, 197*(2), 114–121.

Livneh, H. (1982). On the origins of negative attitudes toward people with disabilities. *Rehabilitation Literature, 43*, 338–347.

Luciano, A., & Meara, E. (2014). Employment status of people with mental illness: National survey data from 2009 and 2010. *Psychiatric Services, 65*(10), 1201–1209.

McAlpine, D. D., & Warner, L. (2002). *Barriers to employment among persons with mental illness: A review of the literature.* Rutgers University.

McDowell, C., & Fossey, E. (2015). Workplace accommodations for people with mental illness: A scoping review. *Journal of Occupational Rehabilitation, 25*(1), 197–206.

Mechanic, D., Bilder, S., & McAlpine, D. D. (2002). Employing persons with serious mental illness. *Health Affairs, 21*(5), 242–253.

National Alliance on Mental Illness. (2014). *Mental illness: NAMI report deplores 80 percent unemployment rate; state rates and ranks listed—model legislation proposed.* https://www.nami.org/Press-Media/Press-Releases/2014/Mental-Illness-NAMI-Report-Deplores-80-Percent-Une

National Center for Education Statistics. (2019). *Children and youth with disabilities.* https://nces.ed.gov/programs/coe/indicator_cgg.asp

Olney, M. F. (2007). Caught in a social safety net: Perspectives of recipients of social security disability programs on employment. *Journal of Applied Rehabilitation Counseling, 38*(2), 5–13,45–46.

Shedler, J., & Westen, D. (2004). Refining personality disorder diagnosis: Integrating science and practice. *American Journal of Psychiatry, 161*(8), 1350–1365.

Sherman, L.J., Lynch, S.E., Teich, J., and Hudock, W.J. (2017, June 15). Availability of supported employment in specialty mental health treatment facilities and facility characteristics: 2014. *Center for Behavioral Health Statistics and Quality,* Substance Abuse and Mental Health Services Administration: Rockville, MD.

Smith, A., & Milson, A. (2011). Social cognitive career theory and adults with psychiatric disabilities: Bringing theory to practice. *Journal of Applied Rehabilitation Counseling, 42*(3), 20–25.

Social Security Administration. (2013). Annual Statistical Report on the Social Security Disability Insurance Program, 2013. Retrieved from: https://www.ssa.gov/policy/docs/statcomps/di_asr/2013/sect01b.html#hLogo

Substance Abuse and Mental Health Services Administration (SAMHSA). (2009). *Supported employment: Building your program* (DHHS Pub. No. SMA-08-4364). Center for Mental Health Services, Substance Abuse and Mental Health Services Administration, U.S. Department of Health and Human Services.

Tschopp, M., Bishop, M., & Mulvihill, M. (2001). Career development of individuals with psychiatric disabilities: An ecological perspective of barriers and interventions. *Journal of Applied Rehabilitation Counseling, 32*(2), 25.

Visser, S., Danielson, M., Bitsko, R., Holbrook, J., Kogan, M., Ghandour, R., Perou, R., & Blumberg, S. (2014). Trends in the parent-report of health care provider-diagnosed and medicated attention-deficit/hyperactivity disorder: United States, 2003–2011. *Journal of the American Academy of Child and Adolescent Psychiatry, 53*(1), 34–46.

World Health Organization (WHO). (2014). *Mental health: A state of well-being.* https://www.who.int/features/factfiles/mental_health/en/

Zunker, V.G. (2008). *Career, work, and mental health: Integrating career and personal counseling.* Sage Publications.

CHAPTER 15

Career Counseling for Ex-Offenders

Brenna Breshears

CHAPTER OVERVIEW

Ex-offenders will experience a variety of difficulties upon release, but the area in which most experience the highest degree of difficulty is reentering into the workforce (Shivy et al., 2007). Therefore, career counselors need to have an understanding of the barriers to returning to work for ex-offenders, as well as strategies and techniques to assist this population. This chapter will discuss and describe the ex-offender population and outline the barriers that ex-offenders may experience when attempting to return to work. Further, this chapter will outline strategies and techniques for career counselors when working with ex-offenders, accommodations in the workplace, and resources career counselors should be aware of and share with ex-offenders.

CHAPTER OBJECTIVES

After reading this chapter, the student will be able to complete the following:

1. Define ex-offender.

2. Identify and discuss the barriers to career counseling and employment for ex-offenders.

3. Discuss strategies and techniques for career counseling ex-offenders.

4. Identify accommodations in the workplace for ex-offenders who return to work.

Introduction

Formerly incarcerated individuals will experience a variety of difficulties upon release, but the area in which most experience the highest degree of difficulty is reentering the workforce (Shivy et al., 2007). The unemployment rate for formerly incarcerated individuals is nearly five times higher than that of the general public (Coullete & Kopf, 2018). Consequently, career counselors need to understand the barriers to returning to work for formerly incarcerated individuals, as well as strategies and techniques to assist this population. This chapter will discuss and describe the formerly incarcerated population and outline the barriers that formerly incarcerated individuals may experience when attempting to return to work.

Further, this chapter will outline strategies and techniques for career counselors when working with formerly incarcerated individuals, accommodations in the workplace, and resources career counselors should be aware of and share with formerly incarcerated individuals.

Who Are Formerly Incarcerated Individuals?

Formerly incarcerated individuals, also referred to as returning citizens, are individuals who have experienced contact with the criminal justice system in various capacities. Although these individuals are often commonly referred to as "felons," "inmates," or "ex-offenders," the terms "formerly incarcerated" and "incarcerated" individuals have been purposefully chosen to embody person-centered language and to account for those who have been wrongfully convicted, as well as those who have been incarcerated without conviction. Whether they have experienced long-term incarceration or short-term incarceration primarily resulting in probation or diversion court, formerly incarcerated individuals are those who have been convicted of a crime and sentenced (also referred to as "adjudicated"), which results in some form of criminal record.

However, in addition to this often public criminal record, formerly incarcerated individuals may experience various unique barriers to employment, such as social stigma, employer bias, lack of community support, gap in work history, limited competitive skills, and trauma related to incarceration (Bennett & Amundson, 2016; De Giorgi, 2018; Shivy et al.; Varghese & Cummings, 2013). Furthermore, over 540,000 individuals are engaged in pretrial detention annually, meaning they have not been sentenced or convicted, yet they may be detained for extensive periods of time in local jails and, therefore, will also likely experience similar barriers to those incarcerated post-conviction (Wagner & Sawyer, 2018).

Currently in the United States, approximately 2.3 million individuals are experiencing some form of incarceration, whether it be in state prisons (56.8%), local jails (26.0%), or various federal facilities (9.6%). While the prevalence of private prisons is increasing nationally, 90% of prisons are operated by state or federal entities, and the by-product of mass incarceration is mass release. It is estimated that 95% of those incarcerated in state prison will eventually be released, and over nine million individuals will be released from jail annually (Wagner & Sawyer, 2018). These numbers are not surprising when recognizing that the United States incarcerates more individuals per capita than any other country in the world, approximately 716 people per 100,000. Although the United States only accounts for 4.4% of the world population, it also accounts for 22% of the world's incarcerated individuals (U.S. Bureau of Justice Statistics, 2015). Approximately 600,000 Americans are released into the community every year, and almost one third of all adults have a prior conviction (Bauer et al., 2016). Considering these staggering numbers, and the fact that employment has been positively correlated with low recidivism rates (Benda et al., 2005; Decker et al., 2015; Hanlon et al., 2000), the need for employment-focused reentry services are clear.

In addition, the rate of mental health diagnoses and psychiatric disability within the formerly incarcerated population is significant; an estimated 40% of individuals experiencing mental illness will experience some form of incarceration within their lifetimes (Batastini et al., 2014). As career counselors trained in employment strategies and counseling theory, the opportunity for service that includes both effective vocational counseling and mental health support is significant and, subsequently, should be the foundation of any interaction with the formerly incarcerated population.

Unlike other stigmatized groups, such as minorities, women, and people with disabilities (PWDs) who are protected by legislation such as the Civil Rights Act of 1964 or the 1990 Americans With Disabilities Act, legal protections related to employment discrimination as a result of criminal records are few, and because many organizations and employers collect data on criminal history through background check procedures prior to employment, the option to conceal involvement with the court system is limited (Bauer et al., 2016). These practices not only increase stigma but also may result in significant anxiety for formerly incarcerated individuals entering the workforce who are fearful that they will be forced to disclose convictions without the opportunity to provide context or demonstrate steps they have taken to rehabilitate.

Barriers

Myriad factors beyond criminal charges contribute to employment barriers for formerly incarcerated individuals, and while it is imperative in the counseling relationship to avoid generalizations regarding this population by recognizing each individual's unique history and lived experiences, decades of research has shown that there are significant commonalties within the formerly incarcerated community related to education, substance use, and mental health. In addition, public policy and legislative practices in the United States have contributed to the disproportionate representation of certain groups within the prison and jail demographics.

Individuals with mental illness are dramatically overrepresented in prison and jail populations, and they have been for decades (Figure 15.1). Following the mass closure of state-run psychiatric hospitals in the 1960s, the availability of inpatient care was greatly reduced. Consequently, a rise in mental health issues among homeless, houseless, and incarcerated populations soon followed. While the intention was to increase community care options, reduce restrictive treatment settings, and address reports of deplorable conditions within state-run hospitals, the reality is that federal and state funding was not enough to serve the growing population, with only 50% of proposed community intervention sites actually being built. In turn, federal funding was not sufficient to support and operate existing treatment centers, leaving individuals without health care few options (Torrey et al., 2010).

Over the past 50 years, there has been a dramatic increase in the rate of incarceration for those with mental illness. Compared to the general population, individuals involved in the criminal justice system are significantly more likely to have a current or past mental health diagnosis, with estimates as high as 56% of state prison inmates, 45% of federal prison inmates, and 64% of jail inmates experiencing a recent history or current symptoms of a mental illness based on a *Diagnostic and Statistical Manual of Mental Disorder, 5th Edition (DSM-5)* clinical diagnoses from a mental health professional (James & Glaze, 2006).

The "War on Drugs" in the 1980s compounded the issue by increasing legislation and policies related to significant prison and jail time for low-level and first-time offenses, further adding to the mass incarceration epidemic. The "Tough on Crime" rhetoric of Richard Nixon, widely recognized today as a racist policy that led to the disproportionate arrest and incarceration of people of color (Alexander, 2010), spurred a trend in sentencing that has directly influenced today's prison and jail demographics (Dumont et al., 2012). The result of providing generous federal funding to local law enforcement and setting new mandatory and lengthy sentences for drug crimes in the 1970s has been an epidemic of disproportionate sentencing. For example, even though illicit drug use is estimated at 9.6% for black Americans and 8.8% among white Americans, blacks are 13 times more likely to face incarceration for drug crimes than whites, and they make up almost 65% of all individuals imprisoned (Substance Abuse Mental Health Service Administration Summary of National Findings, 2010). Today, black Americans are arrested and incarcerated at a greater rate than they were during the Jim Crow Era (Alexander, 2010).

Although the "War on Drugs" does not solely explain the rise in incarceration in this country, it should be noted that between 1985 and 2000, almost two thirds of the federal inmate population and one half of the state prison inmate population were incarcerated for drug-related crimes (Dumont et al., 2012). The effect of disproportionate sentencing has influenced not only incarceration demographics but also increased the stigma and public perception of what a formerly incarcerated individual looks like. For example, research has shown that some employers screen out African American men preemptively over the fear that they have had contact with the court system, regardless of their individual characteristics or qualifications (Flake, 2019).

Just as we must consider the role of racial and cultural components in the context of incarceration, we must apply this lens to gender as well. Although men and women face some similar barriers to reentry, such as housing, transportation, employment, and community support, their paths to incarceration can be categorized uniquely. Women are (a) more likely to be serving time for drug offenses; (b) are more likely to be women of color, in particular African Americans over the age of 30; (c) are mothers (70%); (d) are more likely than men to have to have mental health diagnoses; and (e) are more likely to have experienced a pattern of victimization over the course of their lives (Singh et al., 2019; Snodgrass et al., 2017).

While research regarding the differences between men and women in terms of incarceration and reentry is still emerging, distinct and gender-specific pathways have come to light as a result of feminist-oriented criminology studies. Perhaps the most significant finding is that women's pathways to offending are characterized by a series of gender-specific experiences due in part to the reality that many women offenders in the criminal justice system come from low socioeconomic backgrounds characterized by poverty, poor employment opportunities, and educational attainment. In addition, limited prosocial opportunities to move out of these backgrounds of disadvantage result in some women engaging in antisocial methods of overcoming these socio-structural deficits (Singh et al., 2019.)

In terms of educational attainment, there is significant statistical evidence that points to a trend of low educational involvement and attainment within this population, regardless of gender. A 2003 report by the Bureau of Justice revealed that approximately 41% of currently incarcerated individuals had completed some high school, 23% had obtained a GED, 22% held a high school diploma, and 12% had some level of post-secondary education (Harlow, 2003). Other findings included in this report are as follows: younger inmates were less educated than older inmates, individuals of color were less likely than their white counterparts to have a GED or high school diploma, and those with lower educational attainment were more likely to reoffend. Although there has been an increase in educational opportunities provided during incarceration, low educational attainment continues to be a barrier upon exiting the prison or jail system and entering the workforce. In addition, formerly incarcerated populations include many people with physical, cognitive, and developmental disabilities, both diagnosed and undiagnosed. Prevalence data on disabilities within this population vary widely within studies, making it difficult to estimate the percentage, but particularly those with cognitive, mental health, and substance use issues tend to have a high level of historical contact with the legal system (Harley et al., 2014.)

Finally, beyond the value of employment as a contributor to recidivism reduction (Decker et al., 2015; Lukies et al., 2011), there is often a very real and immediate need for stable income following incarceration. In the last decade, scholars and researchers have compiled a compelling body of evidence supporting the claim that formerly incarcerated individuals face significant and unique financial burdens related directly to contact with the court system. The term "legal financial obligations" (LFOs) coined by Beckett et al. (2008) encompasses myriad monetary sanctions and requirements, including fines, restitution, supervisor fees, and accrued child support (Pleggenkhule, 2018). While not all individuals may accrue significant LFOs, the likelihood that formerly incarcerated individuals will experience some form of immediate financial burden is worthy of consideration in light of the fact that research indicates that only 50% of formerly incarcerated individuals are able to satisfy court-related financial requirements and that as many as 20% report legal debts that outweigh their monthly incomes (Visher et al., 2004) Furthermore, beyond the financial burden, LFOs have been found to limit upward social mobility by compounding existing barriers, such as poor credit, low education levels, and lack of affordable housing (Pleggenkhule, 2017).

Attitudes and Stigma

Despite the known link between unemployment and recidivism, surprisingly few legal protections exist to promote the employment of formerly incarcerated individuals. Although tax breaks are sometimes available to employers that voluntarily hire formerly incarcerated individuals, there is no federal law that prohibits employers from discriminating against formerly incarcerated individuals, and only a handful of states and cities have imposed such limitations, which often apply only to public-sector employment. (Flake, 2019, p. 1082)

Beyond the unique environmental, psychosocial, and cultural barriers formerly incarcerated individuals face, negative attitudes toward hiring individuals with criminal records present perhaps the most significant challenges. To contextualize employer attitudes, it is first helpful to understand the concept of stigma. Jones et al. (1984) first conceptualized stigma as a six-dimensional model consisting of concealability, course, disruptiveness, aesthetics, origin, and peril. *Concealability* can be understood as wither the stigma can be observed, *course* refers to how the stigma may change over time, *disruptiveness* is the level to which the stigma will affect social and interpersonal interactions, *aesthetics* refers to visible characteristics that may affect negative perceptions, *origin* represents whether the stigma is perceived as intentional rather than accidental, and *peril* considers the perceived threat that may be associated with a particular stigma.

For the formerly incarcerated population, all dimensions may be applicable to a discussion of employer stigma, but a selected few are generally understood to have the most impact. For example, while formerly incarcerated status is technically concealable from an observational perspective, physical markers, such as tattoos acquired in prison, could be considered components of *concealability* or aesthetic stigma, as they may be distinguishable from other tattoos, depending on the observer's personal experience and knowledge, and while *course* may pertain to juveniles whose records have been sealed or expunged, or to individuals who will eventually have charges dropped, formerly incarcerated status is primarily permanent and fixed as opposed to changing or dynamic. Therefore, in relation to employer stigma, *disruptiveness*, *origin*, and *peril* are the primary factors influencing attitudes. In particular, origin and peril are most likely to affect this population, as criminal offenses are largely perceived as a fault of character and, regardless of whether crimes committed were violent in nature, a threat to individual and company safety (Young & Powell, 2015).

While the decision to disclose formerly incarcerated status is theoretically the choice of the individual, "forced disclosure" because of eligibility questions at the application stage, gaps in work history, or scheduling considerations because of probation requirements are common. Consequently, formerly incarcerated status is often revealed before the interview stage, resulting in immediate barriers to employment, as well as increased anxiety for those in the application stage of job seeking. Even if individuals are not required to disclose during the application process, they may still face a "disclosure dilemma" after hiring where they must decide whether to reveal their status to employers and coworkers. While disclosing may lessen anxiety for individuals by reducing fear of exposure, it may also lead to stereotyping, discrimination, and social rejection (Bauer et al., 2018). Although some release programs within prison settings may offer strategies for disclosing offender status to potential employers, the reality is that even if given the opportunity to explain the context of the crime and rehabilitative efforts, negative perceptions toward hiring formerly incarcerated individuals are much more common and likely than positive perceptions, and they will, therefore, continue to result in exclusion from the workforce.

Screening processes are the first barrier faced by formerly incarcerated individuals when job seeking, where employers consistently screen out formerly incarcerated individuals during the application process. By looking to research findings from scholars within the human resources field, a troubling picture of widespread employer discrimination begins to emerge. For example, a survey of employers conducted in 2016 by HireRight found that 89% of employers conduct criminal or public record searches, 81% screen contract or temporary workers, and 17% rescreen current employees (HireRight, 2016). Consequently, a majority of employers screen out all formerly incarcerated individuals, regardless of the crime, under the assumption that any conviction will negatively affect workplace performance (Hall et al., 2015). This can be attributed not only to origin and peril stigma but also fear that formerly incarcerated individuals will continue criminal behavior once hired. Furthermore, a recent survey found that nearly all employers screen out individuals who have committed a violent felony, but a similar number of employers also screen out for convictions related to nonviolent offenses, such as fraud or embezzlement. In addition, 52% of employers stated they would exclude individuals who had misdemeanor convictions regarding theft or dishonesty, and 35% stated they would not hire those with drug offenses (Employee Screen IQ, 2014).

In addition, access to jobs for the formerly incarcerated population are affected by state mandatory limitations on employment, which include "blanket exclusions for the formerly incarcerated or those with criminal records, regardless of whether their records are relevant to the job for which they are applying" (Hall et al., 2015, p. 254). While this may partially be attributed to the Negligent Hiring Law, which states that "an employer can be found liable for an injury caused by an employee if the employer knew or should have known of the employee's "propensity for the conduct which cause the injury" (Harley, pg. 14, 2014), there is little evidence to support generalized claims that hiring a formerly incarcerated person will result in workplace injury.

Employer surveys targeting the willingness to hire formerly incarcerated individuals reveal that employers in the manufacturing, construction, and transportation sectors where customer contact was limited; employers with high turnover rates; and employers who sought labor for unskilled jobs were most likely to hire formerly incarcerated individuals. Conversely, while employers who used background checks were less likely to hire formerly incarcerated individuals and most were strongly opposed to hiring individuals with violent offenses, they were more open to hiring those with property or drug crime convictions (Holzer et al., 2004). This information is of importance, as it suggests that vocational counselors working from a demand-side perspective may want to target specific types of employers and jobs based on the specific charges their clients have accrued.

"Ban the Box," a legislative practice that begun in Hawaii in 1998, seeks to reduce employment discrimination by delaying applicants from disclosing formerly incarcerated status until later in the hiring process rather than during the application process by removing the common "check this box if you have committed a crime" question on many applications. Although "Ban the Box" campaigns have increased countrywide in the last decade, empirical research remains inconclusive as to how much this practice actually increases employment for formerly incarcerated individuals, and multiple studies have claimed that ban the box practices may actually increase discriminatory practices by employers who instead preemptively screen out racial minorities based on assumptions that they may have criminal records because of the now well-documented racial disparity rates within arrest and sentencing practices (Flake, 2019).

Tips and Techniques for Working With Formerly Incarcerated Individuals

Any discussion of vocational counseling must include the risk needs responsivity (RNR) model, as it is the globally recognized model used to determine factors that may contribute to continued criminal behavior and incarceration. First introduced by Andrews and Bonta in 1990, the RNR has two basic principles consisting of (1) risk and (2) need. Risk is conceptualized as (a) use of a reliable and validated risk assessment to predict criminal behavior and (b) appropriately matching the level of service to the assessed level of risk. Need is conceptualized as the use of interventions and programs that focus on criminogenic needs, further defined as factors directly relating to offending behavior that are amenable to change (Andrews & Bonta, 2010). Criminogenic factors, indicators, and intervention goals are described in Figure 15.2. The premise of the RNR models is that responsivity should directly address individual factors rather than a "one size fits all" approach. Depending on organization or agency settings, career counselors may be provided with an RNR assessment before beginning the counseling process. For example, if a vocational counselor is working within an agency that provides court-mandated career or mental health counseling for adjudicated individuals, they will most likely be required to develop a treatment plan based on the RNR model. Therefore, an understanding of basic components and implications for individual application should be considered best practice when working with this population.

While there is currently no unified recommendation regarding career counseling theory or modality when working with formerly incarcerated individuals, certain theoretical frameworks lend themselves well to application in this population and are worthy of mention. In particular, the theory of intersectionality, first articulated by Kimberlé Crenshaw in reference to black women, postulates that individuals contain multiple identities that should be considered when identifying discrimination and stigma. For example, black women face discrimination based on their race, as well as their gender, and so the intersection of both of these identities then creates unique barriers that may not be experienced by black men or white women (Crenshaw, 1991). This theory is particularly applicable to formerly incarcerated individuals, as they may hold multiple identities that contribute to both social and employment discrimination, such as race, gender, educational attainment, socioeconomic status, mental health diagnoses, disability status, and history of substance use. The result is a compound affect that not only makes employment barriers more pronounced but also contributes to viewpoints that see these identities as merely variables contributing to recidivism rather than unique lived experiences.

Furthermore, career counseling theories such as social cognitive career theory first articulated by Lent et al. are particularly relevant to this population by providing an ecological client approach that recognizes the importance of self-efficacy, outcome expectations, and interest components as they relate to ability, values, and environmental factors (Lent et al., 1994). In addition, particular modalities, such as cognitive behavior therapy, motivational interviewing, and solution-focused brief therapy, have all been found to be empirically effective with the formerly incarcerated population and should be considered. However, regardless of counselor personal style or theoretical approach, an emphasis on the working alliance offers the greatest chance for successful outcomes within this population.

The influence of a strong working alliance and its relationship with positive outcomes has been documented by many areas in the field of vocational counseling (Chan et al., 1997; Lustig et al., 2002). Defined by Bordin as the collaboration between the consumer and the counselor based on the development of an attachment bond, as well as the commitment to the goals and tasks of counseling (Bordin, 1979), the purpose of the working alliance is not only to create a positive relationship but also to agree on tasks at goals at an early stage to avoid incongruence. For formerly incarcerated individuals, the working alliance presents an opportunity to build a relationship based on equity, informed choice, and empathy for an individual who has likely experienced little to no recent autonomy. Prison environments can be described as total institutions, meaning they are a place of work or residence where a large group of similarly situated people are cut off from the rest of society for a lengthy amount of time and as a result live an enclosed, regulated life that is typically hierarchical in nature (Goffman, 1961). Other examples of total institutions include the military; religious centers, such as convents and monasteries; and psychiatric hospitals. For those recently released from prison, having spent significant time in a total institution can result in confusion, fear, and anxiety related to reentering society, as well as the workplace. For many, making simple choices, such as when and what to eat, when to go to bed, what to wear, and how to spend free time, have not been part of their daily habits. Therefore, a focus on autonomy and an empathetic approach to supported decision making should be implemented at first contact; thus, using a person-centered approach that includes unconditional positive regard, empathy, and genuineness (Rogers, 1956) should be the cornerstone used to build a successful working alliance.

Beyond the ethical considerations necessitating a focus on the working alliance, research from the vocational counseling field shows that (a) employed clients have stronger working alliance than unemployed clients, (b) working alliance is related not only to clients perception of future employment but also to satisfaction with their current jobs, and (c) because vocational counseling tends to be brief, tasks and goals should be defined early to avoid incongruence later on (Lustig et al., 2002). For example, if discrepancies about employment outcomes are not discussed early on in the counseling process, it will not only damage the working alliance but also affect future beliefs about the efficacy of vocational counseling, as well as compound fear-based beliefs about entering the workforce. Because counselor and client personalities tend to be fixed pre-therapy, beliefs and expectations regarding outcomes should be discussed at the onset of any intervention to establish immediate congruence between client and counselor regarding tasks and goals.

Counseling Process

Although formerly incarcerated individuals face many unique barriers to employment, the basic tenets of vocational counseling still apply in many ways. A strong working alliance, emphasis on the structured counseling process, and awareness of the classic counseling stages of change should be implemented with this population while simultaneously including techniques and strategies that directly address the particular experiences of formerly incarcerated individuals. In fact, many barriers formerly incarcerated individuals face, such as "lack of the social skills for presenting themselves positively during an interview, passive approach in searching for employment, lack of confidence to actively job search, assuming the effort of applying for a job is not worth the rejection not knowing how to discuss their legal history in the least damaging way, unawareness of job restrictions and employment saturation and thus spend too much time focused on low probability options, unrealistic expectations for employment for entry-level positions, inability to recognize stress, need of assistance in obtaining state issued identification to complete a 1099 employment form, and difficulty in being contacted by a potential employer when living in shelters or transitional living residences" (Harley, 2016, p. 15) can be directly addressed within the counseling process.

Colling and Davis (2005) conceptualized the counseling process as five unique yet overlapping stages: (1) *attending* (intake), (2) *exploration* (eligibility and planning), (3) *understanding* (planning and service), (4) *action* (service and employment), and (5) *termination* (closure). These stages align closely with the classic psychotherapeutic stages of change—precontemplation, contemplation, preparation, action, and maintenance—and can be used to demonstrate a conceptual guideline for serving the formerly incarcerated population.

The *attending stage* can be used to (a) uphold ethical doctrines of informed consent and informed choice, (b) provide an explanation of the mission of vocation counseling to your clients, (c) develop the working alliance, and (d) assess and client resistance (Colling & Davis, 2005). When working with formerly incarcerated individuals, the attending stage is a critical point in the process that should be used to not only inform and educate them about the counseling process but also to learn about your clients' unique lived experiences. Even though there is an abundance of available statistics related to the characteristics of the formerly incarcerated, generalizing should be avoided, and clients should be encouraged to share and describe their personal experiences, as well as their own perceived barriers. Depending on how much information a counselor has received prior to intake, they may or may not have information regarding specific charges, length of incarceration, probation or parole requirements, co-occurring diagnoses, and so on. The intake stage should be used to establish trust and positive rapport to empower clients to feel comfortable sharing their backgrounds, anxieties, and concerns, as well as hopes and goals. Power dynamics that exist in the criminal justice system may also be present in counseling environments and should be recognized and acknowledged by the counselor at this stage.

The *exploration stage* can be used to (a) learn about the client's world and worldview; (b) explore values, feelings, challenges, needs, and goals; (c) employ microskills and attend to behavior to gather information; (d) look for examples of resilience and identify potential past and present barriers; and (e) gain knowledge of client's medical, vocational, educational, incarceration, and family history (Collings & Davis, 2005).

In addition to strengthening the working alliance, this stage should be used to learn about the unique experiences of the client, as well as identify both real and perceived barriers. For example, a client may have heard misinformation regarding benefits or have misconceptions regarding the labor market. Often, those who have been incarcerated in a state or federal prison will have participated in some form of educational or vocational training with the belief that once released jobs in those fields will be readily available. However, if their training does not fit the current labor market (hoping to use a construction certification but being released during a recession), clients may feel disillusioned or discouraged. This stage should be also be used to identify existing and anticipated LFOs, as well as probation and parole requirements to create a complete picture of the client's legal obligations and to ensure appropriate goals and tasks are determined. At this stage, clients should begin to view their lives from a big picture perspective, with a particular focus on how legal requirements and obligations will affect employment, to successfully begin the planning stage. For those with co-occurring diagnoses, such as substance abuse or significant mental health issues, referrals to appropriate resources should also be established at this time.

The *understanding stage* can be used to (a) encourage clients to consider new possibilities regarding employment, education, and behavior; (b) solidify tasks and goals of the counseling process; and (c) establish realistic expectations for employment. Because of little contact with the general population, as well as possible misinformation perpetuated by those in the corrections field regarding employment expectations, formerly incarcerated individuals may overestimate or underestimate their abilities. At this stage, it is crucial for counselors, based on their understanding and knowledge of their clients' unique lived experiences, as well as educational and vocational training, to present and agree on tasks and goals that are both attainable and realistic by collaborating with their clients. Assessments can be incorporated at this stage to better understand a clients preferred work environment, cognitive functioning, or physical capabilities.

Most importantly, this stage should be used to identify transferable skills acquired both prior to and during incarceration to successfully identify short-term goals related to employment. For example, as previously discussed, formerly incarcerated individuals tend to have lower levels of educational attainment and while employers have indicated a higher likelihood of employing formerly incarcerated individuals with high educational attainment such as a postsecondary degree or vocational certification (Lukies et al., 2011), this may be difficult because financial aid, such as Pell grants, are unavailable for many who have been convicted. For example, a first-time drug offender is ineligible for financial aid for 1 year, while a third-time drug offender is ineligible for life (Harley, 2016).

Therefore, exploration surrounding a client's educational, as well as vocational goals, should be included in this stage to set meaningful tasks. Even though the counselor may not see the results of long-term planning because of the often brief nature of career counseling, an emphasis on thoughtful planning gives clients the foundation to synthesize personal experience and qualifications into goal identification while also increasing personal investment. If clients feel they have set attainable and realistic goals, are engaged in meaningful tasks, and feel unconditional positive regard, they are more likely to remain motivated following case closure.

The *action stage* can be used to continue to recognize barriers and support as they evolve. Implementing a model such as Roessler's 3M model (match, maturity, and mastery) can be used at this stage to ensure that counselors continue to offer support and contribute to their clients' vocational developments. *Match* refers to a proper job-person fit wherein a person not only possesses and uses the skills needed to meet job demands but is also employed in an environment that provides activities or tasks that reinforce their personal preferences (i.e., good at what they do and like what they are doing). *Maturity* refers to the ability to meet developmental challenges that may arise with job tenure and may include job coaching or mentoring from senior employees. Mastery refers to the ability to adjust to day-to-day problems that can negatively affect retention or upward mobility. By using this or similar models, counselors can help clients to establish an appropriate match, meet career maturity challenges, and demonstrate mastery of novel workplace problems (Roessler, 2002). Because many formerly incarcerated individuals have limited or sporadic employment histories, job retention and employee development may not have been previously prioritized. In fact, recent research suggests that a true indicator of recidivism reduction is not based simply on employment but rather type and longevity of employment after release. At this stage, counselors have an opportunity to identify and emphasize the retention strategies with their clients to support long-term competitive employment as a primary goal.

Lastly, the *termination* stage can be used to (a) explore client feelings as the relationship ends, (b) identify further community resources, and (c) encourage the client to continue developing personal autonomy and agency. Most importantly, the counseling process should be used not only to accomplish goals and provide services but also as an opportunity for clients to reduce the fear of change.

Depending on the setting they practice in, counselors may need to acknowledge organizational factors that could potentially affect the counseling process. For example, if working in a state vocation rehabilitation setting where caseloads are high and contact is brief, a more didactic approach may be necessary. However, in this case, all efforts should be made to balance directive and reflective interactions to uphold the tenets of person-centered counseling, as well as support formerly incarcerated individuals in their efforts to practice autonomy and agency.

Finally, from an organizational standpoint, a recent study of almost 600 employers found that while organizational factors, such as geographic location, industry type, and role of responder, did not have significant effect on their willingness to hire, the size of the organization was a favorable predictor in that larger companies were more likely to hire formerly incarcerated individuals than smaller companies (Lukies, et al., 2011). These findings mirror disability-specific studies that find that employers of large companies are more likely to hire PWDs, especially if disability is specifically included in their diversity programs. In addition, mid-level employees, such as human resources managers and supervisors, are more likely to hire PWDs when they have received disability-specific training or education (Burke et al., 2013; Chan et al., 2010). From a demand-side perspective, these findings can also be applied to career counseling for formerly incarcerated individuals by encouraging vocational counselors to build relationships with large companies and by targeting mid-level employees, such as supervisors and human resources managers, for formerly incarcerated persons' psychoeducation efforts.

Summary

Formerly incarcerated individuals face a plethora of unique barriers to employment related to myriad psychosocial, environmental, contextual, and identity-related factors. Therefore, in the words of Rachel Remen, "To *fix* views life as broken, to *help* views life as weak, but to *serve* views life as whole" (Remen, 1999). Consequently, providing ethical and effective career counseling to those who have experienced incarceration demands a holistic approach, giving career and vocational counselors an opportunity to not only work toward employment goals with these vulnerable clients but also to model and practice advocacy by providing culturally appropriate, empowering, and intentional service.

Case Study

You are working with Missy (43 years old, white, cisgender female, lesbian) at the local vocational rehabilitation agency. Missy has recently been released from prison on parole and is meeting with a counselor, having been referred after being diagnosed with depression while in prison. She has been on medication since she attempted suicide while in prison but reports no suicidal ideation now. Missy and her wife have been married for 5 years and are hoping that Missy can get a job that helps them move into a better neighborhood and get on with their lives. However, Missy discloses to you that she is feeling stressed at home because she has developed a new sense of self that does not fit the person she was when she got married. This stress does not make her suicidal, but it does make her consider returning to shoplifting, which put her in prison in the first place.

Discussion Questions

1. Based on intersectional theory, list and describe specific identities your client may hold that could both positively and negatively affect his/her employment prospects.
2. List and describe three strategies career counselors might use to build a strong working alliance with a formerly incarcerated client.

References

Alexander, M. (2010). *The new Jim Crow: Mass incarceration in the age of colorblindness*. New Press.

Andrews, D. A., & Bonta, J. (2010). *The psychology of criminal conduct* (5th ed.). LexisNexis Matthew Bender.

Batastini, A. B., Bolanos, A. D., & Morgan, R. D. (2014). Attitudes toward hiring applicants with mental illness and criminal justice involvement: The impact of education and experience. *International Journal of Law and Psychiatry, 37*(5), 524–533. https://doi.org/10.1016/j.ijlp.2014.02.025

Baur, J. E., Hall, A. V., Daniels, S. R., Buckley, M. R., & Anderson, H. J. (2018). Beyond banning the box: A conceptual model of the stigmatization of ex-offenders in the workplace. *Human Resource Management Review, 28*(2), 204–219. https://doi.org/10.1016/j.hrmr.2017.08.002

Beckett, K. A., Harris, A. M., & Evans, H. (2008). *The assessment and consequences of legal financial obligations in Washington state*. Washington State Minority and Justice Commission.

Benda, B. B., Harm, N. J., & Toombs, N. J. (2005). Survival analysis of recidivism of male and female boot camp graduates using life-course theory. *Journal of Offender Rehabilitation, 40*(3–4), 87–113.

Bennett, A., & Amundson, N. (2016). The need for dynamic models of career development for transitioning offenders. *Journal of Employment Counseling, 53*(2), 60–70. https://doi.org/10.1002/joec.12028

Bordin, E. S. (1979). The generalizability of the psychoanalytic concept of the working alliance. *Psychotherapy: Theory, Research & Practice, 16*(3), 25–260. https://doi.org/10.1037/h0085885

Bureau of Justice Statistics. (2015). NCJ 248768, Special report: Federal sentencing disparity: 2005–2012, http://www.bjs.gov/content/pub/pdf/fsd0512_sum.pdf.

Burke, J., Bezyak, J., Fraser, R. T., Pete, J., Ditchman, N., & Chan, F. (2013). Employers' attitudes towards hiring and retaining people with disabilities: A review of the literature. *Australian Journal of Rehabilitation Counselling, 19*(1), 21–38. https://doi.org/10.1017/jrc.2013.2

Chan, F., Shaw, L. R., McMahon, B. T., Koch, L., & Strauser, D. (1997). A model for enhancing rehabilitation counselor–consumer working relationships. *Rehabilitation Counseling Bulletin, 41*(2), 122–137.

Chan, F., Strauser, D., Gervey, R., & Lee, E. (2010). Introduction to demand-side factors related to employment of people with disabilities. *Journal of Occupational Rehabilitation, 20*(4), 407–411. https://doi.org/10.1007/s10926-010-9243-7

Colling, K., & Davis, A. (2005). The counseling function in vocational rehabilitation. *Journal of Applied Rehabilitation Counseling, 36*(1), 6–11.

Coulette, L., & Kopf, D. (2018). *Out of prison & out of work: Unemployment among formerly incarcerated people*. The Prison Policy Initiative. https://www.prisonpolicy.org/reports/outofwork.html

Crenshaw, K. (1991). Mapping the margins: Intersectionality, identity, politics, and violence against women of color. *Stanford Law Review, 43*, 1241–1279. http://dx.doi.org/10.2307/1229039

Decker, S. H., Ortiz, N., Spohn, C., & Hedberg, E. (2015). Criminal stigma, race, and ethnicity: The consequences of imprisonment for employment. *Journal of Criminal Justice, 43*(2), 108–121. https://doi. org/10.1016/j.jcrimjus.2015.02.002

De Giorgi, A. (2018). Back to nothing: Prisoner reentry and neoliberal neglect. *Social Justice, 44*(1), 83.

Dumont, D. M., Brockmann, B., Dickman, S., Alexander, N., & Rich, J. D. (2012). Public health and the epidemic of incarceration. *Annual Review of Public Health, 33*, 325–339. https://doi.org/10.1146/annurev-publhealth-031811-124614

Flake, D. F. (2019). Do ban-the-box laws really work? *Iowa Law Review, 104*(3), 1079–1127.

Goffman, E. (1961). *Asylums: Essays on the social situation of mental patients and other inmates*. Anchor Books.

Hall, A., Hickox, S., Kuan, J., & Sung, C. (2017). Barriers to employment: Individual and organizational perspectives', research in personnel and human resources management. *Research in Personnel and Human Resources Management, 35.*

Hanlon, T. E., O'Grady, K. E., & Bateman, R. W. (2000). Using the Addiction Severity Index to predict treatment outcome among substance abusing parolees. *Journal of Offender Rehabilitation, 31*(3–4), 67–79.

Harley, D. A. (2014). Adult ex-offender population and employment: A synthesis of the literature on recommendations and best practices. *Journal of Applied Rehabilitation Counseling, 45*(3), 10–21. https://doi.org/10.1891/0047-2220.45.3.10

Harley, D. A., Cabe, B., Woolums, R., & Tumer-Whittaker, T. (2014). Vulnerability and marginalization of adult ex-offenders with disabilities in community and employment reintegration. *Journal of Applied Rehabilitation Counseling, 45*(4), 4–14. https://doi.org/10.1891/0047-2220.45.4.4

Harley, D. A., & Feist-Price, S. (2014). Introduction to special issue: Ex-offender population and employment. *Journal of Applied Rehabilitation Counseling, 45*(4), 3–3. https://doi.org/10.1891/0047-2220.45.4.3

Harlow, C. (2003). *Bureau of Justice Statistics special report: Education and correctional populations.* https://eric-ed-gov.proxy1. cl.msu.edu/?id=ED477377

HireRight. (2016). *Employment screening benchmark report.* https://www.hireright. com/benchmarking

Holzer, H. J., Raphael, S., & Stoll, M. A. (2004). How willing are employers to hire ex-offender? *Focus, 23*(2), 40–43.

James, D., & Glaze, L. (2006). *Bureau of Justice special report: Mental health problems of prison & jail inmates.* https://www. bjs.gov/content/pub/pdf/mhppji.pdf

Jones, E., Farina, A., Hastorf, A., Markus, H., Miller, D. T., & Scott, R. (1984). *Social stigma: the psychology of marked relationships.* Freeman.

Lent, R. Brown, S., & Hackett, G. (1994). Towards a unifying social cognitive theory of career and academic interest, choice, and performance. *Journal of Vocational Behavior, 45*(1), https://doi.org/10.1006/jvbe.1994.1027

Lukies, J., Graffam, J., & Shinkfield, A. J. (2011). The effect of organisational context variables on employer attitudes toward employability of ex-offenders. *International Journal of Offender Therapy and Comparative Criminology, 55*(3), 460–475. https://doi.org/10.1177/0306624X09359933

Lustig, D. C., Strauser, D. R., Dewaine Rice, N., & Rucker, T. F. (2002). The relationship between working alliance and rehabilitation outcomes. *rehabilitation counseling bulletin, 46*(1), 24–32. https://doi.org/10.1177/00343552020460010201

Pleggenkuhle, B. (2018). The financial cost of a criminal conviction: Context and consequences. *Criminal Justice and Behavior, 45*(1), 121–145. doi:10.1177/0093854817734278

Remen, R. N. (1999). Helping, fixing or serving?. *Shambhala Sun,* 25–27.

Rogers, C. (1957). The necessary and sufficient conditions of therapeutic personality change. *Journal of Consulting Psychology, 21*(1), 95–103.

Roessler, R. T. (2002). Improving job tenure outcomes for people with disabilities: The 3M model. *Rehabilitation Counseling Bulletin, 45*(4), 207–212. https://doi.org/10.1177/00343552020450040301

Shivy, V., Wu, J. J., Moon, A. E., Mann, S.C., Holland, J. G., & Eacho, C. (2007). Ex-offenders reentering the workforce. *Journal of Counseling Psychology, 54,* 466–473. 10.1037/0022-0167.54.4.466.

Singh, S., Cale, J., & Armstrong, K. (2019). Breaking the cycle: Understanding the needs of women involved in the criminal justice system and the role of mentoring in promoting desistance. *International Journal of Offender Therapy and Comparative Criminology, 63*(8), 1330–1353. https://doi.org/10.1177/0306624X18818922

Snodgrass, J. L., Jenkins, B. B., & Tate, K. F. (2017). More than a job club, sister: Career intervention for women following incarceration. *Career Development Quarterly, 65*(1), 29–43. https://doi.org/10.1002/cdq.12078

Substance Abuse Mental Health Service Administration Summary of National Findings. (2010). *Results from the 2009 national survey on drug use and health* (NSDUH Ser. H-38A, HHS Publ. No. SMA 10-4856 Findings).

Torrey, E. F., Kennard, A. D., Eslinger, D., Lamb, R., & Pavle, J. (2010). More mentally ill persons are in jails and prisons than hospitals: A survey of the states. *Arlington, VA: Treatment Advocacy Center,* 1–18.

Varghese, F. P., & Cummings, D. L. (2013). Introduction: Why apply vocational psychology to criminal justice populations? *Counseling Psychologist, 41*(7), 961–989. https://doi.org/10.1177/0011000012459363

Visher, C. A., La Vigne, N., & Travis, J. (2004). *Returning home: Understanding the challenges of prisoner reentry: Maryland pilot study: Findings from Baltimore.* Urban Institute Justice Policy Center.

Wagner, P., & Sawyer, W. (2018). *Mass incarceration: The whole pie in 2018.* Prison Policy Initiative. https://www.prisonpolicy.org/factsheets/pie2018.pdf

Young, N. C. J., & Powell, G. N. (2015). Hiring ex-offenders; A theoretical model. *Human Resource Management Review, 25,* 298–312.

PART IV

Additional Career Counseling Considerations

CHAPTER 16

Group Career Counseling

Taryn V. Richardson

CHAPTER OVERVIEW

Group career counseling can provide an opportunity for clients to share their common concerns, explore personal issues, and learn new skills under facilitation of a career counselor (Pyle & Hayden, 2015). Group career counseling has become an accepted method for addressing career-related concerns for a small group of individuals that share the same barriers when it comes to career development and the world of work. This chapter will discuss the following components of group career counseling: goals, key concepts/components, techniques for implementation, and the advantages and limitations of group career counseling.

CHAPTER OBJECTIVES

After reading this chapter, the student will be able to complete the following:

1. Define group career counseling.

2. Identify and discuss the advantages of group career counseling.

3. Discuss the key concepts/components of group career counseling.

4. Discuss the goals of group career counseling groups.

5. Outline techniques for implementing group career counseling.

Pyle and Hayden (2015) described group guidance (i.e., psychoeducational) and group counseling (i.e., problem-oriented) as related concepts of group career counseling. Specifically, guidance groups or psychoeducational groups offer individuals information (i.e., personal, emotional, or occupational/vocational) in a workshop format (Gladding, 2016; Pyle & Hayden, 2015). On the other hand, counseling groups provide an avenue to address interpersonal, intrapersonal, and employment-related concerns (Gladding, 2016). In fact, it has been argued that career counseling groups tend to "resemble classes, seminars, and workshops more than counseling groups, in that leaders rely on direct or indirect instructional activities and neglect group dynamics" (Dagley, 1999, p. 141).

In a seminal piece by Tolbert (1974), who is recognized as one of the first scholars to use the term group career counseling, this concept was described as having the following essential components: (a) knowledge of occupations during career planning, (b) self-awareness, and (c) opportunities for self-exploration (Pyle & Hayden, 2015). Although literature using the term group career counseling is limited, the works of many scholars have conceptualized and highlighted the intersection of career and counseling groups (Pyle, 1986; Pyle & Hayden, 2015; Wittmer & Loesch, 1979). In a conceptual article discussing career guidance groups in school settings, Wittmer and Loesch (1979) stated that career guidance encompasses individuals with diverse backgrounds of knowledge, experience, and interest participating in activities within a workshop format. While largely similar, Pyle and Hayden (2015) asserted that group counseling and group career counseling differ in the following ways:

- Group career counseling relies on external information about educational and occupational options.

- Group career counseling aims to develop action plans.

- Group career counseling strives to improve one's awareness of and adjustment to a career.

Simply put, "group career counseling is every bit as complex as group counseling and possibly even more so because of the added dimension of information processing" (Pyle, 1986, p. 4). Despite the fact that the term group career counseling is not widely used in the literature, the use of group formats in career development has been researched and discussed in the literature over the years. Particularly, groups have been used extensively by counseling professionals with the intent to assist individuals with career-related issues and career development (Kivlighan, 1990).

Goals of Group Career Counseling

This section will discuss some of the key goals of group career counseling. Generally, group career counseling aims to assist individuals with employment-related concerns. Career group members are afforded the opportunity to grow in the following ways: (a) modify attitudes, behaviors, and ideas; (b) examine values to aid in career planning; (c) complete self-assessments to evaluate one's personality traits, strengths, and abilities; (d) understand various careers; (e) navigate career decisions; and (f) receive support during the job search process (Proehl, 1995). In particular, cognitive restructuring, engaging in self-exploration, information seeking, navigating career decisions, and obtaining employment have been identified as goals and will be discussed (Dagley, 1999; Proehl, 1995).

Similar to some approaches used in individual counseling, cognitive restructuring in career counseling groups encourages participants to identify irrational thoughts or beliefs and replace them with healthy attitudes and behaviors (Proehl, 1995). To that end, the integration of cognitive techniques into group career counseling dismantles the cognitive barriers that negatively affect career development (Richman, 1993). Cognitive barriers, such as career indecision, an individual's belief about his/her ability to effectively implement job search activities—also known as job search self-efficacy, self-concept, which refers to individuals' perceptions of their value and worth and irrational beliefs about the world of work and/or themselves (Dahling et al., 2013; Peng & Johanson, 2006; Richman, 1993; Saks et al., 2015, Sue et al., 2010). Cognitive restructuring facilitates coping with any change and incidents occurring in the world of work, challenging maladaptive thoughts or beliefs, and promoting healthy development toward career aspirations (Richman, 1993).

Moreover, group career counseling encourages self-discovery (Proehl, 1995). Career assessments and inventories assist in the examination of values and attributes of group members, which provides data that can be used to enhance career planning (Dobson et al., 2014; Owens et al., 2016). Values influence individuals' perceived preferences for job-related characteristics and rewards (Johnson & Monserud, 2012). In addition, career, personal, and organizational values contribute to work engagement (Sortheix et al., 2013) and predict vocational attainment, choice, and satisfaction (Lechner et al., 2017). Furthermore, research has shown that traits and interests are strong predictors of factors such as vocational choice, work values, and job satisfaction (Schneider et al., 2017).

Group career counseling not only promotes the modification of attitudes and self-exploration but also encourages a collaborative process for gathering information about occupations. Knowledge of occupations "facilitates the development of an accurate representation of the world of work and the making of informed career decisions" (Ferrari et al., 2015, p. 117). This was also echoed by many scholars in the literature. Specifically, increasing occupational knowledge has been found to assist group members in vocational preparation and selection (Proehl, 1995; Rohlfing et al., 2012). Such knowledge also contributes to one's personal and career development. Research on career exploration shows that the level of career knowledge (a) predicts career interests and decision-making self-efficacy; (b) influences career adaptation, satisfaction, and self-construction; and (c) fosters career maturity—one's readiness to make appropriate career decisions—and self-concept (Ferrari et al., 2015).

Another goal of group career counseling is to help individuals navigate career decisions. In fact, "one of the main roles of career counselors is to guide their clients through the decision-making process, helping them make their decisions more effectively" (Gadassi et al., 2012, p. 612). Career decision-making difficulties can be categorized as insufficient, as well as inconsistent information and/or lacking readiness (Santos et al., 2018). On the other hand, career decision-making self-efficacy is one's belief in the ability to achieve in one's career decision-making endeavors (Jiang et al., 2019). Santos et al. (2018) found that high emotional intelligence reduces career decision-making difficulty. Emotional intelligence is defined as the "ability to monitor one's own and others' feelings and emotions, to discriminate among them and to use this information to guide one's thinking and actions" (Salovey & Mayer, 1990, p. 189). Therefore, it is essential to understand the factors contributing to career decision-making difficulty, as they help identify appropriate interventions (Gati et al., 2013).

Ultimately, career counseling groups become a beneficial resource during the job search and employment processes by offering support in resume development, enhancing interviewing skills, and providing opportunities for role play and emotional support (Proehl, 1995). Furthermore, Kondo (2009) highlighted that individuals who participated in job clubs were more likely to obtain employment than those who did not. Introduced in the 1970s, the objective of job clubs is to help individuals obtain employment (Rutter & Jones, 2007). Findings from a study on counselor education students also noted the utility of career counseling groups. Specifically, counseling students indicated that career counseling groups can enhance collaboration and support, as well as provide opportunities to practice job search skills, such as interviewing strategies and networking (Rutter & Jones, 2007).

Components of Group Career Counseling

There are a number of essential components that characterize group career counseling. This section will highlight characteristics of effective group leadership, the stages of group career counseling, the role of curative factors, and the significance of information processing.

Group Leader

Like group counseling, effective leadership in group career counseling requires one to attend to the group process and group content. Group content primarily focuses on the information exchanged during the group, whereas the concept of group process is concerned with interactions and relationships within the group (Gladding, 2016). Leaders of career counseling groups contribute to group members' information-seeking behavior, which is a distinguishing characteristic of such groups (Kivlighan, 1990). Pyle and Hayden (2015) stated, "The leader needs to have an awareness of group process and the skills important to facilitating a group" (p. 9). Thus specific leadership skills will be required as leaders facilitate growth through various stages.

Stages of Group Career Counseling

Pyle and Hayden (2015) described four stages of group career counseling, which include the following: encounter, exploration, working, and action. Each stage encompasses affective and cognitive goals. Table 16.1 outlines Pyle and Hayden's (2015) four-stage model.

Curative Factors

Scholar Irvin Yalom described several evidence-based group variables, also known as therapeutic or curative factors, which influence group members' interactions (Gladding, 2016). The therapeutic factors are (a) installation of hope, (b) universality, (c) imparting of information, (d) altruism, (e) corrective recapitulation of the primary family group, (f) development of socializing techniques, (g) imitative behavior, (h) interpersonal learning, (i) group cohesion, (j) catharsis, and (k) existential factors. According to Pyle and Hayden (2015), these curative factors are also present in group career counseling.

Installation of Hope

Instilling hope describes group members' belief in the therapeutic process (Couch & Childers, 1987). Furthermore, Yalom and Leszcz (2005) stated, "Not only is hope required to keep the client in therapy so that other therapeutic factors may take effect, but faith in a treatment mode can in itself be therapeutically effective" (p. 4). This curative factor promotes involvement and motivation during therapy and self-discovery, which enhances career decisions and satisfaction (Pyle & Hayden, 2015). Installation of hope also contributes to learning in career groups (Kivlighan, 1990).

Universality

Universality occurs when group members understand the shared nature of their experiences and/or problems (Kivlighan & Goldfine, 1991). This experience promotes identification and unification with group members (Gladding, 2016). Universality encourages empathy in group career counseling (Kivlighan, 1990; Pyle & Hayden, 2015). This was echoed by Yalom and Leszcz (2005) when they noted, "Clients experience deep concern about their sense of worth and their ability to relate to others" (p. 7). Furthermore, literature states that career counseling groups help with decision making and foster a space for members to share challenges associated with obtaining and maintaining employment, thus promoting universality (Dagley, 1999).

Imparting of Information

Imparting of information can be accomplished by providing didactic instruction (i.e., formal instruction or psychoeducation) and/or direct advice. Of all curative factors, guidance or imparting information closely

Table 16.1 SUMMARY OF PYLE AND HAYDEN'S FOUR-STAGE MODEL

Stage	Characteristics	Affective Goals	Cognitive Goals	Skills
Encounter	Becoming acquainted with group members. Providing purpose, goals, and expectations (i.e., group norms, participation). Group members may be hesitant.	Group leaders help group members gain a sense of confidence and trust in the group process and leadership. Group members may feel anxious, excited, and explorative.	Group leaders should clarify goals and expectations, discuss confidentiality, and learn about group members. Members learn about the group objectives and meeting times and locations.	Attending (i.e., good eye contact, active listening, and demonstrate respect and interest). Concreteness (i.e., provide clear purpose and outcomes, encouragement, staying on task). Genuineness (i.e., leaders need to be authentic and open, may use humor and self-disclosure).
Exploration	The freshness of the group declines. Group leaders need to help members stay committed, develop a norm. Self-disclosure by members is the primary objective. Lack of participation creates an issue for group leaders.	Group members experience higher levels of comfort and active listening among members (i.e., self-disclosing, less preoccupation with inner thoughts).	Establish a norm of career exploration (i.e., self and world of work). Enhance understanding of career choice, barriers, and decisions.	*Including the three skills from the first stage. Reflection of feeling, clarifying/paraphrasing/summarizing, questioning, self-disclosure, circling, and pairing/linking.
Working	Group members confidently bring problems to the group and assist one another. High morale and participation. Completion of outside group tasks.	Members are receptive to feedback. Also, they provide feedback appropriately. Members are open to career exploration, high career readiness, and assistance from other members.	Leaders enhance occupational knowledge, as well as an understanding of the nature of career decision making and career databases.	*Including the skills from Stages 1 and 2. Accurate empathy, confrontation, feedback, processing experience, and information processing.
Action	Members verbalize a desire to take action, display excitement about the future, and experience positive feelings about the group. The leader discusses the importance of planning beyond the group.	Group members exhibit high energy and morale. Members express feelings of accomplishment, empowerment, and cohesion. Positive feelings about the insight gained are expressed. Members acquire an enhanced understanding of self and the world of work.	Meta-learning takes place. Members apply knowledge, skills, and strengths. Specific implementation plans are developed.	*Including the skills from the first three stages. Drawing conclusions, goal setting/developing the next steps, and bringing closure.

aligns with the aim of group career counseling, which is to share relevant career information (Pyle & Hayden, 2015). Kivlighan (1990) noted that imparting information was a distinctive feature of career counseling groups (e.g., occupational information and test interpretation).

Altruism

"Group therapy is unique in being the only therapy that offers clients the opportunity to be of benefit to others" (Yalom & Leszcz, 2005, p. 13). In particular, group members may alternate between being clients and peer helpers, which promotes support and hope (Yalom & Leszcz, 2005). Altruism is defined as the support one offers to group members by sharing one's experiences and feelings (Gladding, 2016). In addition, altruism assists in goal attainment via knowledge sharing, which enhances members' appreciation for the career group process (Kivlighan, 1990; Pyle & Hayden, 2015).

Recapitulation of the Primary Family Group

Corrective recapitulation of the primary family group is defined as group members re-experiencing and resolving conflicts that may have originated within their family system (Gladding, 2016). According to Yalom and Leszcz (2005), the group mirrors the family system (e.g., authority and sibling authority figures, eliciting strong emotions, and personal revelations). Thus recapitulation of the primary family is a curative factor that allows group members to discuss the role of the family in career decisions and career-related difficulties (Pyle & Hayden, 2015).

Development of Socializing Techniques

Learning basic social skills is a functional curative factor in all groups (Yalom & Leszcz, 2005). Groups may have an indirect (e.g., group expectations for open feedback) or a direct (e.g., preparing to approach a potential employer) emphasis on developing social skills (Yalom & Leszcz, 2005). To that end, role playing and observations in groups may assist members in developing the social skills needed during the job search process and better understand career decision making (Pyle & Hayden, 2015).

Imitative Behavior

Imitative behavior occurs when members of the group learn from others via observation (Yalom & Leszcz, 2005). Specifically, group members model how to healthily navigate their presenting concerns (Gladding, 2016). Group members will be able to "gain insight into the thoughts of their peers as they struggle with a career decision," which enhances their understanding of others' career decision-making processes and presents an opportunity to observe others' progress (Pyle & Hayden, 2015, p. 5).

Interpersonal Learning

Interpersonal learning is a multifaceted curative factor. Particularly, interpersonal learning is best conceptualized in the following ways: (a) by considering the role of interpersonal relationships, (b) by considering the notion of therapy serving as an emotional corrective experience, and (c) viewing the group as a social microcosm (Yalom & Leszcz, 2005). According to Gladding (2016), interpersonal learning is described as "gaining insight and correctively working through past experiences" (p. 46). Group career counseling presents an opportunity for group members to engage in a safe environment that fosters a shared learning experience.

Cohesion

Cohesion is similar to the therapeutic relationship in individual therapy (Yalom & Leszcz, 2005). In particular, cohesion describes "the extent to which the group has bonded and developed a level of trust and confidence that allows for openness and sharing" (Pyle & Hayden, 2015, p. 5). Thus the value of this therapeutic factor cannot be understated as it is needed for other curative factors to function properly (Yalom & Leszcz, 2005). Cohesion promotes the helping relationships that are necessary for group members' development and knowledge attainment. To that point, Kivlighan (1990) argued that cohesion is an essential component of career groups.

Catharsis

Catharsis occurs through the expression and experience of feelings during the group process (Gladding, 2016). This is a vital component of the group's therapeutic process (Yalom & Leszcz, 2005). Catharsis encourages mutual learning and respect, as well as self-disclosure (Kivlighan, 1990; Pyle & Hayden, 2015). Within group career counseling, catharsis provides members the opportunity to openly express any feelings and/or frustrations experienced during career exploration and career planning.

Existential Factors

The concept of existential factors is defined as "accepting responsibility for one's life in basic isolation from others, recognizing one's own mortality and the capriciousness of existence" (Gladding, 2016, p. 46). Simply put, these factors relate to the meaning-making regarding one's existence (Yalom & Leszcz, 2005). In group career counseling, addressing existential factors promotes the reflection of members' career decisions (Pyle & Hayden, 2015). For instance, group members who (a) encounter conflict with parental expectations can become empowered to take ownership of their career decisions and (b) those who encounter issues with committing to a career-related goal or decision may become aware of the source of their uncertainty (Pyle & Hayden, 2015).

Information Processing

Another key concept in group career counseling is information processing. Information processing is the primary distinguishing component of group career counseling and "focuses on the holistic nature of careers, the process of choosing a career path and generalizability of the decision-making process to areas beyond occupations" (Osborne, 2014, p. 152). Furthermore, memory is essential in information processing and problem solving, thus contributing to career decision making (Dipeolu et al., 2015). The theory of cognitive information processing (CIP) approach was developed to assist in present and future vocational choices. Two of the main constructs of CIP include the pyramid of information processing domains and the communication, analysis, synthesis, valuing, and execution (CASVE) cycle (Reardon et al., 2011). The pyramid of information processing domains encompasses career decision making and problem solving, whereas the CASVE cycle is the process involved in career decision making and problem solving. Within group career counseling, information processing helps group members enhance their understanding of occupational information, reflect on process information, and take action beyond the group (Pyle & Hayden, 2015). To that end, Leuty et al. (2015) found that a group career counseling approach with an emphasis on cognitive information processing facilitated a significant decrease in faulty thinking and an increase in decision-making self-efficacy.

Advantages of Group Career Counseling

This section highlights the benefits of group career counseling. Specifically, receiving social support, enhancing intrinsic motivation, having opportunities to practice social skills, and enhancing self-efficacy are benefits of group career counseling. Other advantages include opportunities to give and receive feedback, help members normalize career concerns and anxieties, personalize information, and value mutual sharing and self-expression. Group career counseling is also more time and cost-effective.

Group career counseling offers social support, opportunities to strengthen intrinsic motivation and practice social skills, and it increases self-efficacy (Barclay & Stoltz, 2016; Dagley, 1999). Research shows that social support can enhance group members' performance and effort (Hüffmeier et al., 2014). In particular, Hüffmeier et al. (2014) noted that receiving affective social support, such as praise and reassurance motivates group members' efforts in the group process. That said, "social support should thus be salient in people's beliefs about motivating group work" (Hüffmeier et al., 2014). Moreover, Pyle and Hayden (2015) indicated that group career counseling provides an opportunity to develop and practice social skills needed for engaging with a potential employer. In addition, studies show that an individual's job search self-efficacy can be increased in career groups (i.e., job club). Job search self-efficacy is also associated with job search intention and job offers (Saks et al., 2015). Specifically, job search self-efficacy is a predictor of both job search behavior and job search outcomes, such as job offers and employment. Thus the group members benefit from the following: (a) performance through skill attainment, (b) vicarious learning, and (c) verbal persuasion through praise and encouragement (Sterrett, 1998).

Furthermore, career group counseling provides opportunities to give and receive feedback (Barclay & Stoltz, 2016; Clark et al., 2004). For instance, Di Fabio and Maree (2012) highlighted that members participating in a life design group were able to listen to others and draw on their wisdom and experience. In doing so, members benefited from engaging in a collaborative learning experience where group members were able to obtain feedback from the group leader. Group career counseling also helps group members normalize career concerns and anxiety, as well as personalize information (Pyle & Hayden, 2015). Furthermore, studies have supported the utility of group career counseling. Particularly, research highlighted the value of mutual sharing and the benefit of fostering self-expression of concerns, feelings, and opinions (Maree, 2019). Mutual sharing enhances career adaptability—the ability to cope with career preparation, the world of work, and changes in the workplace and career decision making, while self-expression increases one's ability to cope with career concerns and aid in self and career construction (Maree, 2019; Savickas, 1997).

Group career counseling is also time and cost-efficient (Barclay & Stoltz, 2016; Pyle, 1986). Maree et al. (2018) noted that cost-efficient, group-based approaches make group career counseling accessible to disenfranchised communities (e.g., individuals with low socioeconomic status). To that end, career counseling groups are also beneficial for various populations. Some include college students/athletes (Barclay & Stoltz, 2016; Peng & Johanson, 2006; Rowell et al., 2014), young and old employees (Akkermans et al., 2015; Koivisto et al., 2010; Proehl, 1995), women (Storlie et al., 2018; Sullivan & Mahalik, 2000), international populations (Di Fabio & Maree, 2012; Lam & Santos, 2018), persons with disabilities (Osborne, 2014), and job seekers/unemployed adults (Bhat, 2010). Women survivors of intimate partner violence and individuals from diverse backgrounds have also used career group counseling (Berríos-Allison, 2011; Davidson et al., 2012; Storlie et al., 2018). Research on these populations reveals that participating in group-based career counseling (a) enhanced career search self-efficacy, career adaptability, and career decision making; (b) promoted help-seeking behavior; and (c) encouraged career narratives that provided insight into career development needs.

Group career counseling interventions have also highlighted the benefits of this approach. For instance, individuals who participated in group-based life design reportedly had a decrease in career decision-making challenges, such as lack of information and/or inconsistent information (Di Fabio & Maree, 2012). In addition, group-based life design aided in self-discovery (Barclay & Stoltz, 2016). Furthermore, Kondo (2009) examined the use of job clubs, and it was determined that members benefited from "group learning, increase accountability, networking opportunities, emotional support, helping other members, and enhanced understanding of the context of their experiences" (p. 27). Despite these advantages, it should be noted that there are some limitations, such as concerns about the effect of outcomes based on the length of treatment (McAuliffe & Fredrickson, 1990).

Techniques for Implementing Group Career Counseling

A growing body of literature has emerged within the context of group career counseling that explains the implementation process. To that end, Akkermans et al. (2015) discussed their CareerSkills intervention—designed to facilitate career competency and work-related well-being. Employing a quasi-randomized controlled trial, participants receiving the intervention demonstrated higher levels of career competence across reflective, communicative, and behavioral dimensions. Specifically, these individuals were reflective in terms of their motivations, strengths, and limitations in relation to their personal careers.

Furthermore, participants receiving the intervention were aware of their value in terms of social capital and able to effectively showcase their skills and abilities to the overarching labor market. They rated their ability to actively explore career-related opportunities higher and felt they had a sense of mastery over career outcomes through a process of goal setting and identifying ways to reach those goals. The Career-Skills intervention was beneficial in stimulating a sense of self-efficacy, while also fostering a sense of resilience, which refers to the ability to cope with or bounce back from stressful situations (Smith et al., 2008). Last, increases were observed in the areas of career-related behaviors, perceived employability, and work engagement.

Arguably, much of the successful outcomes of the CareerSkills intervention can be attributed to the methods employed. As the authors indicated, participants engaged in an "active learning process, brainstorming (both in plenary sessions and in subgroup sessions), social modeling, a socially supportive environment, and role-playing" (Akkermans et al., 2015, p. 540). A highly useful strategy in the development of a group career counseling program is the incorporation of activities supported by empirical or theoretical knowledge. In doing so, the group will function from an intentional approach with the objectives, activities, and desired outcomes being formally aligned. This fundamental technique can be widely applied and is also reflected in the career development literature. For instance, Maree (2019) developed a group career construction counseling approach within a high school context, designed to investigate its value in that specific setting. The author was forthright in detailing the relevance and infusion of prior research knowledge in the development of the group format.

Strategies

In addition, techniques are also contingent upon the setting. In particular, individuals in educational settings and community settings require group leaders to use appropriate strategies. Some strategies, as identified by Pyle and Hayden (2015), for implementing group career counseling include the following:

- Educational settings: enhance youths understanding of the world of work by using the American College Test (ACT) World-of-Work Map, provide self-assessment and values clarification opportunities, encourage experiential learning via an internship or shadowing experience, and use informational interviews.

- Community settings: use group counseling principles in employment agencies, businesses, and industries, as well as spiritual and religious settings; enhance employees' morale and make life changes; use techniques, such as asking reflective questions (e.g., what would you do with all the money you need); and assist military service members with transitioning to civilian employment.

Furthermore, the implementation of group career counseling requires consideration for marketing, group member's readiness, group and content design, and outcome assessment (Pyle & Hayden, 2015). Table 16.2 outlines strategies and recommendations for implementing group career counseling as provided by Pyle and Hayden (2015).

Table 16.2 IMPLEMENTATION OF GROUP CAREER COUNSELING

Strategies and Recommendations			
Marketing	**Group Member Readiness**	**Group and Content Design**	**Outcome Assessment**
• Assess the needs of potential participants. • Identify ways to contact potential participants. • Use both local media and print methods of marketing.	• Create an appropriate intake process for individuals at the career exploration stage. • Consider potential members' personalities and comfort in social situations.	• Establish a manageable group size: 4–8 members. • Plan for 90–120 minutes to ensure quality interactions. • The setting should be able to comfortably seat eight people in a circle. • Provide expectations and rules at the first meeting (e.g., confidentiality). • End groups by allowing reflection on group experience. • Assign homework at the end of the group meeting. • Adhere to ethical standards for facilitating groups. • Request verbal and written feedback at the end of the group counseling process. • Use goals as a guide to design content.	• Assess the effect of the intervention. • Outcomes include dysfunctional career-related thoughts and/or client satisfaction.

Summary

Group career counseling assists individuals with career-related issues and career development. Group leaders, especially, help members modify attitudes, behaviors, and ideas, engage in self-exploration, enhance their knowledge about various careers, and navigate career decisions all while receiving support during the job search process. Group career counseling is marked by the significance of information processing, which is facilitated by effective group leadership. Growth and change also occur at various stages of the group process, which is influenced by essential curative factors. Group members benefit from group career counseling in several ways, such as receiving social support, having opportunities to practice social skills, and enhancing self-efficacy. Thus group leaders should (a) develop a screening process to determine if career group counseling is an appropriate intervention, (b) ensure active participation and maximize learning, and (c) consider assessing the effect of the intervention (Pyle & Hayden, 2015).

Discussion Questions

1. Compare and contrast group career counseling and group counseling.
2. What is the importance of curative factors in group career counseling?
3. Briefly discuss the challenges leaders may encounter during the exploration stage of group career counseling.
4. How would you apply what you have learned to develop a group career counseling program? Provide an example to illustrate your plan.
5. Discuss the significance of information processing in group career counseling.

References

Akkermans, J., Brenninkmeijer, V., Schaufeli, W. B., & Blonk, R. W. (2015). It's all about CareerSkills: Effectiveness of a career development intervention for young employees. *Human Resource Management, 54*, 533–551. https://doi.org/10.1002/hrm.21633

Barclay, S. R., & Stoltz, K. B. (2016). The life-design group: A case study assessment. *Career Development Quarterly, 64*, 83–96. https://doi.org/10.1002/cdq.12043

Berríos-Allison, A. C. (2011). Career support group for Latino/a college students. *Journal of College Counseling, 14*, 80–95. https://doi.org/10.1002/j.2161-1882.2011.tb00065.x

Bhat, C. S. (2010). Assisting unemployed adults find suitable work: A group intervention embedded in community and grounded in social action. *Journal for Specialists in Group Work, 35*, 246–254. https://doi.org/10.1080/01933922.2010.492898

Clark, M. A., Severy, L., & Sawyer, S. A. (2004). Creating connections: Using a narrative approach in career group counseling with college students from diverse cultural backgrounds. *Journal of College Counseling, 7*, 24–31. https://doi.org/10.1002/j.2161-1882.2004.tb00256.x

Couch, R. D., & Childers, J. H. (1987). Leadership strategies for instilling and maintaining hope in group counseling. *Journal for Specialists in Group Work, 12*, 138–143. https://doi.org/ 10.1080/01933928708411763

Dagley, J. C. (1999). The restoration of group process in career counseling groups. *Journal of Group Psychotherapy, Psychodrama and Sociometry, 51*(4), 141–157.

Dahling, J. J., Melloy, R., & Thompson, M. N. (2013). Financial strain and regional unemployment as barriers to job search self-efficacy: A test of social cognitive career theory. *Journal of Counseling Psychology, 60*, 210–218. https://doi.org/10.1037/a0031492

Davidson, M. M., Nitzel, C., Duke, A., Baker, C. M., & Bovaird, J. A. (2012). Advancing career counseling and employment support for survivors: An intervention evaluation. *Journal of Counseling Psychology, 59*, 321–328. https://doi.org/10.1037/a0027965

Di Fabio, A., & Maree, J. G. (2012). Group-based life design counseling in an Italian context. *Journal of Vocational Behavior, 80*, 100–107. https://doi.org/10.1016/j.jvb.2011.06.001

Dipeolu, A., Davies, L., Smyth, A., Deutch, S., Saunders, D., & Leierer, S. J. (2015). Cognitive information processing approach to career counseling for individuals with ADHD: A match made in conceptual and clinical heaven! *Career Planning & Adult Development Journal, 31*(4), 12–24.

Dobson, L. K., Gardner, M. K., Metz, A. J., & Gore Jr, P. A. (2014). The relationship between interests and values in career decision making: The need for an alternative method of measuring values. *Journal of Career Assessment, 22*, 113–122. https://doi.org/10.1177/1069072713492929

Ferrari, L., Ginevra, M. C., Santilli, S., Nota, L., Sgaramella, T. M., & Soresi, S. (2015). Career exploration and occupational knowledge in Italian children. *International Journal for Educational and Vocational Guidance, 15*, 113–130. https://doi.org/10.1007/s10775-015-9299-1

Gadassi, R., Gati, I., & Dayan, A. (2012). The adaptability of career decision-making profiles. *Journal of Counseling Psychology, 59*, 612–622. https://doi.org/10.1037/a0029155

Gati, I., Ryzhik, T., & Vertsberger, D. (2013). Preparing young veterans for civilian life: The effects of a workshop on career decision-making difficulties and self-efficacy. *Journal of Vocational Behavior, 83*, 373–385. https://doi.org/10.1016/j.jvb.2013.06.001

Gladding, S. T. (2016). *Groups: A counseling specialty.* Vitalsource. https://www.vitalsource.com/

Hüffmeier, J., Wessolowski, K., van Randenborgh, A., Bothin, J., Schmid-Loertzer, N., & Hertel, G. (2014). Social support from fellow group members triggers additional effort in groups. *European Journal of Social Psychology, 44*, 287–296. https://doi.org/10.1002/ejsp.2021

Jiang, Z., Newman, A., Le, H., Presbitero, A., & Zheng, C. (2019). Career exploration: A review and future research agenda. *Journal of Vocational Behavior, 110*, 338–356. https://doi.org/10.1016/j.jvb.2018.08.008

Johnson, M. K., & Monserud, M. A. (2012). Work value development from adolescence to adulthood. *Advances in Life Course Research, 17*, 45–58. https://doi.org/10.1016/j.alcr.2012.02.002

Kivlighan Jr., D. M. (1990). Career group therapy. *Counseling Psychologist, 18*, 64–79. https://doi.org/10.1177/0011000090181003

Kivlighan Jr, D. M., & Goldfine, D. C. (1991). Endorsement of therapeutic factors as a function of stage of group development and participant interpersonal attitudes. *Journal of Counseling Psychology, 38*, 150–158. https://doi.org/10.1037/0022-0167.38.2.150

Koivisto, P., Vuori, J., & Vinokur, A. D. (2010). Transition to work: Effects of preparedness and goal construction on employment and depressive symptoms. *Journal of Research on Adolescence, 20*, 869–892. https://doi.org/10.1111/j.1532-7795.2010.00667.x

Kondo, C. T. (2009). Benefits of job clubs for executive job seekers: A tale of hares and tortoises. *Journal of Employment Counseling, 46*, 27–37. https://doi:10.1002/j.2161-1920.2009.tb00063.x

Lam, M., & Santos, A. (2018). The impact of a college career intervention program on career decision self-efficacy, career indecision, and decision-making difficulties. *Journal of Career Assessment, 26*, 425–444. https://doi.org/10.1177/1069072717714539

Lechner, C. M., Sortheix, F. M., Göllner, R., & Salmela-Aro, K. (2017). The development of work values during the transition to adulthood: A two-country study. *Journal of Vocational Behavior, 99*, 52–65. https://doi.org/10.1016/j.jvb.2016.12.004

Leuty, M. E., Bullock-Yowell, E., Womack, A., Schmidtman, E., Paulson, D., Andrews Wiebusch, L., & Osborne, L. K. (2015). The integration of science and practice in one training program: Outcomes of a manualized career counseling group. *Counselling Psychology Quarterly, 28*, 286–304. https://doi.org/10.1080/09515070.2015.1053432

Maree, J. G. (2019). Group career construction counseling: A mixed-methods intervention study with high school students. *Career Development Quarterly, 67*, 47–61. https://doi.org/10.1002/cdq.12162

Maree, J. G., Cook, A. V., & Fletcher, L. (2018). Assessment of the value of group-based counselling for career construction. *International Journal of Adolescence and Youth, 23*, 118–132. https://doi.org/10.1080/02673843.2017.1309324

McAuliffe, G. J., & Fredrickson, R. (1990). The effects of program length and participant characteristics on group career-counseling outcomes. *Journal of Employment Counseling, 27*, 19–22. https://doi.org/10.1002/j.2161-1920.1990.tb00259.x

Osborne, L. K. (2014). Using a cognitive information processing approach to group career counseling with visually impaired veterans. *Professional Counselor, 4*, 150–158. https://doi.org/10.15241/lko.4.2.150

Owens, R. L., Motl, T. C., & Krieshok, T. S. (2016). A comparison of strengths and interests protocols in career assessment and counseling. *Journal of Career Assessment, 24*, 605–622. https://doi.org/10.1177/1069072715615854

Peng, H., & Johanson, R. E. (2006). Career maturity and state anxiety of Taiwanese college student athletes given cognitive career-oriented group counseling. *Psychological Reports, 99*, 805–812. https://doi.org/10.2466/PR0.99.3.805–812

Proehl, R. A. (1995). Groups in career development: An added advantage. *Journal of Career Development, 21*, 249–261. https://doi.org/10.1007/BF02105395

Pyle, K. R. (1986). *Group career counseling: Principles and practices.* Educational Resources Information Center, Counseling and Personnel Services Clearinghouse.

Pyle, K. R., & Hayden, S. C. (2015). *Group career counseling: Practices and principles.* National Career Development Association.

Reardon, R. C., Lenz, J. G., Sampson Jr., J. P., & Peterson, G. W. (2011). Big questions facing vocational psychology: A cognitive information processing perspective. *Journal of Career Assessment, 19*, 240–250. https://doi.org/10.1177/1069072710395531

Richman, D. R. (1993). Cognitive career counseling: A rational emotive approach to career development. *Journal of Rational-Emotive and Cognitive-Behavior Therapy, 11*, 91–108. https://doi.org/10.1007/BF01061234

Rohlfing, J. E., Nota, L., Ferrari, L., Soresi, S., & Tracey, T. J. (2012). Relation of occupational knowledge to career interests and competence perceptions in Italian children. *Journal of Vocational Behavior, 81*, 330–337. https://doi.org/10.1016/j.jvb.2012.08.001

Rowell, P. C., Mobley, A. K., Kemer, G., & Giordano, A. (2014). Examination of a group counseling model of career decision making with college students. *Journal of College Counseling, 17*, 163–174. https://doi.org/10.1002/j.2161-1882.2014.00055.x

Rutter, M. E., & Jones, J. V. (2007). The job club redux: A step forward in addressing the career development needs of counselor education students. *Career Development Quarterly, 55*, 280–288. https://doi.org/10.1002/j.2161-0045.2007.tb00084.x

Saks, A. M., Zikic, J., & Koen, J. (2015). Job search self-efficacy: Reconceptualizing the construct and its measurement. *Journal of Vocational Behavior, 86*, 104–114. https://doi.org/10.1016/j.jvb.2014.11.007

Salovey, P., & Mayer, J. D. (1990). Emotional intelligence. *Imagination, Cognition and Personality, 9*, 185–211. https://doi.org/10.2190/DUGG-P24E-52WK-6CDG

Santos, A., Wang, W., & Lewis, J. (2018). Emotional intelligence and career decision-making difficulties: The mediating role of career decision self-efficacy. *Journal of Vocational Behavior, 107*, 295–309. https://doi.org/10.1016/j.jvb.2018.05.008

Savickas, M. L. (1997). Career adaptability: An integrative construct for life-span, life-space theory. *Career Development Quarterly, 45*, 247–259. https://doi.org/10.1002/j.2161-0045.1997.tb00469.x

Schneider, T. J., McLarnon, M. J., & Carswell, J. J. (2017). Career interests, personality, and the dark triad. *Journal of Career Assessment, 25*, 338–351. https://doi.org/10.1177/1069072715616128

Smith, B. W., Dalen, J., Wiggins, K., Tooley, E., Christopher, P., & Bernard, J. (2008). The brief resilience scale: Assessing the ability to bounce back. *International Journal of Behavioral Medicine, 15*, 194–200. https://doi.org/10.1080/10705500802222972

Sortheix, F. M., Dietrich, J., Chow, A., & Salmela-Aro, K. (2013). The role of career values for work engagement during the transition to working life. *Journal of Vocational Behavior, 83*, 466–475. https://doi.org/10.1016/j.jvb.2013.07.003

Sterrett, E. A. (1998). Use of a job club to increase self-efficacy: A case study of return to work. *Journal of Employment Counseling, 35*, 69–78. https://doi.org/10.1002/j.2161-1920.1998.tb00477.x

Storlie, C. A., Hilton, T. L., Duenyas, D., Archer, R., & Glavin, K. (2018). Career narratives of African American female college students: Insights for college counselors. *Journal of College Counseling, 21*, 29–42. https://doi.org/10.1002/jocc.12085

Sue, D., Sue, D. W., Sue, S., & Sue, D. M. (2010). *Understanding abnormal behavior.* Cengage Learning.

Sullivan, K. R., & Mahalik, J. R. (2000). Increasing career self-efficacy for women: Evaluating a group intervention. *Journal of Counseling & Development, 78*, 54–62. https://doi.org/10.1002/j.1556-6676.2000.tb02560.x

Tolbert, E. L. (1974). *Counseling for career development.* Houghton Mifflin.

Wittmer, J. & Loesch L. (1979), *Personalizing career guidance assessment information through group counseling.* National Consortium on Competency-Based Staff Development, Module 35, U.S. Office of Education.

Yalom, I. D., & Leszcz, M. (2005). *The theory and practice of group.* Basic Books.

CHAPTER 17

Career Counseling Intakes, Assessments, and Measurements

Jeong Han Kim

CHAPTER OVERVIEW

Historically, members of minority groups and diverse populations have experienced significant levels of misdirection and diagnosis because of the use of culturally inappropriate assessment and measurement tools (Malgady, 1996). Over time, researchers have diligently worked to address the effect that culture has on the results of assessment and measurement tools, thereby improving the suitability of many assessment and measurement tools for diverse populations. This chapter will discuss the various types of intakes, assessments, and measurements that can be used during the career counseling process. Suggestions and guidelines for the use of assessments and measurements with multicultural and diverse populations will also be discussed.

CHAPTER OBJECTIVES

After reading this chapter, the student will be able to complete the following:

1. Identify and describe various career counseling assessment and measurements.

2. Identify strengths and assets of intake interviews.

3. Identify appropriate assessment and measurement tools for working with diverse populations.

4. Identify and address assessment and measurement-related challenges and limitations faced by members of diverse populations.

5. Implement strategies for working with diverse populations in the area of assessment and measurement.

Intake Interview in Career Counseling

The purpose of the intake interview in career counseling is to identify the (1) client's career goal, (2) demographic characteristics of a client, (3) ultimate career needs, (4) supplementary information relevant to the achievement of the career goal, and (5) challenges and barriers (Kidd, 1996).

The client's career goals in the intake stage are not clear but can be approached from three options: (1) immediate employment, (2) vocational training, and (3) formal education, such as a degree-seeking program. Depending on the client's choice, the focus of assessment and interpretation of the collected information may vary. For example, in an immediate employment case, career assessment may focus on the client's strengths/assets and transferable skills. In a long-term plan, such as seeking a degree, career assessment can be done from a relatively broader perspective, such as exploring career interests, values, aptitude, and so on.

Demographic characteristics often include name, contact information, race/ethnicity, educational background, vocational history, income, reason for the referral, and release for information if there is another source of valuable information relevant to the client's career goal. Demographic information is simple but important in counseling as it provides a quick snapshot of individuals' characteristics or qualifications required by a certain job opportunity. In addition, it further provides cultural information about an individual that has a critical influence on building the collaborative relationship between a client and counselor.

Demographic information is a cultural variable that has an enormous effect on one's career development. The meaning of career in one's life and individual preference may differ widely depending on the societal values associated with a certain job. Three important components in multicultural counseling are awareness (i.e., knowing one's own cultural bias), knowledge (i.e., having cultural knowledge), and skills (i.e., having hands-on skills to work with a certain cultural group). And cultural information collected during the intake interview can be used to gauge cultural differences in a way that helps the relationship building between a counselor and client. However, a counselor should know that demographic variables from a multicultural counseling perspective need be carefully approached with a caution that demographic variables are not always strong predictors of a client's cultural background (Clark, 2016).

Ultimately, career needs mean understanding the nature of the client's needs. Careers address whole aspects of life and reason. Career seeking differs person by person (Szymanski, & Vancollins, 2003). Some may need a career to simply resolve their financial challenges. Some may be looking for a career from a self-actualization perspective. The ultimate goal of career counseling is to provide an opportunity for one to actualize oneself via a career. However, the accomplishment of the ultimate goal is often conflicting when an individual has real concerns, such as urgent financial challenges. In such cases, short-term goals need to be established first, but in a way, one's ultimate career goal is gradually achieved via the successful completion of short-term goals.

Supplementary information is important in that it provides a deeper understanding of the situational context where a client is located in terms of achieving his/her career goal. Examples of supplementary information are social/disability benefits, health conditions and medications, formal/informal networks, housing, and transportation. Addressing issues associated with the supplementary information often brings a complementary effect in accomplishing career goals.

Challenges and barriers, such as childcare issues, anger management, negative influences that hinder one in achieving a career goal both directly and indirectly, thus need to be identified. It is possible that some barriers go beyond the scope of career counseling, and they can be addressed via the referral or service allocation services.

An important key factor, especially during the career counseling intake interview, is to bring "intentionality." The intentional interview is a concept developed in general counseling but applicable to career counseling (Ivey et al., 2014). Intentionality is acting with a sense of capability from among a range of alternative actions. The intentional career counselor can generate alternatives in a given situation and approach a problem from different vantage points, using a variety of skills and personal qualities. Intentionality helps a counselor see clients' strengths, assets, challenges, and barriers in regard to diverse career options and perspectives. Intentional competency develops based on the counselor's ability to predict the consequence and mix various career factors. In summary, intentionality helps counselors and clients get focused, at the same time further allowing counselors to predict clients' responses, thus helping counselors become more flexible. Cultural intentionality also does the same, but it helps you become more culturally open-minded and responsive (Ivey, 1987).

Another important aspect of the intake interview is to provide an orientation of the agency and its services. Every client wants to know what types of services you or your agency can provide and what procedures are used. For example, a typical career counseling procedure can be divided into five steps, including (1) intake, (2) eligibility determination and assessment, (3) plan development, (4) follow-up, and (5) termination. A brief introduction of how each procedure is carried out and the activities involved promotes clients' understanding of the agency that they will be working with. The counselor's role, function, expectation, and style can be addressed during the intake. These are important factors that have influence over the counselor and client relationship. Thus the intake interview can serve to identify conflicting factors between a counselor and client and to proactively remove or address certain factors in advance. In addition, if needed, further assessment needs are also determined. Discussion of these factors helps the counselor and client to be on the same page.

At the end of the intake interview, a counselor also needs to make sure that the client knows what will happen next. This is called "wrapping up." (Summer, 2016). The components that need to be discussed when wrapping up the intake generally include (1) your understanding of the client's career goals and problems, (2) a summary of what you and your client discussed, (3) an activity/task the client should do or accomplish before returning, and (4) information on the next step.

Intake provides valuable time to both the counselor and client in that it is their first meeting and an opportunity to share and communicate expectations. However, a counselor should also know that the first impression plays an important role in developing a collaborative relationship; thus, the counselor should always approach the intake interview professionally with mindfulness (Laungani, 2006).

Career Assessment

At the end of the intake, the counselor should be able to develop a case history relevant to the client. The five most common components addressed in a case history are (1) personal history (e.g., demographics, family, marital, financial), (2) educational history (school, graduation, license/certificate, training), (3) employment history (duties/tasks, part or full time, hobbies, interests), (4) medical history (health condition, medication, disability or illness, restrictions), and (5) present activities (e.g., daily activity, client report of physical problems and limitations). The information needs to be translated and interpreted in terms of the career path that the client has chosen (i.e., immediate employment, further training, formal education). Then a counselor needs to determine whether there is a need for further assessment. This section addresses various assessment options used in career counseling.

Prior to the discussion of career assessment types and instruments, it is important to discuss the therapeutic aspect of the assessment. In career counseling, assessment and evaluation are often interchangeably used; however, each word carries a slightly different connotation. (Fadely, 1987). In comparison to "evaluation," the nature of assessment is more diagnostic, focusing on the identification and determination of client strengths and assets. Evaluation, on the other hand, puts more emphasis on the interactive aspect of assessment procedure. For example, assessment can be done by running an intelligence quotient (IQ) test, and the results will show the strengths or weaknesses of a client. In an evaluation, instead, a client's strengths and weaknesses can be reconceptualized and discussed in terms of the client's career context and development. In the following section, a major area of career assessment is introduced. However, because of the scope of this chapter and page limits, the emphasis is given to the introduction of the assessment area instead of the details of the assessment tool.

Achievement Test

The focus of the achievement test is to evaluate the client's present competency in reading, written expression, and basic mathematics. In addition, because the results are informational in terms of showing a client's academic level in all three areas, the achievement test can also help counselors to select the right future assessments that fit the client's academic level. For instance, there are test inventories that are designed for people who are not English readers and have relatively lower reading levels. Information on a client's academic functioning is valuable information because the degree of literacy has a direct effect on training and placement. For example, many jobs, such as those in the clerical and sales areas, require functional reading and mathematics skills. An accurate understanding of the client's academic functioning enables the counselor to effectively gauge the client's occupational possibilities.

Most commonly, norm-referenced standardized tests are used in the achievement test. These tests yield grade equivalents, standard scores, and percentiles, showing where the client stands. Unlike the norm-referenced test, an informal test does not yield grade equivalents, but it is still a very useful tool to gauge a client's academic skills from a practical standpoint.

Concerning the selection of the achievement test as a part of a career and vocational evaluation, a counselor should also know that the achievement test is not identical to the intelligence test despite it often being used as an achievement test. As noted earlier, the major purpose of the achievement test is to show the grade equivalent of the client's academic skill, while the intelligence test is used to show a client's intellectual potential. The intelligence test can be better used for those with long-term career plans that may require further education before the job search, while the achievement test can be better used for those with a short-term career goal, such as immediate placement.

Commonly used achievement tests include the Wide Range Achievement Test (Jastak & Wilkinson, 1984), Peabody Picture Vocabulary Test, Peabody Individual Achievement Test, Kaufman Brief Intelligence Test, General Ability Measure for Adult, Slosson Intelligence Test, Wechsler Adult Intelligence Scale, and Woodcock-Johnson Intelligence Test. A detailed review of these instruments goes beyond the scope of this chapter, but brief reviews of these instruments are summarized in Table 17.1.

Table 17.1 ACHIEVEMENT TESTS

Test Instrument	Age/Measuring Constructs/Author
Wide Range Achievement Test	Ages: 5–94 years Measuring Constructs: Reading recognition, spelling, arithmetic computation Authors: G. S. Wilkinson and G. J. Robertson
Peabody Picture Vocabulary Test	Age: 2 years 6 month through 90+ years Measuring Constructs: Receptive vocabulary for Standard American English Authors: Lloyd M. Dunn and Douglas M. Dunn.
Peabody Individual Achievement Test	Age: Kindergarten through grade 12 Measuring Constructs: General knowledge (e.g., social), reading recognition, reading comprehension, mathematics, spelling, written expression Author: Most recent version by Frederick C. Markwardt Jr.
Kaufman Brief Intelligence Test	Age: 4–90 Measuring Constructs: Verbal and nonverbal intelligence plus a composite IQ score Authors: Alan S. Kaufman and Nadeen L. Kaufman
General Ability Measure for Adult	Age: 18 and older Measuring Constructs: General cognitive ability (matching, analogies, sequences, construction) Authors: Jack A. Naglieri and Achilles N. Bardos
Slosson Intelligence Test	Age: 4–65 Measuring Constructs: General information, comprehension, quantitative, similarity and differences, vocabulary, auditory memory Author: Richard L. Slosson
Wechsler Adult Intelligence Scale	Age: 16–90 and 6–16 (Wechsler Intelligence Scale for Children) Measuring Constructs: Abstract verbal reasoning, degree of general information, ability to express abstract social conventions and rules, inductive reasoning, problem solving, visual-spatial reasoning, quantitative reasoning, working memory, processing speed Author: David Wechsler
Woodcock-Johnson Intelligence Test	Age: 2 through adulthood Measuring Constructs: Comprehension-knowledge, long-term memory, visual-spatial thinking, auditory processing, fluid reasoning, processing speed, short-term memory, quantitative knowledge, and reading-writing Authors: Richard Woodcock and Mary E. Bonner Johnson

Aptitude Test

The aptitude test is different from the achievement test in that it often measures one's capacity to perform a certain task successfully without previous knowledge. Carroll (1985) said that it is largely constitutional attributes of an individual that make for higher or lower degrees of success in learning. Later, Carroll (1993) stated that the aptitude test "helps in predicting degree of learning beyond a prediction from degree of prior learning," while the achievement text refers to the "degree of learning in some procedure intended to produce learning such as a formal or informal course of instruction" (p. 17). However, a clear distinction between aptitude and achievement still remains uncertain just like the difference between the Scholastic Assessment Test (SAT) and American College Test (ACT). The SAT is often considered an aptitude test while the ACT is closer to an achievement test. From Anastasi and Urbian's (1997) perspective, aptitude and achievement can be viewed in a continuum.

Commonly used aptitude tests include Bennett Mechanical Comprehension Test, Career Ability Placement Survey, Differential Aptitude Test (DAT) Battery, Armed Service Vocational Aptitude Battery (ASVAB), the Wonderlic Personnel Test, The Minnesota Clerical Test, and General Aptitude Test Battery (GATB). Brief summarizes of these tests are presented in Table 17.2.

Table 17.2 APTITUDE TESTS

Test Instrument	Age/Measuring Constructs/Author
Bennet Mechanical Comprehension Test	Age/Readability: 16+ Measuring Constructs: Mechanical comprehension, spatial visualization, knowledge of basic physical and mechanical laws, deduction of how machinery works Author: G. K. Bennett
Career Ability Placement Survey (CAPS)	Age/Readability: Grade 6 through adult Measuring Construct: Mechanical reasoning, spatial relations, verbal reasoning, numerical ability, language usage, word knowledge, perceptual speed and accuracy, manual speed and dexterity Authors: L. F. Knapp and R. R. Knapp
DAT	Age/Readability: Grades 7–12 and adult Measuring Construct: Verbal reasoning, numerical ability, abstract reasoning, mechanical reasoning, space relations, language usage Authors: Alexander G. Wesman, George K. Bennett, and Harold G. Seashore
ASVAB	Age/Readability: Grade 10 + Measuring Construct: General science, arithmetic reasoning, word knowledge, paragraph comprehension, mathematics knowledge, electronic information, automotive and shop information, mechanical comprehension, assembling objects, verbal expression Authors: Randolph K. Harris and Raymond K. Huckell
The Wonderlic Personnel Test	Age/Readability: Requires a sixth-grade reading level Measuring Construct: Skills (perceptual, basic, office and software skills), cognitive ability (problem solving and learning), behavior liability (individual's potential in engaging in counterproductive or unethical behaviors), personality (personal characteristics associated with job performance) Author: Eldon F. Wonderlic
The Minnesota Clerical Test	Age/Readability: Requires second-grade reading level Measuring Construct: Perceptual speed and accuracy related to performing various clerical duties Author: University of Minnesota
GATB	Age/Readability: 18+ and third-grade reading level required Measuring Construct: General intelligence, verbal aptitude, numerical aptitude, spatial aptitude, form perception, clerical perception, motor coordination, finger dexterity, manual dexterity Author: U.S. Employment Service

Test of Personality and Psychological Symptoms

The value of the personality test is that it provides information regarding the individual's behavior in a certain situation, such as career choice, treatment planning, intervention, and any combination of these. For example, cognitive ability is an important predictor of future job performance; however, cognitive ability alone lacks the power to explain why a person who has the capacity to complete a job does not perform well or fails.

Another value of the personality test is that it allows for the consistent prediction of human behavior. Every individual is different and thus will respond to their surroundings in a unique way, making it difficult to predict a person's behavior. However, there is a consensus that a broad pattern of behavior shows some consistency (Epstein, 1979). The personality test also often includes affective elements of an individual, including feelings or emotions, tolerance of stress, anxiety levels, motivation, and social-emotional factors, such as personal relationships and interactions. In real work environments, these factors are very important as they either enable an individual to perform or inhibit an individual's functioning in the workplace.

Commonly used personality assessments include the Minnesota Multiphasic Personality Inventory-2, California Psychological Inventory, Edwards Personal Preference Schedule, 16 Personality Factor Questionnaire, The Myers-Briggs Type Indicator. A brief summary of these instruments is provided in Table 17.3.

Table 17.3 PERSONALITY AND PSYCHOLOGICAL SYMPTOMS TESTS

Test Instrument	Age/Measuring Constructs/Author
Minnesota Multiphasic Personality Inventory-2 (MMPI-2)	Age: 18–20 Measuring Constructs: Hypochondriasis, depression, hysteria, psychopathic deviate, masculinity/femininity, paranoia, psychasthenia, schizophrenia, hypomania Authors: S. R. Hathaway and J. C. McKinley (Original MMPI in 1943); J. N. Butcher, W. G. Dahlstrom, J. R. Graham, A. Tellegen, and B. Kraemmer (MMPI-2, 1989)
California Psychological Inventory	Age: 13+ Measuring Constructs: Dominance, capacity for status, sociability, social presence, self-acceptance, independence, empathy, responsibility, socialization, self-control, good impression, communality, sense of well-being, tolerance, achievement via conformance, achievement via independence, intellectual efficiency, psychological-mindedness, flexibility, femininity-masculinity Author: Harrion Gough
16 Personality Factor Questionnaire	Age: 16+ Measuring Constructs: Warmth, reasoning, emotional stability, dominance, liveliness, rule-consciousness, social boldness, sensitivity, vigilance, abstractedness, privateness, apprehension, openness to change, self-reliance, perfectionism, tension, (intro-)extraversion, anxiety neuroticism, tough-mindedness, independence, self-control Authors: R. B. Cattell, M. Tatsuoka, and H. Eber
Myers-Briggs Type Indicator	Age: 14+ Measuring Constructs: Extraversion/introversion, sensing/intuition, thinking/feeling, judging/perceiving Authors: K. C. Briggs and I. B. Myers

Career Interest Test

Career interest reflects an individual's preference regarding work activities and the environment. Holland's Hexagon (1997), one of the most popular career choice theories, classifies interests into six categories: (1) realistic (doers), (2) investigative (thinker), (3) artistic (creator), (4) social (helper), (5) enterprising (persuader), and (6) conventional (organizer). Many career interest inventories are constructed based on this theory; thus, career interest often tests an individual's preference matched up with work characteristics. The result, then, is associated with Holland's code and provides insight into the area of work that would best fit an individual. Higher motivation, devoted effort, and commitment can be expected when the nature of work matches well with the individual's interest (Van Iddekinge et al., 2011).

Commonly used career interest tests include Career Assessment Inventory, Career Occupational Preference System Inventory, the Strong-Campbell Interest Inventory, the Minnesota Vocational Interest Inventory, and Reading Free Vocational Interest Inventory.

Table 17.4 CAREER INTEREST TESTS

Test Instrument	Age/Measuring Constructs/Author
Career Assessment Inventory	Age: 15+ Measuring Constructs: Basic interest and occupational/nonoccupational scales for 111 occupations Author: Charles B. Johansson
Career Occupational Preference System Inventory	Age: 14+ Measuring Constructs: 14 career clusters, including science-professional and skilled, technology-professional and skilled, consumer economics, outdoor, business-professional and skilled, clerical, communication, arts-professional and skilled, service-professional and skilled Authors: R. R. Knapp and L. Knapp-Lee
Strong-Campbell Interest Inventory	Age: 16+ Measuring Constructs: Individual's interest in six areas, including occupations, subject areas, activities, leisure activities, people, your characteristics Authors: Strong E. K. (original), Holland, J. L. (2004 version)
Minnesota Vocational Interest Inventory	Age: Children and Adults Measuring Constructs: Information on the interest pattern of men in nonprofessional occupations. Author: University of Minnesota
Reading Free Vocational Interest Inventory	Age: 13+ Measuring Constructs: Interest categories include animal care, automotive, building trades, clerical, food service, horticulture, housekeeping, laundry service, materials handling, patient care, personal service Author: R. L. Becker

Work Values

Values are the issues that people think are important to them, and they reflect what an individual wants to actualize in his/her career. Some jobs may require greater responsibility despite relatively low pay, but people who believe in altruism have a better chance of self-actualization in such a job. Work values are traits and qualities that an individual searches for in a career (Zunker, 2016), and they reflect the individual's attitudes, beliefs, and feelings toward a specific occupation (Ros et al., 1999). Work values are a multidimensional construct, and research indicates that work values are related to job retention, peer relationships, and personal qualities, such as integrity and motivation (Wong & Yeun, 2015). They are important factors in career decision making and often assessed prior to providing career guidance. Identifying work values and finding a job that matches well with an individual's values profile increases the chance of self-actualization. Once identified, an individual's work values can be compared to those highly regarded in a certain profession via O*NET (see p. 11).

Various work value assessment tools are available via the Internet and include the Work Value Inventory, Job Characteristic Inventory, and O*NET Career Values Inventory. The O*NET Career Values Inventory is not an actual assessment. It provides six value categories and the list of occupations that correspond to those categories. Brief summarizes of these instruments are presented in Table 17.5.

Table 17.5 WORK VALUE ASSESSMENTS

Test Instrument	Age/Measuring Constructs/Author
Work Value Inventory	Age: 18+ Measuring Constructs: Values relevant to autonomy, creativity, variety, structure, self-development, influence, work-life balance, financial reward, security, prestige, performance, working condition, work relationship and altruism Author: Donald E. Super
Job Characteristic Inventory	Age: NA Measuring Constructs: Skill variety (the extent to which a job requires a variety of employee competencies to carry it out a task), identity (the extent to which a job requires an employee to complete a whole piece of work), task significance (the extent to which an employee sees his/her work as meaningful), autonomy (the extent to which the employee has empowerment and discretion in carrying out his/her tasks), feedback (the extent to which one receives clear information about the effectiveness of performance) Authors: H. P. Sims, A. D. Szilagyi, and R. T. Keller
O*NET Career Values Inventory	Age: NA Measuring Constructs: Achievement (occupations that allow employees to use their strongest ability, giving them a feeling of accomplishment), independence (occupations that allow employees to work on their own and make decisions), recognition (occupations that value advancement and potential for leadership), relationships (occupations that allow employees to provide service to others and work with coworkers in a friendly noncompetitive environment), support (occupations that value supportive management that stands behind employees), working conditions (occupations that value job security and good working conditions). Author: U.S. Department of Labor/Employment and Training Administration

Transferrable Skills Assessment

Transferrable skills are important in that they can be used in various job settings. Transferrable skills are developed through various life experiences, including previous careers—for example, communication, time management, dependability, problem solving, and conflict resolution. Depending on the area of work an individual pursues, there can be a different set of transferrable skills. For example, communication and conflict resolution skills are relevant when working with others. Basic computer, telephone, and greeting skills are transferrable to basic clerical work. Although formal assessment tools, such as the Transferable Skills Scale and Functional Transferable Skill Inventory, exist, these skills are often assumable based on the other assessment results noted earlier.

Table 17.6 TRANSFERABLE SKILLS

Test Instrument	Age/Measuring Constructs/Author
Transferable Skills Scale	Measuring Constructs: Analytical, numerical, interpersonal, organizational, physical, informational, communicative, creative Authors: J. J. Liptak and L. Shatkin
Functional Transferrable Skill Inventory	Measuring Constructs: Skill set relevant to verbal communication, nonverbal communication, written communication, train/consult, analyze, research, plan and organize, counselor and serve, interpersonal relations, leadership, management, financial, administrative, create and innovate Author: N/A., Open Access

Work Sample

Work samples are often used to evaluate an individual's skills and vocational potential, especially for persons with various disabilities (PWDs). Because psychological testing may be ineffective with PWDs in some cases. A work sample provides a more accurate and realistic view of an individual's ability to carry out the required job tasks. Also, language and reading requirements for work samples are generally low and thus suitable for PWDs or language barriers. Compared to psychological testing, testing items in a work sample are often designed based on the job task, such as assembling parts of a product.

The Valpar product is the most commonly used work sample, and the Valpar Component Work Sample includes various subtests to assess a client's performance level in dexterity, spatial perception, mechanical assembly skills, physical and mobility training, and eye-hand-foot coordination. A summary of the Valpar Component Work Sample is presented in Table 17.7.

Table 17.7 VALPAR WORK SAMPLE

Test Instrument	Age/Measuring Constructs/Author
Valpar Work Sample	Age: Job seekers with various disabilities Measuring Constructs: Valpar components most commonly used in allied health profession include: #1 small tools (mechanical), #2 size discrimination, #3 numerical sorting, #4 upper extremity range of motion, #5 clerical comprehension and aptitude, #6 independent problem solving, #7 multilevel sorting, #8 simulated assembly, #9 whole-body range of motion, #10 tri-level measurement, #11 eye-hand-foot coordination, #12 soldering and inspection (electronic), #14 integrated peer performance, #15 electrical circuitry and print reading, #16 drafting, #19 dynamic physical capacities, #201 physical capacities and mobility screening evaluation, #202 mechanical assembly/ alignment and hammering, #204 fine finger dexterity, #205 independent perceptual screen (spatial aptitude) Author: VALPAR International Corporation.

Market Information

Once all necessary assessments are completed, the next step is to conduct a labor market survey. It is a tool that can be used to collect market information to assist clients' career decision making. It focuses on identifying labor market information relevant to certain types of occupations that clients are interested in, including income and salary ranges, market trends, qualifications, and required job tasks. A market information database further provides job descriptions, specific job tasks, salary ranges, future job outlooks, qualifications, and so on. Three databases are the most commonly used: (1) Occupational Information Network (O'NET), (2) *Dictionary of Occupational Titles* (*DOT*), and (3) *Occupational Outlook Handbook* (*OOH*).

O*NET

O*NET online is available via https://www.onetonline.org/. O*NET provides information about job tasks (e.g., developing a plan), technology skills (e.g., internet, office software), knowledge (psychology, education), skills (e.g., listening, monitoring), ability (e.g., oral expression), work activities (e.g., organizing, planning, prioritizing), work context (e.g., face-to-face discussion), education (e.g., master's, PhD), and credentials. It also provides Holland's code information associated with a job. For example, SI indicates the Holland code of social and investigative. Further, information about work styles (e.g., integrity, cooperation) and work values (e.g., relationship) are also provided. Other valuable information includes wages, employment, projected growth, and project job openings. A state-by-state search is also available (Hanson et al., 2001).

DOT

DOT is available at https://occupationalinfo.org/. In addition to an alphabetical search, *DOT* provides a nice classification that includes (1) professional, technical, and managerial; (2) clerical and sales occupations; (3) service jobs; (4) agricultural, fishery, forestry; and related (5) processing occupations, (6) machine trades occupations, (7) benchwork occupations, (8) structural work occupations, and (9) miscellaneous occupations. *DOT* provides occupational titles and definitions. While *DOT's* categorical classification may be used to have a broader understanding of a similar job group, O'NET is better for collecting information about a certain job.

OOH

OOH is available at https://www.bls.gov/ooh/ and managed by the U.S. Department of Labor Statistics. The book covers 25 work groups: (1) architecture and engineering; (2) arts and design; (3) building and ground cleaning; (4) business and financial; (5) community and social service; (6) computer and information technology; (7) construction and extraction; (8) education, training, and library; (9) entertainment and sports; (10) farming, fishing, and forestry; (11) food preparation and serving; (12) health care; (13) installation, maintenance, and repair; (14) legal; (15) life, physical, and social science; (16) management; (17) math; (18) media and communication; (19) military; (20) office and administrative support; (21) personal care and service; (22) production; (23) protective service; (24) sales; and (25) transportation and material moving. In addition to the classification, *OOH* also provides salary and job outlook information.

How to Use Market Information in Career Counseling

Labor market information is a key component to the understanding of the workplace, and it is dynamic, as it helps a job seeker evaluate occupational options from a practical viewpoint. Consider what procedures job seekers go through until they find the best career option. The first is to identify a career to pursue and then analyze the market. For example, what kind of jobs are out there? What career am I interested in? What state or region has the best market for a certain job? After a job seeker has gained a broad idea of his/her preferred occupation, the next is to know the required qualifications for the job and to see whether the job seeker has salable skills to work in the chosen field. During this process, career options can be narrowed down and more in-depth information considered—for example, associate benefits, future outlooks, and trends. Further, from a career assessment perspective, a market database also can be used as a guiding map throughout the process. When a job seeker is not clear about his/her job preference, a counselor can use career interest tests. The results are often associated with the job code provided in the market database. Information on the job description and expected job task also help an individual prepare for the interview. As such, the reason labor market information is a key ingredient for successful career planning is because a market database, such as O*NET or *DOT*, provides the most accurate and updated information on a job whereas information obtained via (in)formal assessment cannot be matched or compared from a practical standpoint.

Selection of Assessment Tools: Reliability and Validity

Two key factors in terms of selecting assessment tools are reliability and validity. Reliability is the extent to which the instrument consistently produces the same result, while validity means the extent that the instrument measures what it purports to measure. In other words, reliability is the degree of consistency of a measure. A test will be reliable when it gives the same repeated result under the same conditions. Validity refers to a test's ability to measure what it is supposed to measure, thus itis about the accuracy of a measure. It is possible that a person with a high IQ would not do well on an achievement test if he/she hasn't had enough educational opportunities. This is how the IQ test is different from an achievement test. If an IQ test is well constructed to measure the pure aspect of the nature of IQ, a person with high intelligence should be able to get a good score regardless of the amount of education. For example, if a test is well designed in terms of its validity, it is possible for a person who received a high IQ score to get a similar score on a different IQ test, but the person may not obtain a similar achievement test score if he/she is exposed to relatively fewer educational opportunities.

If an IQ test is reliable, we expect a similar score whenever we repeat the test to measure one's IQ. If that is the case, then the IQ test used in the assessment is at least a reliable instrument. Validity is different. Suppose that the IQ test you used actually tests one's emotional intelligence (EQ) better. However, to some extent, we have been using it as an IQ test mistakenly. It is possible that the test instrument used in the assessment repeatedly produced similar scores. However, it still does not tell us much about an individual's IQ, as it is better designed to test EQ. In this case, the IQ test used in the assessment is reliable but still not a valid instrument. A valid measure is reliable, but a reliable measure is not always valid.

The way to test reliability and validity goes beyond the scope of this chapter, but it is important, and the following will give you a brief explanation that helps your intuitive understanding of the way it is calculated. The most common ways to test reliability are (1) test-retest, (2) split-half, and (3) internal consistency. Test-retest reliability means that you use a measure on a person or group at one time, and then you use it again on the same measure on the same person or group at a later time. If the test you used is reliable, then the relationship between the two test scores should correlate with each other highly. Regarding the split-half reliability, consider that you developed a test with 100 items and then divided it into two sets, for example, odd versus even testing numbers. Any pair is fine, such as one to 50 as the first set and then 51 to 100 for the second set. The testing scores obtained from the two sets should correlate highly as both sets were designed to test the same construct.

Internal consistency is a bit more complicated. Consider that you developed a test with five items and calculated the average correlation of every possible pair. For example, test item #1 and #2, test item #2 and #3. Because you have five testing times, the possible pairings is 10 pairs. We calculate the correlation of every pair and then compute the average of the correlations of all pairs. The result is often expressed as the Cronbach alpha. Each item is designed to measure the same thing, thus correlation between two items is expected to be high. The theory and testing formula for calculating internal consistency is complicated, but this may help your intuitive understanding. In all testing methods, the correlation .7, or Cronbach alpha .7, is the general cutoff, indicating acceptable reliability. There is also literature that says .6 or above is acceptable and .8 or above is strong (Thorndike, 2001).

There are also various ways to test validity. Face validity means the extent that the testing item seems to test what it purports to measure. For example, I have money to go out with my friend. This testing item has face validity to measure one's financial well-being but no face validity to test one's education level. The field test is often used to ensure face validity in methodology. Content validity means how well the test measures the constructs relevant to the testing construct. The well-being measure is a good example. Well-being is a multidimensional construct, including financial well-being, psychological well-being, family well-being, and physical well-being. If a measure you are using has a testing item that is relevant only to financial well-being, it is not a valid measure to test one's well-being, although it might be a valid measure to test financial well-being. Expert review is a method often used to ensure content validity. When a test is compared to a gold standard measure that is supposed to measure the same construct, then it is criterion validity.

Convergent and divergent validity means how similar or different a measure you are using is in comparison to other instruments that are supposed to measure a similar or different construct. For example, a well-being measure may be closely related to happiness, so the correlation between the two measures should be high. A well-being measure should be different than a stress measure, so the correlation should be low. Discriminant validity and divergent validity are used interchangeably (Betz & Weiss, 2001).

Good testing instruments means a test is psychometrically well validated in terms of reliability and validity, as noted earlier, and such information is provided in its manual. Reliability information is presented in terms of the correlation coefficient or Cronbach alpha (e.g., r or α = .7). Validity information is presented in terms of correlation with other measures—for example, the correlation between character assessment and academic performance. In statistical language, the correlation coefficient r between character assessment and a performance instrument is equal to .7 or higher, for instance. When such mathematical information regarding the validity is not offered (for example, an instrument available via the Internet or agency-developed instrument/checklist), a counselor can look into whether an instrument at least seems to have face and content validity, as those do not necessarily require mathematical calculation.

Culturally Responsive Assessment

Cultural sensitivity is complex because the construct tested in the assessment may have different meanings depending on the culture. First, the content and testing item may be culturally biased. Second, the test administrator or testing procedure may have cultural bias. Third, the bias is related to culturally inappropriate application of the assessment.

First, testing item bias is often associated with the construct and measurement equivalence. Construct equivalence means that a construct tested in a certain instrument has the same meaning in a different culture. For example, work value "being loyal" may mean placing a group/company value over one's values in a certain culture, while in a different culture, this simply means the successful completion of job tasks. Measurement equivalence cares more about whether an instrument is cross-culturally validated in an appropriate manner. These concepts are often discussed in cross-cultural studies, especially to culturally validate a certain instrument in a different culture—for example, the MMPI English versus Korean version. In reality, preparing an alternative instrument that is culturally valid may not be possible. However, it is important for the examiners to know the concept of equivalence and carefully apply this concept throughout the assessment procedure.

Second, testing bias can be addressed by improving test administers' cultural knowledge, awareness, and skills (Sue & Sue, 2013). The test administer needs to have cultural knowledge—how a certain behavior or language is viewed, for example, eye contact. In a certain culture, eye contact is viewed as a sign of disrespect. Punctuality is an ideal and recommended in many cultures, but in a certain cultures, time orientation might be different from general Western culture. Jumping into a point may be appropriate, but in a certain culture, spending more time getting to know each other is important to build collaborative relationships. In addition to cultural knowledge, test administers should also be aware of their own cultural backgrounds and put effort into developing culturally appropriate assessment skills and strategies.

Test accommodation is also another area to improve bias relevant to test procedure. Test accommodation is a modification in testing or testing condition to address issues associated with disabilities. Examples of testing accommodations are as follows:

- presenting instruction in a different format—for example, an examiner may read instructions or use braille;

- a person may be allowed to say the answer to someone who documents answers in writing;

- frequent breaks may be given depending on a person's stamina;

- translators may be allowed for those whose English is not fluent; and

- extended time can be given to complete a test.

Another important factor to consider in determining test accommodation is the nature of the construct tested and the purpose of the assessment. Suppose that you are testing the achievement level of children with autism spectrum disability (ASD) to determine what kinds of accommodations a school should provide. In such a case, testing students' achievements in a regular setting without accommodations is better because it shows where a student stands in comparison to others. Based on the result, options for accommodations can be considered to move up an individual within an average range. On the other hand, accommodations can be used when IQ is tested for a student with high-functioning ASD if the purpose of the assessment is to gauge the intellectual potential of a student.

Third, the ecological approach (Summer, 2016) is recommended in test application. The ecological model emphasizes that cultural factors (race/ethnicity, education, socioenvironmental status, disability, etc.) have influence on every aspect of human life, including intrapersonal, interpersonal, community, physical, health, and so on. Carefully considering cultural factors from multiple dimensions can ensure culturally responsive and accurate interpretation of assessment results.

Summary

A good career plan necessitates an accurate interpretation of an individual's vocational needs, strengths, and weaknesses. An assessment is a clinician's best tool for understanding a client's goals. However, as assessment also requires time and effort from both the client and clinician, being wise and cost-effective by minimizing the unnecessary burden is important. In this regard, the intake interview serves a clinician in designing an effective career assessment plan. To be competent in assessment, a clinician needs to have the necessary knowledge about the constructs that are relevant to a client's career goals and access to the available assessment tools that measure the constructs, as well as assess the pros/cons of the individual assessment tool and cultural variables that have influences throughout the assessment procedure. The text provides an array of information, but it is also important to know that what is presented in this chapter is mostly about the fundamental knowledge component that a clinician must know as the bottom line; the competencies required to apply the knowledge to the practice are often acquired via years of experience.

Assessment requires communication between a clinician and client: the clinician needs to know that his/her characteristics and communication style can have an influence throughout the assessment process. For example, interview/assessment anxiety can be reduced and minimized by explaining the purpose of an assessment. A clarification can be requested and probed when there is a cultural difference that interferes with a relationship between a client and a clinician. The result of an assessment needs to be displayed in a positive and constructive manner. Note that the purpose of an assessment is to understand the assets a client has and help the client to maximize his/her strengths and minimize the effect of weaknesses in achieving his/her career goal.

Case Study: Sample Vocational Assessment Report

This section provides a sample vocational evaluation. It is a fake report to help readers understand career assessment and should be used only as an example.

I. **Client Information**

- Name: Karen Smith
- Address: 3601 4th Street, ABC City, TX, 79430
- Age: 47
- DOB: April 7, 1972
- Referred by Division of Vocational Rehabilitation
- Evaluator: Jake Adams

II. Key Referral Considerations

- Provide career exploration and/or direct placement ideas
- Job goal emphasis: Medical-related work ideas that are light (select) and sedentary in nature
- Provide academic enhancement/job training suggestions
- Identification of immediate work opportunities/employers if no schooling occurs
- Work area preference: ABC County
- Secure new work time line(s): Post-training
- Primary disability factor(s): Physical, possible cognitive and emotional considerations
- Minimum start wage desired: $12+ per hour with benefits
- Willing to give up Social Security Disability Insurance (SSDI) for the right employment situation

III. Identification of Karen's Preferences to Secure Work-Rank Ordered

- First, formalized training (college)
  Program: Medical coding or related
  Best location: ABC Area Technical College
- Second, apply directly to employers with placement assistance (postgraduation)
- Third, use an on-the-job (OJT) training approach (evaluator's suggestion should job search extend itself)

IV. Education/Additional Training Experiences

A. High School Attended: ABC High School, ABC City, ABC College graduated in 1996
Primary coursework: General studies
Overall grades: Above average
Attitude toward school: Enjoyable
Significant courses: Basic coursework only

B. Post–High School Training/Education
Nursing assistant certification acquired from Madison Area Technical College, summer of 1998

V. Work History

A. Most Significant/Meaningful Job
Title: Manager—Fast Food (185.137-010)
Employer: McDonald—three different locations in ABC City
Dates employed: 2012–2014
Duties: Hired new staff, closed and opened stores, counted up receipts, made bank deposits, and inventory control

B. Primary Transferable Skills
Working within a team concept and independently advising others, exchanging ideas/information, assessing/evaluating situations, problem solving, training/teaching/instructing others, supervising others (14+), selling/persuading/influencing others, hiring/firing/interviewing others, motivating/directing others, communicating

continues on next page

needs, answering questions, listening, negotiating, mediating, taking instructions (verbal), helping/serving others, interpreting directions, organizing/scheduling work for others, dealing with the general public, using emotional control/tact, dealing with stress, working with numbers, copying/entering data, verifying receipts, proofing/correcting numbers, inventory control, ordering, keeping records, evaluating/examining information, gathering/collecting information, calculating/computing data, budget management, handling/disassembling, machine setup/operation I control (shake machines, grills, coffee makers), precision, varied and repetitive work ability, sustained attention, working quickly with concentration, meeting production goals/quotas/standards, meeting standards, quality control/inspection of others' work, gross finger and hand-eye coordination, calculator operation, and cash register operation

C. **Additional Job Titles (employed > 6 months)**

- Cashier I/clerk (211.362-01 O)
- Nursing assistant (355.674-014)
- Fast-food worker (311.472-010)

D. **Reference Status**

Counselor would suggest further review of the Oak Park Nursing Home reference because of the Worker's Compensation claim.

E. **Temperaments (Personality Requirements Demonstrated in the Above Job Titles)**

- Performing a VARIETY of duties
- Dealing with PEOPLE
- DIRECTING, controlling, or planning activities of others
- Attaining precise set limits, TOLERANCES, standards
- Making JUDGMENTS and decisions

F. **Additional Transferable Skills/Resume and Interviewing Highlighters**

- Communicating ideas, feelings
- Interviewing, questioning others to obtain information
- Working with special populations (elderly, PWDs)
- Meeting deadlines/quotas
- Working diligently and patiently
- Hobbies: Used to like to bicycle a lot but does a lot of walking now

VI. **Disability Impact on Future Vocational Planning**

A. **Primary Disability**

Karen injured her lower back in August of 2011 and reinjured it in 2014 and had surgery (laminectomy) to repair discs at the L4, L5, and S1 levels performed by Dr. Kay on February 4, 2014. She may have to have another surgery this summer (July) to repair her tailbone. She also has had a history of depression since her early 20s, which has been made worse by the back injury in terms of loss of physical activity and sleep difficulties because of pain (she estimates that she sleeps no more than 4 hours per night).

Additional disabilities identified: Stated that she has anxiety pretty much all the time and a hypothyroid condition. A report by Dr. Thakor came up with a diagnosis of a borderline personality disorder with schizoidal features. A file review also turned up suicide attempts in 2015 and 2016 as well.

Future physical requirements/considerations include the following:

1. Physical strength capabilities

   a. Lift no more than 10 pounds (stationary)

   b. Carry no more than 5 pounds

   c. Push/pull no more than 10–20 pounds

2. Limited/no climbing, balancing, stooping, kneeling, crouching, crawling, reaching above shoulder level, or twisting of torso

3. No working outside in extreme cold/heat, a wet/humid environment, around vibrations, around dust/fumes, around moving mechanical parts, near risk of electrical shock, at unprotected heights, around radiation, around explosives, or around chemicals

4. Average daily pain level is high—stays the same as the day progresses and always set off by physical activities

   a. Physical activities include sitting too long

   b. In addition, weather conditions such as cold fronts, humidity, heat, and low-pressure systems cause symptomology occurrences

   c. Located in the back region, radiating downward in her right leg to the arch in her foot

5. Best mix in a 4-hour workday: Walk, sit, and stand 11 hours each

B. **Current Treatment Methodology**

   Current medical care providers: Dr. Thomas Kay, orthopedic surgeon; Dr. Smily Thaor, psychiatrist Mental Health Center of ABC County (Medication Services Program); Dr. Bailey, general medicine. Additional service providers: Attorney Jason Born who is assisting with the Worker's Compensation settlement/process. Current medications (side effects): Lexapro (none), Klonopin (none), Percocet (drowsiness), and Synthroid (hot flashes).

C. **Acceptance of Disability**

   Karen appears to lack some awareness of the primary effects of her various disabilities. Based on observations made during the evaluation process, there appears to be some duress (e.g., frustration and depression related to her inactivity). While I did not ask Karen about her medication compliance, I suspect based on some of the mannerisms she demonstrated that she just might be self-medicating (e.g., did not/was unable to follow some of the test instructions). This counselor would suggest further discussion on reconsidering future counseling participation. Her only involvement appears to be 15 minutes per month with her psychiatrist; this is not enough / sufficient from this counselor's perspective.

D. **Observable Behaviors by Evaluator**

   Some were apparent: Karen did not fill out most of the pre-sent materials, stating she forgot about them (i.e., I had her fill out the Career Occupational Preference System Interest Inventory (COPS) Interest Test during our session). She also needed to stand up to fill out the aforementioned test because of pain; she misunderstood

continues on next page

the values measurement guide and marked her three top area(s) all as 4s; she was not the best historian when it came to explaining what her disabilities were, and her overall affect was somewhat "flat," which was consistent with file information I reviewed (e.g., schizoidal effects).

VII. Test Results Section—Aptitudes and Interests

A. CAPS Aptitude Test Results

CAPS Test	Stanine Level/ Percentile		Department Of Labor (DOL) Aptitude	GATB EQUIV	Grade Level
1 Mechanical Reasoning (MR)	4	32%	No DOL Correlation	--	
2 Spatial Relations (SR)	1	2%	S=Spatial Ability	40–74	
3 Reading Comprehension (VR)	1	2%	V=Verbal Ability	40–74	
4 Math Ability (NA)	1	2%	N=Numerical Ability	40–74	3.0
5 Grammatical Usage (LU)	2	8%	V=Verbal Ability	40–74	
6 Word Recognition (WK)	4	32%	V=Verbal Ability	76–91	8.0+
7 Perceptual Speed & Accuracy (PSA)	1	2%	P=Form Perception Q=Clerical Perception	40–74	
8 Manual Speed and Dexterity (MSD-Fine Motor)	4	32%	F=Finger Dexterity M=Manual Dexterity	76–91	

B. Test-Taking Perceptions/Observations of the Above Results

1. Ability to Take Tests

Karen feels that she would be a fair test taker if it was required for her to get a job. This evaluator feels that this is an accurate appraisal on Karen's part.

2. Observed Testing Behavior

Karen approached the test devices in a straightforward and deliberate manner. She did need some reassurance and further explanation. She took a little longer than normal to process the instructions than most individuals do. Karen appeared comfortable with this process; however, she finished only one of the tests (SR) ahead of schedule. Karen put forth a very good effort, but her test results do not appear to support her goal of becoming a medical coder (see **Section IX.B.**). Meticulousness, cognitive, medicational, and attentional-related issues could have depressed scores in all tested areas (i.e., testing accommodations such as a solitary testing room in future hiring or school related testing is advisable). Dealing with time pressures in testing situations could also be an issue for Karen (i.e., helping her to secure additional time is also suggested).

C. COPS Interest Test Interpretations

Interests consist of what one wants to do, would be happy doing, and/or what one dreams of doing. According to the COPS interpretation, Karen's best matches are rank ordered as follows:

1. **Communication**

2. **Service-skilled**

3. **Business-professional**

VIII. Interaction Skills/Placement Readiness Appraisal

A. General Overview

Karen displayed a somewhat easygoing but extremely flat-like presence throughout our interviewing session. Her gestures and body language were occasionally fidgety and uneasy, obviously because of pain responses. Her eye contact was used appropriately and reasonably well during our discussion. She demonstrated a good sense of humor. Overall, Karen conveyed a fairly polite and appreciative manner that should appeal to most prospective employers. Her ability to recall information was questionable at times based on her ability to give facts from past events and experiences (e.g., her disability history). In the general area of social interaction capabilities, Karen was somewhat aware of having a good give and take during the interviewing portion of our session, although her overall conversational behaviors tended to be more on the passive/quiet side than talkative. Karen's voice was quite clear and understandable, and her grammar was most acceptable and satisfactory as well.

B. Job-Seeking Skills Analysis

Based on the aforementioned discussion, this evaluator feels that Karen would be a **fair** interviewee. She has an honest and forthright but somewhat reserved personality, which could detract from future job-seeking efforts. Additional work on interviewing techniques is suggested (i.e., Karen needs to become much more animated and outgoing). Overall, I would say that Karen has a solid understanding of the work-related skills and/or abilities that she could offer to prospective employers and, post mock interviewing practice, she should be able to interact reasonably well in most interviewing situations. I would suggest that those individuals who will assist her in her job-seeking efforts do at least a couple of mock interviews with her. She needs to be aware that she is somewhat flat because of her emotional issues/disabilities.

C. Interviewing Impressions

Initial impressions of how Karen would come across in future interviewing sessions include the following personal qualities that should be viewed favorably by prospective employers:

1. Dedicated	5. Autonomous	9. Pleasant
2. Conscientious	6. Methodical	10. Willing to Learn
3. Dependable	7. Far-Sighted	11. People Oriented
4. Honest	8. Congenial	12. Purposeful

D. Self-Confidence

When asked what her self-confidence level for future employment efforts was, Karen responded that it was a 5 on a scale of 1–10. This evaluator feels that Karen's *self-confidence has been diminished considerably* because of the effects of her various disabilities. She appears to be solely focusing on her physical issues when in actuality her emotional issues also appear to be quite significant/involved.

continues on next page

E. Recent Job-Seeking Activity

Karen has casually looked for work but does not appear to have applied anywhere. She did try to apply for a work experience at the Department of Revenue but was not hired.

F. Future Placement Assistance

When given an explanation as to what types of services a placement provider could assist her with, Karen felt that she would be able to best accomplish this process *with* the assistance of a *placement vendor*. This evaluator *strongly agrees* with this perception, especially if OJT/work experience methodologies are recommended. Karen's lack of a recent work history, previous job search difficulties, selective job requirements, possible poor work references (e.g., Oak Park Nursing Home), and interviewing remediation clearly support this type of approach. It looks like we will have to wait until she meets with Dr. Kruse this July to see what her medical status is.

IX. Future Vocational Considerations

A. Work Related

Factors most important to Karen include work environment, minimal/no driving on the job, working indoors, vacation/holiday pay, advancement opportunities, friendly coworkers, can leave job "at the office," working as part of a team, limited driving to and from work, OTJ, accepting responsibility, performing repetitive work, casual work setting, limited job stress, dealing with people, no discrimination, creativity/self-expression, respect/recognition/prestige, making decisions/initiating plans, working under specific instructions, using computer technology, doing clerical related work, learn new skills, and, *especially*, financial rewards (good pay), sick leave/pension benefits, and flexible hours. Additional considerations include working in a mid-sized firm and a minimum starting wage of $10.50 per hour. Karen cited an interest in working in the following occupational areas: *medical coding* or *law enforcement legal area*. Health insurance benefits are also a very important concern.

B. Transportation Issues

Karen stated that she has a driver's license in excellent status, as well the availability of a reliable car. She would commute 10+ miles for work or school options.

C. Learning Style

Karen feels that she can learn either through observing someone demonstrate a job task prior to repeating it or by self-instruction should the need arise. Her WK, reading comprehension ability (VR), and grammatical usage (LU) scores would indicate a *very poor* reading capacity. However, when this issue was more fully examined, a *preference* for *"hands-on" demonstration* was suggested as the best mechanism for learning new job tasks.

D. Stress Factors

Certain job-specific factors have been identified by major research studies as stressors, which can be attributed to job burnout. Based on our diagnostic interview, Karen felt that the following job factors were pertinent:

(E) Emotional Control: Karen can cope with difficult people/situations.

(T) Tedium: Karen is comfortable with repetitive work activities.

(A) Accept Responsibility: Karen prefers to have others make decisions for her.

(S) Sustained Attention: Karen does not work well under production pressures.

E. Knowledge of Work World

Overall, this evaluator feels that Karen has fairly good insight into employer expectations. In regard to accessing her desired job goal identified previously, medical coder, Karen will also need to better examine the labor market need, physical expectations (e.g., sit most of the time), wages to be expected, and stress/emotional implications involved. Karen also appears to be quite methodical in nature (e.g., she completed only one test measure (SR) device).

F. Work Readiness

Karen appears somewhat eager to affect a plan of action. She pretty much has focused in on the medical coding program at Madison Area Technical College, which according to her has a 3-year waiting list.

G. Support Systems

Karen has some agency representatives (lawyer, psychiatrist) who are somewhat supportive in this regard. She appears to be minimally connected with the necessary types of supports that would increase her chances of returning to the labor market. It appears that she has pretty much *isolated* herself from others (e.g., friends and family alike, citing the fact that she can no longer be physically active).

H. Summary Statement of Rehabilitation Process So Far

Karen is somewhat pleased with the help/assistance received thus far. She stated that she does not like the fact that she needs to make all the appointments? The primary impetus to apply for services appears to have come from food stamp program officials who made the suggestion.

X. Job Comparison Process/Interpretations

A. Where the Information Comes From

The author of this report uses the VDARE Process developed by Sink, Fields, and McCroskey. This process requires identifying Karen's *previous* work history experiences (> 6 months) and using the *DOT* to derive a high across the board aptitudinal profile. The next step in the process requires the development of a similar profile, which reflects a current synthesis of test results and information obtained during the evaluation session. The final step in the process is to present the individual's *desired* or *suggested* job goal into a similar aptitudinal profile. The comparative analysis of these previous, current, and targeted profiles gives the evaluator more accurate insight as to future work capabilities, especially if one is a poor anxious test taker.

Aptitudes are defined as the specific capacities or abilities required of an individual to facilitate the learning of some task or job duty. Standard terminology include general learning ability (G), verbal ability (V), numerical ability (N), spatial ability (S), form perception (P), clerical perception (Q), motor coordination (K), finger dexterity (F), manual dexterity (M), eye-hand-foot coordination (E), and color discrimination (C). The following numerical values, in turn, represent the capacity levels expected for job performance (i.e., 1 = Very High, 3 = Average, 5 = Very Low).

continues on next page

B. **Summary of Relevant Information**

Previous Work History:

Aptitudes	Strengths	Skill Level Achieved
G V N S P Q K F M E C	Medium	Semi-Skilled
3 3 3 4 3 2 3 3 3 4 4		

Current Test Result and Physical Capability:

Aptitudes	Strengths	Skill Level Achieved
G V N S P Q K F M E C	Light	Semi-Skilled
4 4 5 5 5 5 3 3 3 3 3		

Targeted Job Goal—Medical Record Technician (079.362-014)

Aptitudes	Strengths	Skill Level Achieved
G V N S P Q K F M E C	Medium	Semi-Skilled
2 2 3 4 4 3 4 3 4 5 5		

C. **Suggested Occupational Focus**

Karen's CAPS test results are fairly inconsistent with the aptitudinal capabilities required for her expressed job goal, medical record technician. This job is, however, very compatible with the COPS interest test interpretations (first ranked), as well as statements made by Karen during the diagnostic interview. Based on the aforementioned, the business-skilled, clerical, and service skilled clusters appear to be the best areas to consider for possible academic enhancements and/or OJT work experience mechanisms that could result in eventual placement-related efforts.

XI. **Personalized Database Options**

The author, through a local labor market analysis and a review of academic curricula, has compiled several different databases that can effectively be integrated and used to best meet an individual's specific needs, requests, etc. Also, each database includes only those jobs that exist in sufficient numbers to be considered as realistic options. They include the following:

- Educational (Technical College and University)
- Career Exploration (Job Family Clusters)
- Civil Service Employment Suggestions
- Personalized (Important Client-Specific Variables)
- Employer Sector Analysis/Direction

In Karen's particular case, it was determined that a combination of Databases A, B, D, and E best meet her needs using the following factors:

- Cluster areas   Business-skilled, clerical, and service-skilled
- Skill potential   Semi-skilled
- Strength level   Light or sedentary

XII. Vocational/OJT/Academic Enhancement Suggestions

A. The following employment and training possibilities are suggested based on Karen's aptitudinal test scores and interest test results. In addition, the Division of Vocational Rehabilitation system usually requests that this report identify immediate work options should educational plans not occur. An **asterisk (*)** indicates additional choices that can be considered as good job matches. "Select" indicates the assumption that individualized employment accommodations will be made. "OJT" indicates some sort of financial incentive is offered to prospective employers and usually involves a placement vendor.

Immediate Job Options

1. Assembler–Small Products (Select/OJT)
2. Office Helper (Select/OJT)
3. File Clerk (Select/OJT)
4. Security Guard (Select)
5. Mail Clerk/Sorter (Select/OJT)
6. Companion (Select)
7. *Survey/Research Worker

B. Educational Enhancement Options: Courses/programs at Madison Area Technical College

1. Involvement with academic support unit(s)
2. Accounting assistant
3. Operations
4. Pharmacy technician

C. Additional Work Options

Please see Addendum #1 (not offered in this case sample) for a listing of those jobs Karen could access with or without the completion of further education or training. Jobs in this listing are rank ordered, beginning with the easiest and ending with those requiring the most training and/or education. Specific Vocational Preparation (SVP) descriptors: 1–2 = Unskilled, 3–4 = Semi-Skilled (Skills Training/OJT), 5–6 = Semi-Skilled (Technical College). These job titles are generated from the previously identified job cluster(s). Please note that computer limitations may result in some suggestions that conflict with Karen's current physical restriction guideline (e.g., maid, waitress (lifting too much)).

D. Additional Educational Options

Please see Addendum #2 (not offered in this case sample) for a listing of educational programs and job titles that Karen could also consider. The wages given are taken directly from the ABC Area Technical College's most recent placement department figures. These courses and job titles are generated from the previously identified job cluster(s) listed in Section X.

continues on next page

E. **Employment Opportunities for Above Job Titles**

Karen could use the following areas as potential employment sectors: electronics manufacturers, hospitals, insurance companies, medical clinics, nursing homes, security agencies, and survey/research firms. Please see Addendum #3 (not offered in this case sample), which lists some specific employers who could conceivably employ Karen in the immediate job options identified in this report. Contact names are included to assist in the job-seeking process. An asterisk (*) in front of a name indicates the CEO, manager, or owner. The primary purpose of the employer database is to give Karen an opportunity to tap into the hidden job market. Every attempt is made to ensure the most current information in this database; however, there could be some errors because of firms closing, relocating, and opening. Personnel managers also have a strong tendency to change jobs quite frequently.

XIII. Client Overview

A. Vocational Strengths:

- Quite personable demeanor, makes a good initial impression
- Willing to start at entry level and work her way up the career ladder
- Stable work history with good references, according to Karen
- Valid driver's license, good driving record, and car is available
- Prior supervisory and training experience
- Prior knowledge of medical terminology and procedures
- Has a basic education (high school)
- Is willing to study to acquire new skills
- From ABC area, has contacts and knows pepole; employment networking could be useful in Karen's eventual placement

B. Obstacles to Employment:

- Could lose some SSDI financial assistance as a result of taking a job
- Confined to sedentary/light work, eliminating a lot of job possibilities
- Multiply disabled, thus compounding job search efforts
- Medical prognosis/treatment modality still seems a bit unsettled (e.g., possible surgery in July)
- Lacks confidence in ability to work
- Gives the impression of being an extremely methodical individual (e.g., completed only one test)
- Probably would not work well under stress and/or pressure situations
- Self-presentation skills need to be improved upon prior to job interviewing (e.g., more animation)
- Poor understanding of current vocational capacities as a result of her disabilities
- Has not worked for more than one and a half years
- Little or no personal support system appears to be available to Karen

- Involved in the Worker's Compensation system
- Not a good test taker
- Difficulty with basic reading and/or computational skills according to CAPS LU, WK, VR, and NA test results

XIV. Recommendations

1. Karen appears to be primarily focused on her back injury as being the one key factor that is holding her back in life (i.e., this counselor would suggest to Karen and her psychiatrist that she needs to deal with her emotional issues better as well). Her present strategy of refusing additional counseling and relying on a brief 15-minute meeting with her doctor is not enough. It also appears that Karen has isolated herself from others (friends and relatives), again blaming her back limitations and inability to do physical activities (e.g., riding a bike with others, as the main reason why this isolation is occurring). Regular counseling involvement with someone whom she can develop a trusting relationship with. This truly needs to occur if Karen is ever to return to the workplace.

2. There also appears to be some significant cognitive impairment going on. When quizzed about her recent neuropsychological examination, Karen had great difficulty describing what transpired or why this occurred. She also cited the fact that she had some sort of seizure difficulties as a child, but they apparently are no longer an issue. She did not do too well on the test instruments I administered. Hopefully, the neuropsychological examination will better elaborate on her academic potential since additional schooling appears to be the primary return to work methodology that she is focusing on (e.g., the medical coding program at ABC Area Technical College). I also gave her additional time (2+ minutes) on the WK and numerical ability (NA) tests, but it really did not improve her scores/results.

3. Karen apparently has a meeting with her surgeon sometime in July to determine whether further surgery is necessary. Securing the results of this meeting will have to be factored into the future scheme of things. Karen did exhibit some pain symptomology (e.g., she sat rather stiffly), and she completed her interest test standing up, using the top of a bookcase in the testing room. Right now, she only cleared herself for sedentary work (10 pounds or less); please note that I increased her options in Addendums #1 and #2 (not offered in this case study) to a light classification in anticipation that her physical condition would improve to at least a light 10–20-pound capacity.

4. While Karen initially stated a willingness to give up her SSDI benefits for the right job/career track (e.g., $10.50 per hour with full benefits), I have some serious reservations about doing/considering this idea. I would suggest that some sort of benefits analysis occur beforehand. It does appear, however, that Karen has her full 9-month trial work period intact, which is a positive. Based on what is gathered (e.g., neuropsychological report and doctor's recommendations), it may be more appropriate to view the acquisition of a part-time job in conjunction with the reception of her SSDI benefits as her best ideal return to work scenario.

5. In regard to her desire to do medical transcriptionist/medical coding types of work, Karen has already found out that there is at least a 3-year waiting list to gain admittance to this program. Based on what Karen told me (needing to alternate her physical positioning equally between standing, sitting, and walking), as well as how she responded to time pressure demands during the testing portion of our assessment, this type of work would not be a good match for her situation. I would also be concerned as to the labor force demand

continues on next page

for this type of activity once all the ABC Area Technical College graduates access the market. A review of the ABC Area Technical College course catalog also stated a physical examination will also be required beforehand.

6. Based on Karen's interest test results and stated desire to work within a medical setting, the clerical sector appears to hold the most promise for future work and/or academic training possibilities. She may already have had what she could best describe as some sort of clerical situational assessment at New Career Directions a few years back, but she really could not expand and/or elaborate too well as to what transpired. I would suggest you consider this option once all the "physical" information is gathered from her doctor this July. I would also be curious as to how Karen follows verbal directions; I had to repeat/re-explain some of the tests. She did two of the tests left to right rather than top to bottom as she was told to do. I also did not ascertain exactly what her typing/keyboarding abilities and software knowledge/expertise were. I called her twice, leaving messages on her answering machine, but she never responded.

7. As stated before, I would suggest that Karen would be most happy doing something in the work realm rather than waiting 3+ years to attend school. Her prior history appears to be quite involved (working 60+ hours per week)—i.e., I suspect work means a lot to her and defines her self-image somewhat. Should she opt for the acquisition of a more immediate job, I would suggest that she be referred to a placement to assist in this process. Vendors should assist Karen with the following issues:

- Finding jobs (hidden job market—Addendum #3)
- Interviewing for jobs (improve presentation level, more animation is needed)
- Develop a resume using some of the transferable skills identified in this report
- Possible implementation of an incentive package should the job search extend itself
- Job follow-up satisfaction
- Review her prior work history and, with her permission, discuss in-depth which work references she will use in this process

8. The intent of this in-depth report is proactive in nature and focuses on a best-case scenario regarding possible future employment options (i.e., it should not be used for litigation purposes). This report is not intended to be a loss of earnings product.

In conclusion, I would like to thank you for this referral. If you have any further questions related to this product, please do not hesitate to call.

References

Anastasi, A., & Urbina, S. (1997). *Psychological testing* (7th ed.). Prentice Hall.

Betz, N. E., & Weiss, D. J. (2001). In B. F. Bolton (Ed.), *Handbook of measurement and evaluation in rehabilitation* (pp. 49–76). Aspen Publisher.

Caroll, J. (1985). Second-language abilities. In R. Sternberg (Ed.), *Human abilities: An information processing approach* (pp. 82–102). Freeman.

Caroll, J. (1993). *Human cognitive abilities: A survey of factor-analytic studies*. Cambridge.

Clark, Madeline E. "The relationship between counselors" multicultural counseling competence and poverty beliefs (2016). [Doctoral dissertation Old Dominion University]. https://doi.org/10.25777/0wyv-wg21

Epstein, S. (1979). The stability of behavior: I. On predicting most of the people much of the time. *Journal of Personality and Social Psychology, 37*(7), 1097–1126. https://dx.doi.org/10.1037/0022-3514.37.7.1097

Fadely, D. C. (1987). *Job coaching in supported work program.* University of Wisconsin-Stout.

Hanson, M. A., Matheson, L. N., & Borman, W. C. (2001). The O'NET occupational information system. In B. F. Bolton (Ed.)., *Handbook of measurement and evaluation in rehabilitation* (pp. 281–310). Aspen Publisher.

Holland, J. L. (1997). *Making vocational choices: A theory of vocational personalities and work environments* (3rd ed.). Psychological Assessment Resources.

Ivey, A. E. (1987). Cultural intentionality: The core of effective helping. *Counselor, 26*(3), 168–172.

Ivey, A. E., Ivey, M. B., & Zalaquett, C. P. (2010). *Intentional interviewing and counseling.* Brooks/Cole.

Jastak, S., & Wilkson, G. S. (1984). Wide Range Achievement Test—Revised. Jastak Associates.

Kidd, J. M. (1996). The career counselling interview. In A. G. Watts, B. Law, J. Killeen, J. M. Kidd, & R. Hawthorn (Eds.), *Rethinking careers education and guidance: Theory, policy and practice* (pp. 189–209). Routledge.

Laungani, P. (2006). The counseling interview: First impression. *Counseling Psychology Quarterly, 15*(1), 107–113.

Malgady, R. G. (1996). The question of cultural bias in assessment and diagnosis of ethnic minority clients: Let's reject the null hypothesis. *Professional Psychology: Research and Practice, 27*(1), 73–77. https://doi.org/10.1037/0735-7028.27.1.73

Ros, M., Schwartz, S. H., & Surkiss, S. (1999). Basic individual values, work values, and the meaning of work. *Applied Psychology: An International Review, 48*(1), 49–71.

Sue, W. D., & Sue, D. (2013). *Counseling the culturally diverse: Theory and practice.* John Wiley & Sons.

Summer, N. (2016). *Fundamentals of case management practice.* Cengage Learning.

Szymanski, E. M., & Vancollins, J. (2003). Career development of people with disabilities: Some new and not-so-new challenges. *Australian Journal of Career Development.* https://doi.org/10.1177/103841620301200103

Thorndike, R. M. (2001). In B. F. Bolton (Ed.)., *Handbook of measurement and evaluation in rehabilitation* (pp. 29–48). Aspen Publisher.

Van Iddekinge, C. H., Roth, P. L., Putka D. J., & Lanivich, S. E. (2011). Are you interested? A meta analysis of relations between vocational interests and employee performance and turnover. *Journal of Applied Psychology, 96*(6), 1167–1194.

VALPAR International Corporation. (1974). VALPAR Component Work Samples. VALPAR International Corporation.

Wong, S. W., & Yuen, M. (2015). Super's work values inventory: Issues of subtest internal consistency using a sample of Chinese university students in Hong Kong. *Journal of Employment Counseling, 52*(1), 29–35. https://doi.org/10.1002/j.2161-1920.2015.00054.x

Zunker, V. G. (2016). *Career counseling: A holistic approach.* Cengage Learning.

CHAPTER 18

Advocating and Marketing to Employers and Human Resources

Rebecca R. Sametz and Danielle Ami Narh

CHAPTER OVERVIEW

The role of a career counselor expands past providing assessments and information to clients about what major they should pursue in college based on what an assessment states about their interests. As the field of career counseling grows and the labor market changes, career counselors are having to adapt to become advocates for their clients and come up with marketing strategies to better assist their clients in a competitive job market (Davos-Klosters, 2014). This chapter will discuss how to become an advocate as a career counselor and provide strategies to assist clients in marketing themselves during the application and interview processes.

CHAPTER OBJECTIVES

After reading this chapter, the student will be able to complete the following:

1. Define advocacy.

2. Implement effective advocacy strategies that can benefit their clients.

3. Outline strategies to assist their clients in marketing themselves to potential employers in a competitive job market.

Marketing to Employers and Human Resources

Developing Partnerships With Employers

Career counselors are educated, trained, and experienced in helping their clients tackle their toughest career problems and achieve their career aspirations (Ginac, 2004). Career counselors typically are experienced in dealing with assessment, performance improvement, career transition, career pathing, workplaces, and work/life balance situations that plague workers at one time or another. Career counselors are experts in tailoring strategies and techniques to the specific needs of people or groups seeking help (Guindon & Richmond, 2005).

Within the current labor market, with the increase of minimum wage and with high employee expectations for entry-level positions increasing, career counselors have to be creative in their strategies and techniques more than ever before. Career counselors may have used a "sales" technique previously to "sell" a client or employer, but this technique is no longer working with employers who have more command over the type of employee they are looking to hire (Guindon & Richmond, 2005). Previously, there were more job openings than there were applicants; now, the job market has switched to not enough jobs for the number of applicants looking for work.

What this means is that career counselors need to adapt not only their techniques but also their overall job duties and responsibilities to be successful in assisting their clients. This is especially true when it comes to social media, which is now a big part of how employers market their companies and products, as well as do recruitment. Therefore, to create a partnership, a career counselor must first ensure that both the career counselor and employer are on the same page when it comes to expectations of applicants.

Cultivating an Equal Exchange of Resources With Employers Through Advocacy

Like any good researcher and counselor, we are trained to work with our clients to set goals and establish the purpose for working together. So wouldn't this be the same for us as career counselors? Therefore, it is important to consider what our goals are as career counselors prior to meeting with our clients. Each day, career counselors strive to assist people in attaining gainful employment and/or valuable work experiences. On the other hand, the goal of employers' is to find the best fit for their companies. However, oftentimes, what an employer is looking for is difficult and vague and does not assist career counselors in understanding how to best assist their clients.

Therefore, for career counselors to be successful in the current labor market climate, they need to cultivate an equal exchange of resources with employers (Neault, 2000). As stated previously, the current labor market supports the idea that employers hold all the cards; it is their game; therefore, we need to play by their rules. We make our best pitch, hoping they will notice that we are on the field before we can even try to be on the same team. What is meant by this is that career counselors need to advocate to employers that we are working toward the same goal. This can occur by setting up an information meeting and inquiring about what the employer is looking for in applicants for various positions within the company and get a feel for the type of environment that the company has and the overall culture.

While this tactic may seem time-consuming, it gives career counselors firsthand knowledge about what the job market within that particular field is requiring of their applicants and enables us to ensure that our clients have the proper skills, abilities, and education to meet the demands of the ever-changing workforce.

Career counselors can learn what they need to learn from employers and human resource professionals through the art of asking questions (Hopkins, 1995). By encouraging employers and human resource professionals to talk, in turn, it encourages them to listen to you and hear what you have to offer within the partnership. Again, the idea is not to go in with an agenda other than to find common ground and understand the employer's expectations of those who are hiring, to gain information about what the labor market is requiring for their applicants, and possibly establish a relationship that can assist you as a career counselor in helping your clients achieve their career goals.

Advocacy

Often, the term or the word "advocacy" has been used to signify the process of fighting for something or a cause. With the term being popular in literature pertaining to social justice, diversity, and inclusion, scholars have identified advocacy as a direct intervention or an action that is an expression of social justice work (Fickling, 2016; Ratts et al., 2010). In recent times, advocacy has become more popular in the counseling literature with its definitions significantly influenced by the areas of community counseling and multicultural counseling (Toporek et al., 2009). The American Counseling Association and National Career Development Association in their codes of ethics articulate that advocacy seeks to remove barriers and obstacles that inhibit access, growth, and development, hence defining advocacy as the promotion of the well-being of individuals, groups, and the counseling profession within systems and organizations (ACA, 2014, p. 20; NCDA, 2015, p. 26).

In defining advocacy, Lewis et al. (1998) identified two clear goals: (a) increasing a client's sense of personal power and (b) promoting environmental changes that reflect greater responsiveness to a client's personal needs (Toporek et al., 2009). In 2001, Toporek and Liu described advocacy as an "action taken by a counseling professional to facilitate the removal of external and institutional barriers to client's well-being" (p. 387). They further explained advocacy as a range of counseling actions that encompasses the process of empowerment to social action. In this process, empowerment includes counselor actions that are geared toward the individual or the client. Here the counselor's main goal and focus is to help the client in identifying and addressing social, institutional, political, and other barriers that affect their well-being. The social action stage includes counselor actions, where the counselor advocates for change in the context of large public areas on behalf of the client.

Although the concept of advocacy is new in the field of counseling, counselors have always been change agents and advocates (Kiselica & Robinson, 2001; Lewis & Bradley, 2000; Toporek et al., 2006). Counselors have made it their responsibility not only to provide face-to-face counseling, but they also have been burdened with making the environment more habitable and conducive for their clients. It was not until the late 1990s that the American Counseling Association (ACA) began the process of codifying advocacy and highlighting the importance of it for both the profession and the work that counselors do with clients (Toporek & Daniels, 2018).

The following are from the 2014 ACA code of ethics[1]:

- Section C Professional Responsibility: Introduction: Counselors are expected to *advocate* to promote changes at the individual, group, institutional, and societal levels that improve the quality of life for individuals and groups and remove potential barriers to the provision or access of appropriate services being offered (p. 8).

  - A.7. Roles and Relationships at Individual, Group, Institutional, and Societal Levels A.7.a: Advocacy: When appropriate, counselors *advocate* at individual, group, institutional, and societal levels to address potential barriers and obstacles that inhibit access and/or the growth and development of clients (p. 5).

  - A.7.b. Confidentiality and Advocacy: Counselors obtain client consent prior to engaging in advocacy efforts on behalf of an identifiable client to improve the provision of services and to work toward removal of systemic barriers or obstacles that inhibit client access, growth, and development (p. 5).

---

[1] Selections from Rebecca L. Toporek and Judy Daniels, American Counseling Association Advocacy Compentencies, pp. 4–10. Copyright © 2018 by American Counseling Association. Reprinted with permission.

The following are from the 2015 NCDA code of ethics:

- A.1. Welfare of Those Served by Career Professionals. A.1.a. Primary Responsibility. The primary responsibility of career professionals is to respect the dignity and to promote the welfare of the individuals to whom they provide service (p. 3).

- A.6.a. Advocacy. When appropriate, career professionals advocate at individual, group, institutional, and societal levels to examine potential barriers and obstacles that inhibit access and/ or the growth and development of clients. A.6.b. Confidentiality and Advocacy Career professionals obtain consent prior to engaging in advocacy efforts on behalf of a client to improve the provision of services and to work toward removal of systemic barriers or obstacles that inhibit client access, growth, and development (p. 5).

- Section C: Professional Responsibility: Career professionals promote change at the individual, group, institutional, and societal levels that improves the quality of life for individuals and groups and removes potential barriers to the provision or access of appropriate services being offered (p. 9).

Advocacy with and on behalf of clients is a major way in which counselors fulfill their core professional value of promoting social justice. The establishment of these codes by these professional associations has solidified this professional recognition.

Becoming an Advocate for Your Clients

Career counselors have a unique vantage point regarding social justice because of the economic and social nature of the work (Flicking, 2016). Advocacy cuts across different career counseling roles and is conceptualized broadly. In this case, it is important as career counselors to adequately delineate and understand advocacy and be able to differentiate advocacy from other career counseling roles, as well as how other career counseling roles are complementary to advocacy. Most importantly, how do we as career counselors and counselors in training become more effective advocates? The next few paragraphs will offer a structure for conceptualizing advocacy and developing advocacy competencies.

Advocacy competence can be thought of as the ability, understanding, and knowledge to carry out advocacy ethically and effectively (Toporek et al., 2009). Knowing the continuum of work done by counselor advocates, the ACA mandated a task force to develop advocacy competencies along two dimensions: level of involvement and setting. Level of involvement includes "acting with" and/or "acting on behalf" and setting includes client/student, school community, and public arena (Lewis et al., 2002). Level of involvement and settings combine to form six domains: (1) client/student empowerment, (2) client/student advocacy, (3) community collaboration, (4) systems advocacy, (5) public information, and (6) social/political advocacy. Lewis et al. (2002) provided detailed suggestions of counselor behaviors consistent with each domain.

In 2018, Toporek and Daniels updated the 2003 ACA advocacy competencies. This update (Table 18.1) expands on the 2003 competencies, clarifying domains and elaborating on specific strategies, knowledge, and skills, as well as explicating the original authors' intentions for inclusion of multicultural and ethical considerations (Toporek & Daniels, 2018).

Table 18.1 ACA ADVOCACY COMPETENCIES DOMAIN

ACA Advocacy Domains		
Individual/Client	Community/Organization	Public Arena
Client Empowerment	Community Collaboration	Collective Action
Client Advocacy	Systems Advocacy	Social/Political Advocacy
Counselor actions must be grounded in multicultural and ethical considerations.		

Original model by Lewis et al. (2003) updated by Toporek and Daniel (2018)

Implementation of Advocacy Competencies: A Case Study

To bring further clarity to how the advocacy competencies play out in the career counseling setting, the following vignette is presented with an accompanying set of thought-provoking questions and approaches based on the advocacy competencies. This is by no means an exhaustive list of approaches a career counselor can take; there are certainly other ways that advocacy can be enacted because of different circumstances, contextual variables, institutions, resources, and relationships.

> A career counselor met with Yaa (a fictional character), a 21-year-old student who identifies as female. Yaa is in her last semester at her university in a social work program. As part of her program requirement, Yaa is currently working as a social work intern at a local homeless shelter. After graduation, she hopes to work as a licensed clinical social worker in a reputable agency that serves individuals with disabilities and their families, including where she is currently interning. When Yaa met with the career counselor, she disclosed that she has been using hearing aids for the past 10 years; however, her hearing was deteriorating. When Yaa started working at the homeless shelter, she made a conscious effort not to let anyone know about her condition; however, one of her colleagues noticed her difficulty when her hearing started deteriorating. Yaa mentioned that she told her colleague about her challenge, and her response was "I am not sure how much longer you can work as a clinical social worker then." She described that it had not hit her that she might not be able to be a clinical social worker, especially because her hearing is deteriorating at a fast pace now. She went on to say that she was aware of the Americans With Disabilities Act accommodations and nondiscrimination policy in most agencies; however, the ability to hear is very essential in clinical social work practices. Yaa indicated that although she has been told by her teachers and supervisors at her internship that she is good at what she does, she felt discouraged, worried, and frustrated as her final semester drew near. She is constantly worried that she will not be able to find a job and is confused about what to do now with regard to her career options.

Individual/Student/Client

Client/Student Empowerment

Within the advocacy competencies, client/student empowerment refers to the efforts of the counselor and client that facilitate the identification of external barriers and development of client self-advocacy skills, strategies, and resources in response to these barriers. Here it is extremely important that the career counselors recognize what sociopolitical, systemic, and environmental factors, as well as internalized oppression, are negatively affecting a client's well-being (Toporek et al., 2009). It is after identifying these factors that the career counselor discovers strategies to help empower clients using the strengths and resources of clients and students.

Toporek and Daniels outlined the following client/student empowerment interventions:

1. Identify the social, political, economic, and cultural factors that affect the client/student. 2. Recognize the significance of counselor's own cultural background and sociopolitical position in relation to power, privilege and oppression and in relation to the client or client communities. 3. Recognize signs indicating that an individual's behaviors and concerns reflect responses to systemic or internalized oppression. 4. At an appropriate developmental level and cultural perspective, help the individual identify the external barriers that affect his, her or their development. 5. Share resources and tools that are appropriate for the client/student's developmental level and issue. 6. Train students and clients in self-advocacy skills. 7. Help students and clients develop self-advocacy action plans. 8. Assist students and clients in carrying out action plans. (2018. p. 4)

These strategies should focus on helping the individual identify resources, strengths, or skills. As an advocacy-oriented counselor, you should deliberate over the following:

- What are the first steps Yaa's career counselor will have to take?

  - What are Yaa's strengths?

  - What should she capitalize on?

- What resources and tools are appropriate for Yaa's progress?

- What basic steps of empowerment will the career counselor take in this case?

Client/Student Advocacy

In this domain, the career counselor focuses on evaluating the need for advocating on behalf of the client and a plan of action. This role is easier to assume in situations where the career counselor has access to resources because of his /her position, when the client has limited language skills, or when the client is not capable of advocating for him/herself because of fear, anxiety, or disability. In this case, it is important for the career counselor to work with the client very closely to develop an initial plan of action for identifying and addressing the barriers, making sure that the plan is consistent with the goals of the client.

Toporek and Daniels outlined the following client/student advocacy interventions:

1. Identify barriers to the well-being of clients and students with attention to issues facing vulnerable groups. 2. Recognize the significance of counselor's own cultural background and sociopolitical position in relation to power, privilege and oppression and in relation to the client or client communities. 3. Identify potential allies for confronting the barriers including those within the organization as well as those who have cultural expertise relevant to the client's issue. 4. Develop an initial plan of action for confronting these barriers in consultation with client and ensuring plan is consistent with client's goals. 5. Communicate plan with client including rationale, and possible outcomes of

advocacy. 6. Negotiate relevant services and education systems on behalf of clients and students. 7. Help clients and students gain access and create a plan to sustain needed resources and supports. 8. Carry out the plan of action and reflect/evaluate effectiveness of advocacy efforts. (2018, p. 5)

As an advocacy-oriented counselor, you should deliberately focus on the following:

- What are Yaa's major barriers?

- What is an example of a plan of action Yaa's career counselor can take?

- What services can the career counselor negotiate on Yaa's behalf?

- How should the career counselor carry out the plan of action?

- How would you evaluate the effectiveness of the advocacy?

Community/School/Organization

Community Collaboration

In community collaboration, the main duty of the career counselor is to work with a group or community to address systemic barriers. Here the career counselor is primarily an ally and contributor of skills, such as communication, training, and research (Toporek & Daniel, 2018). Career counselors use community strengths and systemic interventions to empower the community toward change, advocate to remove obstacles, and increase access to resources (Lewis et al., 2002; Ratts & Hutchins, 2009). Depending on the available resources, the career counselor supports community members by helping them to examine the challenge, develop a plan of action, and reflect on that action. The goal of community collaboration is to develop or obtain access to resources that foster autonomy (Ratts et al., 2010).

Toporek and Daniels outlined collaboration interventions: An advocacy-oriented career counselor should be able to complete the following:

1. Identify environmental factors that impinge upon students' and clients' development. 2. Alert community or school groups with common concerns related to the issue. 3. Develop alliances with groups working for change and explore what has already been done to address the issue. Understand counselor's sociocultural position in relation to the issue, the client group, and allies. 4. Use effective listening skills to gain understanding of the group's goals and help facilitate examination of causes and possible avenues for advocacy. 5. Facilitate understanding of group dynamics, cultural and sociopolitical variations in group members, and how that may affect group decisions as well as variable repercussions for different group members. 6. Identify the strengths and resources that the group members bring to the process of systemic change and communicate recognition of and respect for these strengths and resources. 7. Identify and offer the skills that the counselor can bring to the collaboration as well as any ethical limitations they might have as a professional. 8. Facilitate the group in considering possible outcomes of action, both favorable and unfavorable, and support them in preparing for possible resistance or other challenges. 9. Integrate considerations of the ecological and political context in which the advocacy actions will be taking place. 10. Assess the effectiveness of counselor's collaborative efforts with the community. (2018, p. 6)

Systems Advocacy

In systems advocacy, the career counselor advocates on behalf of groups of clients or students within a community organization or school. Ideally, this form of advocacy may take place where the career counselor has access to the system that the clients don't. The ultimate goal of systems advocacy is to develop strategies that reduce barriers for community members who are seeking resources (Lewis et al., 2002).

Toporek and Daniels outlined systems advocacy interventions: An advocacy-oriented career counselor should be able to complete the following:

> 1. Identify environmental factors impinging on students' or clients' development. 2. Understand the cultural, political, developmental and environmental contexts of the clients or client groups. 3. Understand the counselor's own cultural identity in relation to the group and the target of advocacy including privilege, oppression, communication, values, and intentions. 4. Investigate the issue, population and possible allies and stakeholders. 5. Provide and interpret data as well as share research and expertise to show the urgency for change. 6. In collaboration with other stakeholders, develop a vision to guide change. 7. Analyze the sources of political power and social influence within the system. 8. Develop a step-by-step plan for implementing the change process, attending to possible ethical issues. 9. Develop a plan for dealing with probable responses to change. 10. Recognize and deal with resistance. 11. Assess the effect of counselor's advocacy efforts on the system and constituents. (2018, pp. 7–8)

Public Arena

Collective action (formerly public information) refers to advocacy in which the career counselor collaborates with groups or community organizations as correspondents to address issues that exist on a broad scale or that can be remedied through changing public perception or policies. The career counselor contributes as a group member and lends his/her knowledge and skill to the process of advocacy.

Toporek and Daniels outlined collective action interventions: An advocacy-oriented career counselor should be able to complete the following:

> 1. Recognize the impact of oppression, other barriers, and environmental factors that interfere with healthy development. 2. Identify factors that are protective of healthy development as well as various avenues for enhancing these protective factors through the public arena. 3. Share research and professional expertise with partner client groups and community members in developmentally and culturally appropriate ways. 4. Determine appropriate role within community initiative such as facilitator, researcher, negotiator, etc., aligned with professional and personal skill set. 5. Understand counselor's own cultural identity including positionality related to power, privilege, and oppression and how that influences the ways they work with the community and the targets of advocacy (e.g., decision makers). Participate with and/or facilitate community partners in identifying the source of problems, setting goals, developing an action plan, considering possible outcomes, and implementing the action plan. 6. Prepare written and multimedia materials that provide clear explanations of the role of specific environmental factors in human development in consultation with engaged community or client groups. 7. Communicate information in ways that are ethical and appropriate for the target population. 8. Disseminate information through a variety of media appropriate for the target audience. 9. Collaboratively prepare and present materials

and information to influence decision makers, legislators, and policy makers, ensuring that the community's voice is central. 10. Facilitate the community group in assessing the influence of their public information and advocacy strategies. (2018, pp. 8–9)

Social/Political Advocacy

In this domain, career counselors act as change agents in the systems that affect their own students and clients most directly. They communicate and act on public policy and legislation that directly harms the populations they serve. This experience often leads to the recognition that some of the concerns they have addressed affect people in a much larger arena. Career counselors use their skills to carry out social/political advocacy on behalf of client or student populations, and counselors engage in advocacy strategies often independent of specific clients or client groups to address issues they observe.

Toporek and Daniels outlined collective action interventions: An advocacy-oriented career counselor should be able to complete the following:

> 1. Identify the communities affected by this issue including who makes up the community and whether the community is engaged in advocacy around the issue. Consult with communities affected by the issue to understand their views and experiences, with attention to economic, social and cultural perspectives. 2. Distinguish those problems that can best be resolved through using the counselor's expertise and where the community may have limited access. 3. Identify ways the community may have input into the advocacy process. 4. Identify and collaborate with other professionals as well as other allies who are involved in disseminating public information and may be interested in or already engaging in policy advocacy. 5. Identify appropriate mechanisms and avenues for addressing these problems and distinguish the role of public awareness, legislative, policy and judicial action. 6. Understand counselor's own cultural identity including positionality related to power, privilege, and oppression and how that influences the ways they work with the community and the targets of advocacy (e.g., decision makers). 7. Support existing alliances for change through providing information, support, and expertise. 8. With allies, prepare convincing data and rationales for public awareness campaigns or to lobby legislators and other policy makers. 9. Maintain open dialogue with communities and clients to ensure that the social/political advocacy is consistent with the initial goals. (2018, pp. 9–10)

Summary

As a career counselor, it is important to understand how advocacy fits into your role, as well as the function of advocacy in addressing client and professional issues. It is important that as we go through the advocacy interventions, we have knowledge, skill, and disposition (Trusty & Brown, 2005). It is important to know and understand our clients' needs and wants, know and understand their culture, know their expectations and their visions, know and understand how systems work, and know as many resources as you can or how to locate resources. Be mindful of how you advocate for your clients and respect their wishes. Having important skills enables us to carry out our plan of action seamlessly; these skills include communication skills, problem solving skills, organization skills, collaborative skills, and team building and teamwork skills. Having an advocacy disposition means career counselors are aware of and embrace their professional advocacy roles. With this disposition, career counselor advocates are willing to take risks in helping individual students and groups of students meet their needs.

Discussion Questions

1. What are some strategies that career counselors can engage with their community to increase collaboration?
2. What are some techniques that can be used to allow for the client to create their own plan of action?
3. How can career counselors work with employers to create opportunities for potential clients?
4. What do career counselors bring to the table when working with employers?

References

American Counseling Association (ACA). (2014). *ACA code of ethics*. https://www. counseling.org/resources/aca-code-of-ethics.pdf.

Davos-Klosters. (2014). Matching skills and labour market needs: Building social partnerships for better skills and better jobs. *World Economic Forum*, 1–28. http://www3.weforum.org/docs/GAC/2014/WEF_GAC_Employment_MatchingSkillsLabourMarket_Report_2014.pdf

Fickling, M. J. (2016). An exploration of career counselors' perspectives on advocacy. *Professional Counselor, 6*(2), 174–188.

Ginac, L. (2004, May 1). *Career counseling is a valuable benefit for employees*. National Career Development Association. https://www.ncda.org/aws/NCDA/pt/sd/news_article/4859/_PARENT/CC_layout_details/false

Guindon, M., & Richmond, L. (2005). Practice and research in career counseling and development. *Career Development Quarterly, 54*(2), 90–137.

Hopkins, S. (1995). Marketing career counseling services. *ERIC Digest*, 1–2.

Kiselica, M. S., & Robinson, M. (2001). Bringing advocacy counseling to life: The history, issues, and human dramas of social justice work in counseling. *Journal of Counseling & Development, 79*(4), 387–397.

Lewis, J. A., Arnold, M. S., House, R., & Toporek, R. L. (2002). *ACA advocacy competencies*. Retrieved August 14, 2019, from http://www.counseling.org/Resources/Competencies/Advocacy_Competencies.pdf

Lewis, J., & Bradley, L. J. (2000). *Advocacy in counseling*. Caps Publication.

Lewis, J. A., Lewis, M. D., Daniels, J. A., & D'Andrea, M. J. (1998). *Community counseling: Empowering strategies for a diverse society*. Brooks/Cole.

National Career Development Association. (2015). NCDA code of ethics. *Retrieved on June, 11,* 2018.

Neault, R. A. (2000). Career management: The role of career counsellors in building strategic partnerships between individuals and their employers. *Canadian Journal of Counselling, 34*(3), 218.

Ratts, M. J., Anthony, L., & Santos, K. N. T. (2010). The dimensions of social justice model: Transforming traditional group work into a socially just framework. *Journal for Specialists in Group Work, 35*(2), 160–168. https://doi.org/10.1080/01933921003705974.

Ratts, M.J., & Hutchinson, M. (2009). ACA advocacy competencies: Social justice advocacy at the client/ student level. *Journal of Counseling and Development, 87,* 269–275. doi:10.1002/j.1556-6678.2009. tb00106.x

Toporek, R. L., & Daniel, J. (2018) *Updated ACA advocacy competencies*. Retrieved August 14, 2019 from https://www.counseling.org/docs/default-source/competencies/aca-2018-advocacy-competencies.pdf?sfvrsn=1dca552c_6

Toporek, R. L., Lewis, J. A., & Crethar, H. C. (2009). Promoting systemic change through the ACA advocacy competencies. *Journal of Counseling & Development, 87,* 260–268. https://doi.org/10.1002/j.1556-6678.2009.tb00105.x

Toporek, R. L., & Liu, W. M. (2001). Advocacy in counseling psychology: Critical issues of race, class, and gender. In D. B. Pope-Davis & H. L. K. Coleman (Eds.), *The intersection of race, class, and gender in counseling psychology* (pp. 385–413). Sage Publications.

Trusty, J., & Brown, D. (2005). Advocacy competencies for professional school counselors. *Professional School Counseling, 8,* 259–265.

Index

About the Editors

Rebecca R. Sametz

Rebecca R. Sametz, PhD, LPC, CRC, ETS, VRT, CMCC, is an assistant professor and director of the Master of Science Clinical Rehabilitation Counseling program at Texas Tech University Health Sciences Center. Dr. Sametz obtained her doctorate in rehabilitation counselor education from Michigan State University, and a master of arts in rehabilitation counseling and master of arts in vision rehabilitation therapy from Western Michigan University. She is currently the director of Red Raider Pre-College Summer Academy where she developed a weeklong program for youth with disabilities interested in attending postsecondary education. Previously, Dr. Sametz worked at a nonprofit as a youth career development specialist in which she partnered with local school districts to provide youth with disabilities who were preparing for transition from school to work with community work experiences. In this role, she also provided career counseling and exploration services to youth with disabilities, job placement and development services, and disability education to employers who served as a placement site for youth with disabilities in understanding the disability and low-cost accommodations. The types of disabilities that the youth were commonly diagnosed with were learning disabilities, more specifically, dyslexia, attention deficit and hyperactivity disorder, language processing disorder, dysgraphia, autism spectrum disorder, and dyscalculia. Dr. Sametz's research interests are within the career counseling arena, where she focuses on youth with disabilities transitioning from school to work and adult life, parents of children with disabilities, employer and labor market needs infused within the special education curriculum to best prepare youth with disabilities for the world of work upon graduation, and psychosocial adjustment to disability for individuals with disabilities and veterans.

Mary-Anne M. Joseph

Mary-Anne M. Joseph, PhD, LPC, CRC, is an associate professor in the Department of Rehabilitation Studies at Alabama State University. Dr. Joseph holds a master of science degree in rehabilitation counseling from Winston Salem State University and a doctorate of philosophy in counselor education and supervision from Ohio University. Dr. Joseph is also a certified rehabilitation counselor under the Commission on Rehabilitation Counselor Certification and a licensed professional counselor. Dr. Joseph has been an active member of the National Rehabilitation Association (NRA) for the last 7 years. During this time, she has presented at numerous conferences on a variety of topics. Dr. Joseph has also served as the NRA board representative and president of the Transition Specialties Division of NRA.

About the Contributors

Danielle Ami Narh

Danielle Dede Ami-Narh, PhD, CRC, attained her bachelor of arts degree in psychology and dance studies from the University of Ghana, Legon. She earned her MA in rehabilitation counseling from Michigan State University in 2015 and proceeded to obtain her doctorate from the same university in 2019. Dr. Ami-Narh is a certified rehabilitation counselor (CRC) and has worked with individuals with autism, as well as college-aged individuals with mental disorders. Her research focuses on improving the quality of life for individuals with disabilities and their families in areas where access to resources is limited. Currently, she is involved in developing psychoeducation programs for caregivers of transition-age individuals with autism both in Ghana and the United States. She has a keen interest in global disability issues, disability policies in developing countries, and multicultural issues in the field of rehabilitation counseling. Dr. Ami-Narh is presently a faculty member in the Department of Counselor Education at Emporia State University.

Brenna Breshears

Brenna Breshears is a mental health and vocational counselor residing in Okemos, Michigan, where she serves a diverse population, including those within the substance abuse, formerly incarcerated, and psychiatric disability communities. Her research is focused on the relationship between employment and recidivism, the effect of soft skills training on adjudicated youth, and the effect of social justice informed counselor training on the working alliance.

Jina Chun

Jina Chun, PhD, CRC, is an assistant professor of rehabilitation counseling in the Department of Rehabilitation Psychology and Special Education at the University of Wisconsin-Madison. Before coming to the University of Wisconsin-Madison, she was a postdoctoral research associate of Lifting Individuals and Families Through Empowerment (LIFE) research lab in the Department of Counseling, Educational Psychology, and Special Education at Michigan State University and an adjunct faculty at Western Washington University and Utah State University. She completed her PhD in rehabilitation counselor education at Michigan State University. Her research focuses on psychoeducation programs for caregivers/families of transition-age youth and young adults with neurodevelopmental disabilities, career decision making and its impact on quality of life of transition youth and young adults with disabilities, the interplay of vocational and psychological well-being and career success, multicultural education and training, and evidence-based practice in counseling education.

Brandi N. Cruz

Brandi N. Cruz is a doctoral student in the School of Rehabilitation Services and Counseling at the University of Texas Rio Grande Valley (UTRGV). She is a part-time lecturer to undergraduate students at UTRGV. Ms. Cruz has experience working with people with disabilities in the vocational setting as an employment consultant and case manager. Ms. Cruz's research interests are social media and the effects on young adult's well-being and mental health, the veteran population, career development, and mental health counseling.

Myshalae Euring

Myshalae Euring, PhD, CRC, LPC, holds a doctorate in rehabilitation counseling and counselor education and a master's degree in rehabilitation counseling. She is also a certified rehabilitation counselor and licensed professional counselor associate in the state of North Carolina. Myshalae has devoted her academic and professional career to working with and advocating for individuals with physical, intellectual, and emotional disabilities. She has worked as a counselor, vocational coordinator, and assistant professor of clinical mental health counseling. The populations she serves include adults, children, teens, families, and individuals. Her areas of expertise include women's issues, LGBTQ+, anxiety, depression, addiction, spirituality, trauma and post-traumatic stress disorder, grief and loss, life transitions, and support for caregivers of individuals with physical/intellectual disabilities and mental health issues.

Erin Fearn-Smith

Erin Fearn-Smith, MAPS, MRCAA, is an Australian registered psychologist and rehabilitation counselor teaching in the discipline of rehabilitation counseling at the University of Sydney and working in the area of homelessness intervention with one of Australia's largest not-for-profit organizations, Mission Australia. Erin is undertaking PhD research to identify cognitive impairment and brain injury among people experiencing homelessness and has worked for more than 20 years in social inclusion, housing, and mental health in Australia, New Zealand, and the United Kingdom. Erin lives in the Blue Mountains of New South Wales, Australia, where she parents two children, Bonnie and Finnegan, with her husband, Christopher.

Rene Gonzalez

Rene Gonzalez, PhD, is an associate professor in the School of Rehabilitation Services and Counseling at the UTRGV. Dr. Gonzalez obtained his doctoral degree from the University of Wisconsin-Madison and is a certified rehabilitation counselor (CRC). He teaches undergraduate, graduate, and doctoral courses. Dr. Gonzalez was appointed to the Rehabilitation Council of Texas by Governor Rick Perry and has clinical experience in providing psychotherapy/counseling for predominantly Latinos/Hispanics with various disabling conditions to attain and maintain employment and/or attend postsecondary training. Dr. Gonzalez's areas of expertise include virtues and character strengths, resilience, psychosocial adaptation to chronic illness and disability, and vocational rehabilitation outcomes. Dr. Gonzalez authored and coauthored peer-reviewed publications relative to virtues and character traits, resilience, positive psychology, and psychosocial adaptation to chronic illness and disability, rehabilitation outcomes for individuals with substance use disorders, older persons with diabetes, older stroke survivors, caregiver burden, and Hispanic caregiving.

Nykeisha Grant

Nykeisha Grant, PhD, is an adjunct professor in the Psychology Department at Post University. She earned her bachelor's degree in child development from Claflin University in 2002, a master's in rehabilitation counseling from South Carolina State University in 2004, and her PhD in rehabilitation counselor education from the University of Iowa in 2010. Dr. Grant has practiced rehabilitation counseling in multiple settings in Georgia, North Carolina, and Connecticut. Her research interests are in post-traumatic stress disorder, infidelity, and the oldest old population.

Sara P. Johnston

Sara P. Johnston, PhD, CRC, is an associate professor in the Occupational Therapy Doctorate Program and the Olson Fellow for Global Engaged Learning at Drake University. Her clinical experience is primarily in substance abuse counseling, in particular tobacco and nicotine cessation interventions for clients with psychiatric and cognitive disabilities. She was also employed as a supported community living counselor in Wisconsin and Iowa, and as Americans With Disabilities Act Wisconsin project coordinator. Her current research includes health care disparities related to disability status, caregiver resilience, global health, and ethics in clinical practice.

Jeong Han Kim

Jeon Han Kim, PhD, CRC, is an associate professor in the Department of Clinical Counseling and Mental Health at Texas Tech University Health Science Center. A 2008 University of Wisconsin-Madison PhD graduate in rehabilitation psychology, Dr. Kim, a distinguished national honoree in South Korea, served as a lieutenant in the Republic of Korea Army when he volunteered to diffuse a bomb in 1997. The resulting explosion led to years of intensive rehabilitation for burns, amputation, and hearing loss, and he finally became a man of national merit. Dr. Kim is the founder of the virtue-based psychosocial adaptation model (V-PAM). Traditional theories in psychosocial adaptation to chronic illness and disability (CID) have focused on examining innate psychological disposition, such as personality. However, in his V-PAM, the emphasis is given to virtue, in other words, one's pursuit of excellence and commitment after the onset of CID. From this perspective, adaptation to illness and disability is viewed as a positive by-product of having endured adversities while transforming them into insightful opportunities for renewal. Thus adaptation is no longer determined by innate dispositions; rather, it can be nurtured via the collaborative counseling process. Dr. Kim has also collected extensive clinical experience via independent living, long-term health care under the Medicaid/Medicare waiver program, state/federal vocational rehabilitation, and Veterans Affairs Hospital mental health/addiction/work therapy clinics.

Hung Jen Kuo

Hung Jen Kuo, PhD, CRC, LPC, is an assistant professor of rehabilitation counseling at Michigan State University. He received his PhD from the Rehabilitation Counselor Education at Michigan State University. Before coming to MSU, he was a faculty of Rehabilitation Service program at California State University, Los Angeles. His research interests surround promoting evidence-based practices and improving the quality of life for people with disabilities. Specifically, he is currently involved in several projects concerning educational interventions for transition-aged individuals with autism spectrum disorders (ASD). In addition, with his background and experience in technology, he is also involved in projects using assistive technology (e.g., virtual reality) to promote quality of life for individuals with neurodevelopmental disabilities. His work also includes clinical supervision, psychoeducation for caregivers, and public vocational rehabilitation services.

Trenton Landon

Trenton Landon, PhD, CRC, graduated from Michigan State University with his PhD in rehabilitation counselor education in 2016. Prior to Michigan State, Dr. Landon worked for 7 years as a rehabilitation counselor in a state agency. During his time with the state agency, Dr. Landon was assigned a general caseload but also had the opportunity to work with transition-age youth from three different high schools, participate in the mental health and drug courts programs, and serve as the agency liaison to a state psychiatric hospital. Presently, Dr. Landon teaches master's-level coursework in the Rehabilitation Counseling Program. His research interests include the professional development of counselors, clinical supervision, ethics and ethical decision making, rural rehabilitation, and social inclusion of individuals with disabilities.

Gloria Lee

Gloria Lee, PhD, CRC, is a professor in rehabilitation counseling in the Department of Counseling, Educational Psychology and Special Education, and is the director of the Master of Arts in Rehabilitation Counseling program at Michigan State University. Her research lab, LIFE, Lifting Individuals and Families Through Empowerment; https://msuliferesearch.wordpress.com/, focuses on research in understanding contributing factors and strategies to enhance the psychosocial adjustment of caregiving families and individuals with neurodevelopmental disabilities, including autism spectrum disorder (ASD) and intellectual disabilities at the transition-age. Her various research projects include the development and validation of comprehensive transition psychoeducation interventions, family-school partnership, positive behavior supports and dialectic behavioral therapy for these families and transition-age individuals with ASD.

Allison Levine

Allison Levine, PhD, CRC, is an assistant professor in counselor education at the University of Kentucky. Dr. Levine received her doctorate in rehabilitation counselor education from Michigan State University in 2018. Prior to that, she received a master's degree in education in mental health and rehabilitation from Hofstra University in 2012. Allison's research areas are related to improving counselor education, specifically addressing implicit biases in counselor education, assessment of nonprofessional dispositions of counselor education students, and advancing distance learning in counselor education. Dr. Levine has also developed the Dispositional Development Scale—a tool for evaluating professional dispositions in master's-level counseling students. She is a board member at large for the Rehabilitation Counselors & Educators Association.

Susan Lingle

Susan Lingle, MRC, LPC, LMSW, CRC, CCM, Texas Tech University Health Sciences (TTUHSC) class of 2015, works at Serenity House Drug and Alcohol Treatment Facility as a residential counselor. Ms. Lingle is a licensed professional counselor, licensed master social worker, CRC, and certified case manager. She received her master of rehabilitation counseling from Texas Tech University Health Science Center in 2015 and her master of social work from University of Houston in 2019. Ms. Lingle has worked with a variety of agencies while serving multiple populations, including State Vocational Rehabilitation, in-patient mental health, domestic violence, veterans, persons with disabilities, residential addiction treatment, and home health. As a solution-focused therapist, Ms. Lingle often uses the modality of sand trays with her clients.

Starting in September 2019, Ms. Lingle will be under clinical social work supervision working toward advanced licensure. In addition, she is teaching an online class with TTUHSC as an adjunct instructor for Fall 2019. Ms. Lingle enjoys traveling, learning about history, and spending time with her corgi named Rotten. When asked to describe an overall passion, Susan says that she is extremely passionate that rural Texans have access to the services in which they need.

Serene Lin-Stephens

Serene Lin-Stephens, SFHEA, PCDAA, is a career development learning researcher and consultant for over 20 university courses in multiple disciplines in Australia and Asia and a senior fellow of the Higher Education Academy. She facilitates career development learning for general and discipline-specific cohorts, as well as women in STEM, international students, and low socioeconomic backgrounds. Her current PhD study in the Faculty of Medicine and Health at the University of Sydney focuses on employment-related anxiety. She has received multiple university Teaching Excellence and Service Innovation Awards and the 2019 Presidential Award from the Asia Pacific Career Development Association for her work in building a career glossary in multiple languages.

Emily Lund

Emily M. Lund, PhD, CRC, is an assistant professor of counselor education in the Department of Educational Studies in Psychology, Research Methodology, and Counseling at the University of Alabama. Dr. Lund holds a PhD in rehabilitation counseling (Utah State University), a master's in educational psychology (Texas A&M University), and a bachelor's degree in psychology and social work (University of Montana). She has worked with people with disabilities and their families in a variety of clinical and educational settings. Her primary research interests include interpersonal violence and trauma against people with disabilities, suicide and non-suicidal self-injury in people with disabilities, and the experiences of graduate students with disabilities. She has published and presented extensively on these topics and currently has over 65 peer-reviewed publications.

Michelle McKnight-Lizotte, PhD, CRC, LPC

Michelle McKnight-Lizotte, PhD, CRC, LPC (Idaho), is an assistant professor in rehabilitation counseling and professional school counseling at Utah State University. Dr. Lizotte has a PhD in rehabilitation counselor education (Michigan State University), a MS in rehabilitation counseling (Georgia State University), and a BS in special education (Georgia College and State University). She has been a CRC since 2010 and a licensed professional counselor (Idaho) since 2017. Dr. Lizotte has experience working as a rehabilitation counselor for two state vocational rehabilitation agencies (Colorado and Michigan), specifically with transition youth and individuals with autism. Her research interests relate to the postsecondary and employment experiences of individuals with autism, rural rehabilitation counseling practices, and inclusive postsecondary education programs for students with intellectual disabilities.

Roxanna Pebdani

Roxanna Nasseri Pebdani, PhD, CRC FHEA, is a senior lecturer and course director in the discipline of rehabilitation counseling at the University of Sydney. She is a CRC and a fellow of the Higher Education

Academy. She has authored or coauthored over 20 journal articles and book chapters and has conducted over 30 presentations at local, national, and international conferences. Dr. Pebdani's research interests are in women's issues in disability, specifically pregnancy and fertility. Dr. Pebdani also conducts research on sexuality and disability. Her other streams of research include supervision in counseling and pedagogy in rehabilitation counseling, as well as interdisciplinary research on the effect of exercise on the quality of life of individuals with disabilities. Dr. Pebdani is the mother of two and an avid cyclist.

Taryn V. Richardson

Taryn Richardson, PhD, CRC, NCC, is an assistant professor in the Department of Clinical Counseling and Mental Health at Texas Tech University Health Sciences Center. She obtained her PhD in rehabilitation and counselor education (counselor education and supervision) from the University of Iowa. Dr. Richardson has mental health and vocational rehabilitation experience. She also worked with local colleges and universities to provide prevention services to students and transition-aged youth with intellectual, cognitive, and learning disabilities. Dr. Richardson is committed to the enhancement of the quality of life for persons with disabilities. Her research also focuses on professional identity and development of counseling professionals. She developed a model to explain counselor leaders' development and meaning-making of significant experiences. Another area of Dr. Richardson's research agenda is vocational behavior (e.g., work-related stress, burnout, satisfaction, and emotions in the workplace).

Tyler A. Riddle

Tyler Riddle is a veteran of the U.S. Marine Corps. He completed two combat deployments to Afghanistan, as well as two deployments in support of the Global War on Terror to Jordan and the Republic of Georgia. After his service, he worked as a veteran peer support specialist at a vocational rehabilitation nonprofit supporting veterans with disabilities in obtaining and maintaining employment. He continues to advocate for veterans and their families.

Klarissa Trevino

Klarissa Trevino is a graduate student in the Clinical Rehabilitation Counseling Program in the School of Rehabilitation Services and Counseling at the UTRGV. She is currently employed at a Local Mental Health and Intellectual and Developmental Disability Authority. Ms. Trevino has experience working directly with individuals with intellectual disabilities/related conditions and serious mental illnesses. Her current role is to ensure the quality of services provided to individuals in these populations. Ms. Trevino's research interests are in stress, resiliency, family dynamics, and substance use disorders.

Catherine Troop

Catherine Troop is a doctoral student at the University of Kentucky in clinical rehabilitation counseling, with a research focus on substance use disorders. Catherine has a master's degree in psychology from the University of London and a master's degree in special education from Georgetown College. She is a licensed professional counselor and a licensed clinical alcohol and drug counselor, and she has over 15 years of clinical experience working in a variety of settings.

Quiteya Walker

Quiteya D. Walker, PhD, has 14 years of education and work experience in the field of rehabilitation counseling and mental health counseling. Her work experiences include serving as a postsecondary counselor and disability support service provider at Kirkwood Community College in Iowa City, Iowa. She worked as the director of disability support services at Mississippi University for Women in Columbus, Mississippi. She also worked at ASPIRE Behavioral Health and Developmental Disabilities as a clinical mental health counselor where she provided outpatient treatment to individuals with severe and persistent mental illness. Most recently, she worked as a counselor educator for 7 years at Albany State University. Currently, she is an associate professor in rehabilitation counseling at Winston-Salem State University.

Bernadette Williams York

Bernadette Williams York, PhD, is an associate professor/associate director in the Division of Physical Therapy, Department of Rehabilitation Medicine at the University of Washington in Seattle, Washington. Dr. Williams York received her bachelor of science degree from Tulane University in New Orleans, Louisiana; a master of science degree from the University of Alabama, Birmingham; and a doctor of science degree from Rocky Mountain University in Provo, Utah. Dr. Williams York is a board-certified geriatric specialist and has been a licensed physical therapist for over 30 years. She is also a published author, and her teaching and research interests include health disparities, health care workforce diversity, health promotion, and aging.

Logan Winkelman

Logan Winkelman, PhD, LPC, is an assistant professor and program director for the Master of Science in Clinical Mental Health Counseling Program in the Clinical Counseling and Mental Health Department within the School of Health Professions. She is a licensed professional counselor in the state of Texas and has worked in higher education for the past 7+ years, specializing in career counseling and development. She holds a doctorate in counselor education and supervision from Texas Tech University. She has dedicated time researching marketplace trends in diversity recruiting practices and counseling domestic and international populations assisting individuals in finding employment and advancing their careers in a global economy. Her other research interests include access to mental health and wellness resources, emotional intelligence, biofeedback, and aging and longevity.

Erica L. Wondolowski

Erica L. Wondolowski, PhD, CRC, is an assistant professor of rehabilitation science at Arkansas Tech University. Dr. Wondolowski holds a PhD in rehabilitation counselor education (Michigan State University), a MS in rehabilitation counseling services with a concentration in psychiatric rehabilitation and substance abuse (Springfield College), and a BS in psychology with a concentration in childhood and youth, as well as a minor in sociology (Eastern Connecticut State University). She has been a CRC since 2011 and previously worked for the Massachusetts Rehabilitation Commission. Dr. Wondolowski's research interests include sexual health and expression of persons with disabilities, diversity and inclusion, and social justice law and movements. She has presented extensively on these topics, as well as others at the national, regional, and local levels.